# PARAGUAY

# PARAGUAY

## An Informal History

BY HARRIS GAYLORD WARREN

NORMAN : UNIVERSITY OF OKLAHOMA PRESS : 1949

*By* HARRIS GAYLORD WARREN

*The Sword Was Their Passport: A History of American Filibustering in the Mexican Revolution.* Baton Rouge, 1943.

(With Thomas M. Deam) *The New Guidebook in Civics.* Chicago, 1941.

With others. *Fifth Army History* (9 vols.). Florence, Italy, and Washington, 1944–47.

With others. *Salerno to the Alps: A History of the Fifth Army, 1943–1945* (ed. by Lt. Col. Chester G. Starr, Jr.). Washington, 1948.

TO
THE MEMORY OF
*May Philpott Warren*
AND
*Joseph Allen Warren*

# *Preface*

THIS BOOK is an attempt to bring works in various languages together in a synthesis that will present a view of Paraguay's more than four centuries of history. It will, if I have succeeded, fill a definite need for a one-volume survey in English.

One reason for historical neglect of Paraguay, especially by writers in the United States, may be that the country is not so important as others when measured in statistics. In all of South America, only Ecuador and Uruguay are smaller than its 149,807 square miles; in all of Latin America, only Costa Rica and Panama had fewer than its 1,014,773 people in 1946, and only Nicaragua, Costa Rica, and Honduras had smaller gold and exchange holdings in 1945, or had a foreign trade of less value. United States trade with Paraguay in 1945 was only $8,700,000, less than with any other Latin American country, and our investments were of little significance except to the country itself.

Statistics do not tell the entire story by any means. A country that has fought two major wars within less than a century, that has long been recognized as the diplomatic crossroads of South America, for whose favors both Brazil and Argentina have contended and will contend, whose resources have by no means been exploited to the full, that can still provide homes for thousands of industrious immigrants—such a country is not unimportant. Even if these things were not true, Paraguay would be worth studying for itself alone.

The present volume is a synthesis based largely on secondary accounts, except for documents published by various governments on the War of the Triple Alliance and the Chaco War. Nearly every period and every aspect of Paraguayan history needs to be studied with extensive use of archival materials. A small amount of excellent work has been done in United States, Paraguayan, and Argentine universities, but the field has hardly been touched. In addition to faults entirely my own, this synthesis must necessarily suffer from weaknesses inherent in the materials studied.

I am indebted to the librarians of the Columbus Memorial Library of the Pan American Union, Harvard University, the Boston Public Library, the Library of Congress, Louisiana State University, the University of Texas, the University of Denver, and the University of Mississippi; to Miss Nancy Love Comfort, loan librarian of the University of Mississippi, for her patience and cheerful aid; and to Dr. Edwin Adams Davis, a former colleague at Louisiana State University, whose interest and encouragement were largely responsible for my undertaking what seemed to be a formidable task. My wife, Katherine Fleischmann Warren, read the manuscript and helped considerably in my use of titles in German.

Harris Gaylord Warren

*University, Mississippi,*
*April 2, 1949*

# Contents

Contents

# *Illustrations*

# Maps

# PARAGUAY

# CHAPTER I

# Nature, Miracles, and Myths

THE GARDEN OF EDEN was in Paraguay, a land of paradise before Spanish conquerors sailed up the great rivers. This inviting fiction persists among the Guaranís and the mestizos who forget hordes of stinging insects, poisonous reptiles, savage beasts, and still more savage people; but the fabled garden might well have been on the shores of Lake Ypoa, or perhaps it was a valley hidden among the low hills of Caacupé.

The very name Paraguay is a matter of dispute. Some say that because Indians believed the river to have its source in the flooded lowlands which they called Lake Xarayes, they named it the Paraguay, "Crowned River." Others repeat the tale of Juan García of Asunción who spent many years as an unwilling guest of the Payaguás in the late seventeenth century. García, as travelers will, enjoyed entertaining his friends with stories of his wanderings. Once, so he said, he journeyed with the Payaguás up the Paraguay, across Lake Xarayes, and into another river which boiled out of a mountain through a bat-infested cavern; two days García traveled in the cave, fighting the huge bats, the *andiras*. Again in the open, the river led to another lake so broad that its farthest shores could not be seen. But the great swamps that feed the Paraguay in the wet season are no figments of a fevered imagination, so perhaps it is the Crowned River.

As uncertain in limits as the origin of its name, Paraguay reached far beyond the horizon in all directions: west to the

3

mountains of Peru, north toward the Amazon, east into Brazil, and south even to Patagonia. The Spaniards always were careless about boundary lines. Thrown vaguely under the viceroyalty of Peru, then assigned with equal vagueness to the viceroyalty of La Plata, Paraguay was not of sufficient importance to the kings of Spain for them to bother with accurate geographic definition.

Stretching from northern Argentina to the Amazon basin, the Chaco lying west of the Paraguay River was a land of marvels to the earliest Spaniards who saw it and still is held in some awe. The Quechuas of Peru referred to an abundance of animal life as *chacu;* Spaniards changed the word to *chaco* and so named the lowlands east of the Andes in which mountain tribes sought refuge from the conquerors. Rivers divide the Chaco into three parts. South of the Bermejo is the Chaco Austral; between the Bermejo and the Pilcomayo is the Chaco Central; and north of the Pilcomayo is the Chaco Boreal, over which Bolivia and Paraguay fought their bloody war in the nineteen thirties. The Pilcomayo is a fickle stream that rises in the Bolivian highlands. Some parts of the river are navigable; but its channel changes with every flood, swamps are left as the waters fall away, and huge islands appear overnight.

Early chroniclers invariably remarked on the Chaco floods that covered hundreds of square miles, especially near the mouths of rivers. On such occasions great trees swept downstream, even going on out to the Atlantic. Large sections of the banks were torn out and floated away bearing whatever animal life happened to be present. Sir Woodbine Parish tells of tigers appearing in the streets of Montevideo. Today tigers no longer ride the floods, but high water does occasionally cut off telegraphic communications with Buenos Aires.

Spaniards drank the waters of the rivers and attributed marvelous curative powers to some and shunned others. The Bermejo's water was a veritable elixir of life, a quality imparted by the *yerba de urina* that grew profusely on its banks. Drink of the Bermejo and one would live to a wrinkleless old age, free from "the gravel, the stone, all urinary complaints, the cholic, the gout, the dropsy, and indigestions." Even during the nineteenth cen-

Curing Yerba

Foremost of Paraguayan trees was the yerba, whose coarse green leaves, roasted and powdered, yielded that incomparable tea called *maté*

From *La Plata . . . and Paraguay*
by Thomas J. Page

tury, sailors filled their casks in the Río de la Plata and found the water sweet and palatable after two round trips to England. The water of the Paraguay, while not so clear as that of the Paraná, was credited with clearing the throat and purifying the voice.

The soil of Paraguay was fertile, but a lavish nature had not produced the common fruits and cereals known to Europe. There were no fig, olive, apple, peach, quince, pear, pomegranate, prune, orange, lime, lemon, or citron trees; wheat, barley, anise, peas, lettuce, cabbages, radishes, watermelons, and onions—all were lacking until the Spaniards introduced them.

Foremost of Paraguayan trees, judging by the value of its product, was the yerba, whose coarse green leaves were roasted and powdered. Thus prepared, the product was treated with boiling water and yielded that incomparable tea called *maté*. Thousands of Indians were to die in the *yerbales* gathering leaves after Spaniards developed a taste for maté. The origin of maté is a matter that lies entirely with makers of myths. Some attribute the event to St. Bartholomew; others say that St. Thomas, who the Jesuits insisted had preached in Brazil and Paraguay, taught the preparation and use of yerba. The tea is drunk from a gourd, the maté, which has given its name to the beverage. In curative powers it has no equal, if one believes stories that are told about it. Unfortunately, it did much to cure Paraguay of a numerous native population.

Paraguayan cedars attained such magnificent proportions that those of Lebanon were but pygmies in comparison. Pedro Lozano, a Jesuit historian, had seen two forty-four-foot canoes, each deep enough to conceal a man lying down, made from one tree. Near Salta in Argentina, another Jesuit and his companion came upon a fallen cedar so large that a man on horseback could not see over it. Palm trees of various species covered many leagues. In some the hearts were "so tender and tasteful that one might eat them with much pleasure"; the trunks of others yielded a smooth, intoxicating drink; small, buff-colored coconuts from one species were used to make rosaries. As heavy as lead was the wood of the very tall *palo blanco* (white trunk). The ceibo was extremely light and its pink flowers that turned to deep purple were valued for dyeing wool or linen; its bark cured the jaguar's vicious bite.

Where cedars and pines soared upwards for one hundred feet or more, the shorter lapacho might seem to be something of a shrub. J. P. Robertson, an English merchant banished from Paraguay in 1815, was enthusiastic about this forest oddity: "From the solid trunk of one of these trees a Portuguese scooped out at Villa Real a canoe, which brought down to Assumption a hundred bales of yerba (that is, 22,500 lbs. of Paraguay tea), several hides made up into balls and filled with molasses, a load of deals, seventy packages of tobacco, and eight Paraguay [Payaguá?] sailors, to manage the three masts and sails of the large, but yet elegantly scooped-out trunk of the lapacho-tree." That, surely, was one of the greatest scoops of the century! Resistant, like the *quebracho* (ax-breaker), to rot and insects, lapacho wood went into homes from Buenos Aires to Asunción; huge beams, sometimes polished to a red-marble glow, made Jesuit mission churches defy nature's efforts to return all buildings to earth.

The quebracho was common in the Chaco and in the mission country. Impervious to water and insects, this tough tree provided wood for furniture and buildings. Its only fruit was a "butterfly" which grew in its blossoms and which dropped to the ground, took root, and started another tree. A brew made from quebracho possessed the admirable quality of curing pulmonary diseases. Likewise it had no peer as a cure for venereal disease, the *humor galico,* and for internal ailments.

Great pines, their top branches spread out like the umbrella pines of Italy, grew in forests across Brazil and into Paraguay. The trunk of this noble tree was so symmetrical that it seemed to have been turned on a lathe. Its pine nuts, roasted or boiled, were an important food; balsam from the trunk cured diseases of bone and nerve. Seeds of one species of pine, the *curiybay,* were taken as a purgative to rid the sufferer of "bile and phlegm through vomiting and other evacuations, causing deadly convulsions"; but a swallow of wine or warm water would end such torment. Balsam of the wizard tree, the *ibira paye,* could cure almost anything. Another large tree, the *molle,* yielded a balsam that healed deep wounds, stopped the flow of blood, and calmed the nerves. Molle resin and meal made from its seeds warmed the blood and cured chills, especially when mixed with the alcoholic *chicha.* Incense from the *ayui,* or laurel, vile in odor, gave protection when epidemics swept through the country; a poultice of its leaves, flowers, or bark drew poison from snake or insect bites; a powder made from its roots and taken with warm water dissolved liver stones. Nearly every tree found some use in the weird medical lore of Paraguay. The *paraparay,* a large and beautiful shade tree, offered cures for stomach trouble, open sores, putrid fevers, and mysterious ailments. The tasty melon-like fruit of the *mamon* relieved burning fevers; the sassafras or *apiterebi* relieved urinary obstructions; the *caberá,* growing in swamps or on river banks, produced a resin that was useful in curing toothaches.

Among many useful smaller plants was the wild pineapple (*caraguatá*) which grew long spikes crowned with flowers. Its leaves, used as a thatch, also produced strong fibers for rope or cloth. The fruit could be eaten, or crushed and served as a refreshing drink. Its heavy sap was a source of wine, vinegar, sugar, and syrup. No plant in the province could compare with *mandioca,* elsewhere known as *casava,* which was and is the Paraguayan staff of life. Roots of this plant, except those of one variety, contain a poison when green; but the ubiquitous St. Thomas, the Pay Luma of legend, taught people how to cultivate it and to prepare it for use.

The *macaguá,* name of both bird and plant, bore seeds that were a positive antidote for snakebite. The bird, always at war with snakes, entered combat with one wing held before its head as a shield. If its antagonist succeeded in inflicting a wound, the bird hurried to the macaguá, ate of its seeds, and returned to the attack. Paraguayans, observing this interesting habit, soon discovered that the macaguá cured headaches, fevers, and paroxysms. There were plants to purify the blood, aid digestion, drive away pestilence, improve the appetite, increase ardor, stimulate fading energy, and encourage sleep. Tobacco, called *pey* by the

7

Guaranís, grew abundantly. Flowers in profusion were visited by swarms of bees that made delicious honey and great quantities of wax.

Wild and domestic birds—not nearly so numerous in Paraguay as the *bichos,* insects that make life something of a torment—multiplied with characteristic tropical lavishness. Chickens, ducks, and geese were raised by the Indians; swallows, doves, and other friendly birds followed them in large numbers. Pheasants, partridges, eagles, hawks, buzzards, and waterfowl in wild profusion were found on plains, swamps, and lakes, and in the forests. Even a condensed list of Paraguayan birds would be several pages in length, so riotous was this form of life in an ornithologist's paradise. Chief of scavengers was the *caracará,* a gluttonous bird that cleansed the country of decomposing flesh. Parrots large and small, of dull or brilliant plumage, darkened the skies, filled the air with the sound of whirring wings, and ravaged sown fields. The black *carpintero,* or carpenter bird, with a beak so strong that it dug nests in the hardest of timber, had a colored topknot and a breast splashed with crimson.

Animals common in Europe were unknown to Paraguay before Spaniards entered the country. Pedro de Mendoza introduced horses in 1537 when he left seven stallions and five mares in Argentina, but it was probably Álvar Núñez Cabeza de Vaca who first brought horses into Paraguay proper. By 1600 they were so plentiful that wild herds roamed the pampas and the Chaco. Burros likewise came from Europe, as did all other beasts of burden.

Many species of animals, picturesque if not useful, were native to Paraguay. Several kinds of deer formed bezoar stones in their alimentary tracts. There were wild boars and other swinelike creatures whose navels grew on their backs. They ran in packs behind a leader that summoned them to defense when threatened by an enemy, and they fought savagely, especially against the puma. The lonely anteater found no shortage of food in a country swarming with ants. Among the palm trees, ants often erected conical burrows of clay which measured from four to five feet in diameter at the base and rose to a height of eight to ten feet. The three-toed tapir, large as an ass, with mulish ears and mouth like a calf, was a peaceful creature valued highly for its bezoar stones and extraordinarily tough hide. The Guaranís called the Milky Way the *Camino de Antas,* or Tapir Road. Quite in contrast to the peaceful tapir were the big cats, the mountain lions, jaguars, and pumas. "Whatever valor and cruelty nature denied the lions of Africa, it seems she added to the tiger which is without doubt the king of beasts in all the Indies." This native tiger, actually a jaguar, was an unsociable beast except for cross-breeding with the lion; a union that produced the leopard, so Pedro Lozano insists. Sworn enemy of all creatures, the tiger often attacked men and had a particular liking for Negroes. Not even aquatic animals were safe, since the tiger was a good swimmer. Before white men came, Indians believed that the devil frequently took the tiger's form; but, emboldened by Christianity, they dared to hunt it from horseback, throwing a lariat around the tiger's neck to choke it. Spaniards had great sport hunting the beast with mastiffs, lances, and firearms.

An unknown animal, according to some credulous persons, bore a great *carbúnculo,* or ruby, that shone with marvelous splendor through the darkest of nights. No one ever saw this elusive creature since exposure to its eerie light caused one to lose all sense of direction, and, of course, no one ever killed an *augaipitán,* the "evil spirit that burns like fire." The *quirquincho,* a hoggish-appearing animal protected by a hard shell, was so fond of deer meat that he would lie on his back, make a trough of his belly to catch rain water, then seize and kill any deer so unwise as to drink from this improvised tank.

St. Patrick would have found far more work in Paraguay than in Ireland. Reptiles of all sizes and in great profusion did their part in maintaining an ecological balance. The *cascabel* (bell snake) was a giant rattler whose poisonous bite meant certain death unless the wound were treated promptly. Often growing to lengths in excess of fifteen feet, the *curiyú* (anaconda) could swallow a small deer without chewing it at all. This fearsome creature hunted its prey on the ground or in arboreal highways and crushed its victims into pulp before swallowing them. A hungry curiyú, hanging from a branch over the water, could devour large numbers of fish. Its more loathsome habits, such as lying belly-up in the sun until its gorged stomach rotted and became worm-infested, may be passed by quickly.

In the almost impenetrable swamps lived a huge water snake, eight to twelve feet in length, that could swallow a man without difficulty. Father Antonio Ruiz de Montoya has related two stories about this monster which have yet to be proved. On one occasion, the padre asserts, he saw a snake swallow an Indian; on the next day, this Guaraní Jonah emerged violently, his bones crushed as by a mill. The other Montoya tale has been repeated frequently and rests on the belief that this man-eating snake breeds in human fashion. An Indian woman, "carelessly washing some clothes on the banks of the Paraná, saw one of these beasts and it unexpectedly attacked for the purpose of violating her. The woman was speechless with fright on seeing the huge snake so licentious, and the latter, carrying her to the opposite bank of the river, carried out its lascivious purpose." For three days the woman lay on the bank, unable to move. All this time the snake guarded her carefully, going and coming from the water. Father Montoya found the dying woman, heard her story, and administered the last rites of the Church. Anything could happen in old Paraguay.

A small gray viper, the *frailesca,* measuring fifteen to twenty inches, was vicious and deadly to man and beast; another, similar to the frailesca, wore a crimson stripe on its throat and its skin was mottled black, green, and yellow. Not all Paraguayan snakes were poisonous, but there were so many deadly species that the Indians grew large quantities of spikenard for use as a general antidote.

Rivers and swamps abounded with fish and monsters. The cannibalistic *piraña,* small but vicious, ran in schools that could rip off a man's flesh in a matter of seconds. Even today Paraguayans hesitate to swim in rivers unless protected by a crib. Edible fish existed in such quantities that rivers and lakes never failed to provide food. The *yacaré* (cayman) was a source of excitement and adventure for those brave enough to seek it.

This Paraguayan paradise, so easy to contemplate with shuddering or with rapture from the depths of an easy chair, held great possibilities for civilization. Guaraní Indians, given a few more centuries of isolation from white men, might have developed a high culture. They might, also, have continued their ancient struggle, against a nature that could not be conquered, with no appreciable success. Lush vegetation, swarms of pests, tremendous floods, terrific tropical storms—everything was exaggerated. None of the Indians had conquered their environment, but several tribes had accomplished something much wiser: they had learned to live in rude harmony with nature, however mysterious it might be.

Guaranís believed in spirits big and little, good and bad; they felt that there was something like an immortal soul, but heaven and hell were introduced by Christians. There was no priesthood to provide liaison between man and God, nor could witches, wizards, or magicians fill the gap. If it were possible to examine myths and legends as the Guaranís repeated them before white men came, one might have a better understanding of their religious beliefs. "The study of Guaraní myths," says Eloy Fariña Núñez, "enables us to determine the principal elements in the religious beliefs associated with those myths. In brief, one may assert that the Guaraní religion was monotheistic; that the supreme God of this religion was a pure spirit, undefined, without form; that it recognized the principle of the immortality of the soul and, probably, the existence of a paradise; that it likewise acknowledged the spirit of evil with a limited influence and distinct from the Christian devil, and, finally, that it was a religion without idols, temples, or sacrifices."

Surrounded by exotic plants and animals, fantastic creations of a capricious nature, the Guaranís naturally evolved explanations of how such things came to be. Tupá was the great creator, the spirit whose symbol and home were the golden sun; Añá (or Porá), who took refuge with the goddess Yací in the waning moon, was the great destroyer, the author of plagues and misfortunes. These two deities or their minions were prominent in Guaraní mythology. Tupá created trees and made the forest; he

11

covered the naked banks of streams with grass and flowers; he
made the giant anaconda and the deadly coral, the monkey and
the fox, and every living thing. After long thought he created
man. There was a remote forest where men did not go and Tupá
wished to people it with these new beings. He sent I-Yara, Master
of Waters and his emissary, to fetch him a block of earth from
that area. Tupá shaped the earth with his hands, and from it he
fashioned two figures who were brothers. He gave them sparks
from the sun and they lived. One brother, Pitá, was bronze or red
in color; the other, Morotí, was white. The Master of Waters
then formed two sisters to be their companions, since the creation of women was too mean a task for Tupá.

Pitá and Morotí lived in the forest with their mates, loving and
procreating. Pitá discovered fire and Morotí the art of cooking
meat. These simple people liked the meat so well that they left
their idyllic pursuits to become hunters, fashioning the lance and
bow the better to kill game. Disputes arose over the division of
spoils and soon Pitá and Morotí headed rival camps.

Tupá was angry. He could have destroyed these people whom
Añá threatened to mislead; instead, he decided to teach them
that they were created to live in harmony and not in war. Tupá
summoned Osununú, the thunder, to shake the earth; he sent a
terrible storm that raged through the forest for three days and
three nights. Their quarrels forgotten, the children of Pitá and
Morotí huddled beneath the trees, blinded by lightning and
deafened by thunder. The sun appeared, and from it came I-Yara,
disguised as a dwarf, who led them to a vale in the forest. There
he ordered Pitá and Morotí to embrace. As their children gazed
in astonishment the brothers merged into one body, then
changed into a bush, the lily of the forest, whose red flowers
slowly turn to white in autumn.

On the still surface of a pool in the Jardín Botánico at Asunción
the huge leaves of the water lily *Victoria regia* lie as in eternal
benediction. Common to the rivers of South America, this queen
of aquatic plants delights the eye with its beautiful blossoms,
pervades the air with rare perfume, provides quantities of edible
seeds, and offers its leaves as a platform for frogs and birds. This

is the *irupé* of the Guaranís, the water maize, that came from a love affair between Morotí and Pitá.

These two personifications of color were brothers for the purpose of explaining the forest lily; they are male and female in the myth of *irupé*. Pitá, of course, was a handsome warrior and Morotí was the loveliest of maidens, an incurable coquette. One evening as the young men and women were walking on a river bank, Morotí threw a bracelet into the water and told Pitá to get it to prove his love for her. The warrior disappeared under the waters and did not come back. A sorceress declared that she had seen Pitá in the rich palace of the water witch, the siren who robbed the tribe of so many valiant men. No, Pitá would not return. Morotí must go after him, and she alone could rescue him from the fatal embrace that held him. Morotí tied a rock to her feet and entered the water. Morning came, but still the lovers did not appear. Instead there was a beautiful water lily above the fatal spot, a flower whose outer petals were red for Morotí and whose inner petals were white for Pitá. Tupá had united them in death and had resurrected them in life. Thus the *irupé,* the Queen Victoria, was created.

Each version of the creation begins with the earth, plants, and animals, reaches a climax in the appearance of man, then goes on to an anticlimax to explain the origin of some plant, bird, or animal. The Guaranís cannot agree on some of their stories, especially concerning the origin of maté.

One hundred years after Asunción was founded in 1537, the Spaniards had all but given up hope of finding El Dorado in the land of the Guaraní. The dream died hard, and many a Spaniard died with it in Chaco wastes or drowned in rivers and swamps. There were riches in Paraguay, however, and among them was the leaf of the yerba tree. Maté is as inseparable from Paraguay as oriental tea from England. The leaves, roasted and pulverized, produce a bitter drink which becomes delicious as the taste grows accustomed to it. From Villa Rica, from southern Paraguay and Misiones in Argentina, ton after ton of maté supplied the *porteño* in Buenos Aires, the Gaucho on the pampas, the miner in Peru. Produced in three grades, the *caámini* commanded the highest prices. At the height of maté's fame in the colonial period, Peru alone took 2,500,000 pounds a year and the Gaucho of Argentina refused to be without it. Beef and maté were his diet. Although by no means the elixir of life, maté is a wholesome beverage that contains small quantities of narcotics.

*Caá,* or maté, was one of the trees almost worshiped by the forest-dwelling Guaranís. It is strange that such a plant should have an origin closely linked to Añá, the evil spirit. Shortly before white men arrived in the Plata country, a Guaraní sorcerer learned that by drinking a brew made from yerba leaves he became possessed of powers known to Añá. The tea cleared the drinker's mind and enabled him to communicate with the devil. Jesuits working in Guayrá changed the story, making use of Pay Luma, or Paí Zumé, the legendary benefactor who had preached and taught among the Tupí-Guaraní. This Pay Luma was St. Thomas, they said, who had preached in Paraná. Before leaving his converted children, St. Thomas crushed and roasted the poisonous green yerba leaves and brewed a tea from them. He and his converts drank this brew. Maté, according to the Jesuits, was divine in its origin.

Still another account insists that when Tupá was traveling about the country, he stopped at a hut where a poor old man lived with his daughter and a hen. The Indian killed his chicken to feed the guest. Tupá was so impressed that he made the daughter immortal by changing her into a yerba tree—a peculiar way to show gratitude. But some old Paraguayan will dispute this story. God did not change the girl into a tree: he made her queen of the maté, the Caá Yara, who is young and blonde. And to this day workers in the *yerbales* will swear allegiance to her, promising to touch no other woman if she will aid and protect them. A horrible death awaits the *minero,* the yerba worker, who breaks this vow.

Caá Yara herself has suffered horribly at the hands of myth makers. Some call her Caá Porá, a Diana of the forest who protects her favorite animals from hunters. And Caá Porá has been called a giant who devours the game that hunters kill and cannot find afterwards.

14

One of the most delightful tales about maté begins with the moon goddess, Yací, a divinity who loved to stroll through the forest as a beautiful blonde, nude or clothed in some filmy garment, accompanied by a white maiden, Araí. One time this lovely pair was confronted by a terrible male jaguar. Why did not the two blondes make use of their divinity to escape? Because in human form they had no supernatural powers. They were saved by an arrow that whistled through the air and struck the tiger in the side. Furiously the beast jumped at his enemy, an old Indian hidden behind a tree, who ducked under the jaguar and killed him by plunging an arrow into his heart. This encounter enabled Yací and Araí to get back into their shapes as moon and cloud. They returned that night to visit their savior in his dreams, and Yací told him that she had created a new tree for him, the *caá*, and told him how to prepare tea from it.

The *yedra*, or *hiedra*, a plant whose broad green leaves suffocate trees and eventually cover dead trunks with a false grandeur of life, came from a beautiful woman's ambition. Somewhere on the banks of the Paraná lived a Guaraní tribe whose prowess in war made them invincible. One day there appeared among them a beautiful young widow carrying her orphaned son in her arms. She had been the wife of a chief, but her husband's death caused her to flee in order that his enemies might not kill the boy. The greatest warriors of the tribe sought her love in vain. They wondered at this strange conduct of the beautiful stranger until it was known that she had become the *compañera* of their white-haired chief. The young warriors were angry. How could a young and beautiful woman love the old man? The chief must have forced her to become his woman and she had consented in order that her son might succeed to his stepfather's position. The young woman's love was too much for the old chief: one day he died in her arms. Her sacrifice of youth to ambition had gained nothing for her son. While the funeral was in progress, someone entered the widow's hut and shot an arrow into her son's heart. Again the beautiful creature became an outcast, a wanderer through marsh and forest. Tupá finally took mercy upon her and changed the unhappy woman into a climbing plant, whose green

15

leaves may be seen smothering old trees to death, an eternal reminder that young women and old men should not be too ambitious.

With a cross in each blossom, the passion flower is one of the most beautiful of tropical vines. Devout Spaniards found it to be a natural representation of the passion of Christ. With its thorny crown, its blood-red fruit, and the cross, the plant reminded the conquerors of Calvary. A poem of blues and reds, each fragile blossom is a masterpiece. To the Guaranís this lovely creation is the *burucuyá,* once a pretty Spanish girl who came to America with her father. The *señorita* had an illicit affair with a Guaraní cacique and refused to marry the man selected by her father. For a time the lovers dared not meet, but each night the cacique kept a vigil outside the fort, announcing his presence with notes on a flute. There came a time when Burucuyá no longer heard this musical love message. She pined away longing for her lover. One day the cacique's old mother came out of the brush to tell her that her father had killed the cacique, suspecting that he was the reason for his daughter's refusal to marry. Burucuyá, whose Spanish name has been lost, found her lover's body on its arboreal platform. She dug a grave, told the old woman to bury her with the man whose love had caused his death, and then died of a broken heart. Many months later the passion flower appeared on the grave, a triumph of love over death.

Among the great trees of Paraguay is the *guabirá* whose oval leaves end in a small spike. He who eats fruit of this tree becomes enamored of Paraguay and is content to spend the rest of his life there. Guabirá was a girl, endowed with supernatural powers and a favorite of Tupá and Yací. She decided to become a sorceress and passed all the tests without faltering. She fasted and remained chaste, almost impossible feats among the Guaranís. The final test before the candidate could become a *cuñá-taí,* a medicine woman, caused many an aspirant to abandon both fasting and chastity. She must drink a brew made of maté, a medicinal herb, and *jugo de muerte,* or death juice. This last ingredient was seepage from decomposing bodies that rested on platforms in the trees. Guabirá became a *cuñá-taí.*

16

Dressed in her peculiar costume, Guabirá sat under the sacred tree, the *aguaraibá*. Wearing a hat of plaited feathers, a necklace of feathers and colored seeds, and a jacket of fibers and feathers, the witch must have looked like some rare bird. After inhaling tobacco smoke until she became dizzy, Guabirá could read the future and give meaning to the present. She became a snake charmer of no mean ability. Then she attended the wedding of a Guaraní girl and a Spaniard whose life she had saved. At one stage in the ceremony, Guabirá and the Spaniard disappeared. For many years no one knew what had happened. Finally another witch revealed that the two had fled into the forest to enjoy a passionate honeymoon, after which the Spaniard had tired of Guabirá and had left her to find a white wife. Guabirá was punished for having broken her vow of chastity. She died an outcast; but Tupá changed her body into a tree that produces a yellow fruit. Once a man eats of this fruit, he no longer yearns for the land of his birth, and the maid who loves him need have no fear that her lover will go away.

Another tree, the *izapí*, weeps constantly. Its leaves give off a fine, refreshing mist. This phenomenon is explained by the story of Izapí, a beautiful daughter of a cacique. Izapí either had a heart of stone or lacked tear glands. Nothing could make her weep. She could witness the most horrible disasters without emotion, watch lovers pine away in unrequited passion, and refuse the most pitiful appeals for aid without shedding a tear. Calamities fell on her tribe until at last only a few were left, among them Izapí. This girl, said the wise ones, was the cause of their sorrows because she would not weep. At last a witch invoked the wrath of Añá, who changed her into a tree whose leaves never stop weeping.

The bite of the ñandurié, a vicious snake, is deadly unless one uses an antidote made from the liana *icipó*. The liana and the snake, once were beautiful young sisters, Icipó and Ñandurié, who lived on the upper Paraná and spent many hours making gorgeous lace, the *ñandutí*, when their father was away hunting. One day Aguapé, son of a Guaraní cacique, wrecked his canoe near their hut. While he tarried with the family waiting for the

waters to subside, jealousy rose in the female breasts. Each of
the sisters loved Aguapé, but Aguapé loved neither of the wild
beauties. The girls resorted to love potions and charms to supplement more obvious inducements to ardor. Ñandurié, unable
to suppress her passion, offered her love to Aguapé and received
nothing but scorn in return. Thereupon she poisoned Aguapé's
food, and he went off into the forest to die. Icipó knew the antidote for the poison. She found Aguapé and offered to save him if
he would become her lover. When the warrior refused, Icipó left
him to die in the forest. Then Tupá intervened. He changed
Aguapé into a water hyacinth, whose blue, yellow, and red
flowers decorate the floating islands of the Paraná. The two sisters had to be punished, one for having poisoned Aguapé and the
other for having refused to save his life. Ñandurié became an
ugly, venomous snake and Icipó became a liana whose stems
contain an antidote to the snake's poison.

One story of the creation describes Tupá as having made the
earth and the animals, the beautiful and aromatic flowers, and
then a pair of dusky humans, male and female, from clay on a
river bank. Tupá was indeed surprised to learn some time later
that another god had created a white man and woman. This rival
creation caused Tupá to try again; but as his only materials were
clay and tree trunks, everything he made was dark in color. He
made the green crocodile, the red heron, the yellow snake, and
gorgeously colored butterfles; but he would not be satisfied until
he had made something that was white. Añá, the sagacious devil,
stole a girl from the land of white people and gave her to Tupá.
With this gift Tupá made a white bird, the dove. But the white
dove was ashamed of herself because all other creatures were
colored. Her melancholy coo was a complaint against her sad
fate. At last she sought out Tupá and prayed that he change her
color, but Tupá was too proud of his work to grant this wish. The
dove flew back into the solitude of the forest, where she impaled
herself upon a thorn in a vain attempt to end her unhappy life.
Red blood spread over her breast and the dove fell to the ground
as though dead. Recovering, she saw this splotch reflected in a
pool and hastened to Tupá who liked the change and made it

everlasting. Thus in Paraguay today one sees the wounded doves, snow white but for the crimson spots on their breasts.

In the trees along banks of rivers one may come upon little oven-nests of clay and grass made by a gray bird, the *hornero*, or oven-maker, whose song is beautiful in a land where symphonies of nature eternally praise the Creator. The hornero once was a young warrior who became enamored of a young woman whose golden voice he had heard while hunting. He longed to marry this maiden but seemed destined to espouse the chief's daughter. In the exercises attendant upon gaining manhood, all the young warriors entered contests, the victor automatically becoming the chief's son-in-law. This warrior did not want to marry the girl. His last test was one that required him to fast for several days, an ordeal made difficult by his being wrapped in hides. He survived the test; but when the chief unwound the hides, the young man slowly changed into a bird. He flew off to a tree and warbled a glorious song. The young lady of the forest, too, became a bird, and the couple built an ovenlike nest, a miniature of the hut where the hornero had lived as a man.

Hidden deeply in the woods, the shy *urutaú* sounds his mournful call in the stillness of the night. This weird bird induces melancholy in those who hear its monotonous complaint, a melancholy that epitomizes the sad history of Paraguay. The urutaú was a cacique's daughter who loved a Tupí enemy warrior. Unable to consummate her love, the maiden became a bird that mourns forever in the hidden recesses of the forest.

The work of missionaries among the Guaranís was made easier by a superstition which the fathers may have had a hand in starting. One of the most common denominators of myths is the idea that humans or gods may assume other forms, or may be punished by being changed into some other shape. Thus in European mythology Arachne became a spider, Europa was borne off by a god masquerading as a bull, and a prince cavorted about as a fish. The Guaranís believed that a man might become a tiger, a *yaguareté-abá*, that relished unbaptized natives for dinner. And there were the experiences of Isarakí, the turbulent one, to prove that almost anything could happen.

Something was wrong with Isarakí. As a child the poor fellow couldn't stay at home. He wandered through the woods, quarreled with man and beast, and developed his traits of treachery. He was a daredevil whose wit or strength sufficed to extricate him from the most serious scrapes. In the Chaco he struck up a friendship with an old Indian who taught him many things and told him about Juan Tuyá, who had learned the secret of changing himself into any beast whose form he wished to take. Isarakí sought out the old sorceress who knew the secret. Here was a man the witch rejoiced in, an ally in her war against man. She told him the secret, made the mystic signs, and Isarakí was initiated. His first deed was to become a *yaguareté* that terrorized the forest. After a fox had outwitted the man-tiger, he became a fox and led a band of these wolflike creatures in raids against human settlements. Then he became a snake, and finally a wasp. In this last form he made the mistake of stinging a man who tried to steal his honey, for the wasp died when he lost his stinger; but Isarakí merely returned to his human form. Isarakí, thinking over his adventures, returned to his delighted benefactress with a strange request. He wanted to become a creature ferocious as the tiger, cunning as a fox, loathsome and sneaky as a snake, and vicious as the wasp. "The witch changed him into a white man."

# CHAPTER II

# Guaraní and Guaycurú

T HERE WERE as many Indian tribes in the heart of South America as stars in the Milky Way. This exaggeration by an exasperated chronicler contained an element of truth since the principal nations were divided into tribes, and these in turn fell into smaller units, each of which had one or more names. To the west of the Paraguay River, the Chaco north of the Bermejo was a wild home for the Guaycurús and many other savages; to the east in Paraguay and Brazil lived the Guaraní and other relatives of the Caribes.

In remote ages Indian tribes invaded the North American continent, spread slowly southward until they crossed the Isthmus of Panama, and continued on to Tierra del Fuego, the island tip of South America. Sometime during this process, the great Tupí-Guaraní family occupied a large part of the Amazon and Plata basins. On the upper reaches of the Paraná River system, in the Paranápanema, Tiete, Río Grande, and Paranahiba valleys Guaraní culture developed. Somewhere in these valleys was the center of Guaraní civilization, the nucleus of dispersion. Tribes known as Carios, Tapes, Itatines, Chiriguanos, Guarajos, and many more, were but offshoots of the Guaraní family. Guaranís still cherish "a religious and imaginative cult of Mbaeveraguasú, the resplendent millenial city where the great chiefs dwell and where all Guaranís must go at least once in their lives." This fabled city is the old cultural center, accord-

21

ing to Guillermo Tell Bertoni, but the idea will hardly bear close scrutiny.

Most advanced of all the Guaraní tribes were the Carios, an agricultural people, skilled in weaving cotton and in making domestic implements. Their arts served the Spaniards well. Carios occupied the Asunción area, spread south to the Tebicuary River, north to the Manduvirá, and east for some sixty miles. They possessed objects of gold and silver, apparently obtained in war and trade with Andean peoples of Peru. Their fortified towns protected them from attacks by the river people, the Agaces and Payaguás, and from wild Guaycurús of the Chaco. One of these towns was Lambaré, a few miles south of Asunción, around which were built two wooden palisades twelve feet apart. Ulrich Schmidt, in obvious admiration, describes the outer works: "And at a distance of fifteen feet from this town wall they made pits as deep as the height of three men, one over the other, and put into them (but not above ground) lances of hardwood, with points like that of a needle; and they covered these pits with straw and small gravel, strewing a little earth and grass between, to the intent that when we Christians pursued them, or assaulted their town, we should have fallen blindly into these pitfalls. But at length they digged so many pits that they themselves fell into them."

Paraguayan historians and other social scientists sometimes go to considerable pains in attempting to prove that the Carios possessed admirable cultural traits. Testimony of Europeans who first encountered the tribe is by no means uniformly complimentary, but travelers usually write with an eye to what the reader might enjoy. One may take, as an example, Schmidt's remarks about the Carios: "The men have a little hole in their lips in which they put yellow crystals . . . two spans long and of the thickness of a quill or reed. This people, men and women, young and old, go completely naked as God created them. Among these Indians, the father sells his daughter, the husband his wife if she does not please him, and the brother sells or exchanges his sister. A woman costs a shirt or a bread knife, or a small hoe, or some other thing of that kind. These Carios also eat man's flesh if they can get it. For when they make prisoners in war, male or female, they fatten them as we do swine in Germany. But if the woman be somewhat young and good-looking, they keep her for a year or so, and if during that time she does not live after their desires, they put her to death and eat her, making a solemn banquet of it, and oftentimes this is combined with marriage."

Itatines, living north of the Carios, held the land from modern Bahía Negra north for more than one hundred miles and east to the region of Guayrá. Long before the Spanish conquest, Itatines had attacked the Inca Empire's eastern borders, probably near Chuquisaca, the colonial La Plata, and left a colony of Chiriguanos near the western limits of the Audiencia of Charcas. The Carios, too, are said to have made an expedition against outlying provinces of the Inca Empire a century before Spaniards appeared. Far to the south of Paraguay were the Tapes, an agricultural people well suited to the mission system established among them by Jesuits in the seventeenth century.

The Payaguás, river pirates who lived first on one side and then the other of the Río Paraguay, terrorized the country as far north as Bahía Negra, where the Itatines held them in check; but they bedeviled Spanish settlers for decades. As late as 1815 these half-naked savages lived in *tolderías* north of Asunción, traded with the mestizo and Creole, and treated each with contempt. Masters of swift canoes, fearless and strong, they resisted every civilizing or Christianizing effort. Peculiar ornamentation of the body gave them a distinctive and weird appearance. Males wore wooden discs in their ear lobes, and some of these discs were several inches in diameter. Females, nude from the waist up, loved silver ornaments that hung from the lower lip. Doctors, or medicine men, were always on trial: after the death of three patients treated by a "doctor," the practitioner himself was executed. This perhaps laudable practice has not been adopted by modern Paraguayans. By serving as couriers and vendors of fish and grass, the Payaguás earned enough money to buy liquor to dull their senses to the point that they were perhaps insensible to the filth of their domestic establishments. The dictator Francia, incensed by raids from Chaco Indians, got rid of the Payaguás in 1820 by banishing them to a settlement some 180 miles north of Asunción.

Agaces ruled the river south of Asunción to Corrientes. Together with the Payaguás, they controlled the Paraguay for more than five hundred miles and served as a barrier to attacks by Guaycurús of the Chaco. Agaces were a treacherous lot, even in a land where treachery was common. Larger than most Guaranís, these river marauders refused to use their strength in agricultural pursuits. Fish and meat, supplemented by products demanded as ransom for captives, were their principal foods. Even after obtaining this ransom, the Agaces rarely surrendered their prisoners but indulged in sadistic furies at their expense.

No one can do more than guess how many Guaranís occupied Paraguay—perhaps 100,000, perhaps twice that number. The Asunción area seems to have been a vital center, if not the principal focus, of Guaraní power. Their towns were small aggregations of huts in which lived thirty to sixty families subject to a chief, the *rubichá* (or *mburubichá*). This leader was selected in part because of his oratorical skill in the melodious Guaraní tongue, and his people provided him with food, clothing, housing, and women. A chief's concubines were limited in number only by his own virility. When a prominent person visited the village, its chief as a matter of course sent him one or two of his twenty or thirty concubines. Marital ties were loose among the Guaranís, since their principal business, after hunting and fishing, was war, and permanent wives were held to be a handicap to a warrior. In the matter of clothing the chief was easily satisfied with headdresses, bracelets, and necklaces of feathers which were common articles of adornment for all, except for occasional bands of modesty. Guaranís slept on the ground, on mats, or on rustic beds of branches. Only prominent persons enjoyed the relative comfort of hammocks.

Superstitions, always prominent among primitive peoples, played an important role in Guaraní life. If a pregnant woman ate two ears of corn, she would give birth to twins; if a deer entered and left a village, someone was certain to die; if a toad jumped on a boat, one of its occupants would soon join his ancestors. Pregnant women who ate meat of a large animal would give birth to children with deformed noses, but those who ate small birds would have small babies. Expectant fathers must kill no wild animals, make no arrows, war clubs, or any other war-like instruments. After the baby's birth, the father fasted for fifteen days in deep seclusion to protect the health and future of his child. Viewing the great fecundity of the Guaranís, one wonders how men ever found time to make their arms, and if the women ever ate any meat except that of small birds.

Sorcerers, the *hechiceros,* were in league with Añá, whose appearances to these wizards of the evil eye were accompanied by fearful manifestations of hell's tormented domain. The devil told them what spells to use, how to induce fevers and coughs, stabbing pains and blindness. If these magic rites failed, the *hechicero* might tie a toad, snake, or some other loathsome creature to a tree and let it die of hunger and thirst. As the captive's strength failed, so did that of the bewitched person. These makers of spells were not so powerful as the sorcerers who, while acknowledging human mothers, claimed to be without earthly fathers. These sons of the occult were the prophets, the prognosticators of things to come. They had power to arouse beasts of the forest and to raise tempests on the waters, thus preventing the people from catching game or fish, to dry up the rivers and to send floods raging over the land. They were hypnotists of fearful countenance who had fasted and suffered to win their power from the evil spirit. Medicine men, who made no pretence of sorcery, effected cures by sucking wounds or sores.

Guaranís, it is true, were skilled in primitive agriculture; but it was the women who raised the food and gathered mandioca roots while men spent their time in hunting. Weapons of the chase and of war were the same. Armed with bows and arrows and the macana, a heavy war club, the Guaraní warriors were formidable antagonists. Moises S. Bertoni, author of many scholarly works on the Guaranís, denies that they used arrows in warfare and indignantly rejects all attempts to prove that they were cannibals. Still, there is much evidence to the contrary. A warrior was so skillful with the bow, one chronicler maintains, that "a fly in the air could hardly escape from his arrow." Prisoners of war were eaten at once if old; but young men were fattened for the kill and kept in good humor by delectable maidens.

This custom of preparing a captive for the sacrifice was not unusual among American Indians. The Guaraní practice has been described by Pedro Lozano with evident relish for its gory details, and it has been denied with great vehemence by others. Once the captive warrior had been fattened properly, the entire neighborhood was summoned to partake of the feast, although there was hardly enough meat to go around. After the guests had assembled, the one who had captured the sacrificial victim "came forth with the pomp of a conqueror in the Roman Capitol, dressed in all the finery possible to an always naked people, which amounted to little more than colored plumes. All of his relatives, attired in like array, accompanied him as he entered the stockade with measured step, a *macana* on his shoulder. The unhappy captive, who was to entertain the bystanders with his death, came out tied with two strong ropes by which two robust youths pulled him. He was received at the stockade gate by six old women uglier than harpies, painted red and yellow, and wearing necklaces not of precious stones or pearls but of pointed teeth taken from the bodies of other miserable ones whom they had attended at martyrdom. They were singing and dancing to the sound of clay pans carried in their hands to catch the blood and entrails of the victim. The grave conqueror, on drawing close to the captive, struck with the *macana* a blow that the 'patient' received on his arms which had been left free for that purpose. Other blows fell rather gently, since the longer death were delayed, the greater would be the spectators' pleasure. When the victim at last was exhausted, the conqueror struck a final blow on his head and killed him to the accompaniment of such applause, cheers and whistling that the very air trembled."

The wicked old harpies collected the victim's blood in their pans, then the multitude came to touch the body or to strike it with sticks, for this was the time when the unnamed selected for themselves the appellations by which they were to be known henceforth. Parents, on the birth of children, gave infants rather facetious names suggested by some "physical defect or quality that they recognized in the body of the new-born infant." One with a gray color would be called *cuervo* (raven); one whose voice was hoarse became known as *rana* because he croaked like a frog. But now, at the great celebration, these ridiculous names were discarded for others more suitable. After the naming ceremony was over, the killer cut the body into small pieces. Everyone must partake of the feast, even though his portion be but a fiber or a swallow of broth. Suckling infants also tasted the soup, at which time their mothers might change their names.

Pero Hernández, in Cabeza de Vaca's *Comentarios,* gives a somewhat different version of these cannibalistic rites: "They eat the flesh of their enemies whom they take captive in war, bringing them to their settlements and making great merriment and rejoicing with them, dancing and singing till the captive grows fat. They give him their wives and daughters, in order that he may have every pleasure. It is these wives who take the trouble to fatten him. Those held in the greatest honour among them admit him to their couches, adorn him in various ways according to their custom, and bedeck him with feathers and necklaces of white beads and stones, which are much prized among them. When he begins to grow fat they redouble their efforts; the dancing, singing, and pleasures of all kinds increase. Then the men come; they adorn and make ready three boys of the age of six or seven, placing a little hatchet in their hands. The Indian considered the bravest among them now takes a wooden sword in his hand, called in their language *macana,* and leads the captive to a place where he is made to dance for one hour; the Indian then advances, and with both hands deals him a blow in the loins, and another on the spine to knock him down. It happens sometimes that after striking him six blows on the head they cannot kill him, so hard are their heads . . . . When they have knocked him down the three boys come with their hatchets, and the eldest of them, usually the son of the chief, begins striking blows on his head, the others do the same until the blood flows . . . . As soon as he is dead . . . the old women cut the body in pieces and cook it in their earthenware pots, distributing the flesh among

27

themselves." A fine way to end a year of pleasure and adventures in good eating! Félix de Azara, who read this account in the *Comentarios,* refused to believe that any of the Guaranís were cannibalistic in pre-conquest days.

Fierce in war and cruel to enemies, the Guaraní was kind and hospitable to his own people. No stranger was denied food and shelter. A visitor, or one of the family who had returned from a journey, met with a peculiar reception that had something of a universal quality. The guest or traveler entered the hut and sat at the side of his host without saying a word. Then the women entered, surrounded the seated figures, and burst into loud lamentations. They exhumed from memory the guest's relatives, praised their virtues and deeds, their good fortune, and recalled the manner of their deaths. The women sighed woefully; the men bowed their heads and covered their faces. When a traveler was greeted on his return, the women refrained from vocal exhumation of ancestors but entertained him with a most sorrowful wailing account of all the bad things that had happened since he went away. But these feminine antics ended soon, and the hut immediately became the center of gaiety.

Guaraní gaiety must have been rather peculiar. Dr. Cecilio Báez, in his *Resumen de la historia del Paraguay,* says the Guaranís had no liking for dancing, singing, or playing games; that there was no family life, no friendly gathering to eat and gossip. Some writers insist that Guaranís loved oratory, others hold that they spoke only when necessary, never laughed or displayed joy, and gave vent to sorrow in lamentations but not in tears. Physical suffering brought no complaints or groans. If this characterization is true in general, something certainly happened that wrought a miracle. The modern Guaraní has a keen sense of humor, loves music and games, will shed real tears, talks readily and fast, and is a great storyteller. These traits may be a result of Spanish example and Spanish blood. Dr. Báez is hardly justified in denying a Guaraní love for music, or for a reasonable facsimile. There were such instruments as the reed flute, the bone flute, the shell horn, the war horn, the trumpet, and the calabash guitar to prove that Guaranís made music of a sort. Certainly the Jesuits

Top: Mocovi hunter with Guaycurú-type tonsure
Bottom: Guaycurú warriors with tattoo and wearing painted-
skin robes

After Baucke, reproduced from Vol. I, *Handbook of
South American Indians,* ed. by Julian H. Steward

found them to be apt pupils in learning to sing and to play instruments.

Family life among the Guaranís seems to have been governed by expediency. Polygamy was practiced, not to satisfy sexual desire, but to produce a numerous progeny. Plural marriage, Dr. Bertoni testifies, was not a universal practice. Some tribes were monogamous, and others had a limited polygamy. Wives were well treated in spite of assertions that women were sold lightly by male relatives. Divorce was easy: a woman merely told her consort to be off. Adultery was punishable by death. Children were cherished, not with a great display of affection but with an instinctive love for those who were to continue the race.

Guaranís still retained vestiges of later neolithic culture when Spaniards came to their land. Forests provided bows for arches and shafts for arrows. Stones and bones, shaped to use, served as tools, utensils, and weapons. Fire, produced by friction, had been known for so long that even its origin was lost in hazy legend. Vessels of baked clay were adorned with harmonious designs by woman's skilled fingers; water wolves and jaguars yielded skins for clothing; cotton or vegetable fibers were woven into hammocks; benches of wood, carved with outlines of forest animals or incidents of the chase, were used widely. Basketry and weaving allowed the native artist a chance to execute designs in black and white. Multicolored feathers, combined and woven with intricate artistry, provided headdresses and other ornamentation. Vegetable dyes were used as paint to decorate the body, or to frighten enemies. Guaraní belles knew torso and leg paint centuries before their sophisticated sisters of remote lands used it to substitute for a sun tan. They bathed so frequently that Spaniards were horrified.

Like Indians of both continents, the Guaranís fashioned swift canoes from logs. Their *ygabas*, long and thin, carried from forty to seventy men; an early observer insisted that he had seen one that bore three hundred persons! These canoes, or piraguas, were a principal means of communication. A system of forest paths was used for runners who carried news quickly from tribe to tribe and helped to consolidate the Guaranís.

Perhaps as a part of a recent movement to glorify the Indian, some anthropologists have described the Guaranís in terms far more complimentary than the traditional interpretation of their traits will permit. Juan Natalicio González, in his *Proceso y formación de la cultura paraguaya*, praises the Guaranís for having domesticated such fauna as the chicken, duck, hazel hen, deer, and birds; for having discovered therapeutic qualities of animal products; for scientific precision in zoological and botanical nomenclature; for discovering medicinal uses of plants; and for developing agricultural plants in great numbers. Granted even the majority of these accomplishments, Guaranís could hardly compare with Aztecs, Mayas, Incas, and Toltecs.

Nature in eastern Paraguay, Natalicio González writes, produces a gregarious sense in the inhabitant. There, where trees are as tall as cathedrals, where exuberant forests and lush vegetation press together to form a harmonious, protective whole, individualism tends to be lost. But in the Chaco, individualism rules in nature. Trees more often stand apart, palms shoot from the ground like arrows and spread over the land like an army, each separated from the other. Inhospitable to plant and animal, these sentinels gain no support from one another. The west is an area of two great solitudes, the Andes and the Chaco; the east is a region where falls of classic elegance and perfect beauty mask force with grace. These conflicting regions are bound together by the Río Paraguay. What effect such geographical differences may have on a people's culture, particularly in view of other factors, is hard to say. Certainly Chaco Indians differed considerably from those east of the great river; certainly the heart of Paraguay lies to the east; and strange things happened everywhere.

Across the river in the Chaco several savage tribes wandered among the marshes and lost rivers, over the broad plains covered with tough grasses, and among the islands of trees. Rabbits, small deer, birds, fish, snakes, and lizards were their principal food, while an occasional enemy captive added variety to the diet. Their digestions were good, Charlevoix suggests, because "all of the Indians of South America have very hot stomachs."

None of these tribes was more fierce, none was less lovely than the Guaycurú.

Open to invasion from all sides, possessing a soil and general physical characteristics favorable only to hunting or pastoral pursuits, the Chaco held no attractions for the agricultural Guaranís. Except for sorties to the banks of the Paraguay to protect river communities, the Guaranís let the Guaycurús severely alone; Payaguás and Agaces could be depended upon to protect the river barrier itself. The presence of Guaycurú warriors so close to Guaraní land has been considered beneficial to tribes living east of the river, since the Guaranís, in constant danger of attack, were forced to federate loosely. This loose federation may have promoted cultural development, but the Guaycurús felt no such compulsion. They remained largely unchanged for centuries, in spite of early Franciscan and Jesuit efforts to establish missions among them and in spite of more modern Anglican and Catholic attempts to introduce Christianity to the Chaco Indians. With the end of the Chaco War in 1935, Paraguay made tentative gestures toward colonizing beyond the great river's immediate shores, a development that might continue and expand the Mennonite colonies that began in the nineteen twenties, and which must inevitably press hard on twentieth-century remnants of the Guaycurús. But these things lay far in the future in days before the Spanish conquest.

Man for man, the Guaycurú must have been considerably superior to the Guaraní. A short time before Spaniards came, Mbayás or Albaias crossed over to attack the Itatines in the north of eastern Paraguay and to settle in that region between the Ipané and Apá rivers. Many of the displaced Itatines migrated to the south, settled in Corrientes and Misiones provinces of modern Argentina. These Mbayás, a constant threat to the Spanish colony, were finally conquered in the mid-eighteenth century when Don Rafael de la Moneda was governor. Even before then, in the region of San Pedro, Concepción, and Rosario, the Itatines who remained absorbed the invaders, leaving hardly a trace of Mbayá culture.

In physical aspect alone the Guaycurú might induce nightmares. Men went nude except for a bracelet or belt and a loosely woven cap; women, whose heads were plucked clean of hair, sometimes wore a sort of blacksmith's apron. Why, no one seems to know exactly, since modesty or shame was unknown. In cold weather both sexes wore skin coats and caps. They painted or daubed their bodies in various colors. A boy was black until he became fourteen; for two years thereafter he was red; then he went through the ceremony of becoming a warrior, an initiation conducted by a veteran. The old soldier pulled out the candidate's hair except for a topknot that he tied firmly, jabbed his body with a sharp bone, rubbed his scalp with blood and smeared red earth over him. Now the boy was a warrior and a man. At the age of twenty, another ceremony, with more painting, pricking of the body, and rubbing of the head made the warrior a veteran.

Disfigurement of the body was comparatively mild among the Guaycurús. Lower lips of babies were pierced so that baubles could hang from them; ears were bored and the holes were stretched to enable huge wooden plugs to be inserted eventually. Hairless, with plucked eyebrows to improve the sight, daubed with colored filth, decorated with anything that glittered, the Guaycurú must have presented an appearance sufficient to scare away the devils of rain, thunder, and pestilence.

Among the Chaco tribes were some whose warriors were more than equal to Spaniards deprived of their firearms. The javelin, made of a very tough wood and tipped with barbed horn, was formidable in their hands. Having imbedded the barb in the flesh of an enemy, the warrior pulled him in by means of a rope tied to the handle of his javelin. When the victim arrived, the warrior sawed through his neck with the jawbone of a fish and then scalped the severed head. Famous for their short bursts of speed, the warriors could lasso wild horses in full flight, vault upon their backs, and be off. These attributes were ascribed to several tribes, especially to the Chiriguanos, who were found from Santa Cruz to the Paraguay River. Viceroy Andrés Hurtado de Mendoza in 1556 sent Captain Andrés Manso from Peru to conquer the Chiriguanos in the Chaco south of the Pilcomayo

River. The Indians lulled the Spaniards into a false sense of security, then killed every one of them.

On the shores of Lake Xarayes, more properly called a marsh, lived an Indian nation of the same name. These people were more advanced than the Carios, much more pleasant to contemplate than the Guaycurús. Their towns contained six thousand dwellings and they dominated all tribes in the neighborhood. Unlike most of the aborigines, the Xarayes raised chickens, geese, and rabbits, planted crops, and recognized a king superior to tribal chieftains. Their simple laws decreed death for theft and adultery; prostitutes were compelled to live apart from honest women, but they might leave their sordid calling and marry without suffering any stigma. The Xarayes were feared and respected by the Chiquitos and other tribes, but they were destined to be destroyed by Spanish and Portuguese slave raiders.

Of all the Indians who roamed over Paraguay east and west of the river, only the Guaranís entered effectively, willingly or unwillingly, into colonial development. The Guaranís practically overwhelmed the Europeans racially and had a profound cultural influence upon them.

# CHAPTER III

# White Men from Overseas

OLDEST OF ALL CITIES in the Plata basin, as the proud Paraguayan will find occasion to tell every visitor, Asunción is the center of Paraguayan life. Here is the principal river port where cargoes are loaded for downstream and transshipped for upriver ports; here are the seat of national government, the Congreso, the Cathedral, the university, and the major banks and hotels. The diplomatic and consular corps add luster to society, the Jardín Botánico provides shady drives and a rough golf course, frequent rains clean the streets, and taxi drivers speed madly over streetcar rails. Beautiful villas with delightful patios line Calle España and Avenida Colombia; mestizo women, over-dressed and unshod, peddle delicate *ñandutí* lace.

On the edges of the checkerboard city small orchards of oranges and tangerines are perpetually in blossom. Great, flowering trees are living canyon walls. In the early morning, burros plod solemnly toward the market, unmindful of the drivers' cries and the whip's sharp sting, their loads swaying on shaggy backs, and their long ears swiveling. Women, balancing baskets, bottles, boxes, or bundles on their heads, glide along to and from the market.

For all of its deliberate ways, Asunción is a busy place. Probably one out of every ten Paraguayans lives in the capital city which has a population of perhaps 130,000. The census is neither frequent nor accurate in Paraguay. As becomes a city with more than four centuries of history behind it, Asunción has memories. They are memories of the Guaranís who first lived on the gently rolling hills that drop into the river and look out across the stream to the Pilcomayo and on into the Chaco. They are memories of Ayolas and Irala, of Cabeza de Vaca and the Comuneros, of Francia and the López. There are also memories of bullets spatting into calcimined walls, of telephone poles cut down to form barricades, of violence and oppression.

When wild horses roaming the pampas were the only visible signs of Spanish efforts to seize the gateway to Argentina, Asunción was a flourishing settlement more than one thousand miles above the Plata's mouth. It was Asunción that gave birth to Buenos Aires and Santa Fé, to Corrientes and Concepción del Bermejo, and the Paraguayans will insist, sometimes, that these children were not even *hijos naturales* but the less respectable *ilegítimo* variety. This isolated inland city for three decades was the Spanish crown's homestead in a large part of South America, its outpost to hold back the restless Portuguese in Brazil, its answer to the sneering jibe that Spain could do nothing with a land where gold and silver were not abundant.

In all the ports of Spain there was no greater pilot than Juan Díaz de Solís. He had sailed, in 1508, with Vicente Yañez Pinzón along the east coast of South America, past the Río de la Plata's mouth, an estuary that Pinzón failed to see. Five years later the bankrupt stowaway Vasco Núñez de Balboa had stood "silent on a peak in Darien," looking out upon the South Sea. Now King Ferdinand wished to find the elusive strait that would connect the Atlantic and this South Sea, the Pacific Ocean. To Solís he entrusted three well-provisioned ships that sailed from Spain in October, 1515. On New Year's day in 1516 he found the bay of Rio de Janeiro; a few weeks later he sailed into that vast muddy scar through which waters of half a continent pour into the Atlantic. After his visit this estuary was called the Río de Solís, but now it is known as the Río de la Plata. Indians of the Charrúa nation saw Solís poking about in his longboat and inveigled him ashore on the Uruguayan side. Taking not even the most elementary precautions, Ferdinand's greatest pilot followed the savages

35

into a patch of timber. They ate him. Some persons say that the Plata natives were not cannibals, but Spaniards watching helplessly from their ships told a different story.

After Solís had been killed, his expedition sailed back to Spain. One vessel came to grief near Santa Catharina, called *Yuru minrin* by its Portuguese claimants, and on this disputed island eighteen survivors eventually found refuge. Among them was Aleixo Garcia, one of several Portuguese who had gone with Solís. Garcia readily acquired a good knowledge of Guaraní and with it a desire to visit that fabled land of El Rey Blanco, "The White King," which lay far to the west and which Guaranís and other Indians had attacked. One theory goes so far as to credit a Guaraní invasion with having destroyed the ancient empire of Tiahuanaco early in the tenth century, and there is some reason to believe that Guaraní invasions in the fourteenth and fifteenth centuries threatened outlying parts of Tahuatinsuyu, empire of the Incas. With perhaps five or six companions, Garcia probably left Santa Catharina early in 1524, traveled generally west to discover the falls of Iguassú, crossed the Paraná, and entered the great garden of gorgeous flowers and deep red earth that is Paraguay. It was near the place where Asunción was founded thirteen years later that Garcia enlisted the aid of two thousand warriors to help him in his plan to attack the White King. This army followed the Paraguay north to Corumbá, or possibly not quite so far, before setting out across the Chaco on a route, Charles E. Nowell suggests, that Juan de Ayolas retraced in 1537. Picking up recruits to swell his contingent of Chiriguanos, Garcia reached Bolivia and engaged in plundering. Huayna Cápac, the reigning Inca, fought the invaders so vigorously that Garcia decided to withdraw for a time to safeguard his booty. Francisco Pizarro, later conqueror of Huayna Cápac's sons, was at that time laboriously pushing down the west coast of Colombia. Garcia, back on the Paraguay and thinking himself safe, sent messengers and a small quantity of silver to Santa Catharina to urge his former companions to join him; but, although they received both treasure and message, they had no stomach for the adventure. It was well that they refused, since late in 1525 Garcia and his companions were killed by their allies about 150 miles north of Asunción. Garcia's silver booty remained on the banks of the Paraguay, and there Sebastian Cabot may have seen some of it among the Guaranís.

Aleixo Garcia has several European "firsts" to his credit: first to cross the interior of central South America, first to form an alliance with the Guaranís, first to see the falls of Iguassú, first to enter Paraguay, first to cross the Chaco, first to see any part of the Inca Empire, and at least one of the first to die because of its treasure. His amazing expedition, daring in the extreme, reveals a man worthy of being called *conquistador*. His exploits were to fire the imaginations of Cabot, Ayolas, Irala, and Cabeza de Vaca, and were to cause such confusion among historians that his very existence was sometimes denied. But Aleixo Garcia, shadowy figure that he is, was no wraith born of a poet's dream.

When Charles I, emperor-to-be of the Holy Roman Empire, inherited the crowns of Spain and the Indies, he set new projects afoot to take possession of the Plata basin. There were rich merchants willing to outfit a fleet and the noted pilot Diego García to command it. With three vessels García sailed on August 15, 1526, and reached the future site of São Vicente in January after a voyage of more than five months. In the meantime, the famous chief pilot of Spain, Sebastian Cabot, agreed to follow Magellan's route to the Orient and to return with his ships loaded with "gold, silver, jewelry, pearls, drugs, spices, silks, brocades and other precious things." Cabot's four ships carried more than six hundred men when they sailed from San Lúcar de Barrameda in April, 1526. Félix de Azara recorded that Cabot had three ships and less than three hundred men, among whom were three brothers of Vasco Núñez de Balboa.

Cabot did not see the Orient. Beset by trouble among his men and desiring to win the riches of Peru, he decided to explore the Río de la Plata, which he reached before García arrived. Portuguese at Pernambuco told Cabot in June the story of Aleixo Garcia, the White King, and castaways on Santa Catharina. On this island he found Garcia's companions, confirmed what the Portuguese had told him, and decided to make an effort to con-

quer the Inca Empire or to gain a foothold within it. Sailing into
the Plata, he built a stockade called San Salvador on the Uruguayan shore, left a garrison to defend it, and continued up the
Paraná for about one hundred miles. There he built a fort, Sancti
Spíritu, and left another garrison while he went on up the Paraná
in three vessels, leading the first white men ever to sail that
fabulous river. Past the Paraná-Paraguay junction the Spaniards
made their laborious way. The Guaranís along the Paraná gladly
traded food for trinkets and warned the white men that rapids
lay ahead. Cabot turned back, entered the Paraguay, and sailed
along uneventfully for forty leagues. Then three hundred canoes
bearing Agaces Indians attacked in a narrow part of the river
with disastrous results to themselves and the loss of three Spaniards. "News of this victory spread rapidly through the neighborhood, making the natives happy that the common enemy stronger
than they had met one who humiliated their pride and might
stop the progress of their arms, having vanquished the conqueror
of all." Cabot continued this voyage almost to the site of Asunción. Here he found a Guaraní tribe in possession of silver, perhaps the treasure of Aleixo Garcia. So Cabot named the Paraguay
and he called it the Río de la Plata, the "River of the Silver." His
dream castle soared until its minarets touched the Southern
Cross, for here was a land of wealth that would win for him the
renown his egotistical soul craved.

Civil war threatened when Diego García made his way into
the great river early in 1527. Cabot had no right to be in South
America, but he refused to give up what he considered a rich
prize and persuaded García to join him. He then sent two messengers back to Spain with products of the country, silver, an account of his discoveries, and a request that he be given the right
to conquer. Not waiting for a reply, Cabot sailed for home in
1530, leaving a garrison of 120 men under Nuño de Lara to hold
the fort of Sancti Spíritu. Two years later the fort and most of its
garrison were destroyed by Timbú Indians who were, in the
words of Father José Guevara, "a gentle, affectionate, hospitable
people, good as friends but bad as enemies."

Mangoré, chief of the Timbús, had made many visits to Sancti

Spíritu. He had seen Lucía Miranda, the faithful, "extremely beautiful, honest and chaste" wife of Sebastián Hurtado, and had become her ardent suitor. Lucía had but to leave her husband to become queen of the Timbús. When all of his wiles failed to lure Lucía from the fort, the amorous chieftain plotted to destroy it. While a detachment of soldiers was foraging for supplies, Mangoré appeared at the fort with porters loaded with food. Lara, pleased with the gift, invited the savages to dine and drink. During the festivities, Mangoré's brother Siripo surrounded the fort with Timbú warriors who attacked while guards were being posted. Nuño de Lara fought valiantly and succeeded in killing Mangoré before he fell mortally wounded. A few survivors, led by Captain Rodríguez Mosquera or someone else, reached the Brazilian coast south of São Vicente.

Siripo's warriors killed every Spaniard in sight and pawed over their loot with childish glee. Siripo found Lucía much to his liking when she was brought before him as a captive; in fact, he liked her so much that he waived claim to any other booty. In the Timbú camp he treated her with every consideration and pleaded with her to become his queen; but Lucía held fast to her virtue, an attitude that served only to excite Siripo's passion. Hurtado, who had been out foraging and therefore escaped the massacre, rashly sought out Siripo, who ordered him executed. Lucía saved her husband's life, but only on condition that he should not know her in Biblical fashion. One of Siripo's wives, an old crone who had been discarded, discovered the pair in a knowing embrace one afternoon and hastened to tell the chief. Siripo confirmed the news with his own eyes. In his rage the chief ordered Hurtado to be shot full of arrows, and Lucía Miranda he ordered burned at the stake.

Dr. Cecilio Báez refuses to let us have this bit of romance under the color of history. In his *Historia colonial del Paraguay y Río de la Plata,* Paraguay's energetic historian insists that Sancti Spíritu was destroyed while Cabot and García were upstream, probably in the last half of 1529. They sailed back to Spain because of this tragedy, and en route "they were able to communicate with those fugitives [from the fort]; none of them said that within the destroyed fort there had been a Castilian woman called Lucía Miranda, who was the cause of the catastrophe. This is one of the various legends accepted by the Paraguayan chronicler Ruiz Diaz de Guzmán." The survivors, after quarreling with Portuguese settlers in Brazil, settled on Santa Catharina in 1534.

Embarrassing European wars prevented Charles I, better known by his Holy Roman Empire title of Charles V, from renewing efforts to conquer the Plata basin until 1534. The Portuguese, who were acting as though they intended to press their claim to much of South America, already were becoming bothersome. Charles must do something about Paraguay. Where Solís and Cabot had failed, the aging Pedro de Mendoza, who had the personal fortune if not the ambition to colonize Paraguay's "deserts," might succeed. Fortified with a princely grant of lands, people, and provinces of the Río de la Plata, Indians and all, Mendoza set sail in August, 1535, with 11 vessels, 1,200 men, stallions and mares, and supplies usually assembled for such expeditions. He was to build three forts, open communications with Peru, and colonize. With him as admiral went his brother, Diego de Mendoza, and many other noble reprobates, adventurers, scoundrels, and honest men: Juan de Ayolas, Domingo Martínez de Irala, Juan de Salazar de Espinosa, and more whose biographies are the early history of Argentina and Paraguay. Not far behind such men in importance were the seventy-two horses and mares that survived the voyage.

Great though his name was, Don Pedro de Mendoza proved to be a weak, sickly commander. Deeds attributed to him, such as participation in sacking Rome, may or may not be true; but there is no doubt that he was a failure as a *conquistador*. Quarrels marred the passage from Spain; factions developed—unknown to the sick *adelantado* secluded in his cabin—among the Spaniards, Germans, and Portuguese who made up the expedition. Dividing his fleet at Rio de Janeiro, Don Pedro sent part of it on to the Río de la Plata under his brother's command; the rest remained for a time at anchor in the Brazilian harbor, where Mendoza appointed Juan de Osorio to take over while he attempted to recover from a persistent illness. Well-planted rumors convinced Mendoza that Osorio was plotting rebellion. Without giving his lieutenant a chance to defend himself, the Adelantado ordered his execution and Juan de Ayolas dispatched him with a dagger. The Bavarian Ulrich Schmidt, one of the expedition, wrote that Osorio "was treated wrongly, God Almighty knows it, and may He be merciful to him, for he was a pious, fair-dealing, and valiant warrior, and kept well all the warriors."

Continuing south, the Adelantado rejoined his brother at the island of San Gabriel. After investigating the Uruguayan shore, Mendoza landed on the Argentine side in February, 1536. (For the sake of those who want events to be as old as possible, it may be noted that Azara and all patriotic *porteños* hold that this landing occurred in 1535.) Morale was at low ebb or worse when complete co-operation and high spirits were necessary for success in one of the most difficult enterprises ever undertaken by Spanish conquerors. None of the expected riches were found on those inhospitable banks of the Río de la Plata, a fact that caused many to talk of deserting to Brazil. To discourage this talk, Mendoza decided to settle on the shores of the Riachuelo, a stream difficult to navigate, and named his fort Nuestra Señora del Buen Ayre.

Fish and game abounded in the neighborhood, but so did brave, nomadic Querandí Indians who resented this foreign intrusion. Many expeditions went out in search of food and to explore. One of these, under Juan de Ayolas, left in May to seek a route to Peru. He was gone for two months, a most critical time for the new colony since Indians had inflicted serious losses on the Spaniards. For a fortnight the Querandís had supplied fish and meat, then they became hostile. When they flogged messengers sent to ask for an explanation, Mendoza ordered his brother to chastise the tribe with 300 infantry and 30 cavalry. Twenty-seven Spaniards died in the ensuing battle with 1,000 Indians. Among the dead was Admiral Diego de Mendoza, brought down by a skillful throw of the bola, a long rope to which were attached three thongs bearing stones in pouches at their ends. Thereafter Buenos Aires was under constant siege

41

by thousands of Querandí, Timbú, and Charrúa savages who killed thirty of the garrison, burned four ships, and set fire to all of the thatched huts by shooting flaming arrows into them. The little colony ran out of food, and the men ate everything that had meat on its bones—rats, mice, snakes, and even their deceased comrades. One day three Spaniards stole a horse and ate it. They were hanged as punishment for their crimes, and that night their companions dismembered the corpses and ate the more meaty portions. Eventually well-worn shoes, belts, and hides were considered edible.

During the siege a woman named Maldonata defied an order of the fort's commander that no one could leave the gates. She took refuge in a cave when night closed in upon her. There she found a lioness, probably a jaguar, having such difficulty in whelping that Maldonata acted as midwife. In gratitude for her kindness, the lioness fed Maldonata until nature called that kind beast away. Some Indians found the woman and made her their slave, then Spaniards from the fort rescued her. The commander of the fort raged and stamped his feet until his breastplates creaked. "Take her out and tie her to a tree!" he roared. Maldonata was taken and tied. To satisfy their curiosity concerning her fate, a detachment of soldiers went out two days later and found their victim hungry but in good health, surrounded by lions and tigers who had protected her. The lioness of the cave, of course, was there at her feet. The lady was pardoned, since a Spaniard could not be more inhuman than lions, especially not when God himself had interceded in her behalf. And the man who first told the tale said he had it from Maldonata herself, "not only from the publick voice." Uncle Remus, in this case, was Ruy Díaz de Guzmán who had a lot of fun in writing a history of the Plata area as he wished it had happened. Some of his tales, like this woman-and-the-lioness fable, are too good to ignore; but Ruy Díaz was such a literary fabricator that one hardly knows what to believe in his history.

Ayolas returned from his reconnaissance with reports that Sancti Spíritu was abandoned, but the food that he brought with him revived Mendoza's hopes. He went up river to verify reports

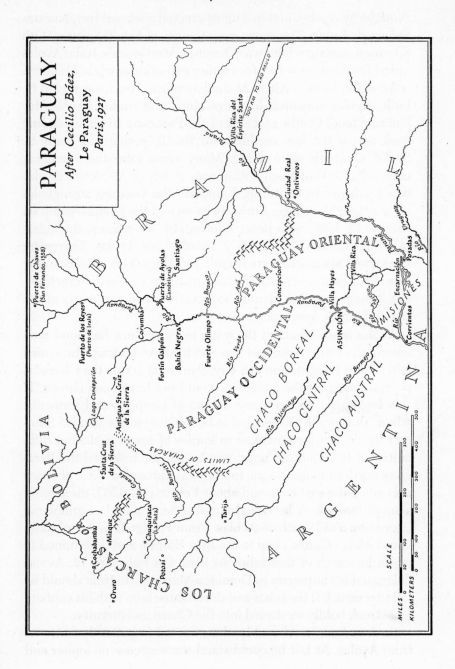

PARAGUAY

After Cecilio Báez,
*Le Paraguay*
Paris, 1927

BRAZIL

BOLIVIA

ARGENTINA

LOS CHARCAS

PARAGUAY ORIENTAL

PARAGUAY OCCIDENTAL

CHACO BOREAL

CHACO CENTRAL

CHACO AUSTRAL

LIMITS OF CHARCAS

MISIONES

Puerto de Chaves (San Fernando, 1558)
Puerto de los Reyes (Puerto de Irala)
Lago Concepción
Antigua Sta. Cruz de la Sierra
Santa Cruz de la Sierra
Mizque
Cochabamba
Oruro
Potosí
Chuquisaca (La Plata)
Tarija
Corumbá
Fortín Galpón
Bahía Negra
Puerto de Ayolas (Candelaria)
Santiago
Fuerte Olimpo
Ontiveros
Ciudad Real
Villa Rica del Espíritu Santo
Concepción
Villa Hayes
Villa Rica
ASUNCIÓN
Encarnación
Posadas
Corrientes

Río Verde
Río Branco
Río Apá
Río Aquidabán
Río Bermejo
Río Pilcomayo
Río Paraguay
Río Paraná
Río Grande
Río Uruguay
Río Tebicuary

1100 KM TO SÃO PAULO

SCALE

MILES
0    50   100    200    300    400    500

KILOMETERS
0  50  100  200  300

43

brought by Ayolas, and in August erected a second fort, Nuestra Señora de Buena Esperanza, near the site of Sancti Spíritu. With fifty men, among whom was Domingo Martínez de Irala, Ayolas sailed from this new fort for further exploration while Mendoza returned to Buenos Aires. At the bay where Asunción was to be built, Ayolas anchored his three ships and traded baubles for Guaraní food. On the east side of the Paraguay River, extending back across the low cordillera to Brazil, perhaps as many as 50,000 Guaranís were living. Many years later the Spaniards counted 27,000 of them within easy reach of Asunción. Ayolas was fortunate in capturing Lambaré, the Guaraní stronghold, after a three-day siege. Emissaries reached the Spanish camp on August 15, 1536, with peace offerings of "six women, the eldest of whom was only eighteen years old," for Ayolas. Thereafter Carios and Spaniards were friends and allies. This alliance in the future suffered severe strain from uprisings by Guaraní factions, but it made possible Spanish explorations and conquests in the heart of South America.

Ayolas inquired about the route to Peru, since he found men among the Carios who had gone with Aleixo Garcia. These men told him to go upstream to a bay, then west across the Chaco. A poorer season for the adventure could not have been chosen. It was late spring in Paraguay, a time of tempests and torments, when "the very devils seemed to be howling in the winds." Summer would bring an increase in hordes of insect pests, but difficulties of this kind did not deter Ayolas. He followed the Paraguay north to Bahía Negra, felt his way through a maze of channels along the east fork, and about February 2, 1537, discovered a small bay which he called Nuestra Señora de la Candelaria, later known as Puerto de Ayolas. From Payaguás he heard more about Aleixo Garcia's trip to the Inca Empire and determined to go on in search of that fabulous land. On February 12, Ayolas delegated his authority to Domingo Martínez de Irala should he fail to return, left the boats and thirty-three men with his captain, and struck boldly westward into the Chaco and eternity.

Back at Buenos Aires, Mendoza waited impatiently for news from Ayolas. At last he could stand the suspense no longer and sent two men, Gonzalo de Mendoza and Juan de Salazar de Espinosa, to investigate. The Adelantado was sick and wanted to die in Spain, so he put to sea after delegating his powers to Ayolas and named Francisco Ruiz Galán to be his lieutenant at Buenos Aires. Storms spoiled his provisions, supplies disappeared, and the Emperor's fine courtier was reduced to eating the flesh of a pregnant bitch. Whereupon, it is said, Mendoza was seized by a frenzy and died, but not until he cursed the fate that had sent him to chase chimeras in the Plata country.

Knowing nothing of their leader's departure, Gonzalo de Mendoza and Salazar went up to join Irala in a search for Ayolas. After a time they grew tired of this fruitless seeking and Irala needed to repair his vessels. The three of them dropped down the Paraguay until they found a place where Irala could make repairs. Irala returned to Candelaria; Mendoza and Salazar went downstream until on the east bank of the Paraguay, where a small peninsula makes a bay, they landed and built a stockade, a *casa fuerte*, in the year 1537, perhaps on August 15, and called it Nuestra Señora de la Asunción in homage to the Virgin Mary. Another version of these events holds that Irala aided in establishing the *casa fuerte*, then went back to Candelaria.

Summer and autumn went by. Irala, keeping his vessels in order, his men under arms, heard nothing from his absent commander. Despair for his fate deepened, a despair heightened by heavy rains that made Candelaria untenable. Irala decided to drop downstream and obtain a more seaworthy vessel at Asunción. He sailed into trouble. Soon after the crude fort was finished, there arrived the great and terrible Captain Francisco Ruiz Galán with men from Buenos Aires, Buena Esperanza, and possibly another fort. As lieutenant governor of Buenos Aires port and second in command to Ayolas, this native of Gaudix might cause trouble for Irala. Ruiz Galán changed his commission to suit himself, a deceit Irala was to suspect. Sure of his strength, the semi-impostor proceeded to Asunción to consolidate his power. For a time Ruiz Galán had things his own way, then Irala arrived looking for a better ship, with only thirty men in his party. Being a practical man who could judge a situation and shrewdly calculate chances, he attempted to avoid a clash with Ruiz Galán even after that pompous captain refused to show his commission. Day after day passed. Irala grew more and more impatient and more stubborn in refusing to bow before threats of his rival. Tired of fencing, Ruiz Galán ordered his sheriff, Juan Pavón, to arrest Irala. Salazar secured the latter's release, and other Spaniards reminded the impostor that his captive was popular with the Indians. Irala at last obtained the brigantine he sought and sailed for Candelaria on August 23, 1538, too late to save Ayolas from death. The frequently repeated charge that Irala deserted his post has no foundation in fact, since his delay at Asunción was not of his choosing. While Irala was away, Ruiz Galán sailed back to Buenos Aires.

Before Pedro de Mendoza left the Plata, he promised to send out aid from Spain. The Court, knowing that a dispute over command would result because of Mendoza's death, sent Alonso Cabrera as *veedor* (inspector) with the relief expedition of three ships and two hundred men. Cabrera's instructions, dated September 12, 1537, ordered him to hold an election for governor if Mendoza had failed to appoint a successor or if the conquerors had not elected one. At Buenos Aires in January, 1539, he heard Ruiz Galán's story and decided to let the colonists decide for themselves which of the claimants they would support. Both Cabrera and Ruiz Galán were in Asunción six months later, where Irala's authority was ratified by popular vote without serious protest. Captain Juan de Salazar, co-founder of Asunción, doffed his cap twice as a sign of obedience. Irala was now lieutenant general and governor of Paraguay, a princely domain that included all of present-day Paraguay, Argentina, Uruguay, most of Chile, and parts of Brazil and Bolivia. Even had there been no designation of powers from Ayolas and no election held by royal command, Irala surely would have emerged as leader by popular demand. Expeditions such as that to Paraguay were always subject to popular will. Spanish adventurers, at once individualists and great lovers of authority, were fiercely democratic. They could and did depose and elect leaders: Vasco Núñez de Balboa on the Isthmus, Francisco Orellana in the Amazon basin, Hernán

South America Divided into Its Principal Parts
From Muratori, *Il cristianesimo felice nelle missioni de' padri della Compagnia di Gesu nel Paraguai*, Venezia, 1743–49. Note the indefinite extent of the area labeled "Paraguay."

Cortés at Vera Cruz, all received their powers from their companions, and all were later confirmed by the King. There was none to challenge Irala when he posted, on June 25, 1539, the documents attesting his authority. Juan de Salazar claimed and received the position of lieutenant to Irala, his second in command, and there was none to oppose him. Now that the government was formed, conquest could proceed. So it was that command passed from Mendoza to Ayolas to Irala.

Domingo Martínez de Irala, true to his trust, prepared a return to Candelaria, where he hoped that Ayolas might still be found. Leaving Captain Gonzalo de Mendoza in command of the fort at Asunción, he sailed from the port with 280 Christians and reached Candelaria on January 16, 1540. There he learned from Indians that the Ayolas party had returned to the Paraguay. Irala dropped down to San Sebastián, some eight leagues to the south. Payaguás in the neighborhood reported that Ayolas was in the interior. Irala set out to find his captain on February 14, leaving Juan de Ortega with seventy men to guard the boats. Through lands flooded to the depth of a man's waist, the rescue expedition pushed on for three dreary weeks. Supplies ran low, and floods deepened. Resorting to a council, Irala asked his officers for advice and their unanimous opinion was to turn back. Irala, of course, was bound by unwritten law and strong custom to obey. His men would follow him anywhere, anywhere they wanted to go! Back at San Sebastián, a Chané boy came into camp with news that Ayolas was dead, murdered by Payaguás, and some of his men were held captive in the Chaco. There was no reason now to remain in the north. Ayolas was dead, Irala was governor. *Rey muerto, rey puesto!* The king is dead, long live the king!

For a few months Irala enjoyed peace while he laid more firmly the foundations of Paraguay. To gain aid from Spain, the Governor sent two Indians to the coast of Brazil with a message for the Franciscan friar, Bernardo de Armenta. It was these Indians who met Álvar Núñez Cabeza de Vaca and guided him to Asunción; but Irala knew nothing of this impending arrival while he wrestled with the problem of what to do about Buenos Aires and its small garrison under Captain Juan Romero. Several considerations counseled abandoning an effort to establish a colony on the Plata: the port was bad, Indians were hostile, the pampas were a "desert," communication with Asunción was slow, and opportunity for disobedience was great. With only 350 men to conquer half a continent, a division of forces was unwise. Buenos Aires must be abandoned.

Upon Captain Juan de Ortega, esteemed as a brother by Irala, fell the task of persuading the men at Buenos Aires to move up the river. He left Asunción in August, 1540, with two well-provisioned brigantines. At Buenos Aires he argued in vain with those who had survived and intended to stay. Irala himself, with three brigantines and the veedor Alonso Cabrera, set out in January, 1541, to effect the removal. The men had been living within the old palisade, while officers bunked in *La Trinidad,* a vessel grounded on the beach. Why keep the men there, since there was no thought of opening a way to Peru from that direction? Spanish attention was fixed on Peru, not on the Plata basin. In June, 1541, Buenos Aires was deserted. A cache of supplies at San Gabriel might serve the awaited fleet from Spain. Irala did not force the men to leave Buenos Aires, but his presence certainly added strength to Cabrera's persuasion. By combining Buenos Aires and Asunción, the colony could count some six hundred men, a sprinkling of women, and a few children. Among the men were several Italians who had been wrecked in the Plata while en route to Peru with a rich cargo. Portugal, Spain, France, Germany, Italy, and England were all represented at Asunción, some illegally perhaps, but still represented. Mestizos, resulting from Indian and white mixtures, soon made their appearance. Irala himself had several Guaraní concubines, but his men needed no example since there were few European women in the colony and the Guaraní women were far from unwilling. Guaraní chieftains, after Salazar's woman had exposed a plot to destroy Asunción, co-operated by providing mates for the white men. Paraguay, international in character in its first years, became a mestizo colony, and not even later immigration has been sufficient to change its racial character.

When the people from Buenos Aires reached the fort at Asunción on September 2, 1541, it was apparent that something more than a blockhouse was needed. Asunción was to be the center of conquest, not merely a post for aiding distressed vessels or for storing supplies. Irala, by the ordinance of September 16, 1541, established a municipality. Juan de Ortega became *alguacil mayor;* Pero Díaz del Valle served as *alcalde mayor;* Juan de Salazar was named as *alcalde de primer voto;* while Alonso Cabrera, García Venegas, and three others were *regidores.* Irala, apparently, submitted these nominations to popular approval. The old stockade came down, palm trees were felled for the expanding town. Sentinels stood guard at night to warn of Indian attacks. The government fixed the value of money, appointed two more chaplains to help serve the church, and assigned 50,000 maravedis to Blas Testanova, a Genoese, as a salary for his medical services. These miscellaneous activities indicate the vigor with which Irala governed.

Having settled the problem of Buenos Aires with a firm hand and with matters well under control at Asunción, Irala ordered ships built and supplies gathered in preparation for carrying out his principal task, the search for a route to Peru. The date of departure for this expedition had been set when a king's whim changed everything. St. Matthew's Day, February 24, 1542, would not soon be forgotten in Asunción, for a message borne by an Indian arrived on that occasion. Álvar Núñez Cabeza de Vaca announced that he was on his way, commissioned adelantado and governor of Paraguay by His Majesty, and asked that aid be sent to soldiers floating down the Paraná. Irala obeyed promptly, putting aside his own plans of conquest. He sent Alvaro de Cháves to inform the new governor that three brigantines under the regidor García Venegas were on their way. Then Irala called in Captains Ortega, Salazar, and Cabrera to form a welcoming committee to meet and to escort Cabeza de Vaca to Asunción. There was to be no lack of pomp and circumstance of rank. Irala's first period as governor was ended; so, too, was the first chapter in the conquest of Paraguay.

# CHAPTER IV

# Cabeza de Vaca, the Great Pedestrian

ÁLVAR NÚÑEZ, native of Jérez de la Frontera in Andalucía, acquired his surname from his mother, Doña Teresa Cabeza de Vaca. During the reign of Ferdinand and Isabella, Don Pedro de Vera borrowed money to finance his conquest of the Canary Islands and, as security for the loan, offered his two sons, one of whom was the father of Álvar Núñez. Don Pedro's grandson could hardly be expected to have great love for the name of Vera, although his blood was of that family of early *conquistadores*.

No mean cavalier, this gentleman of Jérez had distinguished himself in wars against the Moors and in Italy, in the ill-fated attempt of Pánfilo de Narváez to conquer Florida, and in the later period of the Mexican adventure. He was in Spain with eight thousand restless ducats when news arrived that the adelantado Don Pedro de Mendoza had died at sea. Here was a chance to win fame and fortune, and to spend those eight thousand ducats. When Álvar Núñez asked that he be appointed adelantado of the Río de la Plata, the Council of the Indies agreed to issue the commission. He was to be lieutenant governor if Juan de Ayolas survived; if Mendoza's lieutenant was dead, his title was to be governor, captain-general, and adelantado of lands he might discover, conquer, and populate. The council specifically enjoined him to possess the coast south of São Vicente, to settle Santa Catharina Island, which was to be his for twelve years, and to admit no lawyers to the colony.

51

Having assembled an expedition of five ships, four hundred well-armed men, and forty-six horses and mares, Álvar Núñez sailed from Spain on November 2, 1540, trusting that good fortune which had seen him safely across Texas to protect him on the high seas. After a voyage of five months, about the usual time, he arrived at Santa Catharina on March 29, 1541. Here the Governor landed his people and the twenty-six horses that had survived, took possession of the island, treated Indians kindly, and probably learned something of the Guaraní language. Two Franciscans, Bernardo de Armenta and Alonzo Lebrón, who had come out with Alonso Cabrera in 1538 and had labored among the natives, proved to be of great assistance in briefing the new arrivals. They told Cabeza de Vaca about Aleixo Garcia and the White King, of rumors about Buenos Aires and Asunción. In May, Felipe de Cáceres took a caravel to investigate affairs at Buenos Aires, but storms prevented him from reaching that abandoned colony. Nine refugees from the Plata, who had refused to go to Asunción, arrived in a small boat to complain about what had happened since Mendoza's departure and from them Cabeza de Vaca heard a biased story that permanently colored his opinion of Irala. It was Irala's fault, these malcontents cried, that Ayolas had lost his life, although they knew none of the facts; it was Irala's fault that Asunción, founded among the Carios, seethed with suspicion and distrust, although they had never been there.

Believing that his presence was required in Paraguay, the Adelantado sent Pedro Dorantes to explore a route through the interior. Upon Dorantes' return, Álvar Núñez sent Captain Pero Estopiñán Cabeza de Vaca to follow the water route with the ships and 140 men, while he led the others overland by a way well known to the Indians. Perhaps the principal reason for this division of forces was the Governor's fears that horses could not survive a river trip. Aleixo Garcia had made it by land, why not the great pedestrian? With 250 men, Álvar Núñez set out on November 2, 1541. Twenty-seven days later, when summer lay heavy on the land, the party reached the upper Iguassú. After crossing this stream, they met an Indian named Miguel who offered to guide them to Asunción.

Xarayes Indians

From *Viaje al Río de la Plata*
by Ulrich Schmidt

Apparently Cabeza de Vaca handled his men well, since tribe after tribe provided food willingly. Much of his great success with aborigines rested upon a profound understanding of primitive character and upon his insistence that a Spaniard's word, once given, must never be broken. As he went through Indian lands, he took possession of them for his emperor, but not once did he tell the Indians about it. In January, 1542, his route lay across hills and through thickets of reeds. No Indians came with food, but "In the hollows of these reeds there were some white worms, about the length and thickness of a finger; the people fried these for food, obtaining sufficient fat from them to fry them in very well; all ate of them, and thought it excellent food." These juicy, succulent morsels hardly drew highest praise from Pero Hernández, secretary to Cabeza de Vaca, reputed author of the latter's *Comentarios,* and principal literary detractor of Irala. Time and again he recorded how various tribes supplied fruits, fish, meat, maize, fowl, honey, yams, potatoes, and "flour of the pine tree." This meal came from pine nuts borne on trees so large that "four men with their hands joined cannot compass one."

About the middle of January, 1542, Cabeza de Vaca rested his men in a Guaraní village on the Paraná at twenty-five degrees south latitude, in a land of plenty: "They rear plenty of fowls, geese, and other birds; and they have an abundance of game, such as boar, deer, *dantas* [tapirs], partridges, quails, and pheasants; and they have great fisheries in this river. They grow plenty of maize, potatoes, cassava, mandubies, and many other fruits; and from the trees they collect a great quantity of honey." From this paradise the Adelantado wrote to Irala, then went on to follow the Iguassú beyond its great falls and on to the Paraná junction. At the Paraná an assemblage of hostile Guaranís, their bodies smeared with war paint, gathered to dispute their passage but were mollified by diplomacy and presents. Canoe rafts carried the party across with loss of but one man. There were a number of sick and footsore men by this time, so Cabeza de Vaca built rafts to float them and the baggage downstream and wrote to Irala to ask that someone meet them at the Paraguay. As it had in Texas, his fame as a medicine man preceded him until on the last stages of the journey Guaraní welcoming committees waited eagerly for his passing. Truly, all the annals of Spanish conquest tell of few men like Álvar Núñez Cabeza de Vaca.

A new governor might well have had misgivings about the kind of welcome he would receive from the older colonists. No one, however, could complain that Irala and his companions were ungracious when Cabeza de Vaca arrived at Asunción on March 9, since they "showed incredible joy at his arrival." Some probably did feel like celebrating; none knew what was in store for him. "The Spaniards of high rank," Dean Funes wrote, "received the governor in Asunción with more urbanity than pleasure." No one opposed this representative of His Majesty Charles I, certainly not the royal officials who were "Alonzo Cabrera, controller, a native of Loja; Philip de Caceres, accountant, of Madrid; Pedro Dorantes, factor, of Bejar," all of whom accepted the Adelantado without question. Felipe de Cáceres and Pedro Dorantes had come with Cabeza de Vaca and could be expected to be loyal, at least in the beginning. Lafuente Machaín, in his authoritative study of Irala, wrote: "On March 9, 1542, in the presence of General Irala, Royal Officials, and other persons, the Royal Order was presented, which everyone took and put over his head and they swore that they would and did obey it as the letter and command of their King and Lord and then the notary Diego de Olabarrieta read it." Ceremonies of assuming command were completed on March 13, when Cabeza de Vaca took the oath of office in the presence of regidores, members of *cabildo* or town council. Hernando de Ribera, Alonso de Valenzuela, Lope de Ugarte, and Pedro Benítez de Lugo watched their new leader swear "with his right hand placed in the hands of General Irala and Alonso Cabrera."

Enemies of Irala were determined to interpret his every act as one calculated to lessen Cabeza de Vaca's prestige, while his friends could find nothing about their governor to praise. Unfortunately, uncritical historians have accepted Cabeza de Vaca's story, as told in the *Comentarios*, as a full and true account of events in Paraguay. Other *conquistadores* had been placed in circumstances far more difficult than those that confronted

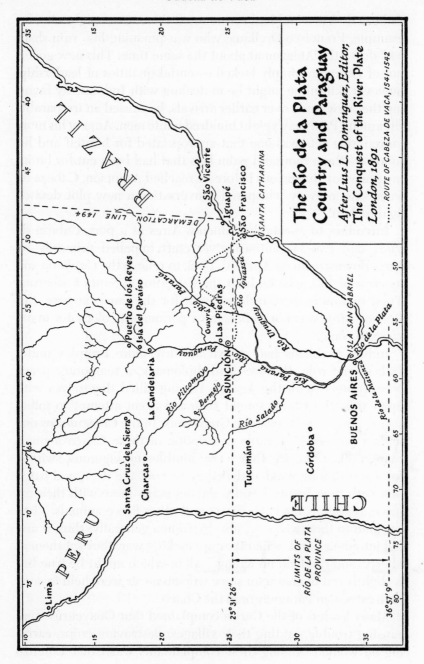

The Río de la Plata
Country and Paraguay

*After Luis L. Domínguez, Editor,*
The Conquest of the River Plate
*London, 1891*

······ ROUTE OF CABEZA DE VACA, 1541-1542

BRAZIL

São Vicente

Iguapé

São Francisco

SANTA CATHARINA

DEMARCATION LINE 1494

Puerto de los Reyes

Isla del Paraíso

Río Paraná

Río Iguassú

Las Piedras

Guayrá

Río Uruguay

ISLA SAN GABRIEL

Río de la Plata

ASUNCIÓN

Paraguay

La Candelaria

Río Pilcomayo

Río Bermejo

Río Paraná

BUENOS AIRES

Río de la Matanza

Santa Cruz de la Sierra

Charcas

Río Salado

Tucumán

Córdoba

PERU

CHILE

Lima

LIMITS OF
RÍO DE LA PLATA
PROVINCE

25° 31' 26"

36° 57' 9"

Cabeza de Vaca and had surmounted them. One might cite, for example, Francisco Orellana, who was pursuing his "vain shadow" down the Amazon at about the same time. This new governor of Paraguay simply lacked essential qualities of leadership, however skillful he might be in dealing with Indians. By favoring the "new" men over earlier arrivals, he caused an irreparable rift among Paraguay's eight hundred white men. Among his more inexcusable acts was one that appropriated for himself and his followers three thousand palm logs that had been cut for building purposes. Suspicious before he reached Asunción, Cabeza de Vaca saw in every whispered conversation a new plot devised against him.

Intending to re-establish Buenos Aires as a port, Cabeza de Vaca sent two brigantines—river craft impelled primarily by oars—downstream on April 16, 1542, to relieve the *Capitana* and its crew of 140, who had left the Governor at Santa Catharina. Then two more were ordered built for the same purpose; but Buenos Aires was not to become a permanent colony for many years to come.

Indian problems had grown steadily more complex under Irala's brief rule. By force and diplomacy, a temporary peace was arranged with the Agaces. Having allied themselves with Spaniards, the Carios sought their aid in an attempt to inflict severe punishment upon the Guaycurús. In the *Comentarios* one finds a far more favorable description of these Chaco nomads than in other sources: they were "nimble and vigorous, swift of foot, and so long-winded that they tire out the deer, and catch him with their hands, besides slaying many more with their arrows, as well as tigers [jaguars] and other fierce animals. They are kind to their wives . . . also to women generally; thus, if any fall into their hands when they are making war, they set them at liberty, and do them no wrong." All of which might be true but is slightly out of character since women never were held in such high esteem in Paraguay or in the Chaco.

Many leaders of the Carios complained that Guaycurús were causing trouble, raiding their villages, destroying crops, carrying off women. Among these complaints was Chief Lorenzo

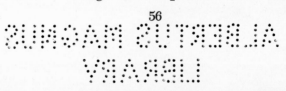

Moquiaracé, father-in-law of García Venegas. As friends and allies of the Carios, the Spaniards had to do something. Cabeza de Vaca conferred with his captains and four priests, "according to custom and law." They recommended war. So it was that on July 13 or 14, 1542, the Adelantado ferried two hundred foot soldiers, fourteen horsemen, and ten thousand Guaraní warriors across the Paraguay for an expedition against marauding Guaycurús. On Sunday night, July 16, a jaguar caused such confusion among the Guaraní vanguard that Spaniards feared a revolt was taking place. Two bullets grazed Cabeza de Vaca's face in the ensuing melee. Never failing in a chance to discredit Irala, Pero Hernández wrote in the *Comentarios* that "these shots were certainly fired maliciously with intent to kill him, and to please Domingo de Irala, whom he had deprived of the command of the province." At daybreak the Guaycurús greeted their enemies with a furious beating of drums, wild cries, boastings of their prowess, and such accurate archery that the Guaraní bowmen fell back until Pedro de Barba came to their support with well-placed artillery fire. Juan de Salazar led a charge of his infantry under the old battle cry of "Santiago!" that had rung in the ears of Atahualpa's retainers at Caxamarca in Peru, that had spurred the men of Cortés on to victory at Tlascala and Cholula in Mexico. Four thousand Guaycurús fled from the field, with Cabeza de Vaca himself leading a wild pursuit; but they rallied when the punitive expedition turned back toward the Paraguay and were credited with killing one thousand Guaraní stragglers.

Guaycurú chieftains sued for peace soon after Cabeza de Vaca returned to Asunción. For a few months there was a truce; but Spanish horses soon appeared in the Chaco and the Guaycurús became splendid horsemen. They carried on an endless war against the Spaniards in frequent raids from which they fled deep into the Chaco when pursued. Not even the patient Jesuit fathers were able to make a lasting impression upon them.

Agaces Indians south of Asunción took advantage of Cabeza de Vaca's absence on the Guaycurú expedition. Their chief Abacote had given the Adelantado, as a token of friendship, one of his daughters and seven or eight other girls to serve all of his needs. Knowing that Gonzalo de Mendoza had but 250 men to protect the colony, Abacote tried to burn it and then, when this effort failed, destroyed outlying homes, pillaged widely, and retreated with several Carios as captives. When summoned to explain this treachery, Abacote sent his son and a few warriors to present his complaints against the Carios. These envoys the Governor threw in jail, executed, or gave to the Carios, a course that won Abacote's enduring hatred in spite of Irala's success in saving a few envoys by hiding them in his home.

One of many stories about Aleixo Garcia attributed to him a son of the same name who had not been killed when the other Portuguese lost their lives after returning from their raid against the Inca Empire. Cabeza de Vaca heard that this son was still a prisoner among Guaranís north of Asunción. To Taberé, chief of the tribe that had murdered Aleixo Garcia, he sent messengers. Taberé killed them all except one whom he sent back with a warning to send no more. Taberé needed a lesson. The Governor sent his nephew, Alonso Riquelme, at the head of three hundred Spaniards and one thousand Guaraní allies to teach Taberé how to behave. Taberé and his allies fought until three thousand of his men were killed and four thousand captured, while the Spaniards lost only fifty killed. Indian losses probably were not nearly so large as reported, but thousands appear more impressive than hundreds in reports for the Emperor's eyes. Of Aleixo Garcia, Jr., nothing was learned, very likely because there never had been such a person.

Cabeza de Vaca made one grand expedition in search of a route to Peru. Impatient to be off, the "old" *conquistadores* moped while their governor concerned himself with Indian troubles. Three of Irala's men, Rodrigo Gómez, Juan de Fustes, and Álvaro de Cháves, offered to make a Chaco reconnaissance. A council agreed that while the main expedition was preparing, Irala should take these men and ninety others in three brigantines to explore for three and one-half months. They were to return in January, 1543. Thrice Domingo Martínez de Irala swore allegiance to the King and to Cabeza de Vaca, then set sail late in October. He dropped Gómez, Fustes, and Cháves at Puerto de las Piedras, 210 miles north of Asunción. These men, accompanied by Chief Aracaré and about one thousand warriors, struck westward through Mbayá territory. After four days they discovered that Aracaré was plotting treachery, so they returned to Las Piedras, found loyal Indians, and again started out. For thirty days they pushed through desolate country, became thoroughly lost, but at last managed to find their way back to the river through great thickets of tall, thorny bushes.

Irala sailed and rowed up the Paraguay until in the first week of January, 1543, he discovered a small bay at about sixteen degrees, thirty minutes south latitude which he named Puerto de los Reyes. He was now more than five hundred kilometers north of Puerto de Ayolas, in territory never before seen by white men who lived to report their discovery. "The land was good and wealthy, such as they had not seen before." People lived in individual dwellings, held Indian slaves, cultivated the land, and grew chickens and ducks. Leaving a guard with his three brigantines, Irala traveled for three days to the west, over hills and through swamps, in land held by the Guaienis tribe. Returning to Puerto de los Reyes, he started back to Asunción, which he reached on February 16, 1543, after having captured and executed Chief Aracaré in obedience to Cabeza de Vaca's orders.

There had been trouble in Asunción, where all of the governor's men had assembled after failing to re-establish Buenos Aires. Rivalries among old and new conquerors became more bitter, and the royal officials were nursing wounded dignity. The accountant, Felipe de Cáceres, had asked for a vessel that might bear dispatches to Spain. Cabeza de Vaca is reported to have said: "When you want to speak to me, get down on your knees with your hat in hand!" Cáceres was not the kneeling kind, even though Alonso Riquelme stood beside the Governor fingering his dagger. As the royal official strode angrily away, he heard Cabeza de Vaca mutter something about a "rapacious Jew." To make matters worse, the Governor quarreled with Alonso Cabrera, another of the royal officials. These two men, Cabrera and Cáceres, did not forget.

Still more trouble delayed the attempt to open communication with Peru, where Don Cristóbal Vaca de Castro was then trying to restore order among quarreling factions. On the night of February 3–4, an Indian woman accidentally started a fire that destroyed more than two hundred huts, four-fifths of the town, in a blaze that lasted four days. The church, convents, granaries, and corrals were lost. Now the execution of Chief Aracaré rose to plague the Spaniards. When Gonzalo de Mendoza, most successful of all in foraging, went out to seek food, he found Taberé, brother of Aracaré, again on the warpath. Irala, who had just returned from the north, led four hundred Spaniards, two thousand Carios, and four brigantines against Taberé. His vessels flew not the royal banner but Cabeza de Vaca's flag. Taberé, putting up a good fight, killed four Spaniards and wounded forty, including Irala. Captain Nufrio de Cháves ended the war, gathered supplies, and took Taberé to Asunción where he agreed to keep the peace.

Discontent continued while conquerors became more and more impatient to be off. Irala's tales of the Xarayes Indians, of Paradise Island, of gold and silver ornaments he had seen, served only to whet avaricious and lascivious appetites. Delay continued while the Governor quarreled with the Cabildo about how to rebuild Asunción after the fire. When Regidor Domingo de Peralta's suggestions were scorned, the Cabildo resigned in a body. In assigning lots for fishing, Cabeza de Vaca followed his own whims, not custom. The treasurer, García Venegas, protested: "It is not objectionable that Your Excellency as governor should appropriate a site, but there is no reason why your captains and friends should enjoy the same privilege." Cabeza de Vaca had enough of these complaints. He was governor, and these rogues should know it. Calling in Captains Juan de Salazar, Gonzalo de Mendoza, Agustín de Campos, Pero Estopiñán, and Pero Hernández, he proposed that they imprison the inspector, Alonso Cabrera, send a priest to confess him, then cut off his head. Salazar and Mendoza refused to have any part in the scheme.

Constantly pressed by old-timers and tenderfeet alike, the Adelantado turned to thoughts of finding a route to some El Dorado. On May 24, 1543, he assembled a council to hear opinions. Since everyone urged the expedition to Puerto de los Reyes, preparations began with the greatest eagerness. Who was to command Asunción in the Governor's absence? Irala and Mendoza suggested Salazar; but Salazar nominated the *alférez* (royal standard bearer), Captain Francisco de Vergara. If gold was to be had, these modest captains wanted their share! By a vote of two to one, Salazar received the honor of guarding Asunción.

A fire, Indian troubles, and spats with subordinates did not end Cabeza de Vaca's trials. The two missionary friars, Armenta and Lebrón, whom he had picked up at Santa Catharina, wanted to go back to Brazil's relative quiet. Upon being refused permission to make the trip, they decided to go without leave, accompanied by a few semi-Christianized girls, who would, of course, cook and take care of camp routine—nothing more. Among the Spaniards were many who entrusted letters to these friars when they slipped out of town on June 10. Someone gave the alarm, probably because the girls were missing, in time for a posse to overtake and return the fugitives to Asunción. With the incriminating letters in his possession, Cabeza de Vaca had what he considered proofs of disloyalty against Martín de Orue, who had lost his place as scribe to Pero Hernández, and Alonso Cabrera, García Venegas, Pedro Dorantes, and Felipe de Cáceres. He could imprison these men but dared not vent his wrath by torturing or executing them for attempting to communicate with Spain.

Cabeza de Vaca's long-delayed expedition got under way on or about September 8, 1543. By river went some 200 men in 10 clumsy brigantines, followed by a flotilla of 120 canoes, each carrying 10 Guaraní warriors. By land another 200 Spaniards, 10 of them mounted, and more natives paralleled their progress. With this group went Pedro Dorantes and Felipe Cáceres, two characters dangerous to leave behind. Again the Adelantado's flag, not his sovereign's, flew from the flagship. At Candelaria, near the modern Corumbá, Payaguás promised to deliver sixty-six man-loads of "plates, crowns, and axes" and small vessels of gold and silver which they had stolen from Ayolas. The Payaguás were lying, of course, and it is doubtful that they had the treasure, none of which was ever recovered. Gonzalo de Mendoza, who could always be counted on to do a hard job well, trailed the leading ships with six vessels and their crews to act as a rear guard. About the middle of October the advance party reached a rapids where quantities of large goldfish (*dorados*) were taken. If one drank for a month broth made of these fish, skin diseases and leprosy would vanish.

Following directions given by Irala, who knew the area well, the expedition arrived at Puerto de los Reyes on November 8, after a voyage of two months. There Cabeza de Vaca, ignoring Irala's discovery, raised a cross under a palm tree and took possession of the land for his king as newly discovered territory; but he did have the grace to name Irala as his camp master. Temporary quarters, protected by a palisade, were built at once, and on September 15 Gonzalo de Mendoza arrived with his group. He had lost only six men in skirmishes with hostile Indians.

Natives at Puerto de los Reyes were well supplied with food and big ears. These Orejones, like peoples of Africa and Asia, loved earrings. They pierced the lobes, inserted gourds and discs of increasing diameter, and eventually had ears that reached to their shoulders. "When they fight, they take these gourds or discs out of their ears and roll them up, or else tie their ears behind their heads." In spite of cotton handicrafts, women delighted the Spaniards by wearing nothing.

From Puerto de los Reyes, the Governor sent Hector de Acuña and Antonio Correa on reconnaissance to the north. They traveled through swamps with great difficulty for three days and at dusk on the fourth day they arrived among Xarayes Indians who greeted them warmly. These Indians were "elegantly attired with parrot's feathers and aprons of white beads to cover their nakedness." Their king, Camire, had heard of Christians and may have been with Aleixo Garcia, at least he knew about the Portuguese adventurer. Among the Xarayes there lived a Guaraní who as a boy had taken part in an expedition against the Inca Empire, perhaps about 1515, to take gold and silver ornaments. Although at first successful, the invaders suffered such severe defeats that two hundred of them took refuge in forests and only one succeeded in returning to the Paraguay. This lad was accepted by the Xarayes, later married one of their women, and now offered to lead the Spaniards back over the route, if he could find it, from Puerto de los Reyes. This story was enough for Acuña and Correa, so weary from their journey that they declined the customary offer of companions for the night.

At last the land of El Dorado seemed within reach. Before November, 1543, had run its course, Cabeza de Vaca, Irala, and more than three hundred men set out for the west. Their way lay through heavy timber, thick canes, low hills, and muddy lagoons, where wild boars, tapirs, and deer abounded. Five days out they met remnants of those Guaranís who had been with the great expedition. The oldest among them were about thirty-five years of age and could not remember how to reach Peru, so young had they been when their fathers were killed. Nine days passed, and rains began, warning of inevitable floods. Just beyond, always only a few leagues beyond, they might reach Tapua-guazú, said to be a rocky hill from which one might see a land rich in precious metals. Should they go on? According to *conquistador* procedure, Cabeza de Vaca summoned his captains to advise him. Their answer was a decided negative, but Francisco de Ribera might push ahead with six men in an effort to find Tapua-guazú. Ribera went on; the rest turned back.

Many Indians had congregated at Puerto de los Reyes, attracted by the strange ships which Captain Juan Romero guarded carefully. Food supplies, already low, practically disappeared when Cabeza de Vaca's party returned. Again he called on Gonzalo de Mendoza, who had "a good tongue," to forage among native villages. It was then December 16. Upstream somewhere, rumor had it, one could find plenty of gold and silver. To investigate this report, the Governor sent Captain Hernando de Ribera with fifty-two men and a brigantine. Among this party, which left on December 20, was Ulrich Schmidt, whose simple but unreliable memoirs were printed in Europe a few years later. Judging by his comments, this German commercial agent enjoyed the trip immensely. About December 21, Ribera arrived at Paradise Island; a week later he met Xarayes who offered to guide him farther; and early in January, Ribera found a cordial welcome at the principal Xarayes village. Schmidt described his hosts with an eye to what would interest European readers: "These Scherues [Xarayes] to whom we now came wear a moustache, and have a wooden ring in the tips of their ears, and the ear is folded around the wooden ring in a wonderful manner. The men have also a large blue crystal in their lips of the shape and size of a draughtsman. And they are painted blue on their bodies from the head to the knees so as to give them the appearance of wearing breeches. But the women are painted otherwise, blue from the breast to the privities, and so artistically, that one could not soon find a painter to do it so well. They are absolutely naked, and are beautiful after their manner, and also commit transgressions in the dark."

Not waiting long to test these transgressions, Ribera went on to see the Xarayes king. A royal welcome, replete with musicians and feasts, awaited him. Always careful to observe the women, Schmidt records that they made subtle cotton mantles, embroidered with animal figures. "These women," he wrote, "are very fair and venerous, very amiable, and very hot too, as it seemed to me." While Schmidt was pleasantly engaged in thermal measurement, Ribera received gifts of gold from the King, who said he had gotten it in war with the fabulous Amazons. Ribera soon went west to search for more gold; but hardships and floods forced him back to the Xarayes villages and then downstream to rejoin his angry commander. Cabeza de Vaca relieved Ribera's men of their booty and would have hanged his lieutenant had not a mutiny threatened. The *Comentarios,* of course, fail to record this part of the story.

Francisco de Ribera rejoined the main party on January 12, 1544, apparently a few days before Hernando de Ribera returned. He had gone seventy leagues to the west, only three leagues short of Tapua-guazú, when many Indians attacked and forced him to retreat. Passing through lands rich in wild fruits, birds, boars, tapirs, and trees filled with honey, he at last had come to a village where many finely wrought articles of gold and silver were displayed. The people there knew about the Inca Empire, about the sea beyond great mountains, about houses that sailed upon it. They told a story, widespread among the Indians, of the Amazon villages. In one of them was a nation of small men who once a year were invited to satisfy the Amazons' desires for children. These Amazons kept the girls borne of such unions and sent the boys back to their anonymous fathers. All of these things, Francisco de Ribera swore, were true according to the Indians.

Gonzalo de Mendoza found only small quantities of food to send back to Puerto de los Reyes. By February, 1544, tribes around the port were so hostile that Spaniards dared not venture beyond their ships and palisade except in force. Hunger and fever dulled the Castilian appetite for precious metals, nightly attacks wore down the will to conquer. Cabeza de Vaca had sent agents to each of the villages. From one of these, Pueblo Grande, Antón Higuera sent word of an imminent uprising. Cabeza de Vaca set out in force to aid Higuera. At Pueblo Grande the people assembled to welcome their supposed friend, but the Governor ordered an attack that caused great slaughter among the Indians and caused a strong alliance to be formed by the tribes. Captain Agustín de Campos treated other villages with like treachery, killed hundreds, and carried off 3,000 slaves. No wonder Gonzalo de Mendoza met resistance wherever he went for supplies. The Spaniards had acted like fools, and Cabeza de Vaca was the worst of the lot. He had failed completely in the greatest test of leadership. When the Indian Francisco, as much a founder of Asunción as any other man and highly esteemed by Irala, remonstrated with the Adelantado, he received a savage blow on the head. Shortly after this injury he died, and Cabeza de Vaca was blamed for his death. It was Francisco, the slave of Gonzalo de Acosta, who had rescued Cabeza de Vaca's rafts on the Paraná.

With rare unanimity the men, led by Felipe de Cáceres, demanded that they return to Asunción lest everyone perish. Late in March the expedition set sail and arrived at the capital on April 18, 1544. Only twenty of the company were in good health; all were half-starved, disappointed, and angry. Cabeza de Vaca had succeeded in alienating the Indians by making war on those who would be friends; he had antagonized his Cario allies by forcing them to be carriers; he had demonstrated his incapacity for leadership; and he had lost an opportunity to colonize a potentially rich area which later fell to Brazil.

Paraguay's first revolution occurred on St. Mark's Day, April 25, 1544, only a week after the expedition's return to Asunción. Exercising their inherent right to depose a governor, the *conquistadores* rid themselves of Álvar Núñez Cabeza de Vaca. At this time Irala was ill but he probably knew what was going on; or, as Father Guevara suggests, Irala feigned illness. There was so much discontent that Irala need not be accused of conspiring against the Governor—the royal officials, each with grievances, could and did hatch the plot. Accompanied by a large group of important men, they forced their way into the house where the Governor lay ill. To Francisco de Mendoza the discredited leader surrendered his sword; to cries of *"Libertad! Libertad! Viva el Rey!"* the rebels bore their captive to jail, confident that the Governor's friends would not be able to help him. Juan de Salazar, living on the outskirts of Asunción, was under guard, as were other leaders of the new men. Pero Estopiñán Cabeza de Vaca, cousin of the Adelantado, followed a course of discretion. On April 26, a mass meeting assembled before Irala's house. Cabeza de Vaca in chains attended this momentous conference to hear Bartolomé González read the charges against him and the request that Irala assume command. There were no objections from the *conquistadores* of Paraguay. Advised of this action, Irala agreed to be governor again, and he swore before God, Saint Mary, the Evangels, and on the sign of the Cross to be faithful to his charge.

Month after month Cabeza de Vaca's friends conspired to free their leader but every plot was discovered. A caravel was being built to take the deposed governor to Spain, since the rebels lacked the courage to kill him or were restrained by Irala's wisdom. After nearly a year in custody, Cabeza de Vaca set sail on March 8, 1545, accompanied by Cabrera and Venegas, two of his bitter enemies, and by an agent of Irala. After a stormy passage the Paraguayan-built caravel reached Spain. Apparently Cabeza de Vaca served a short imprisonment at Oran pending investigation of charges brought against him, was later exonerated, but failed to win compensation for his injuries.

Those who accept Cabeza de Vaca's account of these events generally overlook that even in the *Comentarios* principal blame for the rebellion is assigned not to Irala but to the royal officials. To suppose that Cáceres and Venegas expected to dominate Irala is to deny that *conquistador's* record as an independent leader. There is no doubt that tumults followed the revolt, but it is difficult to believe that Irala and the royal officials "gave public permission to all their friends and partisans to go into the villages and huts of the Indians and take by force their wives, daughters, hammocks, and other of their possessions." These things could be had for the asking, so why resort to force? Irala had been in Paraguay too long to make enemies of the Guaranís by such a policy, particularly when so many great tasks lay before him. Parties formed during Cabeza de Vaca's imprisonment became the basis, according to Dr. Cecilio Báez, for rivalries that were to last nearly two hundred years and gave rise to the Comunero revolts in the eighteenth century. Memories are long in Paraguay, but not that long!

# CHAPTER V

# *Irala, Father of Paraguay*

DOMINGO MARTÍNEZ DE IRALA could trace his ancestry to a family of wealth in the Villa de Vergara in the Basque province of Guipúzcoa. There Martín Pérez de Irala, at the end of the fifteenth century, held the honored position of *escribano real,* a sinecure that went only to first citizens. To Martín Pérez and his wife Doña Marina de Albisúa Toledo were born six children. The second son, Domingo Martínez, affectionately known as "Chomus," was born about 1509. Acting on a royal order of February 17, 1521, Martín Pérez and Doña Marina bestowed their property upon Domingo Martínez as an entailed estate, a *mayorazgo,* in 1529, since their son Pedro had died. The life of an *escribano real* did not appeal to Domingo, filled as he was with the restlessness of youth and a spirit of adventure that swept across the domains of Charles I. To his brother-in-law Domingo transferred the *mayorazgo* in August, 1534. Somehow he had become acquainted with the great lord Don Pedro de Mendoza, who had been named adelantado of the Río de la Plata on July 19 of that year, and won the confidence of Juan de Ayolas. Known to his comrades as Captain Vergara, after his native village, Domingo Martínez de Irala was held in high esteem.

Mendoza's expedition promised adventures to rival those that befell the followers of Cortés and Pizarro. Everyone was talking about the New World where men without a maravedi to their name might become lords of wealth by force of arms. Mendoza did not intend to start an agricultural colony, a circumstance that appealed to men who were looking for high adventure. Instead of seeds, animals, tools, and farmers he carried swords, armor, firearms, and warriors. Peru was his goal, Peru the realm of the White King. Irala might do well on such an expedition.

Mendoza's failure and the death of Ayolas had given Irala an opportunity to show the quality of his leadership, a brief chance temporarily taken away by Cabeza de Vaca. But the rebellion of 1544 had restored him to power. Irala has suffered unjustly at the hands of historians—among whom Félix de Azara is an exception—who relied primarily on the petulant *Comentarios*. Luis L. Domínguez, in his introduction to *The Conquest of the River Plate*, published for the Hakluyt Society, wrote: "Irala, actuated by personal ambition, defeated the plans of Mendoza, deserted Buenos Ayres, abandoned his second in command in the Chaco, occasioning his death and that of all those who accompanied him across that great desert to the confines of Peru, and, when the second Adelantado, Alvar Nuñez, arrived, opposed him by intrigues and conspiracy till he contrived to depose and send him in chains to Spain, under the insidious and calumnious accusation of having committed all sorts of crimes." These charges are convincingly refuted by Ricardo de Lafuente Machaín in his *El Gobernador Domingo Martínez de Irala*, upon which the present account is largely based. The mere fact that Álvar Núñez, after eight years, was acquitted by the Council of the Indies means little. That body, never lenient with *conquistadores*, saw fit to appoint Irala as governor, vindication enough for the father of Paraguay. Ulrich Schmidt, who was in Paraguay from 1535 to 1552, upholds Irala, and so do documents cited by Lafuente Machaín. Schmidt, as one of the old conquerors and a German, might be expected to oppose Cabeza de Vaca, who so greatly antagonized Mendoza's men; but Lafuente Machaín is a competent, objective historian with no reason whatever to present anything but the truth as he found it.

There was much to do in Paraguay after Cabeza de Vaca lost his power. Neither the fallen governor nor Salazar had brought peace with the Agaces, and without peace the men of Asunción must be under arms constantly to defend their allies and themselves. Irala summoned a council of royal officials, captains, and priests, which advised sending Padre Juan Gabriel de Lascano and the linguist Juan de Fustes to treat with Chief Abacote in June, 1545. Negotiations dragged on without success and warfare with the Agaces became normal. Not until 1558, two years after Irala's death, did Captains Alonso Riquelme de Guzmán and Rui García Mosquera put an end to the conflict.

That dream of a *tierra rica*, a rich land, would not leave avaricious minds, nor could Irala forget his old adelantado's command to seek a route to Peru. Everyone wanted to carry out this order, including the Carios; but Irala's council was not in complete agreement on how many should be left behind to protect Asunción, where a base should be established, or whether such a trip should be made at all. Irala decided on July 29, 1545, to override all objections. He arrested some of Cabeza de Vaca's friends who were leading the opposition and thereby checked an incipient rebellion. Plagued by Indian attacks, Irala had to delay his departure for several months, but friendly Indians told Padre Lascano that they knew the way to Peru and would show him how to reach the promised land. Irala then appointed Captains Nufrio de Cháves and García Rodríguez de Vergara to take sixty Spaniards and three thousand Indians to explore the route. Cháves and Rodríguez were gone from October to December, 1545, having made unsuccessful efforts to cross the Mbayá territory west of Puerto San Fernando (Puerto de Cháves.) When these disappointed explorers returned, a rumor gained currency that the whole thing was a trick to lure Spaniards away from Paraguay. Cabeza de Vaca's men might be arrested but they continued to talk.

Comparative peace prevailed early in 1546 and Irala decided to start his great expedition in February, leaving Pedro Dorantes in command at Asunción. After the army had gone a short distance, Felipe de Cáceres caused trouble by charging that Irala had sent Lascano, Cháves, and Rodríguez on a hopeless quest merely to serve his own ends. Divided into two groups by this calumny, the Spaniards barely averted civil war. Padre González

Paniagua pacified the parties but Irala thought it best to turn back. In a few more months opposition to him might die down. He needed every sword the colony could muster.

While waiting for another favorable opportunity, the Governor sent out small exploring parties. One of them, under Cáceres, went downstream to see if a vessel from Spain had arrived and to investigate rumors that Spaniards from Peru had been seen in Paraguay. There was no ship, and the Spaniards, Cáceres learned, belonged to Diego de Rojas' party and had gone back to Peru. One might wonder why Irala should have trusted Cáceres to carry out such a mission in view of his previous opposition. It was a test of loyalty, gave Cáceres something to do, and put him in a position of responsibility. On the advice of his council, Irala sent Captain Nufrio de Cháves in March, 1547, to explore the Pilcomayo River, then called the Araguay. With only thirty men, Cháves ascended the Pilcomayo for forty leagues. He had gone far enough to learn that ships could not navigate the river.

Previous failures merely increased Irala's desire to cross the northern Chaco, swamps and hostile Indians notwithstanding. In July, 1547, he began to organize a body of 250 Spaniards—somewhat more than one-third of Paraguay's European population at the time—and 2,000 friendly Indians. This time he called a council to suggest an interim government, having learned how dangerous it was to ignore the principal captains. Francisco de Mendoza, one of the original Mendoza expedition, had given a good account of himself in spite of a conscience troubled by crimes committed in Spain. Now thirty-two years of age, he was considered wise beyond his years and capable of governing Asunción in Irala's absence. At the end of November, Irala's expedition set out for San Fernando and made such good time that in January, 1548, the great captain was ready to cross the Chaco.

Few details, except for Ulrich Schmidt's hazy relation, are known about this first European expedition, if we except Aleixo Garcia's raid, to cross the Chaco Boreal; but a few facts may be accepted without serious challenge. Captured Indians guided Irala from village to village until he reached the Andean foothills. On September 22, 1548, he sent Captains Nufrio de Cháves, Pedro de Oñate, and two others as messengers to Peruvian officials. Irala was in foreign territory and adelantados, he well knew, rarely welcomed interlopers, brothers or not. He asked, in his message, that Cháves be allowed to take copper, oil, drugs, wine, and flour to Asunción, since the colony had been without contact with Spain for a long time. This request shows that Irala contemplated opening trade relations with Peru, which had been one of the unfulfilled objectives of Pedro de Mendoza and Cabeza de Vaca. It shows, too, a continuity in purpose that has been overlooked in favor of more spectacular aspects of the Plata conquest.

Proceeding on foot, the messengers reached Pocona, a village belonging to the jurisdiction of La Plata, the modern Chuquisaca. To Irala, waiting impatiently for news, Cháves wrote that they were indeed in the viceroyalty of Peru and would go on, but that the party from Asunción should wait four months instead of one, the period previously agreed upon. At Pocona the messengers found Pedro de Guevara, major-domo for Diego Centeño, governor of Las Charcas. Nufrio de Cháves double-crossed Irala. He wrote to Centeño saying that he had come for aid and to ask that someone stronger than Irala be appointed to govern Asunción! Cháves and Oñate went on to Lima with an escort of some fifty Indians. In Irala's camp, in the meantime, there was a division of opinion. Some wished to return at once to Asunción to avoid the rainy season; others advised waiting for the messengers to return; none knew that Cháves hoped to deprive Irala of his command. This conflict in opinion was decided early in November by sending three more messengers into Peru while the expedition waited fifty-five days for some of them to return. Cháves and Oñate reached Lima on December 7, 1548, after what must have been a most difficult trip, and delivered their documents to Pedro de la Gasca, the emissary who had gone out to end the Peruvian tumults. Other messengers also reached Lima with news of Irala's penetration. Pedro de la Gasca summoned his council to consider Cháves' request for a new governor. The council advised him not to interfere in Paraguay's government, since a new governor may have been appointed by the King and there was danger of complicating the situation. Nevertheless, Pedro de la Gasca appointed Diego Centeño to be governor of Paraguay with a new set of officials. He also defined Paraguay's boundaries as running from Cuzco and Charcas on the west, to the Atlantic on the east, north to fourteen degrees and south to twenty-three degrees, thirty-three minutes. Some writers say that Diego Centeño had no stomach for his new job and so informed his superior; others have Centeño applying for the position. In either case, his death in July, 1549, relieved Gasca of an embarrassing situation.

Irala, waiting in Upper Peru (Bolivia) with his expedition, was in a quandary. As his men saw no chance to get rich in Peru, a majority wanted to return to Asunción without waiting for the messengers to rejoin them. Serious quarrels arose over this issue among the *conquistadores* waiting at the gateway to riches, but those riches already were in control of Spaniards willing and able to loot them. Felipe de Cáceres, the *contador*, gathered those who wished to return and gave Irala three days to wait for his emissaries. Spanish democracy worked swiftly. The men deposed Irala on November 10, 1548, elected Gonzalo de Mendoza to lead them, and prepared for the return trip. So the party went back to San Fernando port, leaving the messengers to whatever fate befell them.

At San Fernando the *alcalde mayor* had run into trouble. Captain Diego de Abreu had seized the government of Asunción from Francisco de Mendoza, charging that Irala was dead and that his lieutenant had no more authority, and that a new election must be held. Some of Abreu's followers wanted to kill Mendoza when he went out to hear mass, but Abreu restrained them in favor of more legal proceedings. Abreu, of course, won the election but not without considerable tumult by Mendoza's friends. These tumults caused him to arrest the deposed leader. Abreu's men hanged Francisco de Mendoza in the public plaza after a farcical tribunal condemned him to death. Turmoil in the Chaco, rebellion and murder in Asunción, uncertainty at San Fernando—a little more and Paraguay would be suffering tumults similar to Peru's. Men stationed at San Fernando solved the problem, or at least pointed the way out, by electing Irala as their lieutenant governor and captain-general in March, 1549. Accepting the charge, Irala marched for Asunción at the head of loyal followers. Abreu sent agents to inform him how he had become governor, but that stubborn son of Vergara kept right on going. Late in March, Diego de Abreu and his closest friends went to jail to await trial for their crimes. An assembly of *conquistadores* proclaimed Irala governor of Paraguay, confounding the schemes of Felipe de Cáceres, Abreu, and partisans of Cabeza de Vaca.

Irala had to keep the conquerors busy, a task not too difficult in 1549. Tupí Indians from the upper Paraná were raiding Guaraní villages in Guayrá and gave him good reason for a campaign of pacification. Striking northeast to the falls of the Paraná, he inflicted such defeats on the Tupís that they agreed to keep the peace. More important than this was the opening of formal trade with Portuguese settlers at São Vicente, who could provide cattle, textiles, iron products, and other goods for Asunción, and the establishing of a short route for communication with Spain. Irala returned to Asunción to find Captains Juan de Camargo and Miguel de Urrutia challenging his authority. These captains, it is said, were among the fifty soldiers whom Pedro de la Gasca sent from Peru with Nufrio de Cháves. Although they protested their innocence, Irala was tired of these frequent challenges and perpetual schemes to overthrow him. Urrutia was so hard to kill that the hangman finally strangled him after the rope had broken three times.

Division of the lands and Indians among would-be encomenderos presented a serious problem. Spanish conquerors generally took or received groups of Indians "in trust" to work for them. In exchange for their labor, the Indians were supposed to be protected, indoctrinated, and civilized by their masters, the encomenderos. Irala did not want to impose this quasi slavery, this New-World serfdom, upon his friends and relatives the Carios; but pressure became so strong that in February, 1551, a council agreed to designate certain towns as Christian and to divide the Indians among the Spaniards. These measures were not carried out, but they did keep discontent at a fair minimum until the arrival of Captain Cristóbal de Saavedra with five companions on August 15 diverted their attention. He had come from the coast of Brazil to announce the arrival at Santa Catharina of vessels belonging to the adelantado Diego de Sanabria.

Upon reviewing many accounts from Paraguay, the Council of the Indies in Spain feared the entire conquest of Río de la Plata was in jeopardy. It would not be convenient for Cabeza de Vaca to return to Asunción, so His Majesty on July 22, 1547, had granted the province to Juan de Sanabria of Medellín, a first cousin to Hernán Cortés. When this new adelantado died while struggling to organize his expedition, the King appointed his son Diego to carry on, and to subject Irala to a ninety-day *residencia,* or official inquiry. Diego sent three ships from San Lúcar de Barrameda on April 10, 1550. Doña Mencia Calderón, mother of the Adelantado, her three daughters, and Captain Juan de Salazar de Espinosa sailed with the expedition. These three vessels, with 250 to 300 persons, made the first effort to bring a sizable contingent of white women to Paraguay. Only one, the *San Miguel,* survived the voyage. Off the coast of Santa Catharina it floundered, but Doña Mencia and perhaps threescore others were saved. It was she who sent Captain Saavedra to Asunción for help, apparently in the belief that her son must have gone on to Paraguay. Since there was no vessel at Asunción built to navigate the open sea, Irala could do no more than send Captain Nufrio de Cháves, who had returned from Lima early in 1549, to look for Doña Mencia in the Plata estuary. Just how he had expected her to get there is something of a mystery. Still, Cháves left a cache of food at San Gabriel. Again, in February, 1552, Cháves went to San Gabriel and again he found no one. The party he was looking for, under Doña Mencia's leadership, had established the colony of San Francisco on the coast in order to keep Sanabria's claims alive. When Irala learned definitely that Doña Mencia was not en route to the Plata, he sent aid again, this time by land. After a few months, the absent adelantado's mother abandoned San Francisco and went on to Asunción with her son-in-law,

Hernando de Trejo. Her grandson, Fernando de Trejo, was to become founder of the University of Córdoba.

Irala was having enough trouble in Asunción without having Doña Mencia there to complicate affairs. Many minor plots to overthrow him were brought to light, and one serious conspiracy was ended when the two ringleaders married Irala's mestiza daughters. This matter disposed of, Irala made another attempt to explore the north; but Diego de Abreu started a revolt almost at once, forcing the Governor to abandon the effort. Annoyed by such heckling, Irala executed three of the conspirators and again started for the north. After a few months sterile of accomplishments, he returned to Asunción where Diego de Abreu was still at his old tricks. In desperation, Felipe de Cáceres, who commanded during Irala's absence, had ordered that any one who held intercourse with the persistent rebel should have his feet cut off, any one who fed him would lose his hands. A posse led by a loyal captain finally put an end to Diego de Abreu.

Paraguay's *conquistadores* had nearly completed the difficult transition from warriors to landlords by about 1554. Those who had survived the first expeditions lost their rash enthusiasms over a period of two decades; nearly all had taken Guaraní wives or concubines, had raised families, and were interested in arranging suitable marriages for their children. The colony was too young, of course, not to be interested in further exploration; and Irala, forty-five years old and still vigorous, recognized the danger of an expanding Brazil. His early interest had been in finding a route to Peru and in exploring the upper Paraguay. He turned, in 1554, to the eastern frontiers and sent Captain García Rodríguez de Vergara to found a village on the Atlantic coast. Instead, Ontiveros on the Río Pequiri, a league north of the Falls of Iguassú, resulted. Another *entrada*, under Pedro Dorantes, explored the upper Paraná, Iguassú, and the general area of Guayrá without establishing new settlements. Dorantes was looking for gold and silver. Paraguay was and still is rich in minerals. There were fabulous deposits of diamonds, gold, and semiprecious stones in the Paraguay of Irala's day, but lands containing them fell to grasping, unscrupulous, ambitious Portuguese.

Refusing to abandon the northern lure, Irala sent Captains Cháves and Hernando de Salazar in October, 1554, to seek a route through Itatín territory in the Chaco. While they were gone, a messenger brought great news to Asunción: Irala had been appointed governor by His Majesty! Cháves and Salazar obeyed the Governor's summons to come back for new instructions. Learning that the royal messenger, Bartolomé Justiniano, was being detained by the Portuguese at São Vicente, Irala sent his usually faithful Captain Cháves to obtain the man's release, to protest Portuguese slaving raids into Guayrá, to chastise the Tupís, and to see what renegade Spaniards, partisans of the deceased Diego de Abreu, were doing.

While Cháves was gone in 1555, Irala organized his government without waiting for original documents to prove his authority. The royal officials, Felipe de Cáceres, Pedro Dorantes, and acting treasurer Andrés Fernández the Roman, in turn took the Royal Order in hand, kissed it, placed it upon their heads, and swore fealty to Domingo Martínez de Irala as governor of Paraguay. This venerated document explained that Diego de Sanabria had been lost and Irala, as a loyal vassal and servant, should be governor of Río de la Plata, exercising civil and criminal justice in cities, villages, and places already established or to be founded. A salary of two thousand gold pesos per year was to be Irala's. Prince Philip, who looked after the Indies for Charles I, also required Irala to give every aid to Father Pedro de la Torre, second titular bishop of Paraguay, in the work of serving God and helping the Indians. There were to be no more foraging raids among native villages, a command that effectively ended long-range expeditions.

Cháves was so successful in his mission that the messenger Justiniano reached Asunción in September, 1555. In October came Juan de Salazar de Espinosa, the royal treasurer. With him came several women from Sanabria's expedition, a dozen Spaniards, and six Portuguese who brought with them a few *ganado vacuno*, domesticated cattle, which were of far greater importance to Paraguay than the white women. The bull and his four or five consorts started Paraguay's great cattle industry.

77

Demands for *encomiendas* (permanent grants of Indians) increased quickly with support from the royal officials. Irala succumbed to this pressure in 1556 and divided some 20,000 Indians among 320 men who had aided in the conquest, without considering their nationality or length of service in Paraguay. Among the conquerors were Spaniards, Italians, Portuguese, Flemings, English, French, and Germans. Dissatisfaction arose at once, as shown by letters of protest to the Council of the Indies, in which aggrieved persons pleaded their cause. A wise governor always has enemies. There was so much grumbling that Irala threatened to punish the complainers with a fine of 100,000 maravedis or 100 lashes. This encomienda system may be dated from March 14, 1556, when Irala published an ordinance to regulate relations between *encomenderos* and *encomendados.*

Captain Cháves succeeded in chastising the Tupís in Guayrá and is credited with having founded thirteen Guaraní pueblos in the area; but, by taking many prisoners, he alienated Captain García Rodríguez de Vergara who refused to allow him to enter his village of Ontiveros. Cháves went back to Asunción, after learning that Doña Mencia had moved her people to Ontiveros, and warned Irala against the Portuguese who, aided by rebellious Spaniards, were making frequent trips into Guayrá. Irala strengthened control over Guayrá by sending Captain Rui Díaz de Melgarejo early in 1556 to found Ciudad Real three leagues north of Ontiveros.

Father Pedro Fernández de la Torre reached his diocesan capital on April 2, 1556, a date that may be taken as marking the official establishment of the Paraguayan church. A procession headed by the friars welcomed the prelate, who celebrated the *Te Deum laudamus* in the church. On Saturday, April 5, Irala received the Bishop cordially, but their acquaintance was to be short.

The ship that brought Bishop Fernández waited for supplies at the mouth of the Paraguay, and for passengers and dispatches bound for Spain. Two or three brigantines from Asunción ferried homesick conquerors to the ship. Among the documents sent with them were dispatches from Irala, in one of which he protested against royal orders forbidding new *entradas* among the Indians and asked for permission to carry on the work originally entrusted to Mendoza.

Irala watched the brigantines sail away, then went out to observe the cutting of timber for a cathedral. While thus engaged, the Governor became so ill that he had to be carried to his home in a hammock. Bishop Fernández de la Torre administered the last rites of the Roman Catholic church to Domingo Martínez de Irala, who died on October 3, 1556, in the forty-seventh year of his life.

Paraguay had lost its only great colonial governor. Nearly four centuries have passed since his death, and Paraguay in all of that time has seen none to compare with him. He left a colony firmly founded, inhabited by 1,500 Spaniards and their families; a city comprising three square miles; a cathedral, two parish churches, three convents, and two schools; a textile industry, and the beginning of animal husbandry. He had explored the northern Chaco, subdued hostile Indians, challenged the encroaching Portuguese, changed conquerors into colonizers, established friendly relations with many Guaraní tribes, and sought always "to open the doors of the land" that Paraguay might not be isolated. Cortés and Pizarro may be deemed greater men. Irala reaped no golden harvest, he found no El Dorado; but on his chosen stage, Domingo Martínez de Irala played as heroic a role as any Spanish *conquistador*. No European conquest in the Americas was as humane as the conquest of Paraguay.

Before the notary Juan de Valderas, on March 13, 1556, Irala had signed his last will and testament "In the name of All Mighty God and of the Glorious Virgin Santa María and of all the saints of the celestial court." Commending his soul to Christ and his "body to the earth from which it was formed," Irala asked that he be buried in Asunción's principal church. From his estate was to come money for many masses, in Paraguayan and Spanish churches and monasteries, for his soul, for his parents, and for his relatives. Captains Nufrio de Cháves and Juan de Ortega, who were as brothers to Irala, were named as tutors of his children. In Irala's will one may read: "Item. I say and declare and confess that I have and God has given me in this province certain daughters and sons, who are: Diego Martínez de Yrala and Antonio de Yrala and Doña Ginebra Martínez de Yrala, children of myself and María my servant, daughter of Pedro de Mendoza who was the principal [Guaraní] chief of this land; and Doña Ysabel de Yrala, daughter of Agueda my servant; and Doña Ursula de Yrala, daughter of Leonor my servant; and Martín Pérez de Yrala, son of Scolastica my servant; and Ana de Yrala, daughter of Marina my servant; and María, daughter of Beatriz, servant of Diego de Villalpando, and whereas I own and declare them as my sons and daughters . . . " they were to share in the estate. Marina, Ysabel, Ginebra, and Ursula all married captains. Ursula became the mother of Ruy Díaz de Guzmán, Paraguay's first native chronicler.

There were few who wept when Hernán Cortés, Marqués del Valle, left Mexico forever. Francisco and Gonzalo Pizarro died violent deaths, and there were few who bewailed their passing. But the Cabildo of Asunción certified in 1602 that "even today they weep in this land for Domingo Martínez de Irala."

# CHAPTER VI

# By the Sword of the Word

BISHOP PEDRO FERNÁNDEZ DE LA TORRE had been in Asunción less than a year when Irala died. It was well for the colony that such an able man was present to keep the untamed conquerors within bounds, for these were troubled times in Paraguay.

A Guaraní rebellion in 1560–61 threatened to wipe out settlements on the Paraná and worried the people of Asunción. Riquelme, acting for Governor Juan Vergara, suppressed the uprising by hanging a number of caciques and shooting many of their followers. Vergara then decided to ask authorities at Lima to approve his election; so, like Irala before him, he set out for the west with a large retinue of Indians and Spaniards, including the Bishop and other high officials of Asunción. Vergara reached Lima. Instead of being confirmed in office, he was replaced by Juan Ortíz de Zárate. The new governor went to Spain in 1566 to see Philip II and sent to Asunción a lieutenant, whose trip back across the Chaco was a nightmare of Indian attacks, tragedy, and despair that did not end until the party straggled into Asunción on January 1, 1569.

This acting governor, Felipe de Cáceres, immediately quarreled with the Bishop. Cáceres imprisoned his enemies; the Bishop excommunicated him. Each was afraid that every shadow held an assassin. One day in 1570, as Cáceres was entering the cathedral, the Bishop's men seized him and decorated his wrists

81

and ankles with irons. A year later the Bishop himself conducted Cáceres to Spain, and Paraguay was rid of two capable but headstrong men.

It was a relief for Asunción to receive as governor the energetic Juan de Garay, a native of Biscay who had founded the Argentine city of Santa Fé in 1573. Garay became governor in 1576; and four years later he re-established the city of Buenos Aires, the haughty queen of modern South America. Even Garay's energetic colony-building failed to employ all the energy of Paraguay's Spaniards, who still sought out the Guaraní girls to increase the mestizo population, quarreled among themselves, hatched plots against the governor, and generally neglected the duties of good Christians. Despairing of his people and worried about the heathen Guaraní, the Dominican bishop of Asunción, Alonso Guerra, sent to Córdoba in Argentina a request that Jesuits be ordered to Paraguay.

Men of the cloth went out with every expedition sent by Spain to the New World, since the Spanish rulers were much concerned with spreading the kingdom of God on earth. These men, both good and bad, belonged to the secular and regular clergy. The orders of St. Francis, St. Augustine, St. Ignatius Loyola, St. Dominic, and the Fathers of Mercy went wherever there were converts to be made. They advanced the frontier, reduced savages to a form of civilization, mediated disputes, defied the rapacious encomenderos, and many of them shared the glory of martyrdom with their beloved Master. Where the Spaniard went, there also went the friar; and where the missionary pioneered, the Spaniard generally followed to gain the pecuniary rewards of religious preparation. In modern parlance, the missionaries infiltrated the enemy to prepare for a secular conquest. Their object was to win souls and not to pave the way for exploitation of the indigent natives.

Greatest of all the orders was that founded by St. Ignatius Loyola, the Society of Jesus, which was organized at Rome in 1539. Twelve years later Jesuits were in Brazil, and within a remarkably short time they had spread their influence over a huge area. About the same time, Jesuit missionaries were at work in the western Chaco. Before them had gone such men as St. Francis Solano, the apostle of the Chaco, and Father Luis de Bolaños, who labored among the Guaranís.

Three Jesuits appeared at Asunción in 1588 in response to the Bishop's call. Father Juan Salonio was a Spaniard; Father Manoel de Ortega was a Portuguese; and Father Thomas Fields was either a Scotsman or an Irishman. They spent a few weeks in Asunción, then turned to the Guaranís in eastern Paraguay and on the upper Paraná. For all of their primitive traits, the Guaranís were susceptible to Christian teaching. Perhaps their greatest intellectual achievement was the recognition of an all-supreme being, an impersonal god, that gave the fathers a point of contact when they began to teach essentials of their faith.

Father Salonio remained in Asunción to help in the Lord's work while his two companions established themselves at Ciudad Real on the upper Paraná and went among the Guaranís. After several months of labor in Guayrá, they assured Salonio that 200,000 Indians were on the threshold of Christianity. Perhaps one-tenth of that number would be more nearly correct. Salonio needed Ortega and Fields in Asunción, where, in 1589, a nine-months plague was raging. It is said that one thousand Indians died every month. The plague was still filling graves when Ortega set out for Villa Rica de Espíritu Santo and beyond to baptize wandering Indians of Guayrá, neophytes who accepted his ministrations and repaid him with a plot against his life. Back at Villa Rica, which was a bit more civilized than the wilds of Guayrá, Ortega was joined by Father Fields. At the same time, Fathers Alfonso Barsena and Marcello Lorençana (also called Marcial de Lorenzana) were inviting death in the lands north of Asunción. The splendid results achieved by these five Jesuits led the people of Asunción to erect buildings for a college in the city, a project that was practically completed in 1596 when Father Salonio died.

Father Ortega, who had survived floods, serpents, plots, and a terrible thorn wound in his thigh, was the victim of a vicious calumny in 1596. One of his enemies in Villa Rica informed the Inquisition at Lima that Ortega had violated his confession.

Ignorant of the charge against him, the aging Ortega obeyed the summons from the Holy Office and made his way to Lima. There he spent several months in confinement before brother Jesuits finally secured his release; but it was not until his accuser confessed to the lie that he was restored to the rights and privileges of the Order.

For many years the Jesuits of Peru had been moving here and there across northern Argentina and Paraguay, visiting many tribes, preaching and baptizing, but without being able to claim significant permanent results. This condition dismayed a Jesuit inspector in 1602, who ordered that the area east of the Paraguay and Paraná rivers be left to Brazilian missionaries. At about the same time Asunción was in need of more missionaries, since no one had been sent to replace Father Salonio and the other Jesuits had been recalled from the field. Bishop Martín Ignatius de Loyola asked that they be returned. Thereafter the people of Paraguay often wanted to be rid of Jesuits, but they had to endure them until 1767. Fathers Lorençana and José Cataldino reached Asunción in 1604 and immediately became something other than *simpático* by crying out against oppression of the Indians.

At the root of the quarrel between Spanish settlers and Jesuit missionaries, in Paraguay and other colonies, lay a fundamental conflict in purpose. The colonizer wanted to grow rich by exploiting the cheap labor supply and missionaries alone could subdue the Indians. Jesuits cared not a real, nor even a maravedi, for such base purposes. They would risk their lives to enrich the kingdom of God, but they would never debase Christianity by making it a prelude to slavery. The kings and emperors of Spain time and time again had ordered that the Indians be Christianized, civilized, and protected. Colonists took the attitude *Obedezco pero no cumplo*—I obey but do not comply—while Jesuits obeyed *and* complied. This conflict between colonist and padre was still in its infancy when the first Jesuit missions of Paraguay came into being.

In the province of Misiones in Argentina, between the Paraná and Uruguay rivers, and in southern Paraguay are ruins of an

Ruins of the Jesuit mission of Trinidad near Encarnación

Photographs courtesy Pan American Union

earthly kingdom of God fast being forgotten. In these reminders of prodigious labor, dazzling success, and sudden disaster, one may read the story of the Jesuit missions. For here the men of St. Ignatius Loyola brought a very real Heaven to the Guaranís. They won their battle against a savage nature imbedded deeply in Indian breasts; with the saving grace of their Lord, they revived moribund souls; they wrought a miracle. But not even this work could prevail against jealousy fattened on greed.

Early in the seventeenth century, in the year 1609, when Europe was making ready for the Thirty Years' War, another Jesuit was greeted in Asunción. Governor Hernando Árias de Saavedra and the Bishop were delighted to see him, for Philip III had sent orders the year before that the Indians of Paraguay must be subdued, but only "by the sword of the word." It was the King's desire that the Indians should become his subjects and be happy. The Governor had started the work by engaging the Franciscan Father Luis de Bolaños to Christianize Guaranís around Asunción, to gather them into a "reduction," to protect them and to teach them; but Bolaños, old and tired, had to give up the work, and that is what brought Father Diego de Torres, Jesuit provincial of Chile and Paraguay, to the capital.

Father Torres conferred with the missionaries José Cataldino, Simón Maceta, Antonio Ruiz de Montoya, and others, and exacted a promise from the Bishop and the Governor that the Society of Jesus would have full power in any settlements or reductions that it made. There must be no encomiendas, no *repartimientos*, no slavery for their charges. Armed with these extensive powers, Cataldino and Maceta in 1610 appeared at Villa Rica del Espíritu Santo with their plans well prepared. When the Spaniards in this frontier village fully understood what the missionaries proposed, their opposition became intense. The Jesuits explained that Indians have rights and that the settlers would benefit from a protection of those rights; but the Spaniards regarded Indians as a legitimate labor supply and source of concubines.

On tributaries of the upper Paraná, especially the Paranápanema, in the province of Guayrá where enormous pines and cedars cover the valleys and rolling hills, Cataldino and Maceta gathered two hundred families into their first mission town in 1610 and named it Loreto. Another mission, San Ignacio Guazú, was soon established among the Diaguites between the Paraná and Tebicuary Rivers by Father Lorençana, and then two more in quick succession. Father Roque González de Santa Cruz, after disappointments among the Guaycurús, joined Lorençana in southern Paraguay. Guaranís trusted the black-robed fathers, they became vassals of the King and neophytes in the religion of Christ, and they could have been an effective barrier to Brazil's westward expansion.

Maceta and Cataldino found that the legendary Pay Luma had been before them. This Pay Luma, or Pay Abara, was a holy man who had preached the gospel among the Indians of Brazil and Paraguay many centuries before the discovery. He had taught them the arts of civilization, and everywhere he went converts flocked to prostrate themselves before the cross that he carried. North of Asunción there was a rock that once served as a pulpit for Pay Luma. Like Quetzalcoatl in Mexico, Pay Luma disappeared into the darkness of time, leaving a memory that never died and a prophecy that men of the cross again would come to the Indians of Paraguay.

The missions in Guayrá were destined for stormy times. Don Francisco Álfaro, an inspector sent by Philip III to Asunción in 1613, dismayed Spaniards with his orders protecting the Indians from oppression, and he infuriated them by confirming the King's command that henceforth all Guaycurús and Guaranís were exempt from service to the Spaniards. Only Jesuits might labor among them. These missionaries were in great disfavor with settlers near the frontiers, whose raids on the missions finally caused the Jesuits to move their reductions farther into Guayrá; but this decision, taken about 1618, placed the villages within reach of the São Paulo mamelucos, mestizo offspring of Portuguese or other white fathers and Indian women, who were raiding the hinterland for Indians to sell to owners of fazendas.

Struggling against native apathy and attacks by apostates, and in constant danger from mameluco raids, the Jesuits nevertheless had started a score of missions by 1629. Some were little beyond the planning stage, and in others the Indians had as yet received but a thin veneer of civilization. In the next year a new governor, Don Luis de Céspedes, passed through the missions on his way to Asunción, leaving a wide trail of bitterness behind him. At the time Brazil was a Spanish colony, since Portugal was united with Spain from 1580 to 1640, a fact that explains why a governor could set out for Asunción by way of São Paulo. The Jesuits at Loreto received him well but could get no promise of aid against the mamelucos.

Ever since 1532 the Portuguese government had been attempting to protect the Indians from rapacious settlers. Pope Paul III had recognized the aborigines as humans in 1537, and when the first Jesuits arrived at Bahía twelve years later, they were determined to eliminate Indian slavery no matter how much opposition they encountered. King Sebastian decreed in 1570 that only Indians captured in battle or those known to be cannibals could be enslaved; Philip II did little to modify the status of Indians; Philip III ordered an end to slavery. The furor that greeted this order caused a return to the old captured-in-battle rule, except that such captives could be enslaved for ten years and held in villages. Still the mamelucos went on their raids, their *bandeiras,* to capture more Indians. Eventually they came into conflict with Jesuit reductions in Guayrá.

The dreaded raiders, nine hundred mamelucos and two thousand Indian allies commanded by Antonio Raposo, attacked and laid waste the mission of San Antonio in 1629. With tears streaming down his face, the missionary, Father Pedro de Mola, pleaded for his people, who were shackled in chains. When tears proved unavailing, Father Mola threatened the mamelucos with the wrath of Heaven; but the lawless slavers scorned his threats. Why, if God himself tried to keep them out of Paradise, they would force their way in! Mamelucos remained in the mission area, falling swiftly upon the most poorly protected reductions. Father Maceta gathered many of the refugees under his protection at the mission Jesús-María, for here was the fierce cacique Güyrá Verá. The leader of a large mameluco band, Manoel

Morato, was more than a match for the Indian chieftain. Morato's men pillaged, burned, and killed at Jesús-María, did violence to the virtue of the women, and carried Güyrá Verá in chains to São Paulo.

Chief Güyrá Verá had opposed Jesuit efforts to impose monogamy, asserting that this scandalous foreign doctrine would prevent population growth, and appealed to tradition in his effort to defeat Christian preaching. Jesuits sincerely believed that he held traffic with the Devil and had four personal demons at his command. Güyrá Verá told some neophytes, seduced by Jesuits, that the fathers would be excellent to eat and his mouth watered when he contemplated the calves of Simón Maceta's well-rounded legs. Maceta, when he heard of this carnivorous design, constructed a wooden fort for his protection and never ventured abroad without a strong guard. The *rubichá* repulsed every Christian overture; his arrogance, wrote Father Antonio Ruiz de Montoya, was as great as Lucifer's. Curiosity at last so overcame this stubborn Guaraní that he consented to visit Maceta and Montoya at San Pablo mission. The fathers used this entering wedge to advantage. They moved the mission of Jesús-María to Güyrá Verá's town in January, 1630. The chief, still unreconciled to missionary efforts, organized a plot to kill his enemies, attracted converted chieftains by playing on their pride and fears, and would have succeeded had it not been for the mameluco raid that captured him.

Maceta and another Jesuit, accompanied only by three Indians, followed Morato to São Paulo, where they found no one with power to redress their wrongs. So they hastened on to Rio de Janeiro and then to Bahía, the capital. Here the Captain-General, Don Diego Luis Oliveira, heard them and promised aid; but his hands were more than full. The Dutch had invaded northern Brazil, there were no troops to spare, and the 1,500 Indians stolen from Guayrá missions already had been sold. Oliveira, with a foreign war in progress, could not afford to offend important people by freeing all the captives but he did intervene for Güyrá Verá and a few others. Back at the missions once more, Maceta found the Indians convinced that the entire reduction system was merely a trick to assemble them at points convenient for mameluco raids.

There were a few months of peace in Guayrá; then, in 1631, mamelucos struck again. In one mission only 500 Indians were saved out of 1,500 families. Villa Rica and Asunción refused to send aid to the Jesuits, who at last decided upon a drastic measure: they would gather all the neophytes they could find and with them leave Guayrá forever. The order went out to abandon Loreto and San Ignacio, the only missions remaining intact. Herds of fine black cattle, fields heavy with crops, houses, and finely decorated churches—all were given up. Twenty-five hundred families, numbering possibly 30,000 Indians, made this great migration down the Paraná and its tributaries in 1631, with mamelucos in close pursuit. These fugitives lost all of their canoes and every semblance of order at the falls of the Paraná. Some remained in the region of Iguassú for months, others proceeded down the river searching for a place of refuge. In 1632, there remained not more than 12,000 Indians of the 100,000 that are said to have been in the Guayrá missions.

Stripped of its mission barrier, ineffective though it was, the Paraguayan frontier far east of Asunción became the scene of more devastating raids. In Villa Rica and Ciudad Real, where Spanish encomenderos had sneered at the Jesuits, the fear of God was even less real than fear of the mameluco. Ciudad Real disappeared entirely; Villa Rica lived on in name at several different locations. Small villages were wiped out. These raids continued for several years in which the scourge of hell seemed to hang over Paraguay. There were times when mission Indians met mameluco raiders on equal terms, except that they had no firearms; by 1638, even the missions of the lower Paraná appeared doomed. The Governor of Paraguay, now Don Martín de Ledesma, had no sympathy with them and the Governor of Buenos Aires refused to protect reductions on the Uruguay River.

Still the Jesuits did not despair. While protesting and appealing to the Pope, the Jesuit general, and the King, they continued their work, slowly concentrating their neophytes in southeastern

Paraguay on both sides of the Paraná. Where the great bend of this river comes within less than fifty miles of the Uruguay, the Jesuits decided to construct mission towns that could protect themselves. Their capital became Candelaria, near the present Argentine city of Posadas.

One of the Jesuits, Father Antonio Ruiz de Montoya, went to Spain where he convinced the Council of the Indies that mission Indians should be allowed to bear arms. Every precaution would be taken to prevent their being used against Spaniards. Thereafter, mameluco raids dwindled sharply, and by 1642 the missions were being left strictly alone. A new governor of Paraguay, Don Pedro de Lugo, himself marched at the head of four thousand armed neophytes to intercept a party of mamelucos and routed them completely. Some of the prisoners taken were Tupí Indians, relatives of the Guaranís, who were turned over to the missions to be dealt with as the Jesuits saw fit. Instead of putting their prisoners to death, a fate they had more than earned, the fathers converted them.

Before the end of the century there were some thirty flourishing reductions in the Jesuit mission republic, with a population probably in excess of 100,000. Félix de Azara credits the Jesuits with having founded all but two of these missions. "By the sword of the word" they had conquered the Guaranís and preserved a large area from Portuguese conquest; but the province of Guayrá, well west of the papal Line of Demarcation, was lost forever to the Spanish crown. Not all Guaranís entered missions voluntarily. Azara describes a bit of strategy and duplicity used by the Jesuits to form their last three missions, San Joaquín (1746), San Estanislao (1749), and Belen (1760). Unable to win wild Indians by preaching, a Jesuit sent neophytes among them with gifts to say that the fathers would provide cattle so that they might live without working. For months there was feasting while music and fiestas lulled the savages into a sense of security. At last, more neophytes had gathered than wild Indians. Another Jesuit appeared, captured the unsuspecting guests, and distributed them among pueblos.

Mission villages, or reductions, were built on a modified

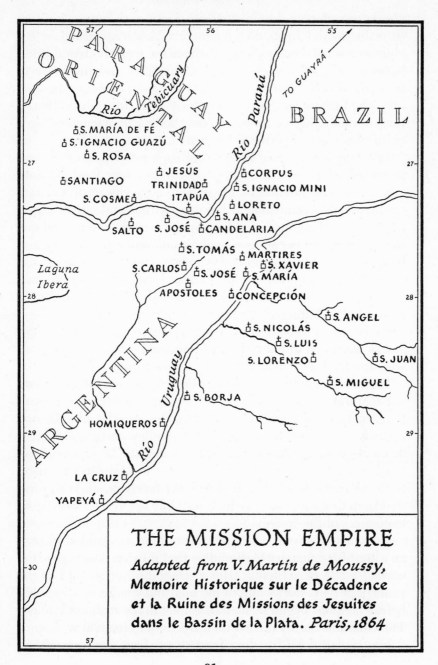

**THE MISSION EMPIRE**

*Adapted from V. Martin de Moussy,*
*Memoire Historique sur le Décadence*
*et la Ruine des Missions des Jesuites*
*dans le Bassin de la Plata. Paris, 1864*

checkerboard plan. Straight streets, lined with houses built on the same model, opened on a square which was formed by the church, arsenal, homes of the missionaries, workshops and storehouses. Each mission contained about 3,500 Indians, more or less, and in each there was usually a senior and a junior missionary. The fathers were extremely busy men, for, in addition to their normal religious functions, they were school teachers, agricultural advisers, overseers, inspectors, judges, and doctors.

Self-sufficiency being the goal of each mission, no food was imported. Meat came from herds of cattle, a few of which were killed daily for general use. There were occasions when Guaraní field workers became hungry before mealtime and satisfied their appetites by slaughtering and eating the oxen they were working. Land, cultivated in common by the community, produced every crop that would grow profitably. Maté, sugar, tobacco, maize, small grain, fruits, vegetables, cotton, honey, wax, and animal products generally were to be found in abundance. The finest maté used in Paraguay, Argentina, Chile, and Peru came from the missions. Production of this tea was so large that surplus stocks were sold at Santa Fé and Asunción where the proceeds were used to buy articles not made in the missions.

Workshops enabled the artisan to practice his skill and to resist temptations presented by hell's ubiquitous master. Beautiful carpets, vessels, and ornaments for the church and daily use, utensils, musical instruments, tools, spindles, carts, and leather products were made by neophytes under the direction of lay brothers sent out for that purpose. There was hardly a common trade, skilled or unskilled, that was not represented. Who profited from this work and production? Only the Jesuits, according to enemies of the system.

Guaranís, always somewhat irresponsible, responded in such an astonishing manner to discipline that mission life became the normal mode of existence after a generation or so, and as the years passed by, stories told by old men and women of savage life before missions began seemed to belong in the realm of fantasy. The Guaranís hardly missed their freedom to roam at will, since it was replaced by freedom from want, fear, and oppression.

How much religion they learned is a matter of conjecture. Two Jesuits in a populous mission, even with helpers, could have done very little real teaching. Most of the Indians knew no Spanish; many padres knew no Guaraní. Everyone was baptized, listened to sermons, partook of communion, and learned passages from an abbreviated catechism. These gestures, mere formalities that meant nothing without understanding, certainly did not make Christians.

Jesuits regulated life for all ages and for both sexes. Religious services at morning, noon, and evening broke the routine of work, provided opportunities to check on the neophytes, and fortified habits of benefit to the Church. Children attended school, where they learned to read and write, sometimes in Spanish and Latin as well as in Guaraní, although visitors suspected that knowledge of Latin consisted solely of being able to pronounce the words without an understanding of their meaning. They worked in shops and fields, each at an appointed task. Women, besides their field work, spun wool and cotton thread for the looms. Their housework, otherwise, was not arduous, since dwellings at first were flimsy affairs, poorly ventilated, and unfurnished except for hammocks. Later, a few more pretentious homes of masonry were constructed and provided with simple but solid furniture.

A system of cultivation, vaguely resembling communal practices under the Incas of Peru, prevailed. Each family received a plot which would produce the necessary food, while orphans, widows, religious personnel, and others whose duties kept them from the fields, were fed from public storehouses that held produce from common plots and surpluses kept against crop failures.

Morals were a source of constant concern to the Jesuits. They made every effort to keep the sexes from mingling too freely, even in the church, where men and women entered and left by different doors and sat apart. Just why so much attention should be given to the matter in such sacred surroundings is difficult to understand, but, after religious services were over in the evening, not even the watchful missionaries could be everywhere. Hard work, full days, adequate recreation, occasional fiestas without *caña*, and constant preaching caused most of the births at a mission to be legitimate. When Azara visited the missions near the end of the eighteenth century, he found morals loose and licentiousness common: "Perhaps there is not an Indian girl ten years of age and up who has said 'No' to any solicitor, be he an old man or young man, free or slave, black or white." Sex was just another physical function, taken as lightly as sleeping or eating. Still, in the nineteenth century, writers could repeat the old tale "that the Fathers were compelled to arouse their flocks somewhat before the working hours, and to insist upon their not preferring Morpheus to Venus, and thus neglecting the duty of begetting souls to be saved." A vicious calumny. No Guaraní, male or female, was ever guilty of such neglect.

The caciques presented a serious problem in the early days of mission life. These leaders took wives more or less at will and cast them off, loaned them to friends, or abandoned them with a casualness that was annoying. For a time the fathers toyed with the idea of requiring caciques to keep the woman of their first liaison, but memories proved short among Guaraní caciques and it was easy to lie. The problem was referred through channels to the provincial, to the general, and at last to the Pope himself. Solomon could have done no better than the Holy Father, who told the Jesuits to use their own judgment. Caciques continued to have an eye for wild beauty.

Lighter aspects of life were not lacking in the missions. Churches were decorated and adorned lavishly in an obvious appeal to a childish love for glitter. Visits by the bishop of Asunción or Buenos Aires were eagerly awaited events. Parties of armed Indians were stationed along the route to protect the prelate on his journey, and when he came within sight of the reduction, cavalry dashed out to meet him and formed an escort which was joined by the Indian officials and missionaries, and then by the infantry "drawn up in order of battle, colours flying, drums beating, fifes and clarions sounding." Women waited at the church, where organs pealed forth their welcome to an accompaniment of clanging bells. Days of the saints were festivals of pomp and circumstance which began with a parade to the church. Thereafter children danced in the public square, bonfires illuminated the streets, and a festive spirit prevailed. At noon of the second day, the celebrating village entertained visitors from neighboring missions who stayed to see the closing event, a procession of the blessed sacrament. Great arches festooned with flowers extended across the streets; birds of brilliant plumage, chained pumas, and bowls of fish marked the route; masses of flowers and sweet-smelling plants lay on the ground; products of the fields, displayed for blessing, revealed God's continuous bounty. Village officials carried the canopy, followed by the royal banner and village militia in solemn array. Fireworks at night brought the festival to a brilliant end.

Every mission village had officials usually found in Spanish towns, although their duties varied somewhat from those of the whites. The cacique and the corregidor held the most prominent places; then came the alcaldes, the alférez, and minor officials. Each mission, also, had its own armed force trained by lay brothers and commanded by the corregidor. Bitter experiences in Guayrá with Brazilian mamelucos and later with hostile Indians and Spaniards would not be repeated. Each reduction had a troop of cavalry and a body of infantry armed with muskets, swords, lances, bows and arrows, small arms, and artillery. When assembled to protect the entire mission republic from danger, these Indian troops commanded fear and respect. A night watch protected the villages from nocturnal surprise and also kept citizens from venturing abroad after curfew.

One of the fairly reliable and smug Englishmen who made two quick visits to Paraguay during the War of the Triple Alliance was Captain Richard F. Burton, who, in his *Letters from the Battle-fields of Paraguay*, wrongly ascribed to the mission system an influence it never possessed: "It is interesting to see how, in the organization of those early times, we find adumbrated the system of Paraguay in the heart of the nineteenth century. Then, and not as vulgarly supposed with Dr. Francia, commenced the isolation which afterwards gave to Paraguay the titles of Japan and 'Chine Américaine.' Then began the sterile, extravagant theocratic despotism which made the race what it still is, an automaton that acts as peasantry and soldiery; not a people but a flock, a *servum pecus* knowing no rule but that of their superiors, and whose history may be summed up in absolute submission, fanaticism, blind obedience, heroic and barbarous devotion to the tyrant that rules it, combined with crass ignorance, hatred of, and contempt for, the foreigner. Then first arose the oligarchy, the slavery of the masses, the incessant *corvées* which still endure, the regimentation of labour, and even the storing of arms and ammunition."

This criticism serves only to reveal depths of ignorance and survivals of anti-Jesuitism in a famous traveler. Had Jesuit missions controlled most of Paraguay, this judgment might have more weight. Distance more than theocracy generated isolationism; inherent faults of Indian and mestizo character, not paternalism, made Paraguay easy prey for ruthless dictators. If the mission system was not the finest thing that ever happened to Paraguay, certainly it was not the worst aspect of colonial life; and since most of the missions were not even located within the limits of modern Paraguay, their influence can be grossly exaggerated. Missions saved the souls of thousands upon thousands of Indians, at least in the eyes of the Church; they brought contentment, care, and civilization to peoples whose lot would have been inevitable peonage or slavery; they redeemed a wilderness, turned a lush "desert" into a garden spot, and saved from extinction the very people whose complaints were unrivaled in bitterness. In spite of all of these accomplishments, the system left little if any permanent influence on life in the countries where it flourished. Modern villages and towns occupy the former sites of many missions; but the high moral tone, the communal enterprises, the benevolent paternalism of the Jesuit fathers vanished long ago.

Spanish settlements in Paraguay and Argentina were threatened by a variety of dangers in the mid seventeenth century. The three foci of Spanish control were at Asunción, Tucumán, and Buenos Aires. Each of these cities was in danger from foreign encroachments or Indian attacks. Asunción was protected on the southeast by Jesuit missions and their militia centering in the area between the Tebicuary and Uruguay rivers, but in the

Chaco west of the Paraguay and in the still unconquered regions north of the city there were wild tribes whose resistance to civilization constituted a menace of considerable proportions. The southernmost missions, between the Uruguay and Paraná rivers, still were in danger from mameluco raids originating in Brazil. Tucumán, constantly exposed to Chaco Indian raids, had no mission protection. When the city was founded first in 1558, Indians lost little time in destroying it. Started again in 1565, Tucumán lost an excellent chance for protection when the encomienda system divided unwilling Indians among the settlers. Buenos Aires, as late as 1664, was a rude village that contained about 1,000 people, among whom were only 211 families. Since communications among the Plata cities and with Peru and Chile were slow and uncertain, Indian conspiracies could be formed with disastrous consequences before mutual aid was forthcoming. Because of its missions, Paraguay was the safest Spanish colony east of the Andes, and even safer than Chile.

Brazilian nibbling at Spanish territory created situations in the Plata basin that were to have serious results for the mission system, and which represented attempts to break the exclusive policies so dear to mercantilist Spain. One of these efforts led to a short-lived colony planted by the Portuguese at Colonia do Sacramento on the Río de la Plata's north bank a few miles below the mouth of the Uruguay. A Portuguese fleet of four vessels had set out in 1679 to establish a port there, and so successful was the attempt that by 1680 Colonia was a respectable fortification that menaced a considerable region. Assembling the military power of the Plata, Governor José de Garro of Buenos Aires sent out an army to destroy Colonia. From the Jesuit missions of Uruguay came some three thousand Indian militia who stormed the fort, killed two hundred or more of its defenders, and captured the remainder. This Indian army well earned the praise of Viceroy Melchior de Liñán y Cisneros of Peru, since it had marched hundreds of miles, defeated the enemy, and cost the royal government not a cent.

Spanish officials at once began to contemplate an extension of the mission system to southern Uruguay; but while the idea was being debated, the Portuguese regent threatened war against Spain if Colonia were not restored. Charles II capitulated, and by 1683 Colonia was even stronger than when the Indian army had destroyed it. The last two decades of the century found Jesuits establishing missions among Chiquitos tribes of the Chaco and repelling mameluco raids, activities that attracted considerable attention at Asunción, Tucumán, and other cities. Colonia on the Plata was left alone until in 1705 the Viceroy of Peru ordered another attack against it. Governor Alfonso Juan de Valdes asked for 4,000 neophytes to aid in the siege of Colonia. By November, 1705, the mission army had arrived to reinforce troops under Baltazar García Ros, who successfully conducted the attack. The Indians left Colonia in the following March, again refusing to accept pay for their services. Each time that Colonia was captured by Spanish colonists, it was returned to Portugal by the Spanish court. Following the Treaty of Utrecht, the Portuguese in 1715 returned to Colonia and made it a thriving smuggling center. They also threatened to seize Uruguay by colonizing near Montevideo in 1723. Although a rebellion in Paraguay was bothering Governor Bruno Mauricio de Závala of Buenos Aires, he summoned mission troops to aid in dislodging the Portuguese and to work on a fortification.

By the treaty of 1750, Portugal agreed to cede Colonia to Spain in exchange for territory east of the Uruguay River which contained seven missions. News of this transfer caused the War of the Seven Reductions, which Jesuits probably inspired. Mission Indians, although not entirely successful in the war, prevented the transfer. Charles III gave Colonia back to Portugal in 1761; Viceroy Pedro de Zevallos took it for Spain in 1762; but in 1763, the Treaty of Paris gave it once more to Portugal. This peculiar game ended in 1777 when the Treaty of San Ildefonso definitely pronounced it a part of Spain's Banda Oriental.

The Black Robes had overreached themselves in their War of the Seven Reductions. As never before, the Spanish court became convinced that this empire within an empire must be overthrown. Charles III, the reforming king of Spain, issued a decree on March 1, 1767, that banished all Jesuits from Spanish dominions.

His council approved the action, and in June the warship *Príncipe* anchored at Buenos Aires with orders for a simultaneous seizure and expulsion of the Jesuits. Francisco Bucareli, intendant of Buenos Aires, appointed July 22 as the day for executing this order.

An inventory of the missions in 1767 revealed how wealthy the Society had become. The reductions in Argentina and Paraguay alone contained 21,036 families. Vast herds of animals included 724,903 cattle, 230,384 sheep, 99,078 horses and mares, 46,936 oxen, 13,905 mules, and 7,505 asses. If one attempts to value the Indian laborers at $200 each, and assigns a nominal value to livestock, buildings, land, and church ornaments and plate, the thirty missions may be said to have been worth about $28,000,000, according to the English merchant J. P. Robertson. Add to this sum the properties existing elsewhere in Latin America, the jewels, precious metals, monasteries, churches, and lands, and the total value of Jesuit holdings reached a figure that would arouse cupidity in any government.

Whether the Jesuits were good or bad for the Indians, there is no denying that their missions in other hands quickly declined until only shambles remained. The Black Robes as a society were wealthy; individually, they were honest and poor. Those who followed them at the missions immediately began to plunder everything of value. Not even church ornaments escaped their avaricious clutches. Mismanagement caused the Indians to desert by thousands; thievery reduced the splendid herds to memory. In 1772, an inventory of livestock revealed only 158,659 cattle, 93,739 sheep, and 8,145 mules. The oxen, horses, and asses had fallen off by about one-half in five years.

Regular and secular clergy and civil administrators sent from Buenos Aires to administer the missions entered a contest of venality in which the Indians were the heaviest losers. Layman and cleric contended for their loyalty so bitterly that the simple neophytes were thoroughly confused. "The result was, that the curate ordered the Indians that obeyed the administrator to be flogged, and the administrator awarded stripes to those who obeyed the curate." Not even the aborigines could endure such treatment forever. Still, the anti-Jesuits blamed the fathers for not having raised their charges to a state of self-reliance. They saw in every disaster new evidence of Jesuit selfishness and oppression, forgetting what happened everywhere else in the colonies. Were the Indians in Peru and Mexico raised to such a high level of civilization by their Spanish masters? Did the Maya of Guatemala become energetic, intelligent citizens under the guidance of Pedro de Alvarado and his kind? Critics of the missions, suffering from a Protestant bias or deluded by snarling devotees of unbridled individual enterprise, refused to see any good in the Jesuits.

A trip through the once thriving missions south of the Tebicuary and the Paraná revealed only the desolation of decay in 1814. Candelaria, capital of the system, had dwindled from 3,064 people to a mere 700. The church was falling into ruins, the roof leaked copiously, ornaments had disappeared, "and even the altar was uncovered by a cloth." Where once flourishing orchards bore fruit for the entire community, nothing but stumps could be seen. The huts, once clean and in good repair, slowly but surely were returning to the earth from which they came. Fields lay untended, overgrown with brush and weeds. Soon the work of ruin would be complete. An era had ended in 1767, when, by a stroke of the pen, a Spanish king destroyed the heroic work of two hundred years.

# CHAPTER VII

# Don Bernardino, Bishop

AFTER THE SEPARATION of Paraguay and Buenos Aires, which was ordered in 1617 and carried out three years later, Don Manuel de Frías became governor at Asunción. Despite a difficult domestic situation—he was separated from his wife, and Bishop Tomás de Torres tried futilely to force a reconciliation, so that pro-Manuel and pro-Leonor parties appeared in Asunción —Frías was sensible of his public duties. Making war on the Payaguás, he dispersed them in several battles, and even the Guaycurús ceased opposition for a while. Then, taking cognizance of the Bishop's complaints, the Audiencia of Charcas ordered Frías to appear for a hearing. He was gone so long that the Cabildo of Asunción complained bitterly about his absence; and when he died in 1627, shortly after his acquittal, there were many who mourned his passing.

Paraguayans, jealous of Jesuit missionary successes and hostile to Jesuit enterprises, found an ally in Governor Luis de Céspedes Jeray, who took office in 1628. He persecuted the Jesuits so persistently that Dean Funes called him "more inhuman than the wild beasts." The new governor's bride, a Portuguese lady of Rio, was escorted to Asunción by mamelucos; and these slave raiders, promised immunity by Governor Céspedes, sold sixty thousand Indians in the Rio market from 1628 to 1630. Thereafter, the Audiencia of Charcas removed Céspedes from office and fined him twelve thousand pesos; but his criminal betrayal of Indians and Jesuits cost Spain and Paraguay a noble province.

Don Martín de Ledesma Valderrama, who became governor in 1636, continued the bitter fight against Jesuit missions. His successor after five years, Don Gregorio de Hinestrosa—who was a native of Chile famed as a fighter against the Araucanians, among whom he had been a captive for fourteen years—partly because of a Franciscan bishop's attitude, was to become a Jesuit ally. Two of his first acts were to expel the Portuguese from Asunción and to call for six hundred Guaraní mission warriors to fight the Guaycurús. And he was to encounter greater and graver troubles.

Of all the strange happenings that made colonial Paraguay the stage for high comedy and low tragedy, the activities of Don Bernardino de Cárdenas are second to none. Don Bernardino was a brilliant Franciscan, native of La Plata (Chuquisaca), whose penchant for indiscretions kept him in difficulty constantly. Dean Funes described him as being "endowed with an easily inflamed temperament, a lively imagination, a happy memory, and uncommon ability." Despairing of holding this erratic cleric within bounds, his superiors sent him to Asunción to be bishop of Paraguay, and Philip IV confirmed the appointment.

Don Bernardino began at once to act the part, although he had made no move to take possession of his diocese; and the Archbishop finally advised him to enter upon his duties while waiting for the papal bulls that would make possible his consecration. Then Don Bernardino, impatient to be consecrated, went to Salta, where Jesuits, on very unsubstantial grounds, decided that the ceremony might be performed. Bishop Don Melchior Maldonado of Tucumán officiated at the consecration, and immediately afterward Bishop Cárdenas embarked for Asunción. This year of 1642 was to initiate a decade of trouble for Paraguay.

The Bishop's welcome was everything that a holy man could desire. Spaniards and Indians lined the banks of the Paraguay as this remarkable prelate approached Asunción and joined generous praise for a man whom they knew only by reputation. That reputation grew quickly. The Bishop aroused sympathy for his devotion to ritual, but his delay in appointing curates to vacant parishes started rumors. Governor Hinestrosa, gentle, modest, and honest, was quite willing to co-operate with the Bishop, even to the extent of abrogating some of the civil power which he exercised under the Viceroy of Peru. A bishop was a powerful official. He could excommunicate cleric and layman alike, levy heavy fines, and threaten the same punishment to anyone who dared to have dealings with a person so cast out of the Church; and he could lay an interdict upon the city, thereby suspending religious activities. These were spiritual weapons of the Church, to be used in moderation lest they incur the contempt of familiarity. No one, not even the governor of Paraguay, would want to incur the animosity of such a powerful prelate.

The first test soon appeared. At Hinestrosa's order, a minor official of the Inquisition had been imprisoned for quarreling with one of the Governor's men. When the Bishop heard of this, he confronted the jailer with a demand for the prisoner's release. The jailer laughed at the Bishop and ignored the chalice with which the prelate sought to overawe him. However, the rector of the Jesuit College persuaded Hinestrosa to release the prisoner. Bishop Cárdenas thereupon gave the fellow clerical garb, demanded and received his confiscated property, and unwisely boasted about his victory. Then he went further. Having seen silver plate in Hinestrosa's house, he expressed a desire to have it for the church. The Governor had the articles delivered in full view of the congregation. Don Bernardino sent the men back with a request that Hinestrosa give still more of his treasures. Again the Governor complied, informing the Bishop that "what's mine is yours."

No sensible Spaniard ever takes such a remark literally; but Don Bernardino was not a sensible man. Before long he was demanding things beyond the Governor's power to deliver. Then, following a series of insults on both sides, the Bishop excommunicated Don Gregorio and other officials, levying, in addition, fines of fifty crowns each against them. However, the incident passed, and Hinestrosa was absolved.

As he had treated the Governor, so did the Bishop deal with others whom he thought had wealth that could be tapped by fines. Eventually this game of excommunication, absolution, and collection of fines had the capital in an uproar. At the height of confusion, in 1643, Cárdenas left Asunción for a while, taking the precaution of again excommunicating Hinestrosa before his departure. Tired of this bickering, the Governor complained to the Audiencia of Charcas, a judicial body, which also received an indictment from the Bishop. Now that the dispute had been taken to a civil court, the vicar general at Asunción lifted the excommunications and interdict, an act that brought the Bishop hurrying back to Yaguarón, near the capital, without visiting the missions as he had intended. Again he declared the city under interdict, and again he excommunicated nearly everyone whose name he could remember. When Hinestrosa begged absolution, Don Bernardino remained haughty and upright, granted a conditional absolution, and fined the Governor 100,000 pounds of maté.

While at Yaguarón, Bishop Cárdenas levied so many fines that, had they been paid in full, his stock of maté would have been the largest in Paraguay. Collecting maté in this fashion was bad enough; but when the Bishop began to collect Indians as well, Hinestrosa again braved apostolic wrath by restoring the workers to their encomenderos. Don Bernardino again excommunicated him. Then the Viceroy of Peru in 1644 ordered Hinestrosa to put an end to the confusion and make the Bishop stay within his spiritual functions, but the Viceroy neglected to suggest weapons for the Governor. Nevertheless, Hinestrosa summoned a military escort and went to see the Bishop. Much to his surprise, Don Bernardino granted absolution and invited his visitor to dinner.

Jesuit chroniclers charge the Franciscan bishop with having reached an understanding with Dominicans to drive the Society of Jesus out of Paraguay. A conspiracy of this sort might well have existed, since Paraguay was not the only colony where Franciscans quarreled with Jesuits, and Cárdenas fully intended to destroy every trace of Jesuit influence within the diocese. He suspended the Jesuits' right to perform public religious ceremonies, challenged the catechism used in mission work, sought directly and indirectly to turn Hinestrosa against them, and made all candidates for holy orders swear obedience to the bishop, even unto death. Every charge he could think of he hurled at the Jesuits: they were robbers, incompetents, apostates, rabble-rousers, traitors, rebels against episcopal authority, seducers of the Indians, and deceivers of the King. He openly announced that he would drive the Jesuits away, confiscate their property and the missions, and divert their revenues into his own treasury. The prospect of having thousands of "reduced" Indians available for their fields and beds aroused lecherous instincts in many a Spaniard who favored the Bishop's design. Don Bernardino actually was prepared to carry out his project, even to ordering boats made ready to carry the Jesuits away, and requested Franciscans, Mercedarians, and Dominicans to be ready for duty.

The great blow was to fall in October, 1644, when the Bishop expected to seize the Jesuit College in Asunción, but Governor Hinestrosa learned of the plot, warned the Jesuits, and then set out to meet the Bishop outside the capital. The prelate knew that his scheme had been revealed, but still he did not know Hinestrosa's attitude and he was not certain of his next move. Hinestrosa suggested, in order to be rid of him, that he start with the missions and then take care of the chapter in Asunción. Cárdenas grasped at the idea and was preparing for his trip to the Paraná when a messenger arrived from the Audiencia of Lima with orders to lift all excommunications and interdicts. These instructions, coming directly from the Viceroy, infuriated the Bishop. He held his temper but not his tongue, with the result that Hinestrosa soon knew that the Bishop planned to remove him from office.

Now was the time for His Majesty's governor to act. Promising 130 soldiers to the Bishop for his descent upon the missions, Hinestrosa secretly sent an urgent call for 600 armed Guaraní militia to come to his aid. And Cárdenas, far from being dismayed by the Audiencia, excommunicated every Jesuit in Paraguay and returned to Yaguarón to prepare his crusade. He had become so suspicious of Hinestrosa that he planned to seize Asunción before going to the missions, although the Governor's soldiers appeared at Yaguarón on schedule. At last the mission detachment arrived, and with it Hinestrosa went to Yaguarón, where he confronted the Bishop in his church. News of important events spread swiftly through the village, and everyone who could hastened to see what would happen.

"What do you want of me?" the Bishop demanded.

"Nothing, my lord, except to banish you from Paraguay," Hinestrosa replied.

"And on what grounds do you base this monstrous action, you who are excommunicated?"

"By the Viceroy's orders! You have attempted rebellion against the King! Adios, my lord," and Hinestrosa strode from the church, still excommunicated.

Cárdenas celebrated mass and then ordered a procession in which he himself carried the Holy Sacrament to the market. Hinestrosa observed this display in silence. He had won the game and knew it; but still he came near to losing all he had gained. The Bishop, promising to lift his excommunications and to leave Paraguay, persuaded him to send the mission Indians away. Then he went to Asunción, barricaded himself in the Franciscan convent, and did everything in his power to arouse the people against the Governor. But Hinestrosa recalled his mission troops, declared the see vacant, prevailed on the canon, Don Cristóbal Sánchez, to take over as grand vicar, and summoned the regular soldiers and militia to gather around the royal standard in the public square. While bells were ringing to proclaim an end to his rule, Bishop Cárdenas decided that he could not demean himself by further residence in a diocese of excommunicates. He celebrated two masses, took leave of his followers, and marched to the river to embark. As he left, he excommunicated his enemies anew and laid an interdict on Asunción. The Franciscan convent rang its bells, but their sound was lost in the tones of those whose loyal tongues clanged for the Governor as Bishop Cárdenas sailed downstream toward Corrientes.

Among the lies spread by the Bishop was a charge that Jesuits had discovered rich veins of gold and were keeping their location a secret. The tale reached Buenos Aires at the time that a similar story was being investigated: An Indian, appropriately named Buenaventura, claimed that he had worked in those mines, but a judicial inquiry branded him a liar. Then came Cárdenas' accusation to resurrect the story. To set such rumors at rest, the governor of Buenos Aires himself went to the missions, where he found not even a grain of gold. Still the "gold mines of Paraguay" persisted in Spanish imagination, and the story has not yet been laid to rest.

At Corrientes, which he reached late in 1644, the exiled bishop appeared to have learned nothing. Here he was in a strategic position, relatively close to Buenos Aires, Tucumán, Asunción, and the missions. He was still the excommunicating, interdicting, anathematizing bishop, who could defy an audiencia's orders with impunity. He wrote to the bishop of Tucumán in January, 1645, to excoriate Don Gregorio Hinestrosa. Summon a council, he pleaded, that will end the Paraguayan schism and punish Jesuit heretics who steal from the King, delude the Indians, preach monstrous heresies, and ally themselves with the devil. Don Melchior de Maldonado, bishop of Tucumán, sent a scathing reply that someone other than Jesuits was at fault. Their gold mines were "an invention of hell," their prosperity was built on sweat and abnegation, and their heresies were buzzings in receptive ears. As to a council, only he and Cárdenas were eligible to attend, and they could never agree.

Governor Hinestrosa carried his complaints to the Council of the Indies and told how he had been reduced to using mission Indians to protect his office from the Bishop's intrigues. Moreover, the Guaraní militia had been called upon in 1646 to defeat a body of Guaycurús whose aim was to destroy Asunción. Had the Bishop had his way, Asunción would be in ashes. From his refuge at Corrientes, however, Cárdenas went on intriguing; and toward the end of 1646 he attempted to return to Asunción, but Hinestrosa stopped him some twenty-five miles away. The Audiencia of Charcas tried to send Cárdenas to Popayán in New Granada, but the Bishop refused to go.

At last, in 1647, Don Diego Escobar Osorio became governor of Paraguay, with strict orders to keep Bishop Cárdenas from molesting the Jesuits. Aided by pleas from the Governor's wife, the Bishop returned to Asunción, still determined to destroy his enemies and to carry out his plans with regard to the mission Indians. The new governor, fearing assassination, entered Asunción with an escort of one thousand armed Indians. The Bishop whittled away at the Jesuits and obtained approval for removing their missionaries from two missions among Itatines far north of Asunción. Then, when Governor Osorio died early in 1649, a mob proclaimed Bishop Cárdenas acting governor. Now that he was supreme in Paraguay, this blight upon the Church spared no means to gain his ends. The Spaniards of Asunción, dreaming still of gold mines and twenty thousand Indians to enslave, supported him. On March 16, 1649, Juan de Villego Villasanti led soldiers into the Jesuit College, whipped the inmates, dragged the sick from their beds, and set the lot of them afloat in canoes on the Paraguay. A mob looted the college, destroying a magnificent altar, tearing off doors, and hacking the pulpit and confessional to pieces, and set fire to the wrecked building.

From a refuge at Corrientes, the Jesuits found a champion in Father Pedro Nolasco, a Mercedarian who became their judge-conservator. While the wheels of justice were turning slowly, the Audiencia of Charcas sent one of its own members, Don Andrés de León Garabito, member of the elite military Order of Santiago, to Asunción as official investigator, captain-general, and governor. While Don Andrés was en route, the Audiencia peremptorily ordered Cárdenas to appear before it, and the Viceroy of Peru backed up the order. Ignoring this summons, the Bishop recruited an army and waited for the next move. Don Sebastián de León y Zárate, acting for the Governor, marched against Asunción with Spanish troops and three thousand Indians loyal to the Jesuits.

The Bishop's army marched out to meet León y Zárate, who read his orders when the opposing troops came together. A volley of musket fire answering, Don Sebastián ordered a charge that sent the Bishop's men in flight toward Asunción. The victor proceeded at once to the cathedral, kissed the Bishop's ring, and ordered him to get out. Nevertheless, Cárdenas remained in

Don Bernardino

Asunción for several months, apparently hoping that something would happen to restore his power. At last, early in 1651, he took his leave of Paraguay and returned to Chuquisaca, his birthplace.

During the next two or three years, Don Andrés found the mission Indians valuable allies in fighting Payaguás and Guaycurús, who, taking advantage of mameluco attacks in 1652, sought to destroy Asunción. A serious pestilence struck the city in 1654 and 1655, accompanied by more Indian attacks. Again the Governor, then Cristóbal de Garay, appealed to mission Indians for aid, and again they came to the rescue. Weakness displayed by Governor Juan Blásquez de Valverde (1656–59) encouraged Indians to rebel under the leadership of a Guaraní cacique, Rodrigo Yaguariguay, chief of Arecayá pueblo. This astute enemy of the Spaniards formed an alliance among nonmission Guaranís who were discontented with their lot as serfs of encomenderos. On a visit to Arecayá and other villages northeast of Asunción, Governor Alonso Sarmiento y Figueroa heard about the incipient rebellion but made the mistake of deposing Rodrigo. That act precipitated the rebellion of 1659–60, which mission Indians again aided in quelling. Had Bishop Bernardino de Cárdenas succeeded in his design to crush the Jesuits, Paraguay's fate would have been far different and its history even more a series of tragedies.

109

# CHAPTER VIII

# Antequera and the Comuneros

PARAGUAY was one of the first of Spain's colonies to attempt independence, perhaps the very first in which a serious revolt occurred with definite intent to throw off metropolitan shackles. Isolated in the heart of South America, considered as a frontier outpost to hold back the Portuguese, and a source of no significant income to the Crown, the province held little interest for kings who were playing a fascinating game of power politics. Even the Crown's concern for Indians was by no means entirely altruistic, and when a man like Bishop Cárdenas could spend years in attempts to destroy the only truly civilizing force in Paraguay, without stern reactions from royal officials, one is inclined to wonder why a strong rebellious movement had not occurred before the seventeen twenties.

Dissatisfaction with the royal rule was not too deep. The King, after all, was far away and his viceroy in Peru was too busy to bother with imposing petty nuisances upon Paraguay. But those Jesuits! Every time a Paraguayan Spaniard thought about the prosperous missions, of their freedom from taxation, of thousands of Indians safe from forced labor on their lands and in their households, he forgot all ideas of charity and cursed the Society of Jesus long and vehemently. The designs of Don Bernardino had been frustrated by a governor who had brought a mission army to enforce his will. These same missions had supplied troops to the governor of Buenos Aires in 1680 and 1705 to capture

Colonia, not as mercenaries to be paid but as subjects of the King who refused to take a single crown for their labors. This demonstration of power and generosity made the Spaniards of Paraguay even more bitter in their denunciations of the Jesuits. Now these insolent clerics had an army at their command, an army that might at any moment lay waste to all of Paraguay. Their hatred found expression in rebellion against the King and plunged Paraguay into confusion for fifteen years.

A new governor, Don Antonio Victoria, was appointed to Paraguay in 1717. For some reason Victoria renounced the commission in favor of Don Diego de los Reyes Balmaceda, mayor of Asunción. When the King confirmed this transfer, he violated both law and tradition. A native of Andalucía, Reyes was a hot-tempered gentleman of mediocre birth and modest fortune, who had plenty of virtue but little else. News of his commission created a buzz of gossip in Asunción, where many a man whose lineage could be traced to persons of noble blood was piqued that Reyes should be elevated to power. The cry went up that Jesuits had seduced Victoria and had brought about the change in appointment.

Don José de Avalos y Mendoza was Asunción's merchant prince, a man whose advice had been followed by previous governors. Don José, indeed, had been the power behind provincial politics for many years, and Reyes sought to placate him with the position of king's lieutenant, the highest office at his disposal. Avalos would have none of it, since he well knew the scorn with which the righteous governor regarded men of his type. Avalos already was a regidor (councilman) and in that capacity he had ample opportunity to build a personal following among the merchants and hacendados. Don José set out to ruin Reyes and thereby started a chain reaction that reached to Buenos Aires and Lima, to Cádiz and Madrid.

Avalos began his campaign by sending a friend to ask a favor which he knew the Governor could not grant, then published an anonymous attack that was heavy with bitter denunciations. He enlisted the aid of Don José de Urrúnaga, a wealthy immigrant and a regidor, who was angered by the Governor's interference with his plans to wrest property from a poor widow. Avalos and Urrúnaga visited Reyes and heaped upon him every invective at their command. Finally, the harassed governor decided to crack the shell of a conspiracy that might be hatching by arresting his detractors in 1719; but from their separate places of confinement, Avalos and Urrúnaga contrived to lay a complaint before the Audiencia of Charcas, using as messenger Avalos's son-in-law. Among their charges was an assertion that Reyes had antagonized and murdered Indians. The preceding governor had allowed Payaguás to settle along the river about five miles below Asunción. Safely established within sight of the capital, those perfidious savages conspired with Guaycurús to destroy the Spaniards. Making nightly forays against isolated homes, the Payaguás robbed, killed, and burned with little opposition, all the while blaming Guaycurús for their crimes. Reyes suspected their activities and sent a small force to remove them to Uruguayan missions; but the soldiers, angered by opposition, massacred the Payaguás.

The charges against Reyes were to bring disgrace to Don José de Antequera y Castro, Knight of Alcántara, member of the Audiencia, and governor-select to succeed Reyes in 1722. Antequera had a plan that would, he hoped, make him master of Paraguay and a wealthy man. Impatient to be on his way, he asked the Audiencia to send him as judge-inquisitor to investigate the charges against Reyes, an appointment contrary to law because he had already been named as the next governor. Antequera arrived in Paraguay on July 30, 1721. José de Avalos met him south of Asunción and told him that Reyes was visiting those terrible centers of iniquity and flourishing commerce, the Jesuit missions. The regidor had arranged to entertain Antequera at the hacienda of a female relative, but the lady became a corpse instead of a hostess. This inconvenience was taken as an omen of ill fortune when on the next day Antequera was welcomed to Asunción by bells announcing to man and God the melancholy news of death.

Avalos and Antequera lost no time in getting down to business. Before Reyes could return from his mission tour, the visitor had a bulky sheaf of signed charges to send off to the Audiencia, suspended the Governor from office, and kept a close watch on all of his movements. Having convinced many former supporters of the Governor that he was unfit for office, Antequera summoned the Cabildo in September to ratify his measures. As the intrigue developed, it became clear that Reyes was to be maneuvered into a dungeon if possible. Every surface aspect of legality was observed in depositions, rehearings, delays, and consultations as the despicable bag of legal tricks was upended and shaken vigorously. So thorough was this work that the Audiencia of Lima, to which the case was transferred from the Audiencia of Charcas, spent ten years in untying Antequera's red tape as a preliminary to vindicating Reyes.

Now Antequera showed his hand in much the same manner that Bishop Cárdenas had done before him: he plotted to gain a monopoly of the maté trade. Not a pound was to leave Paraguay without his permission, and he lowered the price. One market remained, and that one was Governor Antequera. While this maneuver was proceeding, Reyes disguised himself as a slave, escaped from Asunción, and at last reached safety among the missions. From this refuge he went on to Buenos Aires, intending to continue to Spain. In Asunción, Antequera vented his spleen by confiscating the property of Don Diego and his friends, and expelled the Jesuits from their college.

The next move was by the Viceroy of Peru, who reinstated Reyes in February, 1722, ordered Antequera to get out of Paraguay, annulled all that he had done, and reprimanded the Audiencia of Charcas for having believed the lies of such a man. The Audiencia went on believing them. Reyes started back to Asunción with a sublime faith that the Viceroy's order would be enough to rid the province of Antequera, who was indeed between the sword and the wall. An investigation into his maté business and bald stealing of private property was not likely to prove comfortable. Antequera declared the new orders to be forgeries and sent a henchman at the head of two hundred men to arrest Reyes. The priest at Yaguarón warned the deposed governor just in time for him to escape to a mission refuge. Antequera rode the crest successfully for a few months in spite of declining popularity. When one of the noble and virtuous ladies of Asunción spoke openly in favor of Reyes, his rival at first threatened dire consequences and then sought to seduce the beautiful *señora*. But her scornful rebuff made Antequera the laughingstock of Asunción.

For all of his bravado, Antequera was not yet ready for open rebellion. Reyes had sent spies into the capital to distribute copies of his latest commission, an indirect attack that gained some adherents to his cause without causing open opposition to the usurper. Nevertheless, Antequera could not let the challenge pass without at least a gesture of defiance, so he summoned the Cabildo.

"Will you acknowledge this man Reyes whom once you disowned? What does the Viceroy know of conditions here?" he demanded. "It is better to have as your governor one in whom you have confidence than a weak tool of the Jesuits!"

"Don José," protested Don Dionisio de Otazú, the royal standard bearer, "the Viceroy's orders are clear. This commission of Don Diego de Reyes is genuine; it bears the viceregal seal. Refusal to receive Don Diego is rebellion against His Majesty!"

Councilman Juan Caballero de Añasco also held this view, and there were murmurs of assent among the Cabildo. At this critical point, José de Avalos, smooth and insinuating, asked leave to speak.

"*Señores*," he said, "we owe to the Viceroy and to His Majesty full loyalty and obedience. But would we not betray their interests in this province if we refused to do our duty? The Jesuits are in league with Reyes to deprive us of our Indians; they monopolize the traffic in maté. How many of you have been able to buy *caámini* to sell at Santa Fé? Let Reyes return and the King's enemies will triumph. Don José de Antequera offers to protect us. Are we cowards that we refuse to support a judge of the Royal Audiencia?"

Although not fully convinced, the Cabildo voted for Antequera to retain the government until further representations could be made to the Viceroy at Lima. Antequera then became so bold that even Avalos wondered where he would call a halt to his

114

petty tyrannies; nevertheless, he accompanied the Governor and a small army to the Tebicuary River opposite the nearest missions, where Antequera threatened the Jesuits with destruction if they stirred against him. Avalos died of apoplexy on the way back to Asunción, thus depriving Antequera of the one man who might have restrained his excesses, especially when his secret council urged him on to greater lengths. The Audiencia of Charcas received memorials reminiscent of Bishop Cárdenas; and in reply that court, in March, 1723, ordered all persons to refrain from action against the existing government of Paraguay. The Viceroy of Peru, Don José de Armendáriz, Marqués de Castel Fuerte, again ordered Antequera to leave Asunción, told the Audiencia of Charcas that charges against the Jesuits were baseless, and ordered Don Baltasar García Ros at Buenos Aires to enforce his orders. Antequera raged in Asunción. He would keep his government, he declared, in spite of the Viceroy and make Paraguay an independent country.

García Ros had authority to use all the civil and military resources of Río de la Plata to enforce the Viceroy's orders; but first he tried peaceful measures. Reyes left his mission refuge to go to Corrientes where he attempted to communicate with Asunción. Antequera then sent his lieutenant, the alcalde Don Ramón de las Llanas, to kidnap Reyes. The plot succeeded and Reyes made his entry into the capital of Paraguay clad in chains and a nightgown. Antequera then published to all the inhabitants a memorial of the Cabildo to the King which proposed that the Jesuits be expelled and the Indians distributed among the people. Such a proposal was an infallible way to gain support in Paraguay.

Now, in November, 1723, it was García Ros's move. He hurried to Corrientes and called on the Cabildo to come to its senses; but Antequera blocked him by reminding the Cabildo that Reyes and Ros were friends. Seeking support from a general town meeting, Antequera summoned the principal lay and clerical figures to meet in *cabildo abierto* on December 13. Only Dionisio de Otazú spoke against the usurper and no one spoke openly against the King. In order that García Ros might not be badly informed, Antequera sent a hundred armed men to order him out of Paraguay, an act that definitely put him well outside the last wisp of legality which had covered his acts. García Ros summoned two thousand mission Indians and a few score of Spanish militia to meet him on the Tebicuary, and during the night of August 5, 1724, he crossed the river at the head of his troops. Antequera's advanced posts fell back while their commander sent a messenger galloping madly to Asunción and waited for the next move. In the capital the rebel governor fired a signal gun that brought his adherents scurrying to the great square. García Ros, he told them, was advancing upon the city with an army of Indians bent on pillage and rapine. "Your women are to become slaves of these brutes!" he warned. The men joined his army. His next step was to drive the Jesuits out of the city; and on the same day, August 7, he set out for the Tebicuary with a motley army of Spaniards, Indians, Negroes, and various mixtures of the three races. These men were promised plunder and Indians to serve them in all ways.

When the two armies had come within sight of each other, Antequera fired his artillery and García Ros did likewise without damage to either side. The mission troops, without white officers to keep them in line, left their positions at will to swim in the river and to fraternize with the enemy. Antequera waited for his chance, which came on August 25. Having lured a number of Indians toward his lines by promising a fiesta, he sent his cavalry to cut them down as they approached. García Ros, unable to restore order, fled to Buenos Aires. Antequera at once became more violent. He marched upon the four missions lying nearest to Asunción, intending to destroy the villages and to enslave the Indians, but the neophytes fled before he could carry out his plan. In Asunción, the mad governor received a conqueror's welcome for having murdered unarmed Indians. When the Viceroy heard of these events in due time, he issued orders that Antequera should be captured and brought to Lima. In the meantime, Bishop José de Palos, recently arrived at Asunción, succeeded in undermining Antequera's position so seriously that the usurper promised submission to the Governor of Buenos Aires, Don Bruno Mauricio de Závala.

The last of the Payaguás

From *The History of Paraguay,* by
Charles A. Washburn

Závala started for Asunción in January, 1725, to carry out the Viceroy's commands, having taken the precaution of requesting six thousand mission Indians to stand by for orders. While he was approaching Asunción, Antequera sought desperately to rouse the people in his favor; but Bishop Palos threatened to excommunicate anyone who refused obedience to Závala. Antequera knew the game was up. On March 5, 1725, after four years of rebellion, he left Asunción. Závala entered the capital in April to find the people quiet, obedient, and apparently repentant. He undid Antequera's work so far as possible, named a temporary governor, and returned to Buenos Aires. The Bishop wrote to His Majesty a long letter in which he charged Antequera with treason and advised the court to end once and for all the calumnies against the Jesuits which had disturbed the province for a hundred years.

Antequera fled to Córdoba, where he took refuge in a monastery, and eventually reached Chuquisaca. There the Audiencia clapped him in irons and sent him to Lima by way of Potosí, the great mining center. Everywhere the prisoner went, he reviled the Jesuits. In Lima great crowds gathered to see "King Joseph of Paraguay" when he arrived in April, 1726. The Marqués de Castel Fuerte kept him in custody for several years while Spanish justice moved slowly to gather evidence in Paraguay. In his Lima prison, Antequera met one Fernando Mompóz y Zayas and gave him letters to friends in Asunción. Mompóz escaped to Paraguay and pretended to be a lawyer, all the while carrying on a distant intrigue with Antequera. Governor Martín de Barúa (or Burú) was no friend of Paraguayan Jesuits, but he managed to keep out of trouble while waiting for a chance to destroy them. Paraguayan desires to plunder the missions were stifled by a royal order of November 6, 1726, that placed the fifteen missions in the province under control of Buenos Aires; but this decree did not end plots against the Society of Jesus.

An unusual diversion took place on September 15, 1730, when sixty canoes loaded with Payaguá Indians came from *aguas arriba* (upstream) with plunder from Portuguese mines near Cuyabá. The Portuguese had found gold and mercury in Spanish territory and to work the mines had made many slave-hunting expeditions among the Indians. The Payaguás resented these attacks and returned blow for blow. They had pillaged Cuyabá in 1722, and eight years later they intercepted thirty-five canoes loaded with gold and Portuguese en route to São Paulo. Five canoes escaped, but the other thirty yielded a rich booty. Having no desire for gold, the Payaguás began to throw the stuff overboard. One of the few captives told them that they could trade gold for silver ornaments in Asunción and sell the captured slaves there as well. The Indians made such a good trade that they offered to return with more gold held in their *tolderías* (camps); but the mamelucos, angered by these events, declared war to the death against the Payaguás, and by 1734 they had killed most of the men and had sold the women and children into slavery.

Late in 1730, when the order of 1726 was carried into effect, news arrived that another governor was coming, one Ignacio Soroeta, to replace Barúa. Mompóz spread the idea that the commune, the people, need not bow even to the King. Therefore, the commune need not accept a new governor, and if all the people acted together, no one could be held responsible. This democratic idea caused Asunción to be split into two camps, *Comuneros* and *Contrabandos*. Apparently Barúa, too, had eaten of the *guabirá*, the tree whose fruit makes one want to remain in Paraguay; and something must have been wrong with a people who would permit the sly words of a fugitive to divide them. Basically, of course, the Comuneros were seeking a chance to destroy the Jesuits and their missions, regardless of the methods they used. The Comuneros counted among their number the men who had been partisans of Antequera, giving color to the charge that he planned to return to Paraguay after clearing himself in Lima.

The Comunero plot developed swiftly. Barúa's men went out to raise militia to oppose Soroeta. They marched on the city, demanded Barúa and no one else as governor. Barúa was coy; he tried to resign, hypocritically asserting that he wanted Soroeta to be received. Then he became frightened at the prospects and really resigned. Following his action, the Comuneros took over the government and began "bawling through all the streets against the Jesuits." Rioting broke out in such fury that no one was safe out of doors.

In the midst of this turmoil, Soroeta crossed the Tebicuary on his way to Asunción in January, 1731. An escort of four thousand Comuneros met him outside the city. The government remained so firmly in their hands that Soroeta accepted the suggestion that he had pressing business in Buenos Aires. Even then Barúa refused to pick up the staff of office, although Mompóz and he were consulted before the Comuneros acted on any important matter. The rebels selected a junta, or committee, which appointed Don Alonso Reyes as president of the province of Paraguay; but Reyes soon resigned and gave way to Don José Luis Berreiro. This new official, secretly loyal to Philip V, captured Mompóz and sent him to Buenos Aires under arrest. Later, while en route to Lima, the prisoner was rescued by Comuneros, who sent him into Brazil, not because they loved him but because he knew too much. Berreiro himself was soon forced to flee to the missions, and the radical Comuneros were left in full control.

No one in Lima was more surprised than the Marqués de Castel Fuerte when Soroeta walked into his chambers.

"Why aren't you in Asunción?" the Viceroy demanded.

"My lord, no one who values his life can live in that rebellious province," Soroeta assured him. "Not that I am unwilling to do my duty, but when this so-called Commune—"

"Commune!" the Viceroy exclaimed. "Commune! What nonsense is this?"

"Why, your Excellency, the rebels now call themselves a Commune superior even to the King!"

"And who directs this so-called Commune?"

"Fernando Mompóz y Zayas, once your prisoner in Lima, was one of the leaders, but I hear that he has been removed. Don Martín de Barúa, who pretends loyalty and refuses to act openly as governor, really directs the entire business."

"And the Society of Jesus? What do you know of their position in this matter?" the Viceroy inquired.

"The fathers are loyal, the only truly faithful men in all of

119

Paraguay. If I may venture an opinion, your Excellency, it is that Antequera has a hand in guiding the rabble."

"Antequera? Why, he is now in prison! But we shall see."

The Viceroy summoned the Marqués de Casa Conchez, president of the Audiencia of Lima, and asked that Antequera's quarters be searched. This examination revealed nothing until the prisoner's pockets were emptied. There, it is said, the Viceroy found the evidence he needed. The Audiencia rushed through Antequera's trial so fast that on July 5, 1731, he was led through the streets of Lima to the scaffold. A black hood shrouded his head as he sat on a horse draped in somber colors. A herald led the way, reading in a loud voice that Don José de Antequera y Castro, the rebel of Paraguay, must "lose his head on a scaffold." Crowds thronged the great square of Lima shouting for mercy and justice. The Viceroy, fearing a riot, rode forward to lead the guards, then ordered them to shoot Antequera when an attempt to rescue him appeared to be forming. The rebel fell mortally wounded, but the Viceroy ordered his head cut off for good measure.

Consternation seized the Comuneros when they learned of Antequera's fate, since all the ringleaders could expect the same treatment should they fall into the Viceroy's hands. They resolved, however, to have another try at independence and to strike another blow at the Jesuits. On February 19, 1732, an army of two thousand Comuneros sacked the Jesuit College, chased its inmates out of town, and imprisoned the bishop. The governor of Buenos Aires wearily turned to thoughts about restoring order in Paraguay. He summoned mission Indians to the Tebicuary to await the coming of Manuel Agustín de Ruiloba, who, to his misfortune, had been appointed governor of Paraguay. They had a long wait, since Don Manuel did not arrive until July 27, 1733, and their absence from the fields caused untold damage to the mission system.

Governor Ruiloba found time an invaluable ally. Dissension within the commune, the constant threat of an Indian army, and the skillful work of Bishop José de Palos undermined rebel morale. In Asunción he thanked God for his safe arrival, as well

120

he might, and from the cathedral steps he warned the people that their commune was open rebellion. The hydra-headed government of the people was unable at first to rally opposition to this resolute governor who boldly swept malcontents from office. Still, Ruiloba dared not restore the Jesuits to their property in the capital, so deep was resentment against the Society. The displaced officers finally summoned courage to strike in September, 1733. Ruiloba gathered three hundred men to attack the Comuneros, whose army was assembled near Asunción; but his men, except for a few officers who paid with their lives for supporting him, went over to the Comuneros. Ruiloba himself was killed after he had surrendered. This day, September 15, 1733, was the high tide of rebellion in the province.

Another peculiar twist in this tragedy of violence brought Bishop Juan de Arregui of Buenos Aires into the melee. That prelate, an enemy of the Jesuits, had gone to Asunción to be consecrated by Bishop Palos. He remained to intrigue with the Comuneros, who proclaimed him as their governor, an act that sent Bishop Palos fleeing from his diocesan capital. The Comuneros formed a general junta with a defender, Don Juan Ortíz de Vergara, in command and proceeded to confiscate the property of everyone suspected of loyalty to the King, including the Jesuits. Bishop Arregui was merely the hand used by the junta to sign its outrageous edicts until his nerve failed in December and he escaped to Buenos Aires.

Governor Závala in January, 1734, again ordered mission Indians to take the well-beaten path to the Tebicuary River. Don Bruno could have had twelve thousand neophytes to reduce the Comuneros, but he was content with three thousand. Again the Indians sat on the frontier, doing nothing. The Comuneros were torn by factional quarrels; Vergara died at the end of the year but rebellion continued. Závala, no longer trusting to subordinates, finally reached the Tebicuary in January, 1735, and let it be known that this time he would brook no opposition. The small Comunero army fell to pieces in April when Captain Martín José de Echáuri fell upon it. All but two of the leaders were captured, and several paid for their crimes on the scaffold as Governor

121

Echáuri tempered stern justice with occasional lapses of mercy. The rebellion in Paraguay, after fifteen years of turmoil, was over.

Perhaps of all the parties to this strife, the Jesuits and Bishop Palos alone emerged with their honor and integrity unsullied except by the calumnies of their enemies. Through difficult years the missionaries had continued to work with their converts. In 1730, the thirty reductions contained 133,117 Indians; seven years later, famine and disease, occasioned in large part by military service, had reduced the population to about 100,000. Mission Indians had suffered heavily in the King's service, their pastors had shown full loyalty to the Spanish crown; but in 1767 their enemies triumphed over them and the Jesuits were expelled from all of Spain's dominions. Long opposition to the Jesuits in Paraguay, the Comunero rebellion, and the character of the people themselves probably explain why Paraguay, unlike Ecuador and Mexico, escaped devastating civil wars in the next century. The Church, moreover, never did become a dominating political, social, and economic institution in Paraguay, despite more than a dozen missions within the limits of the modern republic.

Strife in Paraguay during the Comunero revolts so encouraged Chaco barbarians that they "carried their ravages to the gates of Asunción." A mission army drove back the marauders when Governor Echáuri requested their aid in 1735. Five years later another governor, Rafael de la Moneda, sought to protect Asunción from raids by Mbayá Indians who came down from the north. There were at the time, according to one estimate, 6,667 mulattoes and free Negroes in Paraguay. Some of these people of color were persuaded to settle several miles north of Asunción in the colony of Emboscada. Moneda set up many frontier posts, crushed a plot in 1747 that threatened to renew the Comunero troubles, and was able to turn a fairly peaceful province over to his successor.

Constant warfare against hostile Indians, civil war, and a stupid imperial economic policy prevented Paraguay from making any significant material progress in the eighteenth century. New towns were founded, new frontier posts appeared, but the population grew slowly. About 1790, Asunción was the only city with some 7,000 people, or maybe not more than 5,500. Three *villas,* 33 *parroquias,* 27 *pueblos de Indios,* and 2 *pueblos de pardos* brought the total to less than 100,000. Paraguay, of all the King's provinces, should have been the easiest to control; but economic, social, religious, and political conditions made it one of the most difficult of all to govern.

# CHAPTER IX

# Aspects of Colonial Society

PARAGUAY'S economy and society were products of environment and racial hybridization. One may readily see traits that are peculiarly all European or all Indian, as well as others that arose from the mixture of Spanish and Guaraní blood. The process of conflict, resistance, and adjustment between the two principal streams, in progress for four centuries, may be slowing down but it has not ended. "The history of the conquest and of the colony," Juan Natalicio González writes, "was guided by this silent, bitter fight, which lay hidden at the root of all daily events, large and small."

The conquerors gained their position of supremacy from a technical superiority, a culture richer than the Guaraní knew; but, isolated from Europe, they were conquered in part by their new habitat while revealing new values to the Guaranís. For their brigantines they used native woods, caraguatá (wild pineapple) fiber for cordage, cotton for sails, the *yzy* for pitch. These things suddenly became of more worth to the Guaranís than "the pile of multi-colored plumes that constituted their treasure before." Spaniards taught their trades to Indians and then to mestizos. Carpenters showed them how to make carts that increased the exchange of goods; cordage makers exploited native fibers; farmers improved native products and introduced new ones; woodworkers took delight in producing furniture from Paraguay's incomparable hardwoods; weavers improved and increased production of cotton cloth. Guaranís, for their part, contributed economic processes, social customs, and a folklore that were absorbed into the Ibero-Guaraní culture.

Deeds of captains great and small are well preserved in history; the little men are forgotten too easily. Men who give orders, not those who carry them out, receive too much of the glory. Who built the brigantines upon which success in Paraguay depended? Who built the houses and the churches? We know some of them. Bastián Alfonso, recruited by Mendoza, could turn his hand either to ships or churches; Pedro Quintero, a ship carpenter, fashioned many a native log into planks; Simón Luis and Fernando Pérez, Portuguese by birth, were skilled workmen; Alonso Rodríguez de Asuaga was a sawyer. With Cabeza de Vaca came the master carpenter Miguel Goceras, the sawyer Pedro Díaz, and the carpenter Pedro López de Aviega. López worked on Cabeza de Vaca's house and brigantine for two months without pay. Sawyers, wood carvers, doormakers, fitters—they were the men who built Asunción. Coopers, like Cristóbal de Beso and Marco Censo, helped in shipbuilding. The yards below Asunción in 1542 had ten brigantines and a caravel on the ways, vessels invaluable in exploring, and the caravel *Comuneros* made a trip to Spain with Cabeza de Vaca a passenger in irons. The impetus given to shipbuilding continued for more than two centuries, and most of the vessels plying rivers of the Plata system as late as 1800 had been built in Paraguay's yards.

Every new expedition brought its quota of artisans to swell the number of those who had come with Mendoza. The cordage maker Juan Medina had many capable apprentices. Old Cristóbal Alonso in 1580 could still regale youngsters with stories of Irala and Ayolas while he made halters, collars, bridles, and harness. Even the basketmakers, Cristóbal López Pequeño and Felipe de Molines, could inspire native workers to greater accomplishments. Shoemakers, of course, were entirely new to Paraguay. The Portuguese Francisco Romero had plenty of work among Mendoza's men without worrying about barefooted Guaranís. Cabeza de Vaca, like a good pedestrian, brought three shoemakers with him in 1542. Weavers, tanners, capmakers and tailors

found more work than they could handle. On his return from
Peru in 1549 or 1550, Nufrio de Cháves brought a tailor, Alonso
de Escobar, and three others of the same skill reached Asunción
sixteen years later.

Isolated as it was from external commerce, Paraguay benefited
singularly by having such artisans in the colony. Clothes brought
by the first settlers lasted but a short time, so introduction of the
European loom kept many a man and a few women from appearing in little but nature's original vestments. The first four varas
(a vara is about thirty-four inches) of cloth woven on the loom
were dedicated to the altar in August, 1539. Their cost was four
fanegas (about six bushels) of maize. Indian women and girls
soon became the principal weavers and made their art a major
home industry. Even they could not meet the demand. Apparel
was so limited that poor girls, although daughters of conquerors,
went abroad half-nude. Even as late as 1725, Paraguayan Comuneros who fought royal troops were dressed primarily in leather
garments; by 1800, foreign textiles were being imported in small
quantities to supplement the native products. Cotton growing,
spinning, and weaving were such old industries that the shortage
of textiles can be explained only by the greatly increased demand.

Metal workers found ample opportunity to practice their
trade. Irala himself took delight in making fishhooks, pins, dag-
gers, and other articles. At least three blacksmiths were among
the conquerors: Juan Álvarez came with Mendoza's expedition;
Francisco Delgado accompanied Cabeza de Vaca to Paraguay;
and Juan Pérez alternated as smith and veterinarian. Antonio de
Pinedo, first locksmith in the colony, was Irala's companion, as
was the swordmaker Galiano de Mayra. Cannon and bells could
be cast by Pedro Morel, who arrived in 1555. Paraguay's iron industry owes its origin to Mendoza's expedition. Richard Lincoln
from Plymouth had "a forge, an anvil, three hammers and two
pairs of tongs" to work with; by 1543, the industry was well established although short of materials. Each ship coming to Asunción brought new supplies of iron, without which all other industry and the conquest itself must have failed. Iron was a principal ingredient in Spanish superiority over the Indians, and thus

in the success of Spain's colonial conquests. Gunpowder was equally important. Juan Rute (John Root), another Englishman who sailed with Mendoza, was a powder maker. Deposits of salt-peter, discovered in Paraguay about 1544, enabled Rute and Juan Cristiano to provide explosives. Arms manufacturing was an art at which mestizos so excelled that by 1573 the only arque-buses in Asunción were of their handiwork.

An irony of history gave to the Portuguese fabulous mineral wealth that should have been Paraguay's. Gold and diamonds in southern Matto Grosso, in territory entered by Irala and Cháves, did everything except to rise up and strike the Spaniards' beards. These riches actually lay exposed, but the conquerors failed to see them. Perhaps it was just as well; but wherever they existed in Spain's colonies, gold and silver mines activated the entire economy. The search for minerals produced only discouraging results, like the discovery of worthless amethysts in Guayrá. Irala used much charcoal and lead in experiments with various ores without finding the great metals of which every conqueror dreamed.

Agriculture flourished mildly as Spaniards took over Guaraní crops and brought in new ones. Chickens and ducks had been kept by Indians to devour insects and to be devoured in turn. Three kinds of hazel hens and birds peculiar to Paraguay were domesticated before the conquest. There were native hogs, but hog raising became prominent only after Spaniards arrived. European hogs, apparently brought over by Mendoza, were taken to Paraguay in 1541 and soon pork became a basic element in the diet. Horses arrived in the Río de la Plata with Mendoza in 1535, and from the seventy-two animals that survived the voyage, thousands descended. None of Mendoza's horses were taken up-stream to Asunción. Cabeza de Vaca, when he entered Asunción in March, 1542, brought with him a score of horses and mares; by 1564, there were so many that Governor Francisco Ortiz de Vergara took more than eight hundred with him to Peru and could have taken two thousand without causing a shortage. It is notable that, while horses were so important in the first conquests of Mexico and Peru, Spanish control was established in Paraguay without them. Not until 1547 were horses taken on an *entrada* to the interior; in less than fifty years, however, they were essential parts of every expedition, and householders were required to keep one at hand for instant use in defense. The horse population grew so fast that Paraguay provided about four thousand for various expeditions from 1582–88. The plodding burros lack proper historical records, but they too played their role in colonial economy. Sheep and goats, brought by Cháves from Peru, multiplied so rapidly that wool was being taxed in 1560.

Cattle banished the specter of hunger from Paraguay. When Juan de Salazar de Espinosa gave up his obedience to Doña Mencia de Calderón to rejoin Irala, two Portuguese were in the party that he led to Asunción. These men, Scipion and Vicente de Goes, hired a herdsman named Gaete to drive a bull and seven cows from the coast of Brazil to Paraguay for a salary of one cow. From this incident came the expression: *"Es más cara que las vacas de Gaete"*—"It is dearer than Gaete's cows." In 1569, Felipe de Cáceres brought a shipment of cattle and sheep to Asunción. Soon Paraguay was sending cattle to other colonies—to Santa Fé, Corrientes, Buenos Aires, and Concepción del Bermejo. Cattle became a principal source of revenue, although the best pastures lay in the mission areas under Jesuit control, another reason why the Black Robes were hated in Asunción.

Maize, beans, and mandioca were staple crops for the colony. When the Spaniards gathered their first harvest in December, 1538, their principal products were 420 fanegas of maize and 45 fanegas of beans. Yields were so good that Alonso Cabrera started collection of taxes in kind in 1539. Cháves, perhaps, introduced sugar cane from Peru, or perhaps the Portuguese brought it from Brazil about 1555. The latter is more likely. A mill was built, the first in the Plata area, and the industry was firmly founded when the first sugar maker arrived in 1575. After Buenos Aires was re-established in 1580, Paraguay provided part of its sugar imports. Oranges, wheat, barley, and grapes were imported from Spain shortly after 1550. Sour oranges were native to Paraguay, but the sweet variety readily adapted itself. Orange trees surrounded every home, filled the air with perfume, and became a symbol of hospitality. "During the long colonial period the orange was never an object of commercial exploitation."

Yerba, the Guaraní *caá,* became not only a symbol of hospitality but of exploitation as well. Thousands of Indians perished in the *yerbales,* the forests of yerba trees or bushes. Efforts to prevent virtual enslavement of *mineros,* as yerba gatherers were called, failed in the face of insatiable greed. Yerba was in such great demand in South America that humanitarian impulses were stifled before they could aid its victims. Even so, it was not the original exploiter but the dealer and speculator who made the profits. At Santa Fé in 1620, twenty-five pounds of yerba brought eight to ten pesos, and up to twenty pesos in Tucumán. The price declined somewhat as production increased, until in 1776 an arroba (twenty-five pounds) sold for less than one peso in Buenos Aires. Little of the money made in the yerba trade reached Asunción.

Wheat raising might have prospered had the natives gained anything from the work. A flour mill at Lambaré, south of Asunción, was grinding in 1600. But mandioca and maize, grown in small patches, retained their ascendancy as food. The wine industry likewise failed to flourish. Jesuit competition, plant disease, and profiteering by dealers are blamed for its decline. Tobacco, which saved many a European colony from failure, played a small role in Paraguay's early economy. Commercial production, begun about 1750, became fashionable for a while; but taxes on exports, particularly at Buenos Aires, ruined the trade by 1800.

Colonial Paraguay might have been a prosperous, flourishing center of Spanish dispersion. A little foresight, a modicum of statesmanship by Spanish officials, attention to reports of governors, and bold remedial action could have made Paraguay a shining jewel in the Bourbon crown. Neglected from the beginning, the colony continued to suffer from a lack of European manufactures, short-sighted trade policies that stifled its commerce, and weakness induced by colonizing other areas.

Each expedition, whether north to Xarayes, west to Peru, east to Guayrá, or south along the rivers, drained Asunción of valuable and almost irreplaceable supplies. Since iron, steel, lead, powder, weapons, and trade goods were always taken, Mendoza's supplies were nearly exhausted when Cabrera arrived in 1539 with two ships from Spain. A short time before, purely by accident, the *Santa María*, en route to Peru, had sought refuge at Buenos Aires. Don León Pancaldo, pilot and principal owner, was in charge of a cargo worth 27,654 ducats: "6 barrels of dried prunes; 12 bags of filberts; 4 pounds of saffron; 21 cases and 141 casks of quincemeats; 70 gallipots and 3 casks of pickles; 6 barrels of Mallorca cheese; 110 *arrobas* [550 gallons] of oil . . . 1 barrel of pickled caper buds, 10 pipes of flour, 164 pipes of wine, 25 barrels of spices, 3 barrels of sugar, and a great quantity of pimientos, cloves, *nuez moscada* [a condiment], cinnamon, and numerous other articles." This shipment saved Buenos Aires from starvation, and its bedraggled conquerors bought "with the imaginary gold that filled their dreams." Shoes, clothing, dry goods, arms, lead, knives, artillery, glass, tools, pens, combs, soap, perfume, toothbrushes, mirrors—the *Santa María's* manifest reads like an inventory of European products of the sixteenth century. Much of the finery soon adorned lovely Guaraní girls in Paraguay.

A period of commercial drought for Paraguayans followed Pancaldo's manna from the *Santa María*. "The vast frontiers of silence and forgetfulness separated them from Spain, and if European events were unknown in Paraguay, less was known in the Peninsula of the fate of those white men lost in the unknown Guaraní forests. More or less they were thought to be swimming in abundance in the fabulous country of metals." No wonder Cabeza de Vaca was welcomed in 1542! But isolation remained a permanent condition while Guaranís and Spaniards learned to live together and to barter native products for European baubles. Two brigantines arrived in 1556 with more needed supplies, the *Todos los Santos* and the *San Marcos*. When these small craft dropped downstream in May, they carried Paraguayan products for transshipment to Spain, the first foreign exports of the colony. Distance, shipping costs, and perils of the sea prevented this trade from developing. The colony in 1579 obtained permission for ships from Cádiz and Seville to trade directly in steel, iron, clothing, and other products, and Juan de Garay re-established Buenos Aires in 1580 partly to promote this traffic. A new era seemed about to begin.

Stupid errors committed in Spain and local jealousies in America ruined Paraguay's trade. Confiscatory taxes discouraged effort; the designation of Santa Fé as the only point of exit for Paraguay killed Asunción's export business. Protest after protest went unheeded, even after pilots protested that Santa Fé could be reached only by sailing several leagues up a shallow tributary of the Paraná. Occasionally Spain relaxed its restrictions, as in 1621 when trade with Brazil was permitted in two ships of one hundred tons each per year. Even then the Buenos Aires Cabildo and governor imposed crippling restrictions on river traffic. Merchants at Buenos Aires, while complaining bitterly about handicaps imposed upon them by Spain, in turn did everything possible to prevent any other city from becoming prosperous. In the end, Paraguay could trade only with Corrientes, Santa Fé, and Buenos Aires. Proceeds from yerba and tobacco dribbled into Paraguay; profits poured into Buenos Aires and other cities. The colony shipped hides, cotton, cloth, honey, sugar, wax, starch, and wood without becoming even mildly prosperous. The total value of exports for 1788–92 has been estimated at 395,108 pesos and of imports at 155,903 pesos, which gave a favorable balance of trade even after taxes and shipping costs were deducted. Still the sum was but a small fraction of what it should have been. One need not wonder that Paraguay was fully ready for independence when Napoleon's peninsular adventure precipitated the crisis that destroyed Spain's colonial empire.

Interior commerce made use of the great river system, the Paraguay, Tebicuary, Jejui, and their tributaries. Old Guaraní roads also served the purposes of trade. The *Camino Real,* called *Tapé Avirú* by the Guaranís, passed from the Atlantic coast through São Vicente in Brazil, crossed Guayrá, and entered Paraguay. More than two hundred leagues long, this road was about five and one-half feet wide and was covered with a fire-resistant grass that marked it clearly. Wheeled traffic eventually destroyed much of it. Another trail led south from Asunción across the Tebicuary. Both of these roads were in use well into the eighteenth century, by which time wheeled vehicles and beasts of burden had revolutionized Paraguayan transport. In spite of carts and burros, Indian carriers were never fully displaced. One may still see barefooted women of the poorer economic class carrying on their heads loads that vary from a small bottle to a huge basket, or barefooted men bending under heavy burdens mounted on their shoulders.

A lack of paper or specie currency handicapped economic life. Taxes were paid in corn, beans, mandioca, hogs, fowls, cotton cloth, and other products. In order to establish a standard for barter and payments, Irala and the royal officials set arbitrary values for certain common articles: fishhooks at one to five maravedis (a maravedi is roughly equivalent to one cent), a cold chisel at sixteen maravedis, a wedge at fifty maravedis, an anvil wedge at one hundred maravedis. The iron wedges, used for many purposes, weighed three and one-half ounces; the anvil wedge (*cuña de ayunque*) weighed seven ounces. To obtain fractional currency, a wedge (*cuña*) was divided into half-ounce pieces valued at about seven maravedis each. Thus iron served the monetary purposes of gold and silver. Its value fluctuated with supply until speculation became rife. One of the Cabildo's important duties was to fix values of important products to serve as exchange standards. When Paraguayans spoke of pesos, they meant imaginary pesos; but, like real pesos, they were divided into eight provincial reales each. For conversion into silver, this imaginary peso was worth only two reales. Various efforts to entice real money into Paraguay failed, and the Spanish government denied every plea for a better currency. In the early republican period, when specie did enter the country, large quantities went into jewelry. People were accustomed to bartering but not to wearing precious baubles.

No one can understand the Paraguayan people without first knowing how this vigorous, friendly, and talented race came into being. The basic origin is really very simple. Conquerors took Indian women, unimpeded by monogamous standards. A Spaniard was satisfied with four Indian women only when he couldn't

Portrait of Ulrich Schmidt, showing his coat of arms

From *Viaje al Río de la Plata*
by Ulrich Schmidt

keep eight, with eight when he couldn't have sixteen, with sixteen—but that's far enough. Nearly every European had five or six, many had fifteen, some boasted twenty or thirty *compañeras*.

The mestizo, offspring of a white and Indian liaison, lost nothing by his mixed parentage. One may use Irala's nine children as an example of what hybridization did for the first or second generation mestizos. Diego, born in 1543, was the son of María, daughter of an Indian chief who took the Christian name Pedro de Mendoza. He was a founder of Corrientes, served as its lieutenant governor and chief justice (*justicia mayor*). Ginebra, Diego's sister, married Pedro de Segura Závala. One son of this union, Juan de Irala, was a captain, a lieutenant of Ruy Díaz de Guzmán, a corregidor, and a talented writer. Isabel, Irala's daughter by Agueda, married twice. Gonzalo de Mendoza, her first husband, sired Captain Hernando de Mendoza, who was a founder of Buenos Aires. With Captain Pedro de la Fuente as her consort, Isabel gave birth to Pedro Hurtado, who became a valiant captain, explorer, lieutenant governor of Paraguay, and *procurador general* (general attorney) for the Río de la Plata provinces. To Ursula Irala, who married Alonso Riquelme de Guzmán y Ponce de León, fell the honor of giving birth to Ruy Díaz de Guzmán. This grandson of Irala's, after a notable career as colonizer, warrior, and official, completed his classic *La Argentina* about 1612.

The process of hybridization had gone so far that mixtures made up a great part of Paraguay's population by 1785. Various names were given by Spaniards to designate different degrees of mixed blood. The *criollo* (creole) was not a mixture, but a person of pure European blood born in the New World. There were three basic crosses among the races: white with Indian, which yielded the mestizo; white with Negro, which gave birth to the mulatto; and Indian with Negro, from which came the zambo. An infinite number of crosses became possible thereafter. The *castizo* was the issue of a white father and a mestiza mother; the *octavón* was the issue of a white father and a *castiza* mother; the *pachuela* was the issue of a white father and an *octavona* mother. Thus the *pachuela* was nearly all white. Conjugal relationships

133

were held lightly indeed, so lightly that priests with consciences were horrified by widespread concubinage and promiscuity. One obvious result was the creation of the Ibero-Guaraní, or, simply, the Paraguayan.

Mestizos enjoyed certain advantages denied to Indians. They paid no tribute, became commanders of troops, founded colonies, held encomiendas, and were officers in provincial government. Certain prohibitions, such as the denial of military careers, were not enforced in Paraguay. Spanish legislation attempted to protect obedient Indians as vassals in the exercise of rights granted to peasants and minors. They could trade, make wills, enter the clergy, and marry white women; they had to do labor on public works but could not be enslaved—in theory. Negroes were never very numerous in Paraguay. They came by way of Brazil and Buenos Aires, perhaps before 1600. Azara reported that there were 5 whites to every Negro or mulatto about 1790, and only 100 slaves to 174 free persons of color. Although Negro slavery existed throughout the colonial period, it was never a serious problem. Colored Paraguayans suffered from few social discriminations except those naturally attributable to economic stratification.

Peninsular Spaniards, called *gachupines* in derision, felt themselves to be vastly superior to creoles and mestizos. Whether layman or cleric, the *gachupín* generally sought and obtained preferment everywhere in Spain's colonies except Paraguay. They sought privilege there, too, but that colony was altogether too democratic to countenance their pretensions. Creoles and mestizos completely controlled society, business, and government, according to some writers; but we find still others who insist that Paraguay's export trade was entirely in the hands of gachupines. A judgment somewhere in between is probably more in agreement with the facts.

Two general types of forced labor, other than slavery, were common to all Spanish colonies. The *encomienda*, a grant of land with its Indians or a grant of Indians exclusive of land, provided an *encomendero*, the holder of an encomienda, with a force of laborers who also paid tribute. It was not a profitable institution in Paraguay and disappeared when a royal decree of May 17, 1803, abolished all encomiendas in the colonies. The *repartimiento* was an allotment of Indians, assigned to someone who needed workers, for a period of sixty days in Paraguay. These Indians were paid a small wage and were not required to labor more than two leagues from their homes. This form of repartimiento was called the *mita,* a Quechua word meaning "turn," since Indians took turns at working. They came from eleven Indian towns (*pueblos de Indios*). Another form of repartimiento was the *yanacona* or *originario,* which meant indefinite personal service without a fixed wage. Yanaconas were suppressed in Paraguay in 1611.

Colonial government centered in Spain, where two bodies exercised control under the monarch. As an agency of government, the Council of the Indies, for all of its inadequacies, must be ranked as one of the greatest institutions of its kind in history. It began formally as a junta in 1511 and was reconstituted on August 1, 1524, as the Supreme Council of the Indies. Over the colonies its power was nearly absolute in all military, political, civil, and criminal matters. The House of Trade (*Casa de Contratación*), formed in 1503, antedated the Council but was in theory subordinate to it. Viceroys in the New World were the king's most powerful representatives, but areas like Paraguay felt only a nominal control, first from the viceroy of Peru and then, after 1776, from the viceroy of Río de la Plata. Adelantados, such as Pedro de Mendoza and Cabeza de Vaca, were practically dictators in their areas under terms of contracts made with the monarch. Later governors of Paraguay lacked the powers of adelantados, had less discretion, and were subject in theory to a viceroy. Under the decree of September 12, 1537, Paraguayan colonists could elect their own governor in case of a vacancy. This privilege made the colony practically autonomous, and explains why many writers referred to it as a republic. The Comunero revolts caused this privilege to be withdrawn.

As an agency of local government, the cabildo held first rank. Technically it should be called the *Cabildo, Justicia y Regimiento.* As *cabildo,* the corporation was a deliberative, executive and legislative body; as *justicia,* it heard and decided civil and criminal cases in original jurisdiction; as *regimiento,* it maintained public order. When leading citizens decided that their cabildo was not functioning properly, they might hold a *cabildo abierto,* an open meeting, and take matters into their own hands. Such meetings were also called by governors to decide especially weighty matters, a practice reminiscent of councils of war called by a *conquistador.* Such meetings, however, had a Spanish rather than an American origin. The number of members in a cabildo varied considerably, and certain officials frequently served in a dual capacity. There were two *alcaldes ordinarios,* somewhat comparable to justices of the peace. One, the *alcalde de primer voto,* voted first in a cabildo meeting but his powers were no greater than those of his colleague, the *alcalde de segundo voto.* There were also *alcaldes de la hermandad,* justices who handled criminal cases primarily and who at times acted as constables. The *alférez real,* royal standard bearer, did more than carry a flag in processions. He defended widows and orphans, aided in supervising and planning military operations, and voted in cabildo meetings. *Regidores* were councilmen for *barrios* or wards, served without pay for two-year terms, and exercised appellate jurisdiction in certain cases. Officers of the cabildo included a city attorney, a property custodian, a controller, a supervisor of weights and measures, and a secretary.

The Asunción Cabildo began in September, 1541, with the election of five regidores. Irala could have appointed them, but he chose the democratic way. This body passed through periods of power and decadence. Until 1625, less than a score of men controlled cabildo elections; then the Audiencia of La Plata (Chuquisaca) ordered that free elections be restored. In that year Ruy Díaz de Guzmán became *alcalde de primer voto.* In succeeding years, the cabildo was Paraguay's aggressive defender, its frustrated champion in bouts with Spain's bureaucratic colonial system. The royal officials—treasurer, collector, and accountant— zealously guarded royal interests, especially in enforcing the many taxes that vexed trade, manufactures, and agriculture.

Forms of government and matters of race or of economics must

136

not blind us to the greatest process in all of Paraguay's history, the appearance of a hybrid culture. Juan Natalicio González, whose splendid *Cultura paraguaya* has been the basis for much of this discussion, writes: "The predominance of native habits gives tone to colonial customs. At first the dominance of the indigenous, above all in private life, is almost absolute. With the hybridization of blood comes the hybridization of habits and character. . . . Clothing, economic structure, and industrial technique are Europeanized; but popular beliefs, cookery, agriculture, the family, much of the pharmacopoeia and medical practices remain Guaraní."

There were alarming times when the first crop of mestizos grew up. If we believe one writer, carrying virgins off to the fields for three days was a favorite diversion. Mestizos feared no one. Neither promises of heaven nor threats of hell restrained them from this promiscuous practice. The reason lay in a loose matriarchy in which European morals did not prevail. How could they, when conquerors disported themselves so freely and Guaraní ethics attached no stigma to an unmarried mother who had sinned for love? Eighteenth-century writers praised domestic virtues of Paraguayan women. Their weeks were spent in household duties, sewing, weaving, gardening, and taking care of ducks and babies. Félix de Azara believed Paraguayan society to be the best in the Río de la Plata area, with few murders and robberies, little drunkenness and gambling to disturb a hard working people. There was so little danger of thievery that most farmhouses had no doors. Mass was poorly attended on Sunday; but after a siesta people went visiting to discuss family matters, love affairs, weather, crops, miracles, and complaints of the flesh, while a servant served maté. Social life in Asunción was more intense, although it followed a pattern similar to that in country towns and homes.

Guaraní legends retained their vitality among a people more pagan than Christian. Around campfires in the forest and the hearths of homes, the hybrid race repeated its twice-told tales. "Yacy Yateré rules in the hot siesta, Pombero in starless nights, Caagüy Pora in the noisy forest, while Curupí collaborates in the

137

cosmic task of incessant creation." Pombero was a gremlin, a spirit who went abroad on dark nights. In the dim light shed by a firefly, one might see his short, stout body. Soft hair in the palms of his hands and on the soles of his feet made his passage noiseless. He could run on all fours or upright with equal ease and with a speed faster than the wind. Friendly with toads, frogs, and snakes, he struck terror into the hearts of wild beasts. Pombero poked his head above window sills, a shameless peeper who loved to frighten lonely people with bloodcurdling sounds. No one could find Pombero. He was a ventriloquist whose voice came from everywhere and he could make himself invisible. Arouse his anger and Pombero would untie your horse, open the corral gate, and wreak mischief without end. By putting a bit of black tobacco in the hollow of a tree, you could win Pombero's good humor and his tricks would end. Keep him happy and he would guard your sleep or protect you on night excursions. Pombero, alas, acquired a taste for strong drink and even today there are times when he might be seen happily drunk beside a cask of *caña!*

Yacy-Yateré slept at night but roamed during the siesta hour when all the world was quiet. While tossing in midday heat, the uneasy sleeper would hear an unearthly whistle—that was Yacy-Yateré, not an unseen bird as some wiseacres insist. This spirit was the personification of the sun's generative power, a Guaraní Eros who carried a golden wand that made him invisible. Yacy-Yateré loved beautiful girls. He would entice them into the forest, play games with them, regale them with gifts. But always there came a time when he no longer could resist the urge to kiss his playmate, and that kiss was fatal.

Caagüy Pora protected nature from man's wanton destruction. Anyone who used nature's gifts unwisely suffered the anger of Caagüy Pora. Really a feminine spirit, this guardian of forest, stream, bird, and beast could assume any form. Only those who truly loved nature ever saw this sylvan goddess in all her enchanting, naked loveliness. Men who killed or destroyed for pleasure incurred her terrible wrath. Natalicio González describes her in poetic words: "Although implacable in her punishments, Caagüy

Pora is really a lovable spirit, chaste and beautiful like Diana, who plays in forest clearings with multicolored butterflies. She saves from death small animals that have lost their mother through the work of some irresponsible hunter. She defends nests from the fury of storms. She keeps little streams that feed creeks from going dry. She runs, with her long hair streaming in the wind, spreading a fresh perfume of water lilies, and her nude and fugitive body, that passes like a white flash, is like the marvelous materialization of the bright daily splendor. Thanks to her, the forest lives eternally and the rivers since their creation have been able to renew the fugitive wealth of their waters without suspension nor rest."

These minor deities lived through the colonial period, personifications of forces recognized by the Guaranís. One sees in the harvest festival of Curuzú Yeguá the homage of a grateful people to Curupí, guardian spirit of crops and fertility. There were, of course, group sports and spectacles peculiarly European in origin which had nothing to do with Guaraní mythology. All classes of society took part in religious processions, attended bullfights until a lack of aggressive animals caused these spectacles to be given up, or watched the *corrida de sortija*. This sport, common in the colonies, required a horseman, whose mount was running at full speed, to pass the point of his lance through a small ring suspended from a wooden arm. There was also the game of "Moors and Christians," in which rival parties jousted with lances. The Moors always lost. In the missions, this *juego de cañas* had mamelucos and Guaranís as rivals.

Paraguayans, whether gachupín, creole, mestizo, or Indian, were by no means deprived of elementary education. Irala provided the first schools, rudimentary, poorly staffed, but still they were an attempt to teach the three basic skills. Any system or whatever one may call it that could produce a writer like Ruy Díaz de Guzmán deserves some respect. The Asunción Cabildo sporadically encouraged education, and it was through grants of public lands that the Jesuit *Colegio* was able to open its doors in 1610. There were individual schoolmasters, both lay and clerical, before then. Father Francisco de Saldivar was teaching at the turn of the century. Bishop Martín Ignacio de Loyola in 1603 started a *Casa de Recogidas y Huerfanas,* a home for abandoned or orphaned girls, whose inmates learned nursing among their other duties. The Jesuit school for boys contributed much to colonial Paraguay. The Cabildo encouraged literate citizens to become teachers. In 1630, Juan Domínguez de la Costa was receiving four pesos per pupil, paid in kind, for teaching reading and writing. The *Colegio Carolino* in Asunción was authorized in 1776, under the name *Real Colegio y Seminario de San Carlos,* and opened in 1780 with Antonio Báez as its rector. Some writers maintain, with more solemnity than veracity, that by 1800 it was difficult to find an illiterate Paraguayan.

Colonial Paraguayans produced prose and poetry of lasting worth, although much of their work is little known. Many songs and ballads, some of which resemble the Mexican *corrido,* were composed by authors whose names will forever remain unknown. The first literati, naturally, were colonizers. Pero Hernández, author of the *Comentarios* of Cabeza de Vaca, wrote simple, virile prose with an eye for what would enhance his chief's reputation. Ulrich Schmidt, native of Straubing, composed his *Viaje al Río de la Plata* before 1554, the first book written in Paraguay; at least, this claim has been made for Schmidt, although it is likely that he wrote the whole thing in Germany after he had left Paraguay. Father Luis de Bolaños, the saintly Franciscan missionary, prepared the first catechism in Guaraní. Father Martín del Barco Centenera wrote *La Argentina* at various times and published it in Lisbon in 1602. This poem is structurally atrocious, meanders like a drunken water bug, but is interesting and informative in spite of obvious faults. Ruy Díaz de Guzmán, Irala's greatest descendant, finished his *La Argentina* in 1612, an epic that has won high praise. Published first in 1835 by Pedro de Angelis, *La Argentina* went through five editions. Félix de Azara, unfortunately, cannot be claimed as a Paraguayan; but this Spanish soldier, geographer, naturalist, and historian performed a great service in writing six important books. His *Descripción e historia del Paraguay y del Río de la Plata* is indispensable for the student of Paraguayan history.

Two natives of Paraguay left their country and won reputations abroad for their learning. They were not by any means the only ones who did so, but the careers of Cañete and Talavera deserve mention. Pedro Vicente Cañete, born in Asunción in 1749, went to Córdoba for his early education and completed his academic work in Chile. Student of law, politics, and history, he served in official positions in Buenos Aires before his return to Asunción in 1781. Three years later he was in Potosí as one of that intendancy's principal officials. His views on government and imperial organization made him *simpático* with ultraconservatives in whose exclusive social circles he moved freely. Transferred to Chuquisaca in 1803, Cañete dominated government in the Audiencia. Because he devoted his great talents to the royal cause, his extensive writings in history, law, and politics have not received just recognition; but Cañete's was colonial Paraguay's most brilliant mind. Another Paraguayan who embraced the royal cause was Manuel Antonio Talavera, son of a gachupín father and a creole mother. Manuel was born in Villa Rica in 1761, attended the Colegio de Nuestra Señora de Monserrat in Córdoba, and, like Cañete, finished his education in Chile. Except for a short period of exile during the early revolutionary movement, Talavera remained in Chile until his death in 1814. As a writer he is remembered primarily for the *Revoluciones de Chile*.

Paraguay produced no poet to compare with Sor Juana Inés de la Cruz, no dramatist like Juan Ruiz de Alarcón. Few great names in literature can be found through nearly three centuries of colonial life, because the mestizo, with few exceptions, did not devote his talents to intellectual activities. Lima, México, Santiago and other cities attracted most of the Europeans who carried Spain's rich culture to the New World. Paraguay remained a distant outpost reached by only occasional flashes of that culture, like sheet lightning reflected in the clouds by some distant storm.

# CHAPTER X

# Viva la República!

LOYALTY TO THE CROWN and the lack of a unifying revolutionary force held the Spanish empire together in an era when liberalism and Napoleon were mutilating the old order in the Western world. The French emperor provided a common cause when he compelled Spain's despicable royal family to surrender its ancient powers in favor of Joseph Bonaparte, and the Spanish Indies became a grand stage for rebellion and civil war. Long before then warnings had come from Asunción.

Paraguay's general condition was described in a memorial sent the King by Governor Agustín Fernando de Pinedo in January, 1777. Encomenderos, he wrote, once conducted themselves well; but their successors, motivated by avarice, had become tyrants who refused to obey royal orders. They left to others their duty of defending Paraguay against Indian raids. Asunción had 5,750 citizens, of whom 2,750 were engaged in agriculture, shipping, or yerba production. Every farmer had to devote eight days a month to military duty; in time of war he had to equip himself for service. This burden was keeping Paraguay poor. River commerce, agriculture, and yerba processing were the principal occupations, with agriculture a poor third. A shortage of money handicapped trade, commerce languished, and farmers were without tools. Maize, mandioca, and fruit were raised for domestic consumption; tobacco, honey, and sugar were exported. The yerba trade could produce one million arrobas a year but was yielding only one-fifth of that amount. Everywhere, from Asunción to the ultimate consumer, taxes were imposed and profits taken. Worth only two reales in Asunción, an arroba sold for thirty pesos in Lima. Reforms were needed: a permanent militia, abolition of encomiendas, permission to resume tobacco manufacture, and strength to repel Portuguese invaders. Pinedo's pleas went unheard, lost in the dust of a crumbling empire. Perhaps Charles III believed that the new viceroyalty of Río de la Plata, created in August, 1776, partly to prevent further Portuguese aggression, would be able to revitalize Paraguay. Less than forty years later, rebellion in the viceroyalty relieved Spain of all responsibility for an area potentially richer than the entire Iberian Peninsula ever had been.

The Spanish court either ignored or was ignorant of the spirit of independence abroad in the viceroyalty of Río de la Plata when there was still time to do something about it. Paraguayans had asserted themselves time after time under leadership of the Asunción Cabildo. They had rebelled against bad governors and against the Jesuits. They had won and defended a huge area for the Spanish crown. They might, under the right combination of circumstances, refuse to lie prostrate at the feet of sovereigns who had spurned them time and again.

Creole leaders of Buenos Aires, having twice won victories against British arms, were in no mood to accept dictation from the Spanish regency that pretended to rule in the name of Ferdinand VII. On May 25, 1810, the Cabildo overthrew the viceroy at Buenos Aires; but outlying provinces—Paraguay, Bolivia, Uruguay, and even Argentine provincial capitals—refused to admit that the *porteños,* the people of Buenos Aires, should control their destinies. Córdoba sent General Santiago Liniers, who had defeated the British in 1806, to oppose a *porteño* army sent to chastise the city. Liniers suffered defeat, and the victorious *porteños* shot him along with several other prisoners. These acts saved Córdoba for Argentina; the other provinces—Paraguay, Uruguay, and Bolivia—were lost forever.

Rumblings that foretold the storm were heard in Paraguay six years before Argentina's famous Twenty-fifth of May. The Governor's favorites became so greedy and their spoliations so open that in 1804 discontented creoles planned to rebel. José Gaspar Rodríguez de Francia, a lawyer of local renown, suggested a memorandum to the Viceroy instead, with the result that the governor of Misiones, Don Bernardo de Velazco, was promoted to Asunción as governor-intendant. In the following year, 1807, Viceroy Liniers appointed Dr. Pedro Somellera as *ad-interim asesor*. A graduate in law from Córdoba, the young secretary struck up a friendship with Francia and brought him into political power through a series of appointments to various offices from 1807 to 1809. A climax to this career came in 1809 when the Asunción Cabildo selected Francia to represent Paraguay at Buenos Aires, where lots were to be drawn for sending delegates to the newly formed Spanish Cortes. When Francia gave false information about his parents for his credentials, an enemy exposed him. Francia did not go to Buenos Aires.

General Bernardo de Velazco y Huidobro, brigadier of the royal armies and captain-general of the mission troops, was the sixtieth and last governor of Paraguay. When he took office in 1806, events already were underway that would end, two decades later, in extinguishing the last vestiges of Spanish power in South America. Velazco fought against the British at Buenos Aires in 1807; he was a friend of Liniers but not of the revolutionary *porteño* rabble and radicals.

Had it not been for the grafting secretary of Governor Velazco's predecessor, one José Espínola y Peña, Paraguay might have joined Buenos Aires in 1810, and Argentina might have been a much greater country, and there might have been no War of the Triple Alliance. The Buenos Aires Junta sent Espínola and Don Luis Márquez to Asunción in June, 1810, to urge Paraguay to follow the port city's lead. It is said that Espínola also bore instructions to overthrow Velazco. Somellera, a *porteño*, was in favor of the scheme; Francia was opposed and retired to his *chacra*, a modest cottage near the capital. Nevertheless, Espínola returned to Buenos Aires with the report that Paraguay wanted action, concerted action against the royalists. This report was only partly true: the Asunción creoles did want action but they did not want action of the sort that would be dominated by the hated *porteños.*

Velazco, knowing well that whatever he did or failed to do might eventually cost him his head, conferred with the Cabildo. That worthy body immediately, and with a fine gesture of democracy, passed the problem to a *cabildo abierto,* an assembly of leading citizens. This group of two hundred or more met on July 24, 1810, voted to remain loyal to the Spanish regency, to continue friendly connections with rebellious Buenos Aires but not to acknowledge its authority, and to create a war committee to defend the province. Velazco, who would with pleasure follow the war committee's recommendations, collected firearms for six thousand men, closed the port to cut off communication with Buenos Aires, stationed armed vessels at the mouth of the Paraguay, and sent militia to guard the Paraná frontier. Buenos Aires accepted the challenge but failed to gauge Paraguayan temper properly. The *porteño* junta declared that certain bad men had conspired to sow seeds of evil in Paraguay. Therefore, on September 27, 1810, it commissioned Don Juan Francisco Agüero, a native of Asunción residing in Buenos Aires, as its agent to tell the Paraguayans what they should know about events in the port city and to warn them against seeking an independent course. If Agüero ever reached Paraguay he had little success. Buenos Aires then tried force.

General Manuel Belgrano soon discovered that the ease-loving Paraguayans would fight to defend their soil. Seven thousand soldiers under skillful leadership might have captured Paraguay; but Belgrano was an amateurish soldier and he had only seven hundred men when he marched overland through the mission country late in 1810 to Candelaria. He crossed the Paraná and advanced to Paraguarí, only forty-five miles from Asunción, where the Paraguayans, perhaps five thousand strong, defeated him badly on January 9, 1811. Belgrano then retreated across the Tebicuary, was defeated again on March 9, and asked for an armistice. While this truce was in effect, the Argentine general "had the chance to plant some ideas of independence and liberty among the Paraguayans that were not long in sprouting." He had the chance, but it is doubtful whether he needed to plant such ideas. The ideological impetus toward independence came from Jean Jacques Rousseau and his colleagues in French liberalism, not from Buenos Aires. Francia had absorbed revolutionary ideas long before Belgrano appeared, and many others favored independence while *porteños* were shouting themselves hoarse for Ferdinand VII. It was Belgrano's invasion, not his ideas, that precipitated open rebellion in Paraguay.

The Gentlemen of the Most Illustrious Cabildo, *Justicia y Regimiento* of Asunción, met on March 28, 1811, to consider the situation. This session voted to send an emissary to Montevideo to inform Viceroy Francisco Xavier Elío about conditions in Paraguay. The Cabildo met again on May 13 to consider Brazilian offers to help Governor Velazco repel Argentine aggression. Lieutenant José de Abreu had arrived on May 9 as the emissary of Captain-General Diego de Souza. Dr. Francia and others suspected that General Velazco was carrying on secret intrigues with Abreu. Anyway, it was a good excuse to start the Governor on his way out of power. With Francia telling him what to do, Captain Pedro Juan Cavallero "pronounced" on May 14; on the following day he sent an ultimatum to Velazco, charging him with a plot to surrender Paraguay to the Portuguese. Velazco replied at once: "I hope the garrison will have occasion to rid itself of the idea that I ever dreamed of delivering this Province to a foreign power." With no loyal troops to call on, the Governor had to accept two "adjuncts" to serve with him as a provisional government: Francia and Captain Juan Baleriano de Zeballos.

What had Velazco done to warrant this rebellion? He had welcomed Abreu. So had the city. After the Brazilian messenger reached the Recoleta, three thousand or more persons of both sexes joined in a procession to Velazco's house. In a conversation of two hours, Velazco assured Abreu that he recognized only Doña Carlota, wife of the Portuguese regent João, as ruler of Spain's provinces. That was treason, indeed, since the Cabildo recognized Ferdinand VII. On May 10, Velazco had suggested that two hundred Portuguese cavalry should be stationed south of the Paraná to protect Paraguay; and on May 11 he summoned the Cabildo and Bishop García Panés to make his request official. Even Lieutenant Colonel Fulgencio Yegros at Itapuá was to be under Diego de Souza's orders. For three days the Cabildo, the Bishop, and the Governor were busy preparing documents to send back to Brazil; and Abreu was busy with "attentions and innumerable visits that the leading people bestowed, having previously given him many presents and a great dance . . . to honor the alliance of the Portuguese with the Paraguayans." These were the acts that caused Francia to plan the revolt of May 14.

Now that Velazco had two advisers, a reply much different from the one he had planned went back to Souza. Paraguay would maintain good relations with Buenos Aires and would gladly accept aid in military supplies, to be paid for as soon as possible, from Brazil. Souza's reply was that he would like to send such supplies but could not do so without royal approval. In the meantime, if Paraguayans would restore Velazco to power and recognize Carlota as eventual heiress to Spain's dominions, there would be plenty of help. Instead of restoring Velazco, the provisional junta set up by the rebels deposed him permanently on May 16.

Francia had succeeded in his revolution but his own power remained to be consolidated. A provincial congress, or general junta, met at Asunción on June 18, 1811, with Francia and Zeballos presiding. It was Francia who wrote and delivered the principal address. There is no need, he said, to detail our complaints. We have been "humiliated, oppressed, degraded and made the object of contempt by the pride and despotism of our rulers. This excess has now reached a point where it is desired to strengthen our chains, to dispose of our liberty, of our fate and of our very persons as one sells a herd of cattle, an hacienda, or a piece of furniture, with no regard for the dignity and rights of a great people, nor for the voice of nature insisting that the unhappy Paraguayans have suffered enough in some three centuries. . . . These unfortunate times of oppression and tyranny have ended at last. The darkness in which we lived has gone and a brilliant dawn begins to show on our horizon. The Province of

Paraguay, emerging from the lethargy of slavery, has recognized and claimed its rights, and is now completely free. . . . This was the only object of our patriotic troops, and of the valiant citizens who took part in the happy revolution of May 14, a great day, a memorable day, that will mark the most significant epoch in the annals of our province. . . . Heaven itself visibly favors the justice of our cause." Our tasks now, Francia continued after expounding a bit of French liberalism, are to form a government, determine our foreign relations, and decide the fate of our former rulers.

The congress acted swiftly and with a harmony never again to be found in Paraguay. On June 19, Mariano Antonio Molas presented several resolutions: Velazco was deposed; in his place should be a five-man junta aided by a secretary. As president of the junta and commander-in-chief, Lieutenant Colonel Fulgencio Yegros was named. His associates were to be Francia, Pedro Juan Cavallero, Francisco Javier Bogarín, and Fernando de la Mora. As for Buenos Aires, that colony had no authority in Paraguay. Commercial restrictions were swept away. Francia was to be Paraguay's delegate to the general congress to be held in Buenos Aires. All members of the government were to swear not to recognize any sovereign other than Ferdinand VII. These and other resolutions became, on June 22, Paraguay's provisional constitution. The new government began to function on June 23 and a new Cabildo of two alcaldes and seven regidores ruled the city.

Don Fulgencio Yegros, president of the Junta, struck a fine figure when he rode through Asunción on his English saddle, his shoulders broadened by fancy epaulettes. But this display could not conceal a deep and ineradicable ignorance that was relieved only by bravery, cunning, and good intent. Don Pedro Juan Cavallero, like Yegros a hero of Belgrano's defeat, had little more to recommend him. Don Fernando de la Mora and Francia bore the burden of organizing a government and of sparring successfully with the wily *porteños.*

Desiring friendly relations with Buenos Aires and perhaps eventual union, the Junta on July 20, 1811, sent a dispatch to the

José Gaspar Rodríguez de Francia
The Immortal *El Supremo* of Paraguay

From *Letters on Paraguay*
by J. P. and W. P. Robertson

old viceregal capital. Paraguay would send a delegate to a general congress but would be independent in the meantime. Buenos Aires replied by sending General Belgrano and Dr. Vicente Anastasio Echeverría as envoys to make some sort of working arrangement with Paraguay. While these *porteños* were en route, military influence in Asunción caused the Junta on September 2 to expel Dr. Bogarín. Francia protested against this act by resigning. No one capable of dealing with Buenos Aires remained, so Cavallero begged Francia to return from his cottage at Ibiraí. The indispensable doctor gallantly accepted the call. Three days later, on September 9, the Buenos Aires envoys wrote from Corrientes asking permission to proceed. Francia replied that they would be welcome provided Buenos Aires recognized Paraguay's independence. While Belgrano and Echeverría were on their way, European Spaniards tried to spring a counterrevolution, led by Pedro Somellera and Pedro Vicente Candevilla. This attempted coup failed on September 16. It was not, as several authors assert, a Machiavellian scheme promoted by Francia as an excuse to initiate a reign of terror. With the conspiracy out of the way, negotiations with the *porteños* went on smoothly. On October 12, 1811, Paraguay signed a treaty with Buenos Aires which freed its commerce of old impediments and paid lip service to the ideal of federation and alliance. Francia withdrew from the Junta again in December and stayed away until November, 1812, when his services once more were required to treat with an envoy from Buenos Aires.

J. P. Robertson, a young Scotsman with an eye for profit, entered Paraguay in 1812 shortly after Francia resigned from the Junta. That he was skillful is borne out by his friendly relations with Fernando de la Mora and, later, with Francia as well. Why anyone should have wanted to visit Paraguay in those years of turmoil, plotting, and insecurity is a mystery that can be solved only by attributing such rashness to a spirit of adventure. Robertson had been at Montevideo in 1806 where he saw the British capture the city by storm. He was not the first nineteenth-century Britisher to seek a fortune in South America, but he was, perhaps, the first British merchant to live in Paraguay.

Robertson's experiences in riding from Buenos Aires to Asunción lead one to believe that Paraguay was in far more danger from domestic discord than from foreign conquest. One could reach the capital after a long voyage up the rivers, a hard trip of about three months. The traveler might also follow the trails on horseback, riding west across the plains from Buenos Aires, then following the right bank of the Paraná to Santa Fé where he crossed the Paraná and continued up the left bank to Corrientes, the sleepy Argentine town just below the junction of the Paraguay and the Paraná. This journey, even at a mad gallop—Robertson maintained that he made twelve or more miles per hour—was slow and uncomfortable. After the posthouses in the pampas were left behind, the traveler was at the mercy of kindly inhabitants in a sparsely settled country where great herds of cattle, horses, and sheep roamed on the open range. Posthouses, such as they were, offered little comfort. One could eat meat, *carne con cuero*, drink maté, smoke cigars and change horses at these stopping places; but the crude wattle huts with thatched roofs were far from being hostelries. If speed were no object, the trip could be made in a high-roofed carriage suspended on leather straps over great wheels. This vehicle served as coach, hotel, and larder.

There were trails but no roads through the plains, swamps, and forests. Deep mudholes lay across the trail between Buenos Aires and Santa Fé and called for great exertion from horses and drivers to prevent the heavy coach from being held fast in the quagmire. In the first year of the Paraguayan Republic, Spanish naval vessels patrolled the Paraná in an effort to cut off shipping. These *marinos* in 1812 and 1813 hovered near Santa Fé to pounce on any boats that attempted to cross the river at that point, and terrorized the river settlements until Colonel José de San Martín, with a force of one hundred mounted grenadiers, defeated twice that number of *marinos* in a battle at the monastery of San Carlos some thirty miles above Rosario.

After he left the monotonous plains of Corrientes and safely crossed the Paraná, the traveler entered a new and rich country. Groves of palms, orchards of limes and oranges, and fig trees lay along the trail. Squirrels chattered in branches festooned with fragrant air plants; birds of brilliant plumage and beautiful songs were seen and heard everywhere; waterfowl covered small lakes. The mud huts of Entre Ríos gave way to low and rambling farm-houses, whose calcimined walls blended or contrasted with the greens of rampant vegetation, set among small fields of tobacco, cotton, mandioca, and melons.

People who lived on such ranchos were generous hosts to the few travelers who ventured into the province. Often the natives were mestizos who spoke Spanish haltingly and used Guaraní by preference. This bilingual accomplishment enabled Para-guayans to converse among themselves without being under-stood by any foreigners who might be present. In rural areas, platforms, some fifteen feet in height, served as a bedroom stage. For some peculiar reason, the omnipresent and omnivorous mos-quito rarely bothered people who thus slept above the ground.

Several of the land approaches to Asunción were through passes made by high embankments thrown up as defenses against Indian attacks. Along these defiles the country people traveled early in the morning, carrying their wares to market. J. P. Robert-son found the roads in 1812 crowded with Guaraní and mestizo traders on foot, riding or guiding burros, and occasionally strug-gling along in a two-wheeled cart. "It was something more than picturesque to see the elegant, lightly-clothed female, with her full bust, roundly-turned arms, small hands, and smaller feet, short petticoat, embroidered tepoi, braided hair, and black eyes, pursuing her course of industry, either with a pitcher of water, a bundle of tobacco, a load of salt, or a parcel of the yucca-root on her head." Well over a century later the scene had changed little. The paths were wider, the feet a bit larger perhaps, the burros were more numerous, and honking *camiones* might usurp the right of way. Square five-gallon cans were perched on the wom-en's heads, but still they were barefooted and the black hair so admired by the British merchant was, as then, wreathed in smoke from short black cigars.

Asunción, capital of all Paraguay, was not an imposing metrop-olis when Governor Velazco was overthrown in 1811. The gov-ernor's palace was a one-story, sprawling structure and less than a dozen private homes could be called substantial. Many buildings were of long, narrow bricks held together by a coarse brown mortar and calcimined in white or shades of salmon. Most of the city's ten thousand people lived in huts or in rooms appended to their shops. The market in the *plaza mayor* was the center of trade. Here the *campesinos,* mostly women, came early in the morning to sell tobacco, honey, mandioca, cotton, corn, flowers, sweets, salt, melons, oranges, chickens, eggs, garlic, *caña,* beef, hay, fish, and a few trinkets. Buzzing flies swarmed around buzzing women bargaining over prices. And old Paí Mbatú, a pretender to holy powers, badgered the vendors into providing him with his daily needs, completely oblivious to the politics of Asunción.

Read the history of Paraguay from 1810 to 1840 and "You will see the Dictator Francia blighting the energies of one of the finest countries in the world. You will see his despotic will changing, abrogating, or destroying all beneficial laws; and you will behold his relentless frown hushing into silence, not only the expression of complaint, but of thought, on the part of his paralysed and terror-stricken countrymen." This judgment of Robertson's may be somewhat harsh, but it is, essentially, true. Francia was austere in both dress and expression. In cool weather his black suit was set off by a scarlet cape. His "countenance was dark, and his black eyes were very penetrating, while his jet hair, combed back from a bold forehead, and hanging in natural ringlets over his shoulders, gave him a dignified and striking air." In his country house near Asunción he lived in seclusion after his quarrel with Yegros and plotted a coup that would make him master of the country. His private library of 250 to 300 volumes contained works on geometry, law, science, and literature and sufficed to give him a reputation for deep learning.

Errors inevitable in establishing any government provided Francia with arguments against the Junta. One of his sharpest weapons was the charge that Fernando de la Mora and Gregorio de la Cerda were planning to sell out to the *porteños.* He could play upon Paraguayan memories of the Comunero revolt, upon their defeat of Belgrano, and paint a glowing picture of Paraguay's future as an independent country. By these means he created so much dissatisfaction that the two suspects resigned.

Near anarchy prevailed in the country when Francia returned to the Junta late in 1812. Armed bands and individual ruffians made life miserable for peaceful citizens. Dr. J. R. Rengger, who arrived in Paraguay in 1819, held Yegros and his companions responsible for these conditions: "To imprison was, in their practice, to govern; to condemn or acquit, as hatred or interest dictated, was their mode of administering justice. They neither respected the old laws, nor would they supply new ones. To complete the disorders of the state, the greatest influence was allowed to women in the conduct of public affairs—and nothing was obtained, except through their intervention. Under the name of patriotism, all this violence was suffered to be perpetrated with impunity. The army, composed of the refuse of the country, arrogated the right of insulting the other inhabitants; and absolutely struck them when they presumed not to take off their hats to a soldier. The officers went so far as to interfere in civil disputes, and to constitute themselves into judges; and being all relatives of those in office, they were allowed to commit the most revolting iniquities."

Francia reorganized the government, removed dozens of incompetent officers, and punished outlaws with unaccustomed vigor. In the month after his return to the Junta, an envoy from Buenos Aires, Don Nicolás Herrera, arrived to revise the treaty of commerce and friendship. Herrera conferred with the Junta, but realized quickly that he was *persona non grata*. Thus his mission, as the Spaniards say, *se fracasó*. After observing their manner of dealing with natives and foreign envoys, Francia had nothing but contempt for Yegros and Cavallero, whose simple and bewildered minds could not grasp the meaning of things as they were and who knew absolutely nothing about government. Paraguay, he decided, must have a strong hand to guide her faltering steps. The Junta summoned a congress to meet in September, 1813, and while delegates were arriving Francia won adherents among army officers and the common people. There was a slight flurry of political activity while three ill-defined groups argued

153

their views. Although he had but few followers in Asunción, influential citizens realized that Francia could not be stopped in his rise to complete power.

The motley congress, when it finally assembled in full strength in October, contained representatives of all classes, including Indian alcaldes who appeared in grotesque finery of cocked hat and beribboned wig, velvet breeches and silver buttons, embroidered drawers and red sash. The sessions were short. A few days sufficed to refuse a treaty with Buenos Aires, and under Francia's direction the deputies on October 15 voted for a consulate composed of Francia and Yegros. Each consul was to serve four months at a time. Here is the place to repeat an old story that tells of two chairs, one labeled "Pompey" and the other "Caesar," being placed for the consuls. Francia took the latter.

Yegros, overshadowed by the brilliant and unscrupulous Francia, had practically no power in the consulate. His rival ignored or outwitted him, built a palace guard, and did all in his power to arouse hostility among the common people toward the small upper classes that Yegros represented. At the beginning of the consulate, Yegros had a plan drawn that provided for each consul to be brigadier general of the army, and each was to have exactly one-half of the troops, arms, and munitions. Francia refused to sign the plan but was willing for Yegros to be called general. Again, in the choice of a secretary of state, Francia dictated the appointment of Don Sebastián Sáenz, one of his creatures. Francia reorganized the army, Francia improved the fiscal system, and Francia set up frontier posts to which he could assign officers whose loyalty he doubted. On one matter the two consuls were in complete agreement: they would have no part in a Brazilian scheme to exterminate José Gervasio Artigas, the Uruguayan Gaucho who threatened Brazil's southern province of Rio Grande do Sul. This decision was but a continuation of the isolationist policy so dear to Francia.

Francia set at ease rumors that he favored the gachupines. Yegros agreed with him in proclaiming in March, 1814, that they could not marry whites. Nor was there any doubt that Francia hated those "refined rogues," the Jesuits. Their missions he regarded as vast plantations worked by underfed Indian slaves for the benefit of the Society. Although their expulsion had brought disaster to the mission country, he believed that Paraguay as a whole benefited. In this respect he revealed the typical creole attitude toward the Black Robes and there was considerable justice in his charges. The Jesuits did have exclusive control over a huge number of Indians for nearly 150 years, yet at the end of their regime the neophytes had made little or no progress toward self-government. They were always children in Jesuit eyes, or perhaps, spiritual slaves. Francia was to demonstrate that the free whites were no better able to govern themselves.

An espionage system, characteristic of Francia's later years, appeared long before the consulate's appointed year had expired. No one knew who was a spy for Francia, but, by observing those who spoke most in his favor, the keen citizen might make a good guess. The maté inspector Orrego, owner of a *pulpería* (saloon), served in that capacity. His jolly, innocent expression and camraderie, his sympathy for all who had complaints to make against the consulate, enabled him to serve his master well. Orrego and his unknown fellow agents served the principal consul faithfully when he became El Supremo.

According to the grant of power in 1813, the consulate was required to summon a congress to meet in the following year to decide on the future course of the government. Consequently, an ignorant, subservient mob of 1,000 delegates poured into Asunción in October, 1814. Most of them were deliriously loyal to Francia, whose name already had become legendary. Francia had drawn up the lists of delegates, the municipal councils merely approved them. There were enemies among those summoned, men who either had to approve the master's proposals or suffer from his anger; but the majority were poor people to whom *Caraí* Francia was nearly equal with God and much more real. The Congress met, quarreled for a few hours, then voted to give one man absolute power for three years. That man, of course, was Francia. One might assume that innocent coincidence accounted for the presence of his guard before the church of San Francisco where the delegates met. Its business over, the delegates went home. Two years later, Francia became dictator for life, a term that ended in 1840. The spirit of the Comuneros was dead. A long and deepening night fell over Paraguayan democracy. Dr. Cecilio Báez explains that "the dictatorship with which Doctor Francia was invested did not include the totality of public power; it meant only, as in ancient Rome, political and military command of the Republic to preserve it from its enemies." In theory, Paraguay's learned historian is correct; but not even he could be blind to the manner in which Francia became absolute.

# CHAPTER XI

# El Supremo

IN ALL OF Paraguay's four centuries of history, no name has been held in greater awe than that of El Supremo. There were those who dared to curse the Supreme One, who muttered angrily against his despotism, his gross and petty tyrannies. They were silenced. El Supremo knew them; his secret police and volunteer spies kept him well informed. El Supremo, so runs the tale, was wont to mingle in disguise among his subjects. Along the rough wharves of the river front, in rooms where the flickering light of candles cast long shadows, on street corners where barefooted men passed the time of day or night, El Supremo went and listened. Thus he learned of petty wrongs and heard the gossip that was Asunción's most cherished pastime.

Always an enemy of the Church as a political institution, Francia bestowed an undue portion of his scorn upon both secular and regular clergy. Whether or not he recognized the fact, Jesuit fathers were in a small way responsible for his very existence. Contemplating Paraguayan lack of skill in cultivating and manufacturing tobacco, the Black Robes urged the governor in 1750 to invite experts from Brazil to teach what they knew of these arts. Among those who accepted his invitation was Don García Rodríguez Francia (or was his name Graciano Rodríguez Franza?), who may have been French, Portuguese, or mameluco. Don García lived near Asunción and to his *chacra* he brought in 1756 Doña María Josefa de Velasco as wife. Doña María was

157

descended from Fulgencio de Yegros y Ledesma, governor of Paraguay from 1764–66. To this couple eventually were born three sons and two daughters, all of whom suffered from intellectual abnormalities, perhaps epilepsy. First of this quintet was a boy, born on January 6, 1766. Like so many things in Francia's career, the date of his birth remains in dispute.

Clergymen directed the boy's education, which began when he was twelve. Three years later, the family moved to Yaguarón, and Don García is said to have entrusted José to the Franciscan Colegio y Seminario de San Carlos in Asunción to study for the priesthood. That would have been in 1781, but the Colegio was not founded until 1783. Without worrying too much about such chronological discrepancies, we can accept the assertion that Francia did graduate from the Colegio de Monserrat at the University of Córdoba, where he was a brilliant, melancholy, pugnacious student who insisted that his name was Francia, not Franza. Enrique Wisner, who zealously gathered data in 1863–64 for his *El dictador del Paraguay,* insists that the future El Supremo left the University in 1785 as a doctor of theology. Others say that theology did not appeal to Francia and he changed his course to law.

Doña María Josefa died while her son was away, and the bereaved husband found solace in the arms of a mistress. José Gaspar upbraided his father for this concubinage when he returned to Yaguarón, refused to continue an ecclesiastical career, refused to live under his father's roof, and demanded his mother's estate. With funds thus obtained, he moved to a cottage near Asunción, buried himself in books, and forgot the family completely. In 1790, or perhaps in 1786, he succeeded in being appointed to the chairs of Latin and theology at the Colegio de San Carlos; but, after two years, the Franciscans tired of their former pupil's anticlerical views and Francia left the school.

Francia became a lawyer about 1792. Just how he prepared himself for the bar is hard to explain unless he had, indeed, studied civil law at Córdoba. No man in the profession had a greater reputation for integrity and a more finely developed sense of justice, but Francia was never popular. He was an introvert, aloof, haughty, and studious among people whose principal care was to enjoy life. Early in his legal career an incident occurred that contributed greatly to his reputation. One who believed himself a friend of Francia went to the young lawyer for aid in concluding a particularly disreputable transaction. The intended victim, Estanislao Macháin, was Francia's enemy, his successful rival for the hand of Petrona Zavala. Burying this animosity, Francia went to Macháin and offered to defend his case. When the litigation came up in court, the judge told the lawyer opposing Francia that the latter must be bribed; but Francia, when the offer was made, is said to have stormed: "Get out of my house with your vile proposals and your filthy gold!" Then he put on his cape and visited the judge. "Sir!" he told him, "You are a disgrace to law and a blight on justice. You are in my power and if you do not tomorrow pronounce in favor of my client, I shall see to it that the place you occupy will crucify you and the symbol of your judicial office will become the emblem of your shame!" Macháin won the case and Francia continued to hate him, just as he hated the Spaniards who had come to Asunción to hold office and to get rich.

If a shred of compassion or a glow of human warmth ever existed in El Supremo's heart, with the possible exception of his unrequited love for Petrona Zavala, no one ever knew it. Perhaps there is no truth in the story, but Paraguayans believed that Francia, long before he became a public figure, had refused to become reconciled with his father, who begged him to come to his deathbed for a last paternal blessing. "Tell my father that I don't care if his soul goes to hell" is what Francia is supposed to have said. His detractors insist that he could not forgive a wrong, real or fancied, so cold, calculating, and vindictive was his character. Patriotic Paraguayan writers want us to believe that El Supremo was as chaste as St. Paul in spite of evidence to the contrary. *Compañeras* shared his bed, but he loved no woman, nor did he ever marry. Children born of his liaisons received nothing but contempt from their father. Justo Pastor Benítez, a Paraguayan scholar whose judgment and ability are of a high order, says of Francia: "During his twenty-six years of dictatorship, his life was as pure and frigid as snow on a mountain top. It was as monotonous, chaste, and comforting as a Christian prayer." Rengger, a contemporary, wrote that this austerity and chastity appeared when Francia became dictator.

Soon after Francia achieved supremacy, he took up quarters in the governor's palace. Here he lived with four servants and followed a regime that allowed no time, so his enemies said, for his two great passions of women and gambling, or for mixing in Asunción society, which he heartily despised. In a land where eating was either a fine art or an occasion for porcine stuffing, the dictator was noted for his frugal fare. His work day was long, since no matter was too small for his attention; his signature must have appeared on a great many documents, very few of which have been preserved. El Supremo scorned love and friendship; praise and calumny alike left him untouched. He entered office a poor man, took only one-third of the annual salary voted by the subservient congress, and died with an estate worth about 35,000 pesos. Francia's honesty was proverbial, and his immunity to bribery was illustrated by his refusal to accept gifts of any kind.

Francia knew Paraguayans and how to control them. He knew their lack of group courage under oppression, their cringing before ruthless authority, their helplessness when deprived of the few creoles who might have led them into rebellion. Political forms, ideals of the American and French revolutions, and techniques of politics meant nothing to the mass of people, who were illiterate, unambitious, and satisfied with their crude living. Francia cared not if the people despised him so long as they feared him; he in turn despised his subjects individually, loved them as Paraguay, and feared no one. He was accustomed to saying that Paraguayans had an extra bone in their necks since he never saw one who held his head upright. If he should have encountered such a bold creature, one of his mounted guards would have bent the head over with a blow of his sword.

To be dictator meant to Francia that his every wish, however unreasonable, must be obeyed immediately. There is a story that on one of his daily trips through Asunción, his horse stumbled slightly on a loose brick in front of an old Spaniard's house.

Francia ordered the householder, José Carísimo, to have it repaired; but the next day, when the brick had not been replaced, El Supremo had the offender jailed, shackled, and fined ten thousand pesos. The Spaniard was fat and the irons sank deep into his flesh. His wife tearfully begged Francia to relieve her husband's sufferings. "Very well," he said. "You shall buy larger irons for him, and if you don't, you too will go to jail." The wife obtained the manacles which Carísimo wore until his friends paid the fine. On another occasion, probably in 1817, El Supremo became enraged on seeing an insulting pasquinade posted on the wall of a house. It was, of course, ridiculous to suppose that the owner, an Argentine named Pascual Echagüe, had dared to post the handbill himself; nevertheless, he went to jail. His wife implored Francia to release her husband, but El Supremo ordered another set of irons for the prisoner, who wore them until he died. Before this victim's suffering ended, a distant relative sought relief for him, an interposition that resulted in his own incarceration and death in prison. Many others who were suspected of posting pasquinades or caricatures were imprisoned or condemned to hard labor. To insult Francia was to insult Paraguay.

Francia's critics grossly exaggerated the dictator's cruelties, and the world learned of them primarily through hostile Argentine and British writers. Men like the Robertsons, foiled in their efforts to become rich through trade with Paraguay, could have had no love for the dictator. They described his despotism in the most severe terms possible, called his summary punishments diabolical crimes, with just enough truth in their charges to prevent reasoned judgment. Before a year had run its course, the Robertsons wrote, "The prisons were groaning with inmates; commerce was paralyzed; vessels were rotting on the river-banks, and produce going to decay in the warehouses; a system of espionage of the most searching kind prevailed; the higher classes were all depressed, the lower brought into notice; while the caprice of the Dictator was the sole rule of government, and the insolence of his soldiers was systematically encouraged as the best means of striking terror into the hearts of the crouching and insulted citizens. Distrust and terror pervaded every habitation; the nearest relations and dearest friends looked as if afraid of each other; despondency or despair were more or less legibly written on every countenance." A strong bill of particulars may be presented to support these accusations.

As it is with all dictators, terror was one of Francia's weapons to maintain his position and thus to insure Paraguayan independence. No one knew when he might be thrown into prison, and El Supremo's jails were not pleasure houses. His less odious prison, for common rogues, was a single-story building about one hundred feet square. The state prisons were located in barracks where troops served as guards. As many as forty inmates could be crowded into each of the eight compartments of the public prison. A flat roof and slits for windows guaranteed the maximum discomfort in Paraguay's subtropical summers. Men and women were thrown together in these filthy, stinking ovens and could look forward to fresh air only when, encumbered by chains and iron bars, they were led out to work. By comparison with the state prisons, these quarters were luxurious. Narrow, underground cells beneath the barracks were the dungeons to which dangerous prisoners were confined. There was no sanitation and no ventilation in these holes where the living were entombed. Governor Velazco and Estanislao Machaín were but two of the many victims who lived out their lives in a state prison.

Hundreds of Francia's victims were shot, hanged, or tortured to death. The more fortunate suffered exile to the penal colony of Tevego, now Fuerte Olimpo, about three hundred miles north of Asunción. "It is a place," J. P. Robertson wrote, "of which the atmosphere is one great mass of malaria, and the heat suffocating, —where the surrounding country is uninterrupted marsh,—where venomous insects and reptiles abound,—and where the fiercest and yet unsubdued tribes of Indians are making continual inroads." Life at Tevego was preferred to a few hours in the dictator's "Chamber of Justice," even though it is generally charged that thousands died there during a period of two decades. Scores of exiles undoubtedly ended their lives at Tevego, but certainly not thousands.

No dictator can be secure from plots to bring his life to a disconcertingly sudden conclusion, and every dictator must take precautions to disappoint those who would increase by one the number of suppliants before the final bar. Francia lived forever in fear of poison in his cigars or his food, of assassins who might succeed in breaking through the guard. Weapons were always at hand, visitors were searched before being ushered into the Presence, and no one of them was allowed to come within arm's reach. When El Supremo rode through the streets on his way to the barrack of San Francisco, all Paraguayans had to be out of sight, so fearful was the dictator of assassination. On one occasion, so Masterman wrote in his *Seven Eventful Years in Paraguay,* "a funeral procession crossed the road as he approached; the bearers immediately dropped the bier, and with the priest and mourners hid themselves behind a hedge at the roadside until he had passed." Edward Lucas White, in his fascinating novel *El Supremo,* repeats the story that Francia never slept two consecutive nights in the same room. The Robertsons move him about from abode to abode. What he had most to fear was not individual anger but conspiracies among his enemies. The greatest of these plots apparently had its origin in 1817 and was not completely crushed until 1821.

Juan Martín de Pueyrredón, supreme director of the Argentine Confederation, was unable to spare an army to subdue Paraguay; but he could and did send a spy into the country after having issued a decree in January, 1817, forbidding the importation of Paraguayan tobacco. Colonel Juan Baltazar Vargas, a Paraguayan, went to Asunción with orders to discover Francia's enemies, unite them into a league, and then overthrow the dictator. Hundreds of respectable citizens in the capital had reason to hate El Supremo. He had deprived them of offices and honors, had thrown their relatives into jail, and had confiscated their properties. Vargas set to work with an ill-concealed enthusiasm that cost him his life in 1818, but his fellow plotters escaped detection until 1820. These brave souls included Juan Arostegui, José Acosta, Juan de los Ríos, Leonardo Guevara, Dr. Marcos Baldovinos, Pedro Montiel, and many more. Juan Bogarín, one of the conspirators in mortal terror of hell, revealed the secret to Father Anastasio Gutiérrez who heard his confession. The despicable friar ordered the penitent to betray the plotters to El Supremo, who struck swiftly. Fifty of Asunción's most distinguished citizens were imprisoned; all surviving members of the old junta and their friends and relatives felt Francia's wrath. More than 175 suspects went to jail. Still the dictator dared not execute the plotters en masse for fear of a spontaneous revolt; instead, he let them starve to death in their own filth while legal processes went on.

Confronted with formal indictments in January, 1821, many of the prisoners denied the guilt attributed to them by their companions, "and then the punishment of the whip was applied to them." Wisner states that this whipping went on in a room in the old Jesuit Colegio a block from the jail. "In said room, which was called the 'Chamber of Justice,' there was a narrow wood bed where the 'patient' was placed face down and tied hand and foot, and the lashes were applied to him on the shoulders by two Guaycurú Indians appointed for that purpose, each armed with a large whip composed of braided thongs of cowhide; and the number of blows that were received never passed 150 to 200, since the greater part of those who were subjected to this punishment became dismayed before reaching the designated numbers." Confessions followed as a matter of course. El Supremo's principal stroke against possible plotters, the Spaniards, fell on June 9, 1821. Assembled in the square before the dictator's quarters, three hundred of them, about one-half of all Spaniards in Asunción, were forced to stand for hours without knowing what was to happen. Francia had them crowded into the public prison where they rotted for eighteen months. Velazco was among this group. After this long imprisonment, the dictator levied a fine of 150,000 pesos on the wealthy survivors and then banished all the poorer ones.

Political prisoners still filled the jails when another Argentine caudillo, Francisco Ramírez of Entre Ríos, sought to stir up rebellion in Paraguay. Ramírez in 1820 apparently intended to invade the country with an army of four thousand men, then turn

José Artigas (1815)
From a portrait by Juan Manuel Blanes, in the Museo Histórico
de Montevideo

Reproduced from *José Artigas*, by Alberto Lasplaces

against the Brazilians who had occupied Uruguay. He had already forced the great Uruguayan caudillo, José Gervasio Artigas, to seek asylum in Paraguay. Another Argentine caudillo, Estanislao López, governor of Santa Fé, ended his temporary alliance with Ramírez and opened negotiations with Buenos Aires. Not knowing what to expect from this new bubble in the political cauldron, Ramírez called off his invasion, probably early in 1821; by that time many Paraguayans were implicated in the scheme. Ramírez had sent a message to Pedro Juan Cavallero, who was to send it on to Fulgencio Yegros, president of the original junta after Velazco's fall. Francia captured this message in July, 1821. He doubled the guard around Yegros, imprisoned Cavallero, and warned departmental commanders to be vigilant. Then he conducted an inquisition in his Chamber of Justice to force prisoners to reveal the names of other plotters. Firing squads were busy for some time. Yegros fell on July 17, Cavallero committed suicide in jail; Fernando de la Mora, Larios Galván, and Estanislao Machaín were among the victims of a purge that lasted for three months, each day of which time brought four to eight executions. Bodies lay exposed to the sun where they fell until nightfall, when relatives were permitted to carry them away. A few brash men dared to protest against this sort of justice. Don Miguel Ibáñez, a strong supporter of Francia and commandant at Villa Concepción, was heard to mutter. He died in jail. Don Ignacio Noceda, another early adherent, received more than one hundred lashes in the Chamber of Justice. Let it be said in Francia's favor that he moderated his policies after 1823; by that time most of his enemies were dead or broken.

During those frightful months, Rengger wrote, "brother was seen to denounce brother—fathers to accuse their children. . . . No one dared to become the depository of his neighbour's secret, lest he should be deemed an accomplice. . . . When friends met, they coldly saluted each other, but did not converse: no more parties—the women even gave up their privilege of speech—the guitar, the inseparable companion of every inhabitant of Paraguay, was mute." El Supremo was harsh, even cruel, but he was not deaf to pleas for mercy nor did he fail in princely gestures.

One of these came on January 6, 1839, when he celebrated his seventy-third birthday by freeing a hundred or more prisoners. Six or seven hundred unfortunates remained in jail. Of this number, it would be impossible to say how many were genuine criminals and how many were there for purely political reasons.

Those terrible days of 1821 seemed to reveal the truth of Francia's observation that Paraguay was not ready for democracy: any people willing to submit to such a purge, who cringed and groveled at El Supremo's feet, had the mentality of slaves and the courage of jackals, a judgment that may be too harsh. Francia ruled a people essentially Indian-white in race, who had been dominated by an extremely small percentage of the population. By crushing this dominating class and by instilling fear among the masses accustomed to mild oppression, he was able to move ahead swiftly to complete control before leaders could possibly develop among the people.

Much of Francia's power rested upon absolute control of a small but efficient army that could suppress rebellion and repel invasions from turbulent Argentina and avaricious Brazil. As in the civilian establishment, El Supremo ruthlessly eliminated all officers of doubtful loyalty or whose social connections might be embarrassing. There were so many in this category that eventually the most capable soldiers were replaced by mediocre men whose principal qualification was a blind loyalty to the dictator. Francia designed the uniforms, drilled and inspected the troops, and obtained their equipment. To supply arms and munitions, he licensed the export of wood to Buenos Aires, while at the same time he encouraged local production. Within the army was the dictator's personal guard, the Corps of Grenadiers, composed of hand-picked and trusted men, which also served as a political police force. The standing army at no time exceeded 6,000 men drawn from a total population of about 300,000. This force could be increased to some 26,000 by calling the militia into service. Frontier guard duty became particularly important after 1816 when Francia feared a new attempt by Argentina to subdue Paraguay, and when raids from Artigas, Estanislao López, or Francisco Ramírez were definite possibilities. A combination of these enemies could have overrun Paraguay, just as a determined Brazilian assault most certainly would have succeeded. Fortunately for Paraguay, Argentine and Uruguayan caudillos did not unite in an invasion, and Brazil was too busy challenging Argentine influence in the Banda Oriental to bother with the hermit state.

Government was a simple matter under the dictator. El Supremo's chief confidant appears to have been his barber, a person whose razor might have made a sharp difference in Francia's career. Anyone who wanted a favor sought first to placate the man who shaved the tyrant, although it is very doubtful if this servant enjoyed any real influence. A minister of finance kept the books, a sort of prefect of police maintained public order, and a secretary doubled as foreign minister and minister of justice. Theoretically, the colonial laws were in effect, but Francia's wish was the final law. To enforce governmental orders, the country was divided into twenty departments, each of which contained districts. The departmental commanders were assisted by police agents in the districts. Two judges attached to the Asunción Cabildo served as a supreme court for the nation. In spite of this rudimentary organization, all government and all justice depended upon Francia's whim: his ministers were puppets, and his departmental commanders dared nothing without express orders from El Supremo. According to the grant of power in October, 1814, Francia's term as dictator was to end after three years; on June 6, 1816, a general congress made him perpetual dictator. This body was to meet whenever the dictator thought it advisable, but there was no provision for anything remotely resembling democracy, no legislative body to which Francia was to answer for his acts. Paraguay's fate was linked firmly to the caprice of one man responsible to no one, although that man was to prove himself one of the most disinterested patriots ever to serve his country.

Paraguay temporarily escaped the political chaos through which neighboring countries careened madly. Francia faced conspiracies at home; a fifth column of Europeans, aristocrats, and Argentine agents; efforts by Buenos Aires to bring Paraguay under its power; attempts by Brazil to steal territory; plans by Argentine caudillos to invade the republic; and severe restrictions or embargoes on Paraguay's principal exports. The dictator wisely adopted policies that practically ended contact with other countries and compelled a broad diversification in agriculture and industry. This isolation exasperated foreign merchants and governments, called forth bitter denunciations, and gave rise to a host of lies so pernicious that Thomas Carlyle, who knew practically nothing about Paraguay, published a defense of El Supremo. Criticize Francia's "China policy" as one will, the fact remains that it preserved Paraguay's independence. His policy of turning the country into a hermit state presented a great contrast to the rest of South America, in which discord, confusion, and civil war prevailed while politicians, crying for liberty and order, sought only power and plunder. In Paraguay there may have been the servility of despair, the docility of a cowed people; there were also peace and order.

El Supremo needed and wanted foreign trade, and he sought to open commerce with the British, whose navy could end Argentine control over the Paraná below Corrientes. To achieve this object, he made proposals to British merchants who had enjoyed considerable experience in Paraguay. In 1814 he proposed that J. P. Robertson should take cotton, tobacco, yerba, sugar, and other Paraguayan products before the House of Commons and there, as agent of El Supremo, invite the opening of formal relations between the two governments. In writing about this incident, Robertson grew very sarcastic. He had visions of appearing at "the bar of the House of Commons; overpowering, with a half-dozen porters, the Usher of the Black Rod; and delivering, in spite of remonstrance and resistance, at once my hide-bound bales of Paraguayan merchandise, and the oration, verbatim, of the First Consul." He might as well have pictured himself paddling barefooted through London streets, hawking cigars and maté. Actually, Robertson seems to have thought well of the scheme and agreed to undertake the mission. But when he reached Buenos Aires in 1814, a series of circumstances largely beyond his control brought the mission to an end.

Buenos Aires needed recruits to fill its armies and hoped to attract some from Paraguay. The Supreme Director of the moment, Carlos M. de Alvear, induced Robertson to put on board a vessel he was sending to Asunción a letter to El Supremo proposing a trade of arms and munitions for recruits. Instead of continuing to Europe, J. P. Robertson decided to conduct his vessel personally. On the way upstream in 1815, this vessel and its owner were captured by a band of Artigueños, bandit followers of José Gervasio Artigas, and the cargo destined for Francia was lost. Released at last through the influence of Captain Jocelyn Percy, commanding H.M.S. *Hotspur,* the unfortunate merchant returned to Buenos Aires and then set out for Uruguay to seek redress from Artigas. This congenital outlaw-patriot-hero then controlled most of Uruguay and Argentina under the title "Protector" and even threatened to overthrow the haughty, pretentious government at Buenos Aires. Robertson found the Uruguayan caudillo "seated on a bullock's skull, at a fire kindled on the mud floor of his hut, eating beef off a spit, and drinking gin out of a cowhorn!" Artigas had no money to meet the claim of six thousand pesos; but he could and did provide the Britisher with a passport to Paraguay.

W. P. Robertson in Asunción had, in the meantime, heard about his brother's misfortune, and so had Francia. The dictator ordered Artigas's subordinates to release the cargo and its owner, but it was British influence that partly turned the trick. Francia, incensed because the British government had failed to guarantee him "a free trade in arms," ordered the Robertsons to get out of Paraguay. Nor was his anger appeased when Artigas spread the rumor, based on Alvear's letter, that Francia was selling Paraguayans to fight for Buenos Aires. Five years later Artigas was a refugee in Francia's power, and it is unlikely that El Supremo forgot this incident.

Francia had good reason to fear free intercourse with foreign countries in spite of his early desire for commerce. He had no illusions about the Bragança empire in Brazil; the United Provinces of Río de la Plata would not forget that Paraguay once was a part of the old viceroyalty; and in none of the neighboring republics was the spirit of conquest dead. The great Simón Bolívar himself in 1825 urged Francia to open friendly relations with the newly formed republics, but El Supremo replied that Paraguay would continue on its chosen course. General Fructuosa Rivera, temporary president of Uruguay, sent envoys to Francia in December, 1838, with some sort of proposal, possibly for an alliance against Buenos Aires. El Supremo refused to let the messengers cross his frontiers, so determined was he to avoid foreign entanglements.

Paraguay's army alone might not be enough to repel a foreign attack, but the danger would be lessened by a strict control over travel. Foreigners might bring in ideas dangerous to dictatorship and certainly they would take out ideas derogatory to El Supremo. Francia forbade emigration, a step that ended the movement to Buenos Aires and forced people into agriculture and other pursuits at home. One result was an increase in the number of "weavers, ironworkers, locksmiths, gunsmiths, shoemakers, saddlers, masons, silversmiths, and goldsmiths." Paraguay, to be strong, must develop its own resources with its own people and capital. Foreigners would exploit the country to the detriment of Paraguayans, who would emigrate to other lands of greater opportunity. Foreign trade, therefore, was limited to one or two ports, and only those products in great abundance should be exported to exchange for things needed.

Before Francia's policy of isolation went into effect, foreign trade was in the hands of some five hundred families. Yerba, tobacco, wood products, and miscellaneous processed goods reached a value of about 1,125,000 pesos annually. It was a small sum, to be sure; but it supported the elite Spanish merchants and a large host of workers. More than one hundred sailing vessels were engaged in the trade. By stopping this commerce, except by special license, the dictator crushed the strongest source of possible opposition to his rule. "The port of Assumption," Rengger wrote, "literally resembled a coast where a hundred ships had run aground. Several of them were carried out by the first swell of the river, but were abandoned by the owners." The loss in revenue he made up through forced contributions, heavy fines, confiscation of church revenues, heavy taxes, escheats to the state of all property owned by foreign-born residents, and through petty impositions.

The Robertsons, canny traders who made large profits in spite of occasional losses, sent an agent, Henry Okes, into the lion's den early in 1820. After a voyage of three months up the river, Okes arrived at Asunción with a cargo that included scientific instruments so dear to the lump of *lapacho* that served as a heart for El Supremo. Delighted with the gift, acceptance of which apparently broke an otherwise inflexible rule, Francia permitted Okes to pass three months in assembling a return shipment. Even then the Englishman, whose connection with the Robertsons was not suspected, was urged to stay on. Okes loaded the vessel but had to leave behind about 37,000 pesos in cash and goods. This property, left with a Spaniard, was confiscated when Francia heard of Okes's death at Buenos Aires in 1821. Another who braved Francia's disfavor was the Spaniard Don José de María, a merchant of Buenos Aires who had married a daughter of Don Antonio Escalada, a patrician son-in-law of San Martín. The Robertsons sent María to Asunción as a partner in 1818 with 200 pesos worth of salt, as ballast for his vessel, which brought 4,000 pesos in Asunción. The voyage netted the English merchants 60,000 pesos. María remained in Asunción, accumulating goods and trying to get out of the country. At last in 1825, with the aid of a request from Sir Woodbine Parish, British consul general at Buenos Aires, María and other foreigners were allowed to depart.

The Argentine Confederation applied economic sanctions against the upstart dictatorship. On January 8, 1817, it prohibited the importation of Paraguayan tobacco; but Francia was not impressed, although his own embargo on exports had led to developing a thriving yerba trade between Brazil and Buenos Aires. El Supremo was not afraid of Brazil. Perhaps he did not appreciate the fact, but Brazilian-Argentine rivalry over Uruguay prevented the *porteños* from carrying out any desires they may have had to avenge Belgrano's defeat, while an Argentine move against Paraguay would have brought Brazilian aid immediately.

On April 5, 1823, Francia signed a treaty with Brazil that gave the latter two ports of entry, Itapuá on the Paraná and Coimbra on the Paraguay north of Asunción. Trade did not flourish, since special licenses must be obtained for each general shipment, and the arrangement was at best but a temporary breach in Francia's system of isolation. Paraguayans might sell yerba and tobacco to the Brazilians, if the seller was also the grower, and if he could get a license. Only whites of unblemished loyalty to Francia need apply for licenses to sell, and only favorites would receive the coveted permits. Brazilian traders, with cargoes bought in Buenos Aires, presented at Itapuá an inventory of their goods which went to Francia with the license. El Supremo selected whatever he wanted from the list, paid whatever he decided the goods were worth, and permitted the merchant to sell the rest. In Asunción, Francia had a shop tended by a government employee where fortunate persons might buy the merchandise.

People who entered Paraguay did so at their own risk, and no one could leave without special permission. Foreigners not approved by Francia found themselves expelled forcibly, thrown into prison, or exiled to some remote village in the country. Many exiles and refugees received a safe refuge; other outlanders were held as unwilling guests. Among the latter were Johann Rudolph Rengger, a Swiss, and his associate Marceline Longchamps. These travelers entered Paraguay in July, 1819, and remained for six years before Francia let them go. They published at Paris in 1827 their *Essai historique sur la révolution du Paraguay*, a work that was actually favorable to Francia but which caused him to counter with a blast at the authors in 1830. They were spies who plotted with Spaniards against the republic, quacks who killed their patients, liars who wove a fabric of falsehoods about the fatherland. Their supposed conversations with Francia were figments of delirium. El Supremo could have stopped these sons of Satan had he desired by refusing to let them leave the country.

Artigas, the Uruguayan who fought in vain against Brazilian and Argentine invaders, was the most famous of Francia's prisoners. This Gaucho, once supreme in a vast area, had not been very friendly toward Paraguay. He had permitted his near-outlaws to stop Francia's ships and to take off Francia's cargoes. When Artigas needed friends in 1817, he had suggested the opening of amicable relations with Paraguay. Francia replied in effect: "Pay me for what you have stolen, then we'll talk of friendship." One of the followers of Artigas incited a rebellion among Indians in southeastern Paraguay, and by the time the fracas was over, twelve mission towns lay in ruins. Enrique Wisner tells the story and it is convincing, except for his assertion that the towns were flourishing. Francia should have sent troops to retaliate; instead, he merely strengthened his forces on the frontier. Artigas apologized for the attack and reprimanded officials responsible for past injuries. In September, 1820, Artigas and five hundred followers, who were fleeing from Francisco Ramírez of Entre Ríos, asked and received permission from Francia to seek asylum in Paraguay. El Supremo, suspicious of Artigas, who had done much to keep the Plata provinces in turmoil, shrewdly guessed that the Uruguayan would hatch some political plot against him; if so, what could be better than to have him under close surveillance? He sent Artigas to live in the village of San Isidro Labrador near the northeastern frontier and gave him a pension of thirty-two pesos a month for a time. Artigas never annoyed his host nor was he persecuted. There the old caudillo lived until 1845, when Carlos Antonio López, successor to Francia, moved him close to Asunción. After thirty years of exile, Artigas died at the age of ninety-two.

An English doctor of unusual ability, who possessed an equally great talent for consumption of alcoholic beverages, appeared at Asunción in July, 1815. This practitioner, one Dr. Parlett, had ruined a promising career in Buenos Aires. Francia, who held Spanish doctors in justifiable low esteem, bade the Englishman to make himself at home. El Supremo wanted a competent person to treat his guards and troops—quacks were good enough for the common herd. Parlett found time to perform seeming miracles of medicine among the Paraguayans. Grateful clients paid him well and were generous with gifts. One miserly merchant, Don Antonio Recalde, voluntarily paid him about one hundred dollars for discovering and removing a *piqué* (chigger) from his daughter's eye. Francia paid him about twenty-five cents for a visit to one of his guards. Parlett could have settled down to a comfortable life; but he grew restless, returned to his old bad habits, and finally died in Asunción in 1825, a short time before El Supremo had decided to release the foreigners he held.

Nearly every foreigner could relate intriguing chapters in the endless story of "what happened to me in Paraguay." Don Manuel Méndez Caldeira, a Uruguayan merchant who arrived in Asunción about 1814, was engaged in a prosperous business that was cut short in 1815 by a decree of exile to Curuguaty. Eleven years later, when El Supremo permitted most of the foreigners to leave, Méndez escaped to Buenos Aires with his family; but for more than a decade he never knew from one day to the next what further misfortunes might lie in store for him. The French naturalist, Aimé Jacques Alexandre Bonpland, arrived in Buenos Aires with his wife in 1817. Two years later he settled near Candelaria in Corrientes, former capital of the Jesuit missions, to raise yerba for the Argentine market. Bonpland prospered in his colony opposite the Paraguayan town of Itapuá until 1821. Then Francia, pretending that the establishment might serve as a jumping-off place for an invasion by Ramírez (who was dead), sent a force that invaded Corrientes, destroyed the colony, killed a few people, and imprisoned Bonpland. The case soon became a *cause célèbre*, with Brazilian, French, and British notables all petitioning for the Frenchman's release. Bonpland actually was quite contented in Paraguay.

For the Church and all its works El Supremo had nothing but disdain. In the first years of his ascendancy, the dictator ordered masses said in one of the barracks and he attended at the cathedral on great occasions; but by 1820 these functions he held to be signs of idiocy. Orders of regular clergy, especially the Jesuits, he considered as locusts on the land. Francia is said to have snorted that if the Pope came to Paraguay, he would make him an altar boy. There is reason to wonder if El Supremo even acknowledged the Almighty as stronger than himself. Paraguayan clergy were noted for their lax behavior. Ignorant, sloven-

174

ly, and lazy, "they lived publicly in concubinage and daily violated the sanctuary of the temples with a thousand abominations." The prior of the Dominicans boasted that "he was the father of twenty-two children by different mothers." On July 2, 1815, Francia moved to bring the clergy completely under his power with a decree that no order of regular clergy could obey any superior officer resident in a foreign country. Only the bishop of Asunción could exercise any authority over them, officers of the orders were to be elected at councils every three or four years by the membership, all officers must have the government's approval, and no council could be held without Francia's permission. This decree proclaimed with a vengeance that the papal bulls, bestowing ecclesiastical control on the Spanish rulers, had been inherited by the republic. The Bishop of Asunción, Monseñor Pedro Benito G. de Panés was a man whose mind was something less than normal. After a priest had asked the Virgin to restore the Bishop's mental health, Francia decided to be rid of the prelate. On October 16, 1819, he deprived the Bishop of all authority over the regular clergy, gave him a pension, and named a favorite as vicar general. Panés fretted unhappily until July, 1838, when El Supremo restored him to office; but he was then ninety years old and died three months later.

Education for the people, classes or masses, had never thrived in Paraguay. Each Jesuit mission had its school, but there was not one public primary school in Asunción until the eighteenth century was nearly worn out. By royal authority, the Real Colegio y Seminario de San Carlos was founded in 1783. In 1805, Don José Gabriel Tellez was struggling to keep Asunción's one public elementary school going; six years later, Tellez resigned because he had no building and was not getting his one hundred pesos a year. This resignation caused the junta, on November 25, 1811, to make provision for a temporary schoolhouse. Francia was not deeply interested in improving the situation. His greatest crime, José Segundo Decoud once said, was in having maintained and perpetuated a state of ignorance. Private schools enabled children of wealthy people to learn the three *R*'s, but formal education was not for the masses. Fearing that the Seminario, Paraguay's only secondary school, might harbor enemies, Francia suppressed it in 1822. The dictator permitted private schools to be operated, although he did not encourage them. There were no newspapers under Francia, not even a newsletter.

Francia's apologists never tire of praising the remarkable self-sufficiency of Paraguay during its enforced isolation. All claimants to land were compelled to prove their titles in 1826, with the result that one-half of the republic's area east of the Río Paraguay was declared public domain. Areas once idle were brought into cultivation, new crops supplied food formerly imported from Buenos Aires, cotton became an important staple and gave rise to a respectable industry, while cattle and horse raising for the first time achieved the status of major enterprises. When a plague of locusts swarmed across Paraguay from the Chaco in 1826, Francia summoned all males from fourteen to sixty to combat the invasion. The locusts won. Undismayed, El Supremo ordered the farmers to replant immediately. The fall harvest in March and April, 1827, was so abundant that the two-crop year became established, according to Rengger who places this event in 1819–20. Actually there was nothing new in this practice, since the Spaniards had harvested two crops a year before 1540.

During the refreshing autumn days of 1840, El Supremo could look back on a long career with a great satisfaction. No foreign enemy had challenged his country's independence, no declared domestic enemy had succeeded in overthrowing him. Things left undone were appalling in number, as they are at all times and in all countries. A fertile land fairly ached to be wooed by man; a fertile people could not rise above the level apparently predetermined by a mysterious destiny. Francia had held high ideals of achievement; he had threatened, coerced, and driven his people. If the furrow he traced in the sea closed swiftly, at least his footprints on the beach were deep and lasting.

El Supremo could not know the future, but he knew that for him the future was coming swiftly. As he made short rides from the cavalry barracks, his seventy-four years protested more and more. He began in June, 1840, to burn his papers, an act of destruction that was to deny him forever an accurate biography and to deny historians a measure of professional glee that comes from sifting yesterday's ashes. Asunción's raw, wet winter was too much for the old dictator to bear. He rode for the last time on August 30; on September 20, El Supremo became El Difunto.

Beside the high altar in the Church of the Incarnation, El Supremo's body was buried. Father Don Manuel Antonio Pérez commended his soul to God with words of praise. *Requiescat in pace!* But he could not rest in peace. Vandals opened the sepulcher and threw his body into the Paraguay River. Tradition has it that Payaguás "disinterred the tyrant's corpse and threw it into a miry arroyo that flowed out near the one today known as Chacarita." The body died and was torn from the grave; but the spirit of El Supremo will forever be close to the heart of Paraguay.

A dictator, as Cecilio Báez observes in his *Ensayo sobre el Doctor Francia,* is a complex being. A study of Oliver Cromwell reveals the complexity of the dictatorial character. Francia also was a complex man, an ardent partisan, a republican who derived his political ideas from Rosseau's *Social Contract.* He believed that man, by compact, gave up his natural independence for social security, that all political organization is based on popular sovereignty exercised in democratic processes, and that all men, being free and equal, have the right to promote their welfare through a government freely established. These principles were far too advanced for Paraguayans en masse to absorb; or, one should say, Paraguayans were not ready to assume responsibilities arising from exercised rights or privileges. Perhaps, as Báez suggests, great ideas are disseminated to the people through great minds. Francia was to be such a disseminator for principles of the French Revolution. He interpreted the Revolution for Paraguay, became its victorious leader, and succeeded in preserving independence for his country. His policy of isolation, forced upon him by circumstances, was not adopted through preference. Paraguay lost in material wealth to be gained from commercial intercourse; the country gained a more diversified economy, an invaluable self-reliance, and internal harmony while civil and international wars kept its neighbors in turmoil. El Supremo needs no greater eulogy.

# CHAPTER XII

# Carlos Antonio López, Heir To Francia

SLOWLY TRUTH insinuated itself into Paraguayan minds: El Supremo was dead and he had left no heir to his powers. Perhaps he had been convinced that no one in the country could take his place; perhaps he did not care. One might expect that a tremendous social explosion would have taken place, so long had self-expression and self-government been suppressed; but the internal pressure necessary for such an outpouring of popular will simply did not exist. There was no popular will and never had been. Paraguay's "crown" lay in red clay dust, waiting for recovery by a hard-riding hero.

Heroes were timid about asserting themselves. Francia's secretary persuaded four reluctant corps commanders to form an interim junta, with himself as secretary. The junta, suspicious of his ambitions, threw him in jail where the terrified fellow committed suicide. For six months governmental affairs were in confusion; then, on March 12, 1841, Paraguayans to the number of five hundred assembled at Asunción. Behind their deliberations was the persuasive influence of Carlos Antonio López. This congress set up a dual consulate for a three-year period, in which López played the leading role with Colonel Mariano Roque Alonso, a nonentity who retained that status, as his silent partner.

Among the first acts of the Extraordinary Congress were decisions to declare an end to Francia's trade embargo and to sign a commercial treaty with rebellious Corrientes province of Argentina. This treaty aroused the ire of Juan Manuel Rosas, still, unfortunately for Argentina, the dictator at Buenos Aires. When, in December, 1842, the Consulate suggested a treaty with Argentina, Rosas replied by closing the Río de la Plata to Paraguayan shipping. He would reopen the river when and if Corrientes behaved. Paraguay obtained a constitution in 1844 which ended the Consulate and provided for a president; but it came far from establishing a democracy or even a republic in the true sense, although Andrés Gelly vigorously presents a contrary opinion. The president controlled all services of the government, including the Congress. He was king in all but name.

Francia's successor was born about 1787 to a Spanish creole father and a mestiza mother who is said to have been part Guaycurú, or, perhaps, Círilo López was a mestizo and his wife an octoroon. Living in poverty on the outskirts of Asunción, the shoemaker father could not send his rather ugly but bright son, one of eight children, to school. A friend of the family provided the small sum necessary to keep Carlos Antonio in the Colegio de San Carlos in Asunción, where he learned enough to become a teacher and lawyer of sorts. Don Carlos had enough sense to keep his mouth shut about El Supremo most of the time, and he married well. Doña Juana Paula Carillo was no beauty, she loved ease and good food, and her father was well off. This girl, it was rumored, was Carrillo's stepdaughter by whom he had a child. Charles Ames Washburn, in his *History of Paraguay*, repeats with suspicious relish the story that Carlos Antonio received Juana Paula and her *estancia* dowry on condition that he give the child his name. However that may be, the *estancia*, some 120 miles from Asunción, served as a place of exile for López during Francia's last years. Don Carlos and his wife brought forth several children. Francisco Solano was the first, if we discount the scandal about his birth. The second son, Venancio, and the fourth child, Angel Benigno, were to be sacrifices to Francisco Solano's terror in later years. The two daughters, Inocencia and Rafaela, were destined to lose their husbands in a similar manner.

In personal appearance López certainly was no Adonis. Con-

179

temporary foreigners disagree about his personality. One author refers to "chops flapping over his cravat," a face with a porcine expression. Another calls him a stout, respectable-looking chap. One leg apparently reached ground slightly ahead of the other, causing His Excellency to remain seated in the presence of visitors. He wore a hat, indoors and out, for no apparent reason. Suspicion came naturally to him, especially suspicions of foreigners. Although he invited them to Paraguay, used them in his service, and often followed their advice, they never won his confidence completely.

Preferment fell naturally to the López boys. Why not, since their father was dictator? Commerce was an easy road to wealth; herds of cattle and broad pastures for grazing were theirs for the asking. All of the sons and daughters were spoiled brats, but no one, not even their father, dared to put them in their proper places. Francisco Solano was born on July 24, 1826. Only fourteen when El Supremo died, he had little formal education. Marco Antonio Maíz, Miguel Albornoz, and his father seem to have been his principal tutors. After 1845 he had no teachers but is said to have been a tireless reader. He was a brigadier general at eighteen, and at twenty-three he boasted that military science held no secrets unknown to him. This vain but capable braggart became his father's favorite and was, probably, the dictator's principal adviser. Venancio and Benigno, the other sons, were just as capable as Francisco and just as lecherous—especially Venancio, who regarded every pretty girl as fair prey and Paraguay was full of pretty girls.

Ladies of the unlovely López family also displayed remarkable business perspicacity. George Thompson, officer in the Paraguayan army, aide-de-camp to Francisco Solano, Knight of the Order of Merit of Paraguay, knew the family well. In *The War in Paraguay*, Thompson says the distaff side "established an exchange, where torn paper-money, which would no longer pass, was bought at a discount of sixpence on the dollar [peso], and by their connection they changed it at the treasury for new paper at the full value. They also lent money on jewellery at a large profit, and anything they liked they kept, without any reference to the

Carlos Antonio López

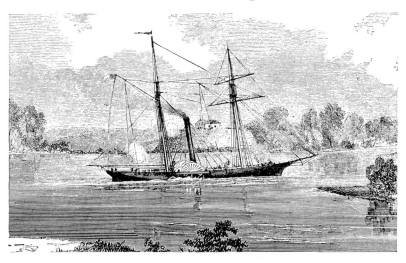

Attack on the *Water Witch*

From *La Plata . . . and Paraguay*
by Thomas J. Page

owner's wishes." They didn't do quite as well as China's "Holy Family" a century later, but their grafting was not bad considering Paraguay's poverty.

Carlos Antonio López inherited a country rapidly increasing in population. Always unreliable estimates report such figures as these: 1795—97,480; 1818—300,000; 1825—200,000; 1838—300,-000; 1840—220,000; 1848—600,000; 1857—1,337,449; and 1865—400,000. One can conclude, with reasonable safety, that there were several thousand people in Paraguay. The 1840 figure comes from a census ordered by Francia and may be accepted as approximately correct. Cecilio Báez, in *Le Paraguay*, accepts the figure 525,000 as about right for 1864.

Captain Richard Francis Burton, in his *Letters from the Battlefields of Paraguay*, asserts that Francia's dictatorship had left only ruins, that López was the organizer of Paraguay. This generalization is hardly tenable in view of Francia's public works program, his insistence on self-sufficiency, his organization of the army, his careful and honest handling of finances. But it is true that Francia, for all of his grand schemes, died without having greatly improved Paraguay's transportation system. López remedied this failure in part by building three short highways and a railway. The latter, one of the first in South America, was begun in 1858 by an English engineer and reached Paraguarí, on its projected route to Villa Rica, in 1861. This railway was to be of great value to Francisco Solano López in the War of the Triple Alliance.

Government under Carlos Antonio was far milder than Paraguay had known for nearly three decades. The new president, *El Excelentísimo*, insisted that he was merely the representative of the supreme government, not the government itself. Still it made little difference to the Paraguayans, used to the exactions of Francia. Their constitution remained a document only; their congress was completely subservient to the Most Excellent One and offered few objections to renewing his term of office, or to rubber-stamping his laws. Nevertheless, it was a kind of progress that Paraguay needed if a reasonable facsimile of democracy was ever to exist in the country.

Carlos Antonio was a dictator whose rule was nearly as absolute as Francia's but he wanted and needed support from the better people. There were still some six hundred prisoners in El Supremo's jails when the consulate began. These victims were liberated quickly. One of the prisoners was Father Marco Antonio Maíz, whom López honored with the title of Professor of Latin and Philosophy. Espionage continued as before, albeit the state police were less efficient. Departments of government, with puppet ministers, relieved Carlos Antonio of many details of administration, while the rudiments of a judicial system appeared for the trial of cases. There were laws and decrees, among which should be noted those that abolished torture, slavery, and confiscation of goods in 1842. Two decades later people were still being tortured, their goods were being confiscated, and slavery definitely existed until 1870. In 1842, likewise, Congress declared with vehemence if not conviction: "The Republic of Paraguay shall never be the patrimony of one person or family." The López family owned and operated Paraguay as a private estate until 1869.

All of El Supremo's contempt for the clergy seems justified and his harsh treatment mild when one contemplates the fathers who sunned their ample figures under Carlos Antonio's favor. Masterman found the Paraguayans steeped in religious ignorance and floundering in idolatry under a bishop who believed that Cain and Abel were sons of Noah. Priests, he declared, were "ignorant and immoral, great cockfighters and gamblers, possessing vast influence over the women, a power which they turn to the basest of purposes." Carlos Antonio did not improve the situation much by having his brother León Basilio, a Franciscan, appointed to a bishopric; but he did give Asunción a new cathedral to replace the old one that dated back 285 years to 1557. Remnants of the mission system had survived many vicissitudes after the Jesuit expulsion in 1767. In eleven of the original establishments that were in Paraguay north of the Paraná, López found some six thousand Guaranís clinging to their old reductions in 1848. Simply by ordering the Indians to disperse, the dictator delivered a *coup de grace* to the hoary vestiges of a famous epoch.

One sees the boast *"Soy Paraguayo, puedo leer!"* ("I am a Paraguayan, I can read!") repeated so frequently that it is easy to credit an educational achievement without much basis in fact. Carlos Antonio did expand a primary school system until by 1860 there were about twenty thousand boys in some five hundred schools, and in 1861 every justice of the peace was ordered "to send to school all children between nine and ten who had no excuse for staying away." Teachers carried on in inadequate houses or sheds without walls. They received mere token salaries, many were ignorant priests, and the others rarely had any training for the profession. Their product could not have been very outstanding. One finds, in fact, complaints that even government officials were unable to penetrate the mysteries of simple arithmetic. If literacy means no more than a mechanical ability to read and to write, a few thousand Paraguayans became semi-literate under López; but illiteracy was worse in 1862 than in 1840. Education languished in spite of certain halfhearted gestures. About 1841, the Congress ordered twelve thousand pesos from Francia's uncollected salary to be given to the Academia Literaria, which Marco Antonio Maíz directed. About 1858, López sent sixteen young men to study in Europe, but he made no great effort to improve secondary or higher education. Private schools had met with little interference from Francia; López hedged them with regulations. Dr. Báez charges López with not wanting Paraguayans to become well educated for fear that they might not continue fit subjects of a tyrant. One might search in vain for a native with an academic degree in any profession. For Paraguayans who could read, the government published a weekly paper, *El Paraguayo Independiente,* which began in April, 1845, apparently to counter Argentine slurs. This paper became *El Semanario* in August, 1852, and continued under the younger López. A complete file of these two official organs, together with the war journals *Lambaré* and *Centinela,* should be worth a small fortune.

Don Carlos loved Paraguay—so much, in fact, that he owned about one-half of the land. The government, synonymous with the dictator, held the titles; income from the land mingled with state revenues until all distinction was lost. As an *estanciero*, López owned 300,000 cattle and thousands of horses. Commerce, too, became concentrated in the presidential family which set extremely profitable prices. Yerba, declared a government monopoly in 1846, yielded fabulous profits when it was bought for one cent a pound and sold at six to twenty-five cents. Although this and other income could be drawn upon freely for personal uses, López kept Paraguay free of public debt. He was the state and the state was his. Income from the yerba monopoly, tithes, stamped paper, a land tax, customs duties, and the treasure inherited from Francia provided ample funds. Enforced peace, relatively fair treatment of foreigners, and increased agricultural production helped to improve commerce to such a degree that the volume of foreign trade tripled from 1850 to 1860. The López trade monopoly could not easily be broken by smuggling. Along the east bank of the Paraguay the dictator built a string of eight *guardias*, each containing a *mangrullo* (watch tower) forty to sixty feet in height, from which troops surveyed the river and land frontiers zealously. A stockade enclosed patches of corn, orange trees, and mandioca. In each of the spaces between the *guardias* were two smaller posts, the *piquetes*, where a squad of soldiers maintained land and water patrols.

Carlos Antonio ended Francia's monkish seclusion for the country in 1845. In spite of a natural antipathy against them, he invited, even urged, foreigners to enter Paraguayan service. Many Englishmen, much to their future discomfiture, accepted the invitation and, as engineers, surgeons, and mechanics, contributed greatly to Paraguayan prosperity. The fortress of Humaitá was planned primarily by two Englishmen and an Austrian, although João Calogeras insists that Brazilians did the work. At any rate, foreigners of English, Irish, French, and German origin provided much of the genius and labor that enabled Francisco Solano López to fight the devastating war of 1864–1870. An English firm, Messrs. J. and A. Blyth, rounded up mechanics for Paraguay, making all manner of false promises. Among them was Alonzo Taylor, a stonemason who went on a four-year contract in 1850. Taylor worked at various jobs—in the arsenal, on the railway station, at Francisco Solano's palace, at the Luque soap works, and elsewhere. He was a victim of the younger López but escaped with his life. The arsenal at Asunción was almost entirely the work of Englishmen.

Foreigners who entered Paraguay submitted to rather rigorous restrictions regarding travel, protection by their governments, marriage with Paraguayan women, and property rights. These handicaps were not sufficient to discourage individual and even mass immigration. A contract signed at Bordeaux by Francisco Solano López, who was in Europe from 1853 to 1854, resulted in a colony of French immigrants, near what is now Villa Hayes, on the Pilcomayo River. Begun as Nuevo Burdeos in 1855, this colony started to fail from the beginning. Its site was unfavorable, its members were poor pioneers for a subtropical land, and López had no interest or no opportunity to make it but one in a series of Chaco colonies that would have ended Indian nuisances. Carlos Antonio, indeed, made life miserable for the French immigrants and did everything possible to make it fail.

Opening formal relations proved to be a difficult and, at times, annoying process, especially with the dictator Rosas. That tyrant of Río de la Plata closed the Paraná to vessels bound for Paraguay in 1845. In the preceding year, López had asked that Rosas recognize Paraguay's independence; Rosas refused the request and López renewed his treaty with Corrientes. Rosas drew the blockade tighter. Brazilians began to meddle in the dispute, hoping to make Paraguay an ally against Rosas and end Argentina's competition for the favors of Uruguay. On December 4, 1845, López declared war against Rosas. He sent an army corps, commanded by Brigadier General Francisco Solano López, then overflowing with the genius and wisdom of nineteen years, to cooperate with Correntino forces. The corps, preceded by a Correntino unit, crossed the Paraná. In January, 1846, General Justo José Urquiza defeated the Correntinos. General López scurried back across the Paraná with his corps intact, its weapons unused. After this experience, Carlos Antonio in September decided to be neutral in the Argentine civil war and accepted the mediation offered by William A. Harris, American chargé in Buenos Aires.

Time and Urquiza worked for him, since six years later Rosas went down to defeat and into exile.

Before this happy event, López had been considerably annoyed with Brazil. His envoy, Juan Andrés Gelly, failed to obtain a satisfactory boundary treaty. Formal relations ended for a few months in 1849, and López even went so far as to eject Brazilian garrisons from territory claimed by Paraguay. López, not certain of either friend or foe, enlarged his army, increased the number of frontier forts, and put pressure on English artisans to get the new arsenal into production. Brazil decided to renew flirtations in 1850 when, on December 25, the two countries signed a treaty of alliance that united the elephant and the gnat against Rosas; in 1852, Rosas was driven from power by Urquiza, but López contributed nothing to that result.

The fall of Rosas ended Paraguay's international solitude. Argentina, Great Britain, France, Sardinia, Prussia, and the United States all signed treaties with López between 1852 and 1860. The treaty with Argentina in 1852 fixed the Paraná as the boundary, surrendering Paraguay's claims to Misiones. Formal diplomacy with Europe and the United States was begun; the great rivers of the Plata system were opened to foreign vessels. Soon an American naval officer, commanding the *Water Witch*, would make the name of his vessel famous in Paraguay's relations with the United States, small though the incident was that precipitated the argument. And twenty-five years later, President Rutherford B. Hayes was to hand down an arbitral decision favoring Paraguay in the dispute with Argentina over part of the Chaco north of the Pilcomayo River. Between these two events, on the heels of the first, an American minister was to be accused as ringleader of a plot to assassinate the younger López. These things lay in the future; the present of 1853 promised a new era for Paraguay.

As a part of his foreign policy, López wanted to make Paraguay known to Europe. He chose Francisco Solano to carry out this task and commissioned him to buy warships and engage foreign artisans to work in Paraguay. Accompanied by his brother Angel Benigno and Juan Andrés Gelly as secretaries, and four officers, López left Asunción June 12, 1853, on the *Independencia del Paraguay*. The party reached Southampton in September, went to London, and then on to Paris to be received by Napoleon III. According to O'Leary's account, López on one occasion put some French troops through their paces, much to Napoleon's amazement. From Paris this Paraguayan legation went to Madrid in 1854 in a vain attempt to obtain a treaty. A small warship, the *Tacuarí*, which López had purchased in London, picked up the legation at Bordeaux on November 11, 1854, and dropped anchor at Asunción on the following January 21. This voyage to Europe, Carlos Pereyra says, "strengthened the perceptions of his fervent patriotism."

The heir apparent returned to Asunción to find his father engaged in a serious dispute with Brazil, which desired free navigation of the Paraguay in order to reach Matto Grosso, and a settlement of the northern boundary. Brazil claimed south to the Apá; Paraguay had equally good if not better title north to the Branco. A Brazilian admiral, Dom Pedro Ferreira de Oliveira, appeared below Humaitá on February 20, 1855, with a menacing force of twenty gunboats bearing 130 pieces of artillery, 2,061 marines, and 3,000 infantry. Knowing this force was on the way, López had sent his son to concentrate 6,000 men at Humaitá, which he fortified hastily, and then told the Brazilian admiral to keep his distance.

López attempted to end his dispute with Brazil over the northern boundary by sending his faithful foreign minister, José Berges, to treat with the wily José Maria da Silva Paranhos. For once the Brazilian met a man of nearly equal astuteness. The treaty signed in April, 1856, provided for discussion about free navigation of the Paraguay and Paraná rivers and for arbitration of the boundary within six years. López did not want to ratify this arrangement that placed in jeopardy territory clearly belonging to Paraguay, but when the Crimean War ended he feared that France would protest vigorously against his treatment of colonists at Nuevo Burdeos. Therefore, he ratified the treaty, fully expecting, as he told the British consul, that war was inevitable. López issued decrees to hamper Brazilian navigation of the Paraguay until Dom Pedro II and his ministers were so sorely vexed that they sent Silva Paranhos to Asunción. This envoy visited Urquiza, just to scare López, signed a treaty freeing the Plata rivers to navigation by all nations, and called for "the closest union between the Empire and the Confederation." When Silva Paranhos reached Asunción in January, 1858, López knew he was isolated. He had his son Francisco treat with the Brazilian and sign a convention agreeing to freedom of navigation. Brazil, by means of skillful but tricky diplomacy, had outwitted López, a fact that Francisco Solano would never forget. In 1859, Brazilian steamers inaugurated regular communication from Rio de Janeiro to Cuyabá in Matto Grosso. The six-year clause in the treaty of 1856 expired with no arbitration of the boundary. López would not go through with it, and Brazil's chargé left Asunción in a huff. There the dispute rested. When the astute dictator lay dying on September 10, 1862, he said to his son Francisco Solano: "There are many pending questions to ventilate; but do not try to solve them by the sword but by the pen, *chiefly with Brazil.*" These were Carlos Antonio's last words. His son, according to Washburn, asked Padre Fidel Maíz: "Is he dead?" And upon being assured of the fact, hastened to a closet to take possession of his father's papers while Benigno López held the old dictator in his arms.

Brazil's six-year treaty with Paraguay was but a play for time in which almost anything might happen. Whatever it was, Brazil did not intend to lose the game. In the meantime, López further increased his army and Brazil strengthened its defenses in Matto Grosso north of the Branco. An armed clash with Brazil over territorial questions definitely was brewing, but when and where it would come could not be foreseen. Carlos Antonio and Francisco Solano must have believed that war was inevitable, although neither wished to precipitate the struggle if a peaceful settlement, meeting Paraguay's demands, could be made. When the war did come, Francisco Solano blundered sadly in antagonizing Argentina, his only possible ally, by betting on the wrong side in Uruguay.

Paraguay's relations with Great Britain reached the tongue-sticking-out stage after a few years of stiff friendship. Two years of life remained in the treaty of 1853 when an impatient English envoy, W. D. Christie, arrived in 1858 to negotiate a renewal. He expected to finish his work in twenty days, twenty days in a country where at least that much time is necessary just to think about getting ready for something. The envoy left without the treaty. Then came the Canstatt affair.

Carlos Antonio liked the theater, even Paraguay's theater. Perhaps a group of natives planned to highlight a performance by shooting His Excellency as an added attraction. At least that is what the dictator asserted on February 18, 1859. One of the score accused of being involved in this uncharitable scheme was Santiago (James) Canstatt—merchant, adventurer, pilot, and dandy—supposedly an agent of Paraguayan exiles in Buenos Aires, and also supposedly half-English in his uncertain origin, who had arrived with a Uruguayan passport in 1852. What really lay behind the trumped-up conspiracy was an embezzlement. One of the Decoud brothers (there were four of them) had been an agent for López in selling maté in Buenos Aires. Over a period of years this agent had stolen a large sum from his employer. When all efforts to lure the embezzler to Asunción failed, the conspiracy was hatched in order that López might confiscate Decoud's property. Unfortunately, too, Carlos Decoud was a rival of Francisco Solano's for the favors of Carmelita. López imprisoned Canstatt, two of the Decouds, and six or seven others. When the British consul, C. A. Henderson, intervened on behalf of Canstatt, who claimed to be an English citizen, the dictator temporized and refused to release him. Edward Thornton, British chargé at Buenos Aires, executed a neat coup. Francisco Solano was in the Argentine capital ready to return home after successfully mediating in a dispute between the Entre Ríos caudillo Urquiza and Buenos Aires. Thornton persuaded the British admiral to use two warships, *Buzzard* and *Grappler*, to apprehend the Paraguayan *Tacuarí*, Captain Pedro Ignacio Meza, on which Carlos Antonio's son was sailing upstream on November 29, 1859. Francisco Solano got ashore, after deciding that the English crew could not be trusted for a fight, went overland to Paraná and then by boat to Asunción where he helped his father rage at the British. Canstatt gained his freedom and an indemnity; the brothers Decoud were shot.

Relations between Paraguay and the United States began cordially in 1845 but soon changed drastically, primarily because of disputes with the enthusiastic Hopkins and over the *Water Witch*. Edward Augustus Hopkins first appeared in Paraguay in 1845 as a special representative of the United States. He came at an opportune time, when López was reversing Francia's former policy of hibernation. Hopkins saw a chance to help the dictator and to make a fortune at the same time. This son of an Episcopalian bishop, one-time church organist and sailor, was a restless rover whose brilliant mind caused him to see great opportunities for commerce with South America. One day after resigning from the navy on June 19, 1845, much to the relief of his superior officers, Hopkins persuaded President James K. Polk to name him special agent to Paraguay. He was twenty-two years old, filled with zeal, quick of temper, enthusiastic, possessed of boundless energy, and daring to the point of rashness. James Buchanan, Polk's secretary of state, instructed his boy agent to determine whether Paraguay should be recognized. In a sense the mission was secret, since Hopkins was not to reveal his official character unless necessary. Special Agent Hopkins, like Cabeza de Vaca before him, walked from Brazil to Asunción, not to save time but to get an intimate knowledge of the country. At the capital Hopkins presented himself as an important man, assured López that the United States would recognize him very soon, and in November, 1845, wrote to Buchanan that Paraguay was "the richest, and the strongest nation of the new world" after the United States.

Hopkins did more than exude optimism during his first visit, which lasted only two months. He offered to mediate in Paraguay's dispute with Rosas, then read the latter a stern lesson on how he should behave. Although later disavowed by William Brent, Jr., American chargé in Buenos Aires, and by Buchanan, Hopkins soared on to greater things: a revival of Bolívar's dream for a league or congress to settle all inter-American disputes. Disavowal of his actions did not daunt this Algeresque adventurer. In the next five years he made long visits to Paraguay and other countries, met prominent people, and explored the Paraguay and Paraná by canoe. "He came," Harold F. Peterson asserts, "to know Paraguay better, perhaps, than any Paraguayan; certainly he was the best-informed American on its politics and resources." At home sporadically, he wrote articles praising Paraguay's possibilities, urging trade relations, and telling its history. He was the foremost "good neighbor" of a decade that brought filibustering expeditions from the United States against Mexico, Central America, and Cuba. Hopkins wanted a good diplomatic service, scientific expeditions, and enforcement of the Monroe Doctrine as its spokesman had intended. For himself, he asked López to grant a fifteen-year monopoly of steam navigation on rivers of Paraguay to a company he would form; a monopoly on industrial machinery to be introduced as a start toward manufacturing bricks, tobacco, lumber, and textiles.

Constantly asking American officials for a consul's commission, Hopkins at last was rewarded with the office on February 14, 1851. At that moment he was in Paraguay about to be named by López as Paraguay's special minister to the United States. The dictator made this appointment on February 25, and instructed his agent at length on what he should do. These instructions stated that Hopkins's long residence in Paraguay, his familiarity with all aspects of the republic, and his high character made him the ideal person to represent López in Washington. Troubles with Argentina, perhaps, caused this search for a new friend. Had not American consuls mediated the dispute in 1846? With war again threatening, Paraguay needed outside support. A minister from the United States would be welcomed, one who might sign a commercial treaty in Asunción. Hopkins was to impress upon the United States Government that Paraguay wanted peace, was tired of isolation and constant preparation for war. Too, he was to find out what agents of Rosas were doing in various countries. A bribe was held out: Hopkins had asked repeatedly for a monopoly of steam navigation on the Paraguay. Such a monopoly should not be given to the citizen of a country that had not recognized

Paraguay's independence; but wouldn't it be splendid if Hopkins should return in a steamer of the best construction? Should his mission succeed, Hopkins would receive a ten-year monopoly. Moreover, since the world was so ignorant about South America's interior, Paraguay would welcome and aid a scientific and nautical expedition. Hopkins was to cause trouble; the scientific expedition would cause trouble; and López' failure to ratify the treaty of 1853 was to cause more trouble.

Back home in 1852, Hopkins pressed for all that López wanted and largely succeeded. He formed the United States and Paraguay Navigation Company with $100,000 of Rhode Island capital. As agent for the corporation, Hopkins was to receive a share of the profits and a moderate salary. As American consul in Asunción and agent for the company, his affairs might have prospered. The river steamer *Paraguay*, first to be sent by the company, carried machinery of various kinds: "steam engines, road scrapers, paper-cutting machines . . . a steam sawmill, a sugar-mill," and many workmen. But the *Paraguay* foundered off Brazil and lost most of the cargo. With what he could salvage, Hopkins arrived at Asunción on October 17, 1853, to be greeted warmly by López. Work of many types began at once under Hopkins's direction, at Asunción and ten miles south of the capital. The steam sawmill was going, bricks were made, tobacco manufactured. Things went smoothly for a while; but in July, 1854, López began to frown severely. The scowl had begun earlier, followed by attempts to appropriate Hopkins's enterprises, and amazing charges that Hopkins was a smuggler. One day a Paraguayan soldier struck Hopkins's brother with a saber. Hopkins, whip in hand and wearing riding clothes, furiously demanded that López punish the offender. López, conciliatory at first, became angry when Hopkins insisted that the *Semanario* publish an account of the punishment. That was the end of Hopkins in Paraguay but not in South America. López revoked his consular exequatur, confiscated the company's charter, and expelled his once great and good friend. Louis Bamberger, who served as American consul in Asunción from December, 1855, to August, 1862, had little to do. The United States and Paraguay Navigation Company complained long and loudly to Washington without effect until 1858, but by that time troubles had arisen involving the *Water Witch.*

One of the objects of Brazil and Argentina's riparian provinces was to open the Plata system to navigation. This was accomplished by Urquiza in a decree dated August 28, 1852. "The seal of many navigable waters, offering communication with the Atlantic to a region of country embracing not less than 800,000 square miles was thus broken." Since there was so little data about the Plata rivers, the United States undertook a scientific survey, which was entrusted to Lieutenant Thomas Jefferson Page in February, 1853. Among other duties, Page was charged with negotiating a treaty of commerce and navigation with Paraguay. The *Water Witch,* assigned for this expedition, was a sidewheel steamer of four hundred tons which drew nine feet of water and was armed with three bronze howitzers. At Rio de Janeiro in April the Brazilian government authorized Page to ascend as far as Albuquerque and later granted permission to explore any tributaries of the Paraguay that might flow through Brazilian territory. Page reached Asunción in October, was well received by López, and gained a promise of aid in fuel and supplies. López, the lieutenant observed, was "highly intelligent, well read, and familiar with the policy of foreign governments; he is also an accomplished, but, as I afterward discovered, unscrupulous diplomatist." Page was still at Asunción when Hopkins arrived bearing a commission as vice-consul.

Page sailed up to Corumbá in Brazilian territory, then turned back to Asunción. López, however, had become suspicious of Hopkins in the meantime and, in a petulant mood, reprimanded Page for having gone beyond Paraguayan limits. Brazil, he said, would soon demand the same privilege. Nevertheless, López permitted Page to proceed with explorations of the Bermejo in a smaller vessel built at Asunción. Page had great success in charting streams and in collecting specimens of minerals and animal life. When López had become so seriously involved with Hopkins that the company was forced to cease operations, Page tried to mediate the trouble. López would not listen to him. Hopkins and his companions prepared to leave on the *Water Witch* if López refused to issue passports. The dictator consented, however, merely requiring that members of the company obtain passports and a permit from the *aduana* (customs) to ship out their property. Before the men could get away, police mistreated some of them and Page complained to López without effect. When Hopkins was ready to go, he discovered that López wanted all of the company's papers, including deeds to land purchased. In spite of all difficulties, Page extricated the men safely. López, he reported, was frightened. Expecting a bombardment, he was prepared to run away in his carriage, an act so completely out of character that the story is probably false.

López had signed a treaty with the United States on March 4, 1853, and had ratified it a few days later. Technical errors were so numerous that the United States Senate corrected them and Secretary of State William L. Marcy charged Page with exchanging ratifications of the corrected version; but when Page's messenger, in October, 1854, carried to Asunción a note in English without its Spanish translation, Paraguay's foreign minister refused to read it. In November, 1856, Commissioner Richard Fitzpatrick from Buenos Aires explained the corrections to Foreign Minister Nicolás Vázquez; the Paraguayan informed him that López had ratified the treaty in its original form and there the matter rested.

Once the *Water Witch* was out of sight, López issued orders closing Paraguayan rivers to foreign warships. Page obtained supplies in Buenos Aires preparatory to exploring the Paraná, a stream that was as international as a river could be. He himself went up the Salado at the end of January, 1855, leaving Lieutenant William N. Jeffers to sail the *Water Witch* up the Paraná. A few miles beyond the confluence, the Paraná-Paraguay junction, was the Paraguayan post of Itapirú. When the vessel was opposite this post on February 1, it was challenged in Spanish. Jeffers, after getting his ship off a sand bar, followed the channel near the Paraguayan shore and refused to stop. A shot from the fort killed the helmsman and carried away the tiller. Jeffers returned the fire, probably killing several Paraguayans, then sailed back to report. Page, of course, was furious and wanted to knock Itapirú into rubble. He informed Commodore W. D. Salter of this insult; but Salter, who had the *Germantown* and *Savannah* at Rio, refused to take any action.

Complaints from the United States and Paraguay Navigation Company were now linked with the treaty affair and the *Water Witch* incident. President Buchanan, in his message to Congress in December, 1857, complained of these matters and asked for authority to deal firmly with Carlos Antonio López. Congress in June, 1858, voted $10,000 to pay expenses of a chastisement, and on October 17, James B. Bowlin sailed from New York to set matters right. Bowlin was not lonesome. Twenty-five hundred men, on a score of warships armed with two hundred guns, went along. Toward the end of 1858, Bowlin reached Asunción escorted by a small part of his fleet. Things went along smoothly. Paraguay agreed to pay $10,000 to survivors of the *Water Witch's* helmsman; a treaty, granting navigation of the Paraguay, was signed on February 4, 1859; claims of the United States and Paraguay Navigation Company were to be arbitrated. Bowlin's instructions authorized him to accept $500,000 cash indemnity or to insist on $1,000,000 if force were necessary. When General Urquiza heard of the expedition's arrival at Montevideo, he became alarmed because of possible ill effects on Entre Ríos of a Paraguayan-American war, so Washburn believed. Someone, maybe Bowlin himself, let a copy of the instructions get to Urquiza who either sent or took them to López, urging him to avoid a conflict and to haggle for a low indemnity. Thus, López was well prepared to deal with Bowlin. Denying that Paraguay owed Hopkins anything, still the dictator offered to pay $250,000 to be rid of the affair. Bowlin, as naïve a negotiator as ever set foot in Paraguay, magnanimously offered to submit the case to arbitration.

Hopkins and his friends lost out completely in proceedings of the arbitral commission which met at Washington in June, 1860, to hear complaints presented by the company's attorneys. J. Mandeille Carlisle defended Paraguay against claims for more than $1,000,000 in real and imaginary damages. Cave Johnson and José Berges, who heard the case, decided that Paraguay did not owe the company anything. Hopkins, they held, had failed to comply with a decree of August, 1854, that required every foreign commercial agent and enterprise to obtain a Paraguayan license. Hopkins actually had asked for a license, but López had denied it. The commissioners refused to take cognizance of a mere supposition that Paraguay would issue licenses to all who applied. Berges contended that in buying a sawmill site at San Antonio, Hopkins had not paid the real owners; moreover, in this purchase and others the company had not obtained the government's consent. Johnson rapped the company's collective knuckles for clamoring about its losses until the United States had taken up the matter, for the "prodigious if not criminal exaggerations of demands that increased constantly, thanks to its loose bookkeeping methods; the malevolent and premeditated attacks upon the Paraguayan president and people—all for the simple purpose of putting money into the claimant's pockets."

There was nothing criminal about the company's demands, although they were exaggerated. Pressed by Hopkins, President Buchanan asked the Senate to review the arbitral decision; the Senate, knowing that it lacked power to do so, quite properly refused. The company did not rest. President Lincoln, in July, 1861, instructed Charles Ames Washburn to take up the matter; López refused to reopen the case. After the Paraguayan defeat in the War of the Triple Alliance, Secretary Bayard told Chargé E. Bacon to present the subject once more. This time Paraguay's foreign minister, José S. Decoud, agreed on August 12, 1887, to pay $90,000 in gold to the company; but the Congress refused to vote the appropriation. A new protocol in May, 1888, was again rejected, and Hopkins died in Washington a few months later. For the United States to have pressed a claim of this sort, after an adverse arbitral decision, was disgraceful, no matter how stupid Bowlin had been.

When Carlos Antonio, fat and aging, knew that life was drawing to a close, he prepared a decree that in effect bequeathed the government to his son Francisco Solano. This decree was perfectly legal since the subservient Congress had granted López the right to name a temporary successor; but Francisco Solano López was disqualified by the Constitution, which stated that the government was not to be the patrimony of any family. For many years Paraguay had been a patrimony of the López family and would continue to be under Francisco Solano.

Paraguay's astute dictator died on September 10, 1862. With great pomp he was buried before the altar in the church of La Santísima Trinidad four miles from the capital. With him was buried Paraguay, for eight years later the people of his country were on the verge of extinction. Carlos Antonio had tried to be a wise dictator. He had ended Francia's policy of seclusion, improved transportation, built an army, increased foreign trade, and achieved diplomatic success in contests with powerful adversaries. He was, probably, the best of the three dictators who ruled the country for more than fifty years. In the *Bulletin* of the Pan American Union, a journal that exudes honeyed phrases about everything and nothing bad about anything, María Irene Johnson wrote of Carlos Antonio: "He had an extraordinary soul; it dreamed of greatness, and made titanic efforts to surmount obstacles, to overcome difficulties. He was not a product of his environment; rather he led a redemptive crusade against it." Most of this exuberant encomium is sheer nonsense. No one was more Paraguayan, more a product of his environment.

# CHAPTER XIII

# Francisco Solano López and Power Politics

ACCORDING to the terms of Carlos Antonio's decree, a triumvirate was to rule until the people should choose a new president. Francisco Solano as vice-president dominated not only the triumvirate but also the Congress that met to settle the succession. His infantry and cavalry surrounded the government house, prepared for any eventuality. Two men who dared to suggest that Paraguay's constitution made him ineligible missed the next day's session and all others. One should note that some writers deny the triumvirate story and maintain that Francisco seized the government immediately after his father's death. The presbyter Fidel Maíz is authority for the statement that Carlos Antonio first named his younger son Benigno as vice-president to summon the Congress, but that Francisco Solano hurried from Humaitá when he heard of the appointment and forced the old dictator to name him instead. However it really happened, the second López took office formally on October 16, 1862, as Supreme Chief and General of the Armies of the Republic of Paraguay. The new Supremo delayed only a few weeks in beginning his reign of suppression. By December, 1862, Fidel Maíz and more than four hundred others whose loyalty was suspect, were in prison or under guard, and among them was Benigno López who suffered home arrest on one of his *estancias*.

An objective attitude about this second López is almost im-

198

possible to achieve. Many volumes have been written to condemn him as the vilest excretion of his country; a few have gone to the other extreme. In this latter class falls that rhapsody by Juan E. O'Leary, *El Mariscal Solano López,* a panegyric all the more remarkable since its author's mother and many relatives were tortured by López. Rebaudi attributes the change in O'Leary, from a bitter anti-Lopista to a craven worshiper, to a gift by Enrique López of fifty leagues of land. O'Leary's introduction should be quoted in full, not because of its truthfulness but as an example of blind ecstasy. We may sample a few effusive passages: "Ridiculed by the diatribe of his enemies, exalted by the praises of his admirers, he has known in life and afterward in death the most resplendent heights of glory and the deepest shadows of condemnation. Meanwhile, his cyclopean figure has remained alone but firmly set on its high pedestal, defying the hurricane of passion and the destructive action of time, without anything being able to cast it down, nor anyone being able to detract from his tragic grandeur. . . . Over his gigantic tomb, over his mountain mausoleum, there has always burned . . . 'a funeral lamp that no wind will ever extinguish.' And through its tremulous and uncertain splendors posterity has seen him as in a dim twilight, limned magnificently on the far horizon, treading the earth with his human feet, touching the sky with his great brow thoughtful in Promethean sorrow." Let San Martín and Bolívar stand aside with bared heads while Francisco Solano López passes in glory, his marshal's baton borne on a platter of diamonds by Dom Pedro II. There is a new star in the heavens, another sparkling gem in that divine crown of immortals.

Paraguay's third dictator had a character more than just complex. Masterman, who knew him well and hated him intensely, still described him rather impartially: "Personally, he is not a man of very commanding presence, being but five feet four in height, and extremely stout—latterly most unwieldily so. His face is very flat, with but little nobility of feature, head rather good, but narrow in front, and greatly developed posteriorly. There is a very ominous breadth and solidity in the lower part of his face, a peculiarity derived from his Guaycuru ancestry, and which gives the index to his character—a cruel, sensual face, which the eyes, placed rather too close together, do not improve. His manners when he was pleased were remarkably gracious; but when enraged . . . his expression was perfectly ferocious; the savage Indian broke through the thin varnish of civilization, as the Cossack shows in an angry Russian. His address was good, both in public and private, although his articulation was imperfect from the loss of the lower teeth, and he spoke in so low a tone . . . that only those standing near him could catch the purport of what he said." Lieutenant Colonel George Thompson knew López through a residence of eleven years in Paraguay and served him faithfully in peace and in war. This self-taught military engineer reveals the dictator as a lover of luxury, fine clothes, good food, delicate wines, and expensive tobacco. He was selfish, morose, lazy, sly, dignified, proud, strong willed, and intelligent. López could speak Spanish, French, Guaraní, and some English. In manners the dictator could be smooth, as suave as any cultured European, a gentleman outwardly at least. There was room in his heart for affection, which he showed toward Madame Lynch's children if not toward his other numerous offspring.

Not even O'Leary could say that his hero's life was as pure and chaste as snow on a mountain top. Before a small cottage beyond the capital, in the days of Carlos Antonio's dictatorship, there was a black wooden cross decorated with delicate lace and beautiful flowers. When no one was near to see, a sobbing girl, lovely and dressed in mourning, knelt at this roadside shrine to vent her anguish in solitude. She was Carmelita, once the belle of Asunción, the betrothed of Don Carlos Decoud. Francisco Solano's passion led him to suggest a liaison which Carmelita scorned. Shortly after this rebuke, Don Carlos Decoud and his brother were arrested, charged with plotting to assassinate the dictator. They were, of course, executed. The naked body of Don Carlos was thrown into the street before his mother's home. There Carmelita saw it. The black cross became a monument to the murdered lover and Carmelita's sobs blended with the eternal mournful plaint of the lonely *urutaú*, a warning to other girls who might resist Francisco's lecherous advances.

Carmelita was but one among brave girls who defied the López family. More pitiful, if possible, was the case of Pancha Garmendia, an orphan who grew to be "the pride and jewel of Asunción." Many young men vied for her hand, but all were frightened away by Francisco Solano, who longed to despoil her as he had so many others. Panchita preferred death's embrace. The scorned profligate waited until he became president to gain his revenge. Then he imprisoned Pancha Garmendia, subjected her to torture of the worst sort, but failed to break her spirit. At last two lance thrusts ended her life. This maid of Asunción, pure to the end, was eulogized by Padre Fidel Maíz, himself a torturer without equal: "Pancha Garmendia, the beautiful and unfortunate Pancha, is the honor and the glory of her sex. She is the maid of Paraguay as Joan of Arc is the maid of Orleans"

Any effort to arrive at an appreciation of Francisco Solano's character must take into account his bestiality during the War of the Triple Alliance. Suspicious of everyone about him, the fiendish dictator put hundreds of innocent victims to torture before execution ended their agony. Ordinary flogging, heavy manacles, starvation, and other modes of torture were but child's play compared with the *uruguayana* that played a prominent role in breaking men's backs and wills. Alonzo Taylor, an English stonemason, described this device and its use from personal experience: "I sat on the ground with my knees up, my legs were first tied tightly together, and then my hands behind me, with the palms outwards. A musket was then fastened under my knees; six more of them, tied together in a bundle, were then put on my shoulders, and they were looped together with hide ropes at one end; they then made a running loop on the other side, from the lower musket to the other; and two soldiers hauling on the end of it, forced my face down to my knees, and secured it so." After a few hours in this device, a prisoner generally was willing to confess his guilt to anything. If, as it sometimes did, the *uruguayana* treatment failed, the prisoner's fingers could be crushed with a mallet.

During the war, when all but López knew Paraguay was beaten beyond question, the dictator believed he had uncovered

201

a gigantic conspiracy against his life and country, which he identified as one. To the twisted mind of López, a hideous spider sat at the center of the web, a spider named Charles Ames Washburn, American minister to Paraguay. Hundreds were arrested and executed because of this imaginary plot. According to official count, 596 prisoners perished from June 19 to December 14, 1868. No compassion, no consideration for sister or brother, for age or sex, interfered with the president's sadistic rampage. His sniveling underlings, fearful for their own lives, zealously endeavored to excel in a cruelty they knew was pleasing to their master. They were but agents of a vile monster whom no special pleading can excuse.

Earlier in the conflict, López became furious at defeats suffered by his army. Dr. Báez wrote: "He established his residence at San Fernando; from there, he organized the tortures and massacres of imaginary conspirators and traitors to the country. According to the authentic journal of the Chief of the General Staff, General [Francisco Isidoro] Resquín, and the assertion of Don José Falcon, the number of executions of distinguished persons for imaginary crimes reached 1,000, without counting the seven or eight thousand soldiers shot for minor offenses, and the hundreds of families sacrificed by the lancers, for no purpose except to despoil them of their jewels and silver. Among the tyrant's victims, one counts hundreds of distinguished women and young ladies, whose only crime was in being mothers, wives, daughters or sisters of supposed conspirators." These are harsh words, but Paraguay's outstanding historian did not stop there. "He who had given a first impression of an active and energetic man, threw himself into the arms of a favorite, the Englishwoman Elisa Alicia Lynch; he abandoned the fate of the nation to the hazards of a war that he had provoked." Nor could one trust the dictator's promises: "Since López had drafted all males over eleven years of age, women were compelled to volunteer for work in the fields to feed and clothe the soldiers. They cultivated mandioca, corn, and calabashes to feed them; to clothe them, they cultivated cotton. The tyrant issued decrees, offering prizes to the poor women who wove that textile; those prizes were never paid to anyone, and all war work, during five years, was given free by the people. During that time, the tyrant forcibly collected gold and silver coin and family jewels to enrich the mother of his bastards."

His critics charge, in brief, that López used the war as an excuse to enrich himself at the expense of wealthy families, drummed up the conspiracy hoax to eliminate property holders, ordered consuls abroad to send money in their possession to various European accounts, seized religious vessels for his private use, sent government money to London for his private account, used the army to build houses for his concubines and children, and constantly appropriated public money for Eliza Lynch.

Severe critics of Francisco Solano have acknowledged his occasional generosity, his offhand clemency to prisoners, his gestures of liberality. They have also accused him of harboring a profound jealousy and distrust toward his brothers and other relatives, a jealousy certainly unbecoming a man who saw in his mirror the Napoleon of Paraguay. Without undue exercise of the imagination, one may admit his absolute loyalty to his country. Ideas of treason, if at any time he had them, never were revealed in his acts. Brazil and Argentina were "ever ready to build for him a bridge of gold" during the War of the Triple Alliance; López, although addicted to the good living that could have been his for the rest of his life by accepting their offer, scorned all overtures of that kind. The dictator coddled a love for finery, for scarlet ponchos fringed in gold, boots of the best leather, silver spurs, rich furniture, and even a crown Napoleonic in pattern. A plaster model of the royal headgear reached Buenos Aires from Paris. Perhaps the crown was the idea of Madame Lynch, who undoubtedly preferred to be an emperor's rather than a dictator's mistress.

A beautiful adventuress mounted on a spirited horse led Paraguayan women into battle during the War of the Triple Alliance, according to absurd legend. This fabled equestrienne was Eliza Alicia Lynch, a brilliant and lovely (if somewhat damaged) colleen who was born in Ireland of a good family in 1835. At the age of fifteen she married a French officer, Jean Louis Armand de

Quatrefages, and lived with him for three years. After her husband left her, probably for good reason, Eliza made a Russian aristocrat happy, according to stories circulated by her detractors. Eliza's story is different. Her health was bad, her marriage was not entirely legal. She went back to England to live for a while with her mother, then stayed with her uncle and his family. She then went to Paris with her mother, lived chastely, and met López in 1853. The future dictator fell in love with Eliza; and she, ambitious to the extreme, saw in the bemedaled Paraguayan the vehicle that would carry her off to castles of paradise floating on clouds of gorgeous hue. She became his mistress, followed him to Paraguay, and amazed natives with her resplendent gowns, striking beauty, linguistic skill, sumptuous dinners, and ability to carry champagne with dignity.

Madame Lynch, as she was called, had comfortable quarters in what is now a wing of the Hotel Paraguay on Calle España; at least, that is the story. She bore López some five or six children, kept him tolerant if not in love, and remained fairly serene in spite of an increasingly stout figure and a "duplicity of chin." As a "woman on horseback," Eliza was no more of an Amazon than Helen of Troy. It is, likewise, ridiculous to say that she fought through the Paraguayan War by her lover's side. She did stay with him at Humaitá, fled with him to the Aquidabán, and at last buried him with one of her sons in a shallow grave at Cerro Corá. But as to fighting, that is another matter. Perhaps she was fond of her paramour monster. Without him, her position in Asunción's society was uncomfortable, since the better people usually married before their children were born. Madame Lynch, denied the comfort of a formal liaison, had to be content with a somewhat less secure status.

Eliza, young and beautiful, arrived in Paraguay early in 1855 with a capital of 800 ounces in gold. She multiplied this modest sum as though by magic during fourteen years. Besides many houses, she acquired 437,500 hectares south of the Pilcomayo and 5,000,000 hectares east of the Paraguay through gifts from her paramour. In 1865, when warfare threatened disaster, López sent large sums out of the country on the French warship *La*

*Decidée.* Still other treasures in jewels, gold, and silver were said to have been sent to the United States, where López and his mistress may have expected to spend their last years. When Asunción was evacuated in February, 1868, many families deposited their remaining valuables in the American Legation, where even Eliza kept several chests for a time. During the conspiracy of 1868, valuables of hundreds of victims, tortured by Padre Fidel Maíz and Major Silvestre Aveiro, passed into Madame Lynch's hands and were sent out from Angostura at the end of the year. Indeed, Charles A. Washburn charges that hundreds of people were tortured and killed to enrich "this bad, selfish, pitiless woman." When General M. T. McMahon, Washburn's successor as United States minister, left Paraguay in July, 1869, he carried, Cecilio Báez charges, 4,400 ounces of gold and 5,600 silver dollars to be deposited in the Bank of England to the account of Dr. William Stewart. The physician had given Eliza a statement that the treasure belonged to her. Chests that could not be exported were buried along the route López followed in his last flight, and those who buried them went down with the treasure. Even today Paraguayans speak of ghosts that guard the hidden treasures of López.

Knowing that his crimson career was drawing to a close, López gave to General McMahon a codicil dated December 23, 1868, bequeathing all of his property to Eliza Lynch. At the end of the war in 1870, that adventuress was deported to Europe. She lived in France for several years, ran through her wealth, did penance at Jerusalem, and finally died in poverty. No one exercised over Francisco Solano López an influence greater than Eliza's. She was faithful to her master and played a leading part in the tragedy of Paraguay.

Asunción must have seemed rather drab to Eliza Lynch after Parisian excitements, but Francisco Solano promised to change things. He wanted to be a builder. Grandiose structures must rise in Asunción to proclaim to the world how great was López. A theater of walls and arches, but without a roof since the architect didn't know how to put one on; the palace, imposing but incomplete; a railway station, post office, and customs house, all in various stages of construction, remained as monuments to hope if not to its fulfillment. The city's twenty thousand people still lived in one-story houses as they had in the time of Francia. A languishing river trade used the dilapidated quay that was separated from the city by a muddy stream. An old bridge over this obstacle threatened to collapse at any moment. On the right, as one crossed the bridge going toward the heart of town, stood the half-completed arsenal. López wisely refused to be his own engineer and had employed an Englishman, W. Whytehead, to supervise the work; but Whytehead died about 1865, leaving the building unfinished.

Beyond it was a colonnaded hospital, where George Frederick Masterman, author of the fascinating *Seven Eventful Years in Paraguay*, presided as chief military apothecary and lecturer on materia medica. The presence of an eight-gun battery between the hospital and the river caused Masterman considerable concern. The customs house, "so hideous, that one can only regret that it was ever commenced," apparently bothered him even more. He, like the Robertsons and other consciously superior Englishmen, found his sense of proportion outraged by Paraguayan inattention to form and symmetry. Francia's city planning had remedied some defects in street patterns, since the rectangular system made for fairly uniform roadways, though sand still substituted for pavement. Ravines, such an eyesore to El Supremo, continued their errant ways and served as efficient sewers in wet weather. Along these streets were lined the low houses that reminded the traveler of Pompeii with their Roman-style bricks, thick walls, large doorways, pillared courtyards, and beamed ceilings.

Captain Burton, who visited Asunción during the War of 1864–70, found little in the capital to praise: "Public conveniences are nowhere; the streets are wretched; drainage had not been dreamed of; and every third building, from the chapel to the theatre, is unfinished. The shops were miserable stores, like those of the 'camp-towns' in the Argentine Republic. The post-office consisted of two small rooms in a private house. The barracks and churches, the dungeons, and the squares for reviews, are preposterous. Every larger house belongs to the reigning family Lopez. The lieges, if not in the caserne or the violon, must content themselves with the vilest ranchos, lean-tos, and tiled roofs supported, not by walls, but by posts. Nor may they display their misery: it must be masked from the eye of opulence by the long dead brick walls that connect palace with palace. A large and expensively-built arsenal, riverside docks, a tramway, and a railway, have thrown over the whole affair a thin varnish of civilization; but the veneering is of the newest and the most palpable: the pretensions to progress are simply skin-deep, and the slightest scratch shows under the Paraguayan Republic the Jesuiticized Guarani."

Let the Englishman deprecate as he might, the "Jesuiticized Guarani" was not an unlovely person. Generous, happy in a childlike simplicity, fond of music and dancing, keenly aware of life's brevity and determined to use its opportunities to the utmost, the Paraguayan men and women possessed a dignity and a generosity of spirit worthy of admiration by the most sophisticated of people. Common men and women dressed simply and comfortably. Thompson's description of their dress is characteristic of foreign comment and observation: "The Paraguayan costume was, for the men, a tall black hat, such as is at present worn in Europe, a shirt with the front and cuffs beautifully embroidered, a pair of white drawers, with a foot of fringe down to the ground, and three or four inches of embroidery above the fringe. Over these a 'chiripa' or sort of sheet, wrapped round the legs from the waist down to above the embroidery on the drawers, and secured by a scarlet silk sash; no shoes, and a 'poncho' hanging over the shoulder. The women wore a white chemise with short sleeves, embroidered and edged with lace, and the top of the chemise embroidered all round in black silk. They wore nothing over their chemise down to the waist, where a scarlet sash secured a white petticoat embroidered with a broad black band halfway down. They had no shoes. These costumes were only worn by the country people and by those of the lower class in town. The women's chemises, called *tüpoi*, are very beautiful and look charming. The ladies and gentlemen in town dressed like Europeans, and the ladies showed generally very good taste. They were very ladylike and graceful, and anyone going to a ball in Asuncion might have almost imagined himself in Paris."

Paraguayans could have been happy had it not been for their political immaturity that gave rise to oppressive dictatorships, and the interplay of rivalry between Brazil and Argentina. The Brazilian historian, Antonio Baptista Pereira, in his essay *Civilización contra barbarie,* cleverly states: "Francia was the major premise, Carlos Antonio López the minor, and Solano López the conclusion of the Paraguayan syllogism." This syllogism ended in the War of the Triple Alliance, a conflict caused by power politics in the Plata basin. What López might have done had there been no war is an interesting and, of course, entirely useless conjecture.

One must not suppose that Francisco Solano López alone caused the war that all but destroyed his country. The late Dr. Pelham Horton Box, in *The Origins of the Paraguayan War,* displayed extraordinary energy and skill in presenting the most reasonable explanation of the war's causes that has appeared in print. There were long-standing disputes with Argentina over freedom of river navigation and boundaries. Paraguay, by being Brazil's tool, had allied herself with Corrientes against the Argentine Confederation. By refusing to accept the Apá as a northern boundary and by failing to help in the overthrow of Rosas, Paraguay incurred Brazil's enmity. Twice, in 1850 and again in 1855, Carlos Antonio López had ejected Brazilian garrisons from territory claimed by Paraguay, and war was narrowly averted in the latter year. Brazil had forced Paraguay to grant free navigation of its river in 1858. These matters alone would have been enough to cause war. Add to them Paraguay's loss of the missions south of the Paraná to Argentina and Brazil, and the Uruguayan political vortex, and one wonders why war had not come sooner.

*La República Oriental del Uruguay,* the Eastern Republic of the Uruguay, went through birth pains agonizing in the extreme. The story has been told over and over again, but there is no way to make this complicated account either simple or sensible. Fortunately, and perhaps by doing violence to historical canons, one may pass over the long rivalry of Argentina and Brazil with generalizations about Paraguay's position in that conflict. Francia, by steering clear of foreign entanglements, avoided involvement in Uruguay's political chaos. Carlos Antonio López was not so wise, but he managed to end his dictatorship without more than a gesture at war with disunited Argentina. Very nearly involved in the league to overthrow Rosas, he recognized the danger in time to maintain a precarious neutrality. Francisco Solano López possessed little of his father's wisdom and luck, and as a result started the most destructive war in the history of South America.

After the fall of Rosas in 1852, Buenos Aires refused to enter the Argentine Confederation, and seven years later went to war against the other provinces. Defeated in this attempt, Buenos Aires accepted mediation by Carlos Antonio López long enough to make another effort to defeat Urquiza's Gauchos. Francisco Solano, acting as mediator, won high praise from Bartolomé Mitre and many others for his efforts. Buenos Aires had become the asylum of Venancio Flores and his extreme *Colorados* (Reds), who had lost out in the effort to control Uruguay. Mitre and other leaders of Buenos Aires promoted their plans to regain power in Montevideo. There were raids from Buenos Aires against Montevideo, from Montevideo against Buenos Aires. Extreme cruelty by the Uruguayan *Blancos* (Whites) in disemboweling captives early in 1858 lost them much support. Finally, the Blanco government severed relations with Buenos Aires and asked Urquiza and Dom Pedro II for aid in 1858 against their rival across the Plata. Then followed a short reconciliation between Buenos Aires and the Argentine Confederation. Mitre became governor of Buenos Aires in 1860, fought Urquiza in 1861, and by February, 1862, was in control of nearly all of Argentina and became president later in the year. Nevertheless, Argentine unity had not yet been achieved.

Venancio Flores, the Uruguayan Colorado exile, and his friends had fought well for Mitre. The next step would be to deal with the Uruguayan Blanco party. Soon Flores was preparing an expedition to overthrow the Blanco President Bernardo P. Berro, who fully appreciated Uruguay's vulnerability, exposed as the country was to Argentina and Brazil. Uruguayans and Brazilians on the frontier had long engaged in murdering one another for various reasons or for none other than sheer deviltry. Since Berro had observed strict neutrality in 1862, a fact recognized by Mitre, the Argentine president promised that he would try to prevent Uruguay's peace from being disturbed. But how could he pay his debt to Venancio Flores and keep this promise? How could he prevent Urquiza and Entre Ríos from supporting the Blancos? Observing preparations by Flores, the Blancos sent Dr. Octavio Lapido to protest to Mitre. Prove that Flores is plotting a revolt, Mitre told him, and I'll intern my great and good friend. Lapido produced proof, and even the newspapers printed enough to have convinced the most confirmed skeptic; Mitre did nothing, perhaps because he knew that President Berro had tricked Flores into replying to an invitation from a Colorado in Uruguay to join a revolt, perhaps because *porteño* opinion overwhelmingly supported Flores. While Mitre was in Rosario, where he went to inaugurate the Córdoba railway in April, 1863, Flores landed in Uruguay. On the night of April 19, he and three companions galloped off to join Gaucho friends. Soon five hundred of these hard-riding cowboy fighters were heading for the Brazilian frontier, where, they knew, others would gather to aid them. Still, in spite of open sympathy in Buenos Aires, Mitre and his foreign minister, Dr. Rufino de Elizalde, knew nothing officially. Dr. Andrés Lamas went from Montevideo to complain about gunrunning to Flores, and, although he found Elizalde evasive, he followed instructions from Montevideo to press the matter. European diplomats joined the verbal fray, but the American minister, Robert C. Kirk, held a discreet silence.

Events moved swiftly after June, 1863. In that month Uruguay seized contraband of war on an Argentine vessel; Argentina demanded reparation; Uruguay was conciliatory; Argentina was bellicose, refused to arbitrate the dispute, and threatened war. On June 22, Argentina blockaded the Uruguay River; on June 23, Uruguay broke off diplomatic relations; on June 29, the two countries agreed to salute each other with twenty-one guns. Mitre had backed up just short of war because he did not trust

Urquiza, who might lead Entre Ríos to help Uruguay, and perhaps because Uruguay had told Francisco Solano López about the trouble. President Berro had sent Lapido to Asunción, where the envoy promised López an equal part with Brazil in mediating the dispute. Mitre refused to accept this upstart as a mediator with a scornful "One might as well invoke the mediation of China." So the protocol, arranged by Brazil's minister João Alves Loureiro, lapsed—primarily because of Uruguayan commitments to López. Smuggling to Flores continued. An expedition, captured by Uruguay in November, 1863, caused another rupture in relations. Mitre ordered forts built on Martín García Island at the mouth of the Uruguay and increased his army. In March, 1864, Mitre sent José Mármol to effect an agreement with Brazil.

Dom Pedro II inherited a three-fold policy and carried it on consistently: encroachment on Paraguayan territory, intervention in Uruguay, and opposition to Argentina's plan for resurrecting the old viceroyalty of La Plata. Many Colorados had taken refuge in southern Brazil, ready and anxious to help Flores; many Brazilian Gaucho generals, later famous in the War of the Triple Alliance, were there and could not be ignored. It is possible that Rio Grande slave owners hoped to see slavery re-established in Uruguay, and that they would profit greatly from holdings in that republic as well as from capturing slaves who had sought freedom there. General Felipe Souza Netto, helping Flores with one thousand Gauchos, went to Rio late in 1863 to impress his desires upon Pedro II's government which had been attempting to remain neutral in the Uruguayan civil war. Brazilian officials resented Uruguay's attempt to drag López into the quarrel but continued efforts to prevent the civil conflict from spreading and refused to pick a quarrel with Argentina. Things changed early in 1864 when imperialistic Liberals dominated Brazil's Chamber of Deputies. With General Netto abetting them, these fighting cocks demanded a reckoning with Uruguay. Mármol from Argentina was in Rio de Janeiro, assuring Brazil of Mitre's friendship. In May, a special envoy, José Antonio Saraiva, arrived in Uruguay from Brazil to announce that a Brazilian army on the frontier would prevent Uruguayan violations of the border and to demand reparations for damages. Vice-Admiral Joaquím Márquez Lisboa, the Baron de Tamandaré, went to Montevideo with a squadron of five ships at the same time.

Uruguay's president was now Atanasio Cruz Aguirre, a patriotic but rash Blanco, whose advisers counted heavily on López for support against both Brazil and Argentina. Don Juan José de Herrera, Uruguay's foreign minister, has the doubtful honor of being the architect of this scheme, although López was far from reluctant. Saraiva was tactful in handling his task. He knew that Uruguay's civil war was but a sputtering fuse on a bomb whose explosion would shake South America. In an exchange of notes, Herrera emerged with a measure of triumph: he made Brazil's demands appear ridiculous, a sad error in view of imperialistic clamor in Rio. Saraiva made ready for every eventuality by asking and receiving broad powers in an attempt to preserve peace.

Argentina entered the picture again. At Mitre's request, Britain's minister, Edward Thornton, accompanied Elizalde to Montevideo for talks with Saraiva and Herrera in June, 1864. Time was fast running out. Thornton, Saraiva, and Elizalde, mobilizing public opinion in favor of peace in the civil war, succeeded in persuading President Aguirre to grant favorable terms to Flores and to promise a free election. Flores accepted on June 18 and a truce began in Uruguay; but, since Aguirre refused to reconstitute his ministry before Flores disbanded his troops, civil war was resumed. Saraiva had failed to pacify Uruguay, but he could make Argentina friendly to Brazil. Upon conferring with Mitre, he suggested joint intervention. Mitre would not go so far but promised not to oppose Brazilian intervention. Now Andrés Lamas, Uruguay's great envoy to Buenos Aires, warned Aguirre that Brazil would present an ultimatum. His advice to anticipate its terms was sound, but Aguirre refused to take it. Saraiva delivered the ultimatum on August 4, 1864; before the end of August, he signed a protocol with Argentina bringing the two countries into agreement on Uruguay. On August 26, 1864, a Brazilian gunboat fired on Uruguay's steamer *Villa del Salto*. The long-feared war had begun, "the great storm that," as Dr. Box observed, "beginning with the 'coercive measures' of Brazil against

212

Madame Lynch

Francisco Solano López

their small neighbor, was to sweep for half a decade across the lands of the Río de la Plata in a drama of war and revolution, of blood and tears, from Montevideo to the ultimate fastnesses of Cerro Cora."

Well might one wonder what Francisco Solano López had to do with all this trouble in and about Uruguay. For many years Uruguay had sought an alliance with Paraguay. Carlos Antonio López, hating Brazil and Argentina, still refused an alliance. The Blanco diplomat, Octavio Lapido, went to Asunción in July, 1863, in a vain attempt to persuade Francisco Solano to sign an alliance against Argentina. Lapido urged López to demand explanations from Mitre, hoping for aid in Uruguay's attempt to form an alliance with Paraguay and the Argentine provinces of Entre Ríos, Corrientes, and any others that wouuld come in. Mitre, of course, knew of these schemes. By agreeing to give Brazil a free hand in Uruguay, he was displaying the skill of a statesman. Should war come, Argentina would not be alone; but had Mitre tried to oppose Brazil, internal politics in Argentina would destroy the union he sought so diligently to cement.

López was no novice in diplomacy. Lapido may have thought he was toying with José Berges and his master, but the dictator had schemes of his own. By sending to Mitre originals of Lapido's confidential dispatches, which revealed how bitterly the Blancos hated Buenos Aires, López apparently hoped to precipitate a crisis. Then perhaps Mitre would ask López to mediate the dispute. That would put Paraguay in a central position, would give Francisco Solano a chance to strut. This amazing but calculated step increased Mitre's suspicion of López, and the latter openly condemned Argentine aid to Flores, according to the United States minister in Asunción, the much maligned but colorful Charles A. Washburn.

Note after note passed between Asunción and Buenos Aires. Mitre and Elizalde were firm, even conciliatory, in dealing with López and Berges. Apparently convinced that war was inevitable, López established the military camp at Cerro León in March, 1864. By August, he had 64,000 partially trained men and Washburn believed he was preparing an army to defend the imperial crown of which he dreamed. At any event, the army existed, probably as a threat to Argentina, certainly to give Paraguay strength to make its voice heard in affairs of Río de la Plata. When Brazil presented its ultimatum to Uruguay in August, the Uruguayan minister at Asunción, Vázquez Sagastume, asked López to intervene. That request brought the protest of August 30, which informed Brazil that Paraguay could not stand by with indifference. Were the people of Paraguay ready to back López in a war against Brazil? If one could believe *El Semanario*, they were. That official organ published many protestations of loyalty; but, as Washburn wrote to W. H. Seward, "if any one were to refuse to sign such a paper he would soon find himself in a prison heavily loaded with fetters."

War in Uruguay developed swiftly in October, 1864. General Menna Barreto came down by land from the north along the Uruguay River, after having delayed three months in crossing the frontier; Admiral Tamandaré sailed up from the south. Paysandú, defended by Leandro Gómez, was under siege about December 1. By that time Francisco Solano had seized the Brazilian steamer *Marquez de Olinda,* an event that occurred on November 12. Two days later the Brazilian minister to Paraguay, César Sauvan Vianna de Lima, demanded his passports and received them with help from Washburn. The War of the Triple Alliance had begun.

Brazilian diplomacy was now directed toward bringing Argentina into the war. Pedro II's government sent its great Silva Paranhos to Buenos Aires in an effort to remedy diplomatic blunders committed by Tamandaré. Mitre wanted to remain neutral. Urquiza in Entre Ríos was still an uncertain quantity and was having difficulty in preventing his followers from joining the Uruguayan Blancos. Silva Paranhos, for the moment, was desperate. He feared that López might gain an initial advantage by attacking Rio Grande do Sul, that resentment over Paysandú would alienate Argentina. Brazil needed Uruguay as a base for war against López, and Silva Paranhos obtained it by forcing Flores to promise aid in return for Brazil's assistance against the Blancos. Thereafter, Brazil had to defeat the Blancos as soon as possible, put Flores in power, and proceed to attack Paraguay. Mitre was ready to mediate; but President Aguirre, by refusing all representations from the diplomatic corps in that matter, lost his last chance to isolate Brazil politically and morally. Andrés Lamas, Uruguay's brilliant minister to Argentina, had met another rebuff by mediocre but more powerful politicians. Now he could do nothing but weep while the great catastrophe ran its course. He saw "The genius of destruction . . . stretching its black wings over Montevideo" while Brazil and the Colorados were "sacrificing our Montevideo on the altars of Paraguay!" Aguirre expected Urquiza and López to rush to his aid; neither did so. Urquiza remained inactive; López invaded Matto Grosso north of Paraguay. In the middle of February, 1865, Tomás Villalba succeeded Aguirre as president of Uruguay and soon signed a protocol with Brazil that made Flores dictator.

Silva Paranhos, having liquidated the Uruguayan war, increased his efforts to bring Argentina into the alliance against Paraguay. Mitre was between a dozen devils and innumerable whirlpools. As Dr. Box saw it, "Once war had broken out between Paraguay and Brazil, the Río de la Plata became a veritable powder magazine of which the components were the Uruguayan revolution; the war of Brazil and Flores against the Montevidean Government; the war of Paraguay against Brazil; the intrigues of Brazilian agents lavishing money in Buenos Aires; the open campaign against Paraguay and López in the Buenos Aires press; the strained relations between Argentina and Paraguay originating in the demands for explanations of the attitude of Mitre's Government towards Uruguay; the propaganda against López conducted by the Committee of Liberal Paraguayans in Buenos Aires; the sympathy of Mitre's Cabinet for Brazil in her struggle with the Blancos and Paraguay; the widespread sympathy for Paraguay and the Montevidean Government in the provinces of Argentina—a sympathy embodied in the small expedition to help the Blancos headed by Colonel Waldino Urquiza, the son of the great *caudillo* of Entre Ríos." No wonder Mitre wanted to remain neutral. In a series of notes to Urquiza, he came to an agreement with that great patriot on Argentina's role. Neutrality it would be, but war if anyone violated Argentine territory. López, by demanding permission to cross Corrientes, committed a blunder; by declaring war, he joined ranks with idiots. A hand-picked Paraguayan congress assembled on March 5, 1865. On March 18, it approved war against Argentina on four grounds: refusal of permission to cross Corrientes, denial of title to Misiones, Argentine support of Paraguayan exiles, and Argentina's journalistic support of Brazil.

Dom Pedro II could also complain about journalistic insults. The Brazilian historian, Antonio Baptista Pereira, attributes to Don José Berges a great anti-Brazilian campaign of vilification. Berges, he says, was worth a legion. In this work he had help from Juan Bautista Alberdi, a friend of Francisco Solano López and Argentina's most noted political scientist, who hated Brazil with ever increasing venom and who never tired of warning against Dom Pedro's empire. Alberdi and Berges, both in London during 1865, probably planned their anti-Brazilian propaganda together. Berges then went to the United States to organize more antipathy toward Brazil in the world's press. When war came, great newspapers were sympathetic toward Paraguay. Berges, understanding the value of propaganda, instructed Paraguayan agents in Argentina to miss no opportunity to point out that a free Paraguay was fighting a slave empire, and it is possible that Brazil's abolition movement was hastened by such criticism. But who was López to pose as a champion of human rights? Paraguay's abolition decree of 1845 was a dead letter until 1870, and Argentine writers maintain that fifty thousand "slaves of the nation" were in arms—an absurd figure, unless all Paraguayans were slaves.

Any attempt to disguise the war as one of a free people against slavery is ridiculous. That disaster, which crushed Paraguay as surely as Germany was smashed in World War II, had its origin in Brazilian encroachments upon Paraguayan territory, in Brazilian and Argentine meddling in Uruguay, in Paraguay's desire to play a decisive role in politics of the Río de la Plata. But López precipitated the war, and upon him must rest much of the blame for what happened to Paraguay.

# CHAPTER XIV

# War of the Triple Alliance

ONE'S IMAGINATION may be fired to the point of delirium in contemplating a war of more than four years during which little Paraguay fought heroically against three enemies. Uruguay's contribution to the conflict was negligible, to be sure; but Argentina and Brazil, the most powerful states in South America, and at the time, in all Latin America, possessed resources sufficient to have crushed a nation several times the size of Paraguay. If other facts are disregarded for the moment, Paraguay's achievement in holding such opponents at bay for so long assumes the stature of a miracle. The world may have been astonished; patriotic Paraguayans regarded their heroic resistance as part of the natural order of things. In explaining why Paraguay fought so well, Manuel Domínguez, in *El alma de la raza*, concludes that the Paraguayan was superior to the invader in race, native intelligence, sagacity, generosity, physique, sobriety, agility, endurance, military spirit, fraternal union, democratic equality, and so on. "Paraguay was superior," he says, "to each ally as a nation. It was not, like the Argentine Republic, a heterogeneous amalgam of *porteños* and provincials, federals and unitarists who hated one another to the death; it was not, like Brazil, broken into republicans and imperialists, into masters and millions of slaves."

López, believing that Paraguay was ready for war, pursued a course that led inevitably to defeat, devastation, immense suffering, and territorial losses for his country. Without straining his resources unduly, the dictator could field an army of 30,000; with a little effort, he could increase it to 60,000; and, by pulling in boys and old men, his army would exceed 100,000. This military strength was formidable for a country whose population was about 525,000. Moreover, forts guarding the Paraguay at Humaitá and other places were strengthened until it was doubtful if any South American flotilla could force a passage. Gunboats on the Paraguay and Paraná were not numerous, perhaps a dozen in all that could co-operate with shore batteries. A telegraph line 270 miles long connected Asunción with the Humaitá defensive system; communications, nevertheless, left much to be desired. Manufacturing industries were few, although leather-working establishments turned out military equipment and the arsenal at Asunción intensified its production.

While Brazilians were preparing for their siege of the Uruguayan port of Paysandú, López continued to hesitate. On November 10, 1864, a Brazilian steamer, the *Marquez de Olinda*, stopped at Asunción en route to Corumbá, bearing the governor of Matto Grosso, Colonel Federico Carneiro de Campos, to his post. Brazilian vessels had been plying the river freely for several years and it was the only feasible route to Matto Grosso. López let the attractive river boat depart, then suddenly precipitated the war that all but annihilated Paraguay. He sent the gunboat *Tacuarí* to bring the *Marquez* and its two thousand muskets back to Asunción on November 12, where it soon became a Paraguayan gunboat. The steamer's crew and Governor Campos went to prison; some of the crew were released after a few months, but Campos died in 1867, still a prisoner.

*Porteños* of Buenos Aires, always contemptuous of anything outside the city limits, were somewhat amazed with the Paraguayan action, and few really intelligent people expected Argentina to become involved. López they had scorned as an uncouth barbarian with ridiculous pretensions, a keeper of harems in wigwams, but those who knew anything about military matters could not scorn the Paraguayan Army. Military might has always attracted wider respect in Latin America than any other attribute of a people, and by this standard Argentina, with its insignificant standing army and provinces of doubtful loyalty, could not command high regard from her neighbors. Paraguay's first campaign, the invasion of Matto Grosso, allowed a few weeks for taking stock of the situation, and in this time President Mitre apparently became convinced that Argentina should cast its lot with Brazil if neutrality proved impossible.

Now that war had begun, López might have helped the Blancos with an expeditionary force sent to Uruguay across Argentine territory, or by a roundabout route through Brazil. It might seem that a campaign north of Paraguay in Matto Grosso would be of no more value to the Uruguayan Blancos than a sanitary campaign among the Chaco savages, but López knew what he was doing. Brazilians, preparing for years to defend southern Matto Grosso, had stored large quantities of munitions and a hundred or more brass guns within easy reach of Paraguay. They had neglected to station enough troops in the province to defend it, arrogant in the belief that the mosquito could not hurt the crocodile. López, needing those military supplies and the prestige of a quick victory, sent two forces into the province in December, 1864. A river-borne contingent of 3,000 men sailed on eight vessels and anchored below Coimbra on December 26. A reconnaissance in force the next day failed miserably except to prove that the Brazilian garrison might fight. Coimbra, indeed, could have held out for some time, if not indefinitely, against the Paraguayans had its cowardly commander not ordered a retreat after the first clash. Colonel Vicente Barrios, the Paraguayan leader, soon had thirty-two brass guns and plenty of munitions to send back to Asunción. Albuquerque and Corumbá, on up the river, offered practically no resistance. At Corumbá, Barrios allowed his men to commit the customary excesses of rape, pillage, plunder, and murder. Soldiers on the *Ypora* decorated the shrouds of their ship with strings of Brazilian ears, a barbarity that earned them a reprimand from López, whose sense of propriety warned him that severed ears should not be advertised so blatantly when foreign observers were around. Discounting ears, women, and personal plunder, the Paraguayans picked up enough munitions of war in Matto Grosso to supply the entire army for many months.

López continued to recruit men while the Matto Grosso campaign was under way, and by April, 1865, he had a poorly equipped army of 80,000 men, more or less. About two in five had firearms; the others carried lances and knives. Throughout the war López had to depend more on his artillery than on his infantry, except in the first months, partly because much of the fighting was defensive and partly because the infantry was never fully armed. There is reason to believe that Paraguay would have stood the war better had its army been smaller, since so many workers were taken from the fields that agricultural production suffered severely. Some 15,000 men, roughly equivalent to a modern reinforced division, were stationed in the swampy Humaitá defense system where they died by the score from disease and malnutrition.

So much has been written about the heroic Paraguayan soldier that one more word or two must be devoted to him. No people could love their country with greater devotion than the natives of Paraguay, and it was not only blind obedience to authority that made them willing to die in its defense. One sometimes competent observer, Sir Richard F. Burton, found the Paraguayan soldier an interesting subject: "The figure is somewhat short and stout, but well put together, with neat, shapely, and remarkably small extremities. The brachycephalic head is covered with a long straight curtain of blue-black hair, whilst the beard and mustachios are rare, except in case of mixed breeds. The face is full, flat, and circular; the cheekbones are high, and laterally salient; the forehead is low, remarkably contrasting with the broad, long, heavy, and highly-developed chin; and the eyes are often oblique, being raised at the exterior canthi, with light or dark-brown pupils, well-marked eyebrows, and long, full, and curling lashes." Essentially a vegetarian, the Paraguayan did not thrive on a heavy meat diet made necessary by the lack of agricultural hands. A contempt for death and the conviction that every Paraguayan was fully equal to six of his enemies, made him a foe to be feared and respected. He was deadly in patrol work

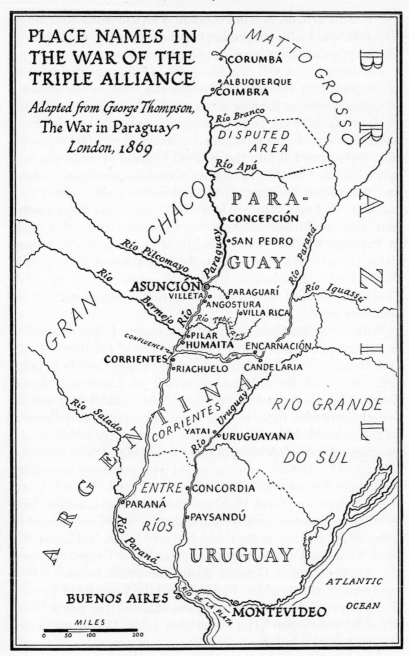

PLACE NAMES IN
THE WAR OF THE
TRIPLE ALLIANCE

*Adapted from George Thompson,*
*The War in Paraguay*
*London, 1869*

MATTO GROSSO

CORUMBÁ

ÁLBUQUERQUE
COIMBRA

*Río Branco*

DISPUTED
AREA

*Río Apá*

BRAZIL

CHACO

PARA-
CONCEPCIÓN

SAN PEDRO

*Río Pilcomayo*

*Río Paraguay*

GUAY

*Río Paraná*

GRAN

ASUNCIÓN
VILLETA
ANGOSTURA

*Río Bermejo*

*Río Tebicuary*

PARAGUARÍ

VILLA RICA

*Río Iguassú*

CONFLUENCE

PILAR
HUMAITÁ

ENCARNACIÓN

CORRIENTES

RIACHUELO

CANDELARIA

*Río Salado*

ARGENTINA

CORRIENTES

*Río Uruguay*

YATAI
URUGUAYANA

*Río*

RIO GRANDE

DO SUL

ENTRE
PARANÁ

CONCORDIA

PAYSANDÚ

RÍOS

*Río Paraná*

URUGUAY

ATLANTIC

BUENOS AIRES

*Río de la Plata*

MONTEVIDEO

OCEAN

MILES

0    50   100        200

221

and gloried in hand-to-hand combat. A lack of intelligent initiative, combined with unthinking dependence upon unreliable officers, appears to have been his greatest weakness.

The Paraguayan will or willingness to fight persisted in spite of demoralizing conditions. Disease ran wild in the stinking hospitals where, as the war progressed, a few fortunate victims lay by twos on rough beds. Others were consigned to the floors and suffered under open colonnades. At one time 1,000 wounded men were crowded into the general hospital at Asunción in a space intended for 300. Epidemics of measles, smallpox, cholera, and pneumonia among civilians and military alike added to a mortality that may have reached 50,000 before any major battles had been fought. Suffering agonies in heroic silence, thousands of Paraguayans died under conditions of indescribable horror. Paraguay may well take pride in the stoic heroism of her people during the López holocaust, but how the country can be proud of Francisco Solano López is a mystery that defies everything resembling logic.

With the Matto Grosso campaign a success, López demanded Argentine permission to cross the province of Corrientes to attack Brazil at a vital spot. Refusal of this request, made in January, 1865, and the subsequent attack on Corrientes, found Urquiza in full support of President Mitre. Had López not invaded Corrientes, there is some reason to suppose that Urquiza might have aided him against Brazil, a country for which he had nothing but hatred. Adding blunder to blunder, López captured the city of Corrientes, an undefended river port lying some sixty kilometers downstream from Humaitá, on April 13, 1865. A few weeks before, on March 18, Mitre had permitted arms for Paraguay to clear customs and declared that he would not consent to a Brazilian blockade of the rivers, but now López had forced the issue. On May 1, 1865, Argentina, Brazil, and Uruguay formed the Triple Alliance. General Bartolomé Mitre became Allied land commander-in-chief; Vice-Admiral the Viscount of Tamandaré, favorite of Dom Pedro II, commanded the naval force. Mitre set the slogan: "The barracks in a day, Corrientes in two weeks, Asunción in three months!"

Argentine leaders and people, like their Brazilian allies, grossly underestimated the task before them. Newspapers, including *La Prensa, La Nación,* and *La Tribuna,* expressed their contempt, echoing an Uruguayan statement that "only a nation of sheep would become enthusiastic by having the impotency and degradation of its enemies pictured to it." In vain did Mitre's former agent to Paraguay, Anarcasis Lanús, warn against belittling Paraguay's military power. By April 24, an Argentine battalion was on its way to Corrientes, whose governor ordered to arms all males from sixteen to sixty. An outburst of war hysteria in Rosario caused the Paraguayan consul to be imprisoned; a mob tore the Paraguayan flag to shreds and used the coat of arms and a picture of López for target practice. In Entre Ríos, after revealing that López had made overtures to him, Urquiza got together 8,000 men, equipped them with supplies from Buenos Aires, then watched them melt away in mass desertions at the critical moment. Other gestures to raise a division in Entre Ríos came to nothing, although Urquiza sold enough cattle and horses to the Allies to make him quite wealthy. There was even a rumor that Mitre, unwilling to trust the great caudillo, bought these animals to prevent him from raising an army. None of the many rumors got at the truth, which was that Entre Ríos would follow Urquiza but would not fight a *porteño* war.

The alliance against Paraguay seems appalling and the odds insuperable only when one discounts the serious difficulties that confronted the Allies. They must attack up the Río Paraguay against strongly fortified positions, since no highways or railways led into Paraguay, or make a difficult Paraná crossing between the confluence and Encarnación. Men, munitions, and supplies must be transported over long distances. Brazil and Argentina, traditional enemies, inevitably found it difficult to work together harmoniously, and strong opposition parties in each country launched bitter attacks against Pedro II and President Mitre. Convinced from the beginning that Paraguay would have to be conquered "palm by palm," although it proved to be a "swamp by swamp" affair, Brazilian commanders lacked the military genius necessary to bring the war to a quick conclusion. Mitre, the first

Allied ground commander, was an amateurish bungler. López, equally inept as an offensive strategist and tactician but clever on defense, had a great advantage in being at home and in fighting the war on ground of his own choice.

Marshal López, to use his grandest self-bestowed title, had the country with him. This support, regardless of how he won it, was something his enemies found difficult to understand. The Allies proclaimed that their war was against the tyrant and not against the people, an old and ridiculous bromide that has done service so often as to be suspect in every age. Madame Lynch rallied the women to give a tithe of their jewelry to the government, although apparently most of these baubles found their way into if not on Madame's chest. Fiestas, parades, harangues, dances, and general synthetic enthusiasm confirmed a belief that Brazil and Argentina, countries that were little more than names to the isolated peasantry, must bow quickly before the *mariscal's* genius. Of course López was a genius. Had he not himself proclaimed it in his official paper, *El Semanario?*

An abundance of ignorance, overconfidence, and downright stupidity existed on both sides. Brazilians and Argentines looked upon Paraguay with contempt; Paraguayans regarded their enemies with a similar sentiment. None of the combatants fully appreciated the enemy's capabilities, and the ease with which Matto Grosso fell filled strutting Paraguayan officers with greatly exaggerated self-esteem. López had too much confidence in himself. There were, as it proved, few chances for him to crush his enemies; but they had a number of opportunities which were allowed to pass by without any effort to use them. No set of allies ever frittered away its advantages with greater profligacy than Argentina, Brazil, and Uruguay. The ineptness of their commanders was in itself a crime against civilization: a war that might have ended within a year dragged on and on until the eventual victors had lost heavily and Paraguay lay completely prostrate, its population reduced by perhaps 60 per cent.

López had one over-all plan of campaign. General Wenceslao Robles would march down the Paraná with 25,000 men while Colonel Antonio de la Cruz Estigarribia went down the Uruguay with 12,500. These two forces were to meet on the Uruguayan frontier. The Paraguayan fleet, paralleling Robles, would try to clear the river. This combined movement was too poorly co-ordinated, too badly led, and too late to succeed. It also presupposed that Uruguayan Blancos in Rio Grande do Sul would come to Estigarribia's aid, and that Entre Ríos and Corrientes would rebel against Mitre and help Robles. Neither of these conditions materialized.

While Robles marched down the left bank of the Paraná, Captain Pedro Ignacio Meza tried to capture a Brazilian fleet of nine vessels that had blockaded the Paraná from a comparatively safe position opposite the Arroyo Riachuelo, some ten miles below Corrientes. At this time, according to Lieutenant Colonel George Thompson, the fortress of Humaitá and its outer works had only ninety guns in all, less than the Brazilian fleet carried. An attack pressed with skill and persistence might have eliminated the "Sebastopol of South America," since the defenders were exposed to enemy fire except at one battery that mounted sixteen guns. Humaitá's fame apparently frightened the Brazilians but their fleet didn't worry López.

In good spirits, 500 men of the Sixth Battalion manned the Paraguayan fleet of nine gunboats on June 10, 1865. Everything was ready, almost. López did not forget to make a speech, to which his soldiers replied with a promise to bring the ironclads back to Asunción. Had grappling irons been remembered, it is possible that the promise would have been kept. The plan of attack was simple. During the night the Paraguayans would steam down the river, reach a point below the Brazilians as dawn broke, then turn and attack upstream. Each vessel was to tie to a Brazilian, board it, and bring the prize to Asunción. The Paraguayan flotilla mounted thirty-four guns, plus six 68-pounders towed on as many *chatas* (barges). One of the gunboats became disabled on the way, leaving eight vessels with thirty guns to go on.

Captain Meza, commanding the fleet, failed to gauge his arrival at the proper moment. Dawn had broken long since when the astonished Brazilians saw the enemy bearing down on them below Corrientes. The fleets exchanged lead compliments at a

225

distance that favored the superior Brazilian guns. Instead of turning at once, Captain Meza then went on to the Riachuelo, giving the enemy time to weigh anchor and to assume a more favorable position. One Paraguayan gunboat, the *Jejui,* was put out of action and anchored at Riachuelo; another ran aground. As the Brazilians bore down on their daring opponents, three of the Paraguayan ships, the *Marquez de Olinda,* the *Tacuarí* and the *Salto,* attacked the *Paranahyba* ineffectually. The *Tacuarí* and the *Salto* could have grappled had someone remembered to put the grappling irons aboard. As it was, about thirty Paraguayan soldiers jumped on board from the *Salto* and momentarily captured the *Paranahyba.* One story, a bit too good for credibility, is that the Brazilian soldiers rushed below deck or jumped overboard; but the Paraguayan sergeant, instead of fastening the hatches, marched up and down beating reveille on a drum. His martial rolls brought Brazilians pouring out of the hold, and Paraguayans took their turn at jumping overboard. The truth seems to be that the Brazilian flagship *Amazonas* came alongside, swept the *Paranahyba's* deck with grape, and killed two-thirds of the boarding party. The *Amazonas* then rammed the *Paraguayi* and played a prominent role in breaking up the battle, from which four Paraguayan boats managed to escape. Fortunately for Captain Meza, a Brazilian shot removed him from all danger of the Marshal-President's vengeance.

This attack by converted merchant paddle steamers against modern ironclads seems quixotic. Thompson reports a Brazilian confession that the battle was "touch and go," and might have been a Paraguayan victory had Meza "immediately gone alongside instead of running down past" the enemy. And Masterman is not far from being correct in saying that the "battle of four hours and a half really decided the war, for it gave the Allies command of the river. If those nine vessels had been captured," he continues, "I am certain that López would have been victorious for he would have instantly appeared before Buenos Ayres or Monte Video, and, by threatening a bombardment, compelled them to make terms with him." And, he might have noted, General Robles had 25,000 or more soldiers on the east bank of the

Paraná near Bella Vista, ready to fight their way through Entre Ríos. When news of the Riachuelo disaster reached this land force, Robles hurried back to a point near Corrientes, where he wasted his time in futile marching up and down the river bank. Here, on July 23, López sent his minister of war, General Vicente Barrios, to arrest Robles on just charges of insubordination.

Allied control of the rivers was never seriously challenged after Riachuelo. No fleet flying Paraguayan colors would bombard capitals on the Río de la Plata, no grand army would threaten Uruguay. Still Colonel Estigarribia invaded Brazil early in August. He had not heard about the Riachuelo disaster. The Colonel struck across from Itapuá to the Uruguay River, captured San Borja and Uruguayana on the left bank in Rio Grande do Sul, then waited while a quarreling Allied army, mollified by a visit from Dom Pedro II, prepared to attack. Estigarribia had made the mistake of leaving more than 2,000 of his troops on the west side, where they were cut to pieces by Uruguayans under General Flores on August 17 in the battle of Yatay. Outnumbered greatly, completely isolated from Paraguay, and wondering what had happened to Robles, Estigarribia gave up the rest of his troops at Uruguayana on September 18. So ended the grand López offensive with the loss of about "13,000 men, 5 steamers, 10 barges, 42 pieces of artillery and 18 flags." Paraguayans captured after the battles of Yatay and Uruguayana suffered various fates. Some were sold as slaves, others were formed into battalions and forced to serve the Allies, and probably several hundred were butchered. López blamed everyone but himself for these disasters. Commanding officers, when he could get his hands on them, suffered torture and execution. Their relatives met the same fate, or were exiled after confiscation of their property. Measures typical of the dictator at bay, these actions would have broken the spirit of any people less tenacious than the Paraguayans.

Not until April, 1866, did the Allies invade Paraguay. They recovered Corrientes, after Estigarribia's surrender, in November, 1865; but even then the Brazilians hesitated for five days before a town defended only by dummy guns. General Francisco

Isidoro Resquín, successor to Robles, had been permitted to withdraw his 27,000 men without interference. Paso Pucú, a narrow and relatively dry strip of land southeast of Humaitá between the Río Paraguay and the Estero de Ñeembucú, became headquarters for López while the Allies gave him plenty of time to improve its defenses. Mitre continued to hope desperately for peace while an Allied army of 62,000 men, made up of 40,000 Brazilians, 18,-000 Argentines, and 4,000 Uruguayans, lay inactive at the bend of the Paraná, protected by batteries set up on a circular island lying at the confluence. López sent 1,200 men to make a futile dawn attack against this island on April 10, 1866. Apparently 800 gained the island; 500 remained killed, wounded, or as prisoners, and nearly all who returned were wounded. Emboldened by this little success, which cost them 1,000 casualties, the Allies began to cross the Paraná a week later.

López probably did not know it, but his raid of April 10 came at an annoying time for the Allies. General Mitre had called a council of war at Corrientes on February 25, at which he expressed a desire to by-pass the swampy areas of Paso la Patria at the confluence; Admiral Tamandaré argued that his fleet could provide better protection for a landing if it were tried at Paso la Patria. Mitre preferred to land farther up the Paraná, outflank the Humaitá defenses, and march directly on Asunción. Had he done so, the war must have ended very soon. By April 16, D-day for the invasion, the Allied fleet of sixty-five steamers, forty-eight sailing vessels, and numerous small craft was the largest ever assembled on the rivers. López expected an attempt to be made at Fort Itapirú, which lay up the Paraná some ten miles from the confluence, and defended the spot with infantry and cavalry. He also detached 3,000 men to watch Baron Porto Alegre, who appeared across the Paraná opposite Itapuá with 9,300 troops on April 15, and sent an infantry battalion and a cavalry squadron to guard the confluence.

Allied troops began to fill the boats long before daylight on April 16. Fifteen thousand Brazilians were to have the honor of securing a beachhead. Gunboats ran up to Itapirú and silenced its small batteries while transports headed straight across the

Bartolomé Mitre

From Mitre's *Historia de San Martín*

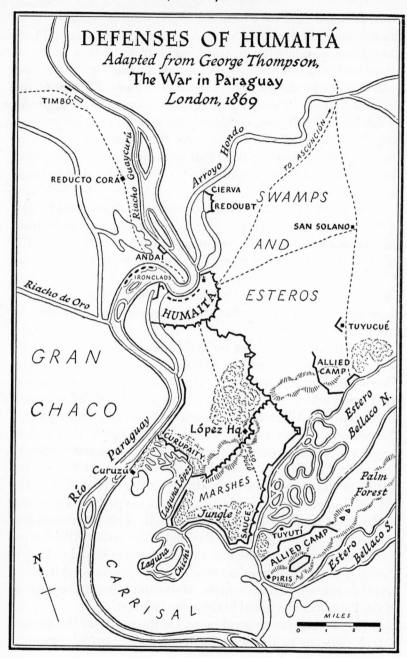

DEFENSES OF HUMAITÁ
Adapted from George Thompson,
The War in Paraguay
London, 1869

river. In midstream they turned sharply, went down to the confluence, and sailed up the Paraguay for a mile or so. General Luis
Osorio, commanding the invasion, led his troops ashore and went
ahead with a handful of men on reconnaissance, "trading in that
critical moment the august role of Agamemnon for that of the
brilliant Achilles." General José Ignacio Garmendia, in throwing
in this bit of Greek lore, condemns the general-in-chief for such
stupid exposure. Osorio looked over the ground, decided that
the invasion was impossible in that area, and gave orders to stop
the flow of troops; but Captain Vieira Ferreira refused to inter-
rupt the landing.

News of the Brazilian invasion reached López quickly. His
nearest mobile troops were at Itapirú, a dozen or more miles from
the beachhead. While this contingent hastened to challenge the
landing, the small guard already on the ground fell back slowly.
A heavy rain ended the battle early in the afternoon, and when
General Flores landed his Uruguayans under cover of darkness,
there was no opposition other than occasional wild shooting by
Paraguayan snipers.

López demonstrated his foolhardiness on April 17 when he
sent 3,000 men to attack the 15,000 invaders under Osorio and
Flores. His long left flank was exposed to fire from gunboats in
the Paraná which might do some damage, but a well-led assault
might rout the Allies as they struggled to organize a defense in
the swampy, muddy land they held. The Paraguayans, outnumbered and outmaneuvered, fought with characteristic bravery
but suffered total defeat. Casualties of 400 dead and 100 wounded
testify to the ferocity of their attacks. After this action of the
Fluvial, López abandoned Itapirú to take up prepared positions
in the outer works of the Humaitá system. This movement was
completed on April 19; three days later the entire Allied army
was setting up camp in the former Paraguayan ground of Paso la
Patria. General Garmendia, recalling this landing with bated
breath, wrote: "San Martín in the Andes and Mitre in the passage
of the Paraná are weighed in the same balance."

Paso la Patria was no great prize. On the north lay the flooded
Estero Bellaco; to the west an impassable *carrizal* (swamp)

bounded the camp; lagoons laced the land on the other sides. Three passes, Sidra, Carreta, and Piris, bridged the Estero Bellaco on the way to Humaitá. Mitre ordered Flores to hold these passes with 1,300 Uruguayans and 1,900 Brazilians while the Allied army completed its concentration. Behind this screen, the Brazilians took up positions on the left along the river, while Argentines held the right.

May 2, 1866, was a beautiful day. Allied soldiers frolicked in the autumn sunshine, unmindful that their carefree bantering would soon give way to cries of terror and death. A scouting party ran into a fire fight with what it thought was a Paraguayan patrol but apparently attached no significance to the encounter. Unknown to the Allies, López was concentrating his infantry, artillery, and cavalry for an attack against the Brazilian left and the Argentine right, an attempted double envelopment. At high noon the Paraguayan troops poured through the poorly guarded passes, screaming like maniacs, and fell on the vanguard with 6,000 men. Battalion after battalion broke and fled under the fierce assault, their commanders taken completely by surprise. López had given orders for his men to pillage, and they did so with a vengeance. While they were thus pleasantly engaged, General Osorio came to the rescue with the Sixth Brazilian Division and other units. Disorganized Paraguayans fled from the field as best they could, having lost between 2,500 and 3,000 men as against 1,500 for the Allies. What was the sense of it all? Why attack an army of 40,000 with but 6,000 men, with no provision to cover their inevitable retreat? The entire army could not have been used in the attack because the passes were too narrow, but López could have used at least part of the 30,000 men at Tuyutí to good advantage. At best it was a rash gamble; at worst it was a stupid blunder.

While López learned nothing from his defeat on May 2, Allied leaders at last had one fact pounded home: Paraguayans might have bad leadership, but they could and would fight undismayed by odds, completely indifferent to death. Thereafter Allied vigilance increased, reconnaissance became routine, and an Allied council decided when the next battle would be fought. "The en-

231

thusiasm was great," Garmendia burbled, "because the spirit of our soldiers was noble and generous, they knew that their cause was holy and that they were going to shed their blood in the fight against the last despotism, which like a belch from the old colonial barbarity was becoming a menace in a corner of America." Paraguayans, this same Argentine glorifier of war proclaimed, were merely driven by tyrannical terror.

General Mitre and his council fixed May 20 as D-day for the attempt to force the passes and drive López back from Tuyutí. Once across Estero Bellaco, an attack on Tuyutí would follow with little delay as the second phase. Paso Sidra in the center was a key point that seemed to be held lightly by a small detachment of troops entrenched behind a crude earthen parapet, to the right of which was a small patch of palms that would offer refuge for the defenders if they should be hard pressed. The apparent lack of concentration near the passes led Allied commanders to believe that López would try to draw them into an ambush farther back on more favorable ground.

After dawn on May 20, three Allied columns advanced toward the passes. General Flores led Uruguayans against Paso Sidra with a reinforced Brazilian infantry division in reserve. Flores, behind an artillery concentration, seized his objective and sent the Brazilians on to capture the defenses in a swift push over open ground. Paraguayan fire was brisk but ineffective, and the defenders dispersed into the convenient woods. On the Allied right, Argentine cavalry seized Paso Carreta with ease. López had abandoned Tuyutí to take refuge within the quadrilateral defenses of the Humaitá system. General Garmendia could see no sense whatever in the Paraguayan dictator's tactics. He could have inflicted heavy losses at the passes; instead, he retreated with only token resistance.

López lost the war on May 24, 1866, if one can fix upon any date for the turning point. On that day occurred the battle of Tuyutí, also known as the battle of Estero Bellaco. The Allies were still busy with setting up camp and in preparing for their own attack, a combination that offered a strategic time for López to strike. Argentines on the Allied right, Uruguayans and Brazilians in the center and on the left, formed a crude arc south of the *bañados* (swamp lands) that gradually merged into Estero Rojas (or Estero Bellaco del Norte). The Allies were vulnerable to a strong attack delivered with persistence and followed up vigorously. Colonel Enrique Wisner de Morgenstern counseled caution and defense instead of rashness and offense; López wanted to strike. The Allies had about 32,000 men, including 18,000 Brazilians, 12,000 Argentines, and 1,400 Uruguayans divided among seventy-five infantry battalions and seventy cavalry squadrons, and supported by eighty pieces of artillery. General Juan Andrés Gelly y Obes was *ad interim* commander of the Argentines, Flores still led the Uruguayan vanguard, and General Luis Osorio commanded the Brazilians. For the Paraguayans, López was commander-in-chief, chief of staff, and all other things at once. Facing the Brazilians on the Allied left were 7,000 infantry and 1,000 cavalry under General Barrios; Major José Eduvigis Díaz, with 4,000 infantry and cavalry, was in the center; General Resquín faced the Argentines with 8,000 men. Reserves brought the total to 23,640, according to Garmendia. The Paraguayan plan called for Barrios and Resquín to envelop the Allied flanks while Díaz struck the center. On the night of May 23, Paraguayan forces moved into position ready to attack.

A beautiful, cloudless autumn day, with a sky blue as the Argentine flag, was the twenty-fourth of May. Before nightfall 6,000 mutilated bodies would await funeral pyres. The Allies did not suspect an impending attack in spite of reports of Paraguayan cavalry movements at dawn, so engrossed was Mitre with plans for his own advance. He had alerted the Allied army for an attack later in the day and troops were moving into position when the Paraguayans struck at eleven-thirty, more than two hours late. General Resquín's attack against the Argentines enjoyed preliminary success because of surprise; but reinforcements, well-placed artillery, and skillful cavalry maneuvers decided the outcome. Although General Barrios threw his men against the Brazilians with such ferocity that the outcome was in doubt for some time, his lack of reserves won the fight for Osorio. The battle seemed to be over by two o'clock when firing was heard to the left rear. It was the last desperate fling by Barrios, who had sent parts of two cavalry regiments supported by infantry to turn the Brazilian flank. More than a dozen Brazilian battalions, hastily thrown into the breach, trapped and annihilated the Paraguayans.

Losses were stupendous in view of numbers engaged. López left 5,000 dead on the field, lost 350 captured, and had 8,000 wounded. If these estimates are correct, Paraguayan casualties were 13,350 out of less than 20,000 in the attack. The Allies suffered 3,913 casualties, of which 971 were killed. Brazilian casualties alone were over 3,000. Although one may question Garmendia's assertion that "The battle of Tuyutí will always be the greatest South American military event," there is no doubt about its being one of the bloodiest. That May 24 may well be remembered by Paraguayans, for in the land between the two arms of Estero Bellaco, López lost his chance to save Paraguay from defeat. Masterman attributed a great significance to the Paraguayan loss: "That battle of the Bellaco may be said to have annihilated the Spanish race in Paraguay. In the front ranks were the males of all the best families in the country, and they were killed almost to a man; hundreds of families, in the capital especially, had not a husband, father, son, or brother left. Old men who had been left in Humaitá, Indians, slaves, and boys now filled the attenuated ranks of the national army." Disposal of the dead presented something of a problem: "The Allies buried some of their own dead, but they heaped up the Paraguayan corpses in alternate layers, with wood, in piles of from 50 to 100, and burnt them. They complained that the Paraguayans were so lean that they would not burn." Thompson, who made this observation, was on the ground. He also adds a gruesome detail from a reconnaissance made six weeks after the battle: "The woods and the spaces between them were still full of the corpses from the Battle of May 24. These bodies were not decomposed, but completely mummified, the skin having dried on to the bones, and the bodies looking tawny and thin."

The tragedy of errors ran on and on, partly because Allied military and naval commanders lacked mutual confidence. As commander of the Brazilian forces in November, 1866, and commander-in-chief in the following February, the Duke of Caxias displayed great heroism on occasions; but to call him, as does João Pandiá Calogeras, a great strategist, is to stretch the term until it screams. López goaded the Allies into fighting again, from July 16 to 18, and inflicted 5,000 casualties while losing 2,500. Then Mitre and his allies, principally Brazilians, attacked and captured the battery of Curuzú on the river midway between the Paraná-Paraguay junction and Humaitá, in a battle from September 1-3, 1866. López, again having suffered heavily, fell back to Curupaity, close to his main works, and asked Mitre for a conference to discuss an armistice. This meeting occurred on September 12 and failed completely because of Allied insistence that López get out of Paraguay.

Apparently believing that López had pulled back to Humaitá, General Mitre ordered an all-out assault on Curupaity to take place on September 22. Brazilian troops did gain a part of the line in the attack but the Argentine battalions suffered heavy casualties in the main effort, and more than 4,000 Allied soldiers were left on the field. Something seems to be wrong with the figures, since the Paraguayan losses are given as only 54. Here was a chance for López, it would seem, to pursue and rout his enemy completely. Had he not wasted most of his army in April and May, it is likely that the dictator would have done so; now he could do little without the protection of his field fortifications.

Curupaity was a victory for Paraguay that made ultimate defeat certain, since there was now no hope of continuing the conciliation efforts that had begun after Curuzú. The official paper, *El Semanario*, bloated with fulsome praise of Paraguay's savior. Again came a forced contribution of jewels and gold. Six leading citizens went down the river to deliver gifts to Marshal López. The poor fellows, terrified and abashed in such an august presence, stammered and stuttered their pat speeches, and one of them even shouted "Viva Dom Pedro!" No one, of course, needs to believe this story.

Drooping disconsolately under bedraggled laurels, the Allies entrenched before Curupaity continued their river blockade and

235

snarled at one another. For eighteen months the fleet bombarded Curupaity almost daily; on occasions, two thousand shells dropped on Paraguayan positions in the early hours of dawn. From Curuzú, also, two batteries added to the weight of metal delivered to López. Paraguayans welcomed the noise of firing with derisive tooting on their *turututus* and were diligent in recovering thousands of unexploded shells and tons of splinters to be returned with proper emphasis in the future. Although Thompson improved the trenches that practically enclosed the Paraguayan position, to the east lay a large and completely undefended area through which an enemy flanking movement could have succeeded with ease.

Foreign and native ingenuity did much to overcome serious shortages caused by this long blockade. Women revived the arts of spinning and weaving cotton and wool for clothing. A foreigner set up a crude paper factory that used cotton and wild pineapple fibers; excellent parchment from sheepskins served for official documents. A black bean yielded ink when treated with ashes; soldiers made their own soap; salt, always in short supply, came partly from river mud and partly from a thick-leaved tree. Gunpowder of poor quality was made from sulphur extracted from iron pyrites and saltpeter "manufactured from urine and decomposed animal substances." The arsenal at Asunción, under English engineers, designed and cast guns, changed rifling and breeches to accommodate recovered enemy ammunition, and displayed rare ingenuity in solving a succession of difficult problems.

Military aviation, as it had in the American Civil War, now played a small role. After one expensive balloon proved useless, two Americans made a successful ascent in June, 1867. These men, James Allen and his brother, directed fourteen or more ascents to an altitude of about fifty feet. When pot shots failed to destroy this aerial reconnaissance, Paraguayans used a crude smoke screen with good effect. At last, on August 15, gunboats finally passed Curupaity and anchored below the triple-chain boom protecting Humaitá.

Carlos Antonio López had begun to fortify this position in

1855 when trouble loomed with Brazil and the United States. Colonels Wisner and Thompson helped to complete its defenses for the younger López, who fully appreciated the possibilities of a fortress lying on the great horseshoe bend of the Paraguay. Built on high ground twenty or thirty feet above the river, bounded on either side by swamps, armed with an estimated two hundred guns or more, Humaitá was famed in Europe and America as the Gibraltar or Sebastopol of South America. Its batteries actually were arrayed in a slipshod manner; the guns were of various calibers, various dates, and more various reliability; protective field works were crude in the extreme. Thatched brick or adobe barracks, little better than animal sheds, housed the disease-ridden garrison. Fairly comfortable quarters for the dictator, Madame Lynch, and the bishop fell far short of being luxurious. A telegraph line connecting with Asunción enabled López to while away many hours "sending and receiving messages about the most trivial matters." Frogs made the nights hideous with their croaking; glittering fireflies wove dizzy patterns with their cold, brilliant lights; mosquitoes clouded the moisture-laden air.

Across from Humaitá and upstream about ten miles, the old *piquete* of Timbó on the Chaco side aided in guarding the river. Little more than a redoubt, this fortification had some forty field guns of different calibers which were mounted on raised platforms and were protected by a rough system of ditches and parapets. Huts and sheds housed the small garrison and the inevitable contingent of fleas and other vermin. Timbó, useless after the evacuation of Humaitá, was stripped and abandoned early in 1868.

After the Brazilian ironclads had dared to scurry past the batteries of Curupaity, they anchored at a safe distance from Humaitá and occasionally bombarded a church, the only structure visible to gunners. Since no troops in significant numbers could be landed along the river, the Allies would have to fight through the outer ring of Paraguayan defenses, or change the direction of their attack. The latter course was the only intelligent one to adopt; and López, who constantly expected a flanking movement around his left, was surprised that Allied strategists failed to take advantage of their opportunity. So were intelligent observers of the war, who could hardly understand why Mitre and then Caxias chose to mire down their armies in the swamps and periodically flooded lowlands on the lower reaches of the Paraguay and to fight on ground chosen by López. Compared with such campaigning, a single envelopment to the right would have been simple, especially with command of the river unchallenged. Mitre and Caxias, inept novices in military science, took the hard way.

López, before evacuating Curupaity, took one last major fling at his enemies, whose principal forces were divided by the northern Estero Bellaco. Tuyutí, part of the main Allied camp, was an inviting objective. At dawn on November 3, 1867, Paraguayans attacked so suddenly with 8,000 men and boys that the Allies were thrown into great confusion. Some of the troops fled back to the Paraná, where they competed with officers and camp followers for transportation across the stream. Following orders, the Paraguayans practically disbanded to loot the rich stores. This disorganization saved the Allies from a major defeat. Reinforcements rushed up and forced the enemy to retreat, leaving about 1,200 men on the field. Allied losses were about 1,700 killed, wounded, and captured, in addition to heavy destruction and capture of stores, munitions, and artillery. A well-organized attack would have disrupted most of the Allied army, but López was blind to the opportunity. The dictator then shortened his defenses by pulling back most of the troops in the advanced line of trenches to newer and shorter works running through the high ground of Paso Pucú.

Cholera took a heavy toll among the Brazilian and Argentine troops in 1867, a loss made up by replacements that brought their strength to about 48,000 men. There was a strong cavalry, plenty of arms and munitions were available, and complete command of the river to Humaitá guaranteed an essential supply line. López was reduced to some 15,000 troops, half of whom were boys or old men. In Humaitá itself, Colonel Paulino Alen had 3,000 half-starved and nearly naked soldiers to man fifteen thousand yards of trenches; the rest of the army was distributed generally to the southeast of the river fort. Time to starve was granted by the timorous attackers, who, when their ironclads finally ran over the torpedo-loaded chains during high water on February 18, 1868, had little inclination to force the issue. López knew that to hold Humaitá and Curupaity would be impossible. In evacuating the latter, he planned and carried out his most skillful military feat of the war. Dummy guns, a desultory fire, marching and countermarching of troops, kept the Allies confused while López sent his artillery across the Paraguay on barges. López himself left Paso Pucú on March 2 and was in the Chaco the next day. The ragged army marched up the Chaco side under great difficulties, then recrossed the Paraguay to fortify San Fernando, just north of the Río Tebicuary.

For at least a month the Brazilian-Argentine leaders did not know that Curupaity had been left with only a skeleton force. Apparently suspecting the Paraguayan game at last, Caxias ordered a reconnaissance in force on March 21 against the old Curupaity line. The small guard acquitted itself well in beating back the attack at one point, but on March 22 the defenders withdrew to Humaitá, where Colonel Alen held on faithfully while his supplies steadily ran out. With communications to López cut off and no hope of relief, the Colonel tried to commit suicide but bungled the attempt. About the same time, when observers on the ironclads reported that Humaitá was being evacuated, Caxias decided to cover himself with glory by storming the works on July 16. Somewhere between 6,000 and 12,000 men took part in the attack which resulted in the loss of 2,000 Allied troops. It was the last gasp from Humaitá. Evacuation in earnest on July 24 left only those too weak to escape. Brazilian troops in the Chaco captured about one-half of the garrison after the fugitives had exhausted their strength and ammunition. López treated the escaped fragment as a group of traitors, tortured and then shot Colonel Alen, and executed the wife and mother of Alen's second in command, who had surrendered his fugitives on August 5. No one could serve López, with the exception of a few who escaped his wrath by a miracle.

While Humaitá was being liquidated, López strengthened his camp at San Fernando. He sent Colonel Thompson to set up the battery Fortín at the Tebicuary-Paraguay junction, then he himself moved to San Fernando. Here, "on a little spot of dry ground about thirty yards square," the commander's house was built; an army of 8,000 camped in the mud. And here, also, López tortured and executed scores of "conspirators." Thompson amused himself at Fortín with target practice on Allied ships that twice ventured to run by the battery.

Humaitá's fall in July caused López to withdraw up the Paraguay to Villeta, a village some thirty kilometers south of Asunción. A rear guard at San Fernando inflicted more than 200 casualties on Brazilian attackers in August, 1868, as a reminder that the stricken viper could still sting. Below Villeta, at Angostura, Thompson took command of the last position he was to prepare during the war. Allied troops, following slowly, landed on the west side of the river in the Chaco, built a road to outflank the Villeta position, and then laid siege to it. López, it was rumored, now turned to liquor and religion for solace and amused himself by torturing and executing loyal citizens by the score. Like Francia, López let his vengeance strike even those who were his most devoted followers. Englishmen who had served Paraguay well, including George Frederick Masterman, suffered incarceration and torture on the flimsiest excuses. The common run of prisoners, crowded into moldy, vermin-infested dungeons, were subjected to tortures that would have done justice to a Nazi death camp. Cholera, endemic in the prisons, spread to the army and among civilians so swiftly that Asunción lost a fourth of its population from this cause alone in 1868.

How López treated prisoners, both Paraguayan and foreign, would be a tale of cruelty that would vary only slightly in detail. A few foreigners escaped miraculously. One of them was R. von Fischer-Treuenfeld, who built the telegraph line from Asunción to Humaitá. Accused of complicity in the nonexistent plot to overthrow López, he was arrested in October, 1868. At Las Lomas, near Villeta, he was treated unusually well, far better than the dictator's brothers, José Berges, and many more. The

German escaped with his life by a lucky whim. Dr. William Stewart, captured by Brazilians, was another of the lucky men. This English adventurer lived to become quite wealthy in Paraguay, although after the Brazilians occupied Asunción on January 5, 1869, he lost ten thousand dollars to the pillaging soldiers.

Advancing Allied troops forced López to move his principal prisoners, including his closest relatives, back from San Fernando to Villeta. During the course of this movement, in September, 1868, the select few—those charged with conspiracy—joined a thousand or more prisoners also on the march. Masterman, who was there as a victim, wrote: "Men, women, and children, in three divisions, were hemmed in by soldiers on foot and on horseback, fully armed and with sticks in their hands, with which they thrashed those outside and those that fell from exhaustion; whilst the officers, with drawn swords, rode amongst them, dealing out blows right and left in wanton cruelty. . . . The red rays of the setting sun flashed now and then from whirling sword blades within it, and more constantly from the line of bayonets without; small groups were detached in the rear, from which the horrible din, in the distance a confused roar, swelled loudest; heavy blows, dull thuds, or quick incisive lashes resounded on all sides, with an incessant clanking of fetters, groans, shouts, cries, and curses; it reminded me of the close of a battle, when there were but the helpless fugitives to slaughter." Venancio and Benigno López were held at Las Lomas, as were Doña Inocencia de Barrios and Doña Rafaela de Bedoya, sisters of López, whose husbands had been tortured and shot.

The charge that López tortured his sisters and at least threatened his mother, cannot be proved beyond doubt. General M. T. McMahon, United States minister following Washburn, testified to a Congressional committee that while he was in Paraguay (December, 1868, to May, 1869), López treated his mother and sisters as "the first ladies in the land. . . . Their residence was at that time a few miles from Piribebuy, and when I left, my house, being one of the best in Piribebuy, was given over to the mother of the president, where she lived with her daughters, and on many occasions it occurred to me that his devotion to her was

241

exceedingly filial." Washburn, on the other hand, testified that these women were held prisoners in their house, and Dr. Stewart asserted that he saw the dictator's sisters taken to jail.

Four ironclads ran past the Angostura batteries on October 1, 1868, and were joined by several others a month later at their anchorage off Villeta. In November, 32,000 Brazilians landed above Villeta; on December 5, they won a bridge over a small stream barring the road to Paraguayan lines. After a few pitched battles, in which the Paraguayan army dwindled from 8,000 to 3,000, Caxias launched an attack against the dictator's headquarters. In this battle of Lomas Valentinas, or Pikisiry, from December 21–27, the Paraguayan army was annihilated. López fled to the north. Caxias could have pursued and captured him; but the Brazilian commander was more concerned about entering Asunción and declaring the war at an end, which he did on January 5, 1869.

But the war was not over. In the cordillera east of Asunción, near the pilgrimage village of Caacupé, López gathered a handful of troops and continued a guerrilla war while scores of women and children died of starvation. Luis Felipe María Fernando Gaston de Orleans, the Comte d'Eu, son-in-law of Dom Pedro II, took over the Allied command in 1869. At least, he was no worse than Caxias, and most of the fighting was over. His armies all but encircled López in August; still the prey escaped. After a fugitive existence of a few months, he was surprised at last on the banks of the Río Aquidaban, more than two hundred kilometers north of Asunción. Historians refuse to agree on how López died, just as they quarrel about his life. Some insist that José Diabo, a common soldier, killed the dictator with a lance thrust on March 1, 1870; others say that López suffered an abdominal wound during a skirmish, and that the lance thrust was the *coup de grace*. "He died like a knight of the Middle Ages," as Pedro Calmon says.

A conflict of such length and ferocity might be thought to have ravaged the Paraguayan countryside, but there was little material damage. At El Pilar (Ñeembucú), which fell to the Brazilians in September, 1867, the conquerors plundered nearly everything worth moving. Other centers of population, including Asunción, suffered from the soldier's ancient prerogative. Captain Burton throws part of the blame on "Basque and Italian sutlers" and admits that his own countrymen "also distinguished themselves: one walked off with a church bell; and two others, having dressed up a life-sized image from a crucifix in blue jacket and duck pants, walked it down arm-and-arm to the port, pretending that their comrade was much the worse for liquor." Admit such plundering, the destruction of livestock, and occasional firing of a farm home, still the area of active operations was too small to have wrought large-scale destruction.

Paraguay's greatest loss was in man power. Although reliable statistics do not exist, we can accept the estimate of 525,000 as Paraguay's population in 1865 with relative equanimity. The figure so often cited, 1,337,449, for 1857 is obviously greatly exaggerated. A count made in 1871, under supervision of the victors, found 221,079 people in the country. Of these survivors, 106,254 were women, 86,079 were children, and 28,746 were men. Although the balance, for simple biological reasons, righted itself within not more than two generations, the belief persisted for many years that Paraguay's excess of women over men was caused entirely by the war. Competition for a man's favors developed quickly among the surviving women, a condition that led to rampant promiscuity, illegitimacy, and male laziness. These characteristics were by no means new phenomena in the world.

The nation lost about 55,000 square miles of territory to Argentina and Brazil, was charged with a huge indemnity it never paid, and sank to the bottom rank of South American republics. Burton's eulogy was earned at a terrific price: "Seldom has aught more impressive been presented to the gaze of the world than this tragedy; this unflinching struggle maintained for so long a period against overwhelming odds, and to the very verge of racial annihilation; the bulldog tenacity and semi-compulsory heroism of a Red-skin Sparta, whose only vulnerable point, the line of her river, . . . has been defended with a stubbornness of purpose, a savage valour, and an enduring desperation rare in the annals of mankind."

# PARAGUAY

Well might a maiden, lamenting the loss of lover, family, and friends, cry to the mournful gray bird, the *urutaú:*

> Weep, weep, *urutaú,*
> in branches of the *yatay,*
> no more is there a Paraguay
> where I was born, like you.
> Weep, weep, *urutaú.*

# CHAPTER XV

# Diplomat in Difficulties

CHARLES AMES WASHBURN, whose actions during the War of the Triple Alliance antagonized both López and his enemies, belonged to a family whose sons achieved fame and wealth. The future commissioner and minister to Paraguay was born in Maine in 1822, was graduated from Bowdoin College in 1848, and was admitted to the bar in Wisconsin. Always a restless young man, and often dependent upon his brothers for support, he answered California's call in 1850. Three years later he became a newspaper editor, and in 1861 President Lincoln paid part of his debt to the Washburn family by nominating him as commissioner to Paraguay. This rank was raised to minister plenipotentiary in 1862. Author of two mediocre novels, *Philip Thaxter* (1861) and *Gomery of Montgomery* (1865), Washburn published his two-volume *History of Paraguay* in 1871. Before his death in 1889, he invented the typograph and other machines and wrote various articles and more books. Charles Ames Washburn was one among thousands who possessed everything except the character and judgment that makes for greatness.

Lincoln's secretary of state, William H. Seward, was not too greatly occupied with his attempts to become a prime minister to be concerned with Paraguayan affairs. President Buchanan had not been satisfied with arbitral proceedings relative to the United States and Paraguay Navigation Company's claims, but had contented himself with refusing to announce the negative award by proclamation. Lincoln's administration, assuming that the matter was not settled, decided to send a resident commissioner to Paraguay to reopen negotiations. The post was unimportant and its first incumbent fell in the same category. Washburn left the United States on July 27, 1861, and reached Asunción on November 14. Because of the Civil War in the United States, Carlos Antonio López could afford to be defiant. He refused either to treat with an agent of the company or to discuss the matter with Washburn, and Francisco Solano continued his father's policy in that regard when he became dictator in 1862.

For some time Washburn had little to do except enjoy the country, where adobe houses, he observed, "have an air of refreshing coolness, and the dense orange-groves that stand near, with awnings of grape-vines, and the luxurious vegetation, the abounding fruit, with the general appearance of indolence and unthriftiness among the people, give one the idea that this must be a suburb to the Castle of Indolence, and that the whole life of the people is but one dream of lazy idleness and harmless delights." These adobe houses were crude structures of two or three rooms covered with thatch. Small hovels for servants, many orange trees, and a rude sugar mill and shed stood near by the *estancia* owner's home. Only small patches of land were cultivated to produce cane, corn, cotton, mandioca, and tobacco. Cattle often grazed in common on the plains and were so plentiful that meat was extremely cheap. Proceeds from tobacco sales provided money for maté, clothes, and jewelry. Favorite dishes were *puchero*, a stew with beef or chicken with rice, boiled mandioca, *chipa* (corn or mandioca bread), and a *dulce* for dessert. Oranges were so plentiful as to be practically worthless in rural areas.

Time passed pleasantly as the United States commissioner became acquainted with the foreign colony, which included many Englishmen who were inclined to sympathize with the Confederacy in the Civil War. Washburn acquired a large house near the Church of the Incarnation, for which, its owner charged, he failed to pay rent. Here he became acquainted with José Mauricio Casal, who lived at Limpio, about twenty miles away.

Don José, a widower, once was very wealthy: "The silver plate which the house contained was to be estimated by hundreds of pounds, if not by the ton. The richest silks, brocades, and damasks wrought with gold and silver threads were bought and stored away, while the necessary furniture and fixtures of the house would, perhaps, not all be of the value of one hundred dollars." Casal had kept in Francia's favor, probably through large gifts to the state; but the López family stripped him of *estancias*, silver plate, and all but the thatched adobe house he lived in. Washburn passed many hours there, hunting, taking siestas, drinking maté, smoking, and listening to Don José's pretty daughters sing plaintive, melancholy ballads in Spanish and Guaraní. There was also time to make excursions through the country, including a trip to the *yerbales* in April, 1863. Washburn's description of yerba preparation, in his *History of Paraguay*, is a classic account of that great Paraguayan industry.

Another friend was Doña Carmelita Gill de Corbal, whose brother fought at Humaitá and whose husband, a wealthy man, was forced into the ranks as a barefooted private and died early in the war. Doña Carmelita, hating López intensely, enjoyed telling her woes to the sympathetic American. Mrs. William Stewart, wife of the English doctor, was always a welcome visitor at the legation, and Washburn succeeded in delivering some six thousand dollars' worth of silver and jewels to her brother-in-law in Buenos Aires when he left the country. Doña Juana Carillo de López, mother of Francisco Solano, and her daughter Rafaela apparently confided their troubles to the American minister. Washburn knew Madame Lynch well, and his opinion of the dictator's Irish mistress is revealed in his request that General McMahon should let him know "something of Mrs. Lynch and her brats."

Critics of Charles Ames Washburn have charged that he lacked qualities essential for success in diplomacy, that he did not possess the finesse, courage, and iron nerves necessary for his Paraguayan mission. In the autumn of 1868, when Captain Burton saw him in Buenos Aires, Washburn was nearly a nervous wreck: "Many of his assertions were those of a man who was hardly responsible for his actions." But when one recalls what diplomats endured at Asunción, it is a wonder that the minister was even partially coherent. If he was not our most skillful militia diplomat, to borrow a phrase from John Adams, he was far from being the worst. Considering conditions in Paraguay, there is little basis for condemning him. He kept his government well informed about events; he refused to be bluffed or intimidated by the worst despot in the New World; he defied López when defiance might well have meant death; and he found time to work, with Porter Cornelius Bliss doing most of the research, on his history, which, in spite of inevitable prejudices, remains one of the best accounts in English of Paraguay's history to 1868.

Washburn served with satisfaction to both governments until January 16, 1865, when he took a leave of absence. Just why he selected that critical time to leave his post is hard to say. His fiancée, who returned with him as a bride, could have waited, in view of the international situation. Paraguay was at war, Washburn's health was no worse than it had ever been, and he certainly had no great financial interests at home that needed his attention, although he may have been dreaming about enlisting capital to invest in a street railway. He departed from the United States on his return trip in September, arrived at Rio de Janeiro about October 1, and found that he would need naval assistance to get through the Allied blockade on the Paraguay River.

Washburn's request for aid was directed to Rear Admiral S. W. Godon, who had assumed command of the South Atlantic Squadron (*Susquehanna, Juniata, Nipsic, Shawnut, Wasp,* and *Shamokin*) on June 21, 1865. Nettled by the minister's pompous attitude, Godon replied that he had no vessel able to make the trip but that the *Wasp* was expected shortly. Washburn waited impatiently, then went on to Buenos Aires, arriving on November 4. Godon's excuse was a lame one, since the *Shamokin* was well able to make the trip and coal was available at Montevideo, Buenos Aires, Rosario, and Corrientes. He hesitated to become involved in efforts to force passage through the Allied blockade, assumed responsibility for deciding that Washburn was not needed in Asunción, considered himself America's principal representative in the Plata area, and regarded civilian diplomats as political humbugs. The Allies, of course, were unwilling for the American minister to re-enter Paraguay, since it was feared that his presence would lend moral support to López. In view of international law governing such matters and provisions of the United States treaty with Argentina, however, Godon had every right to ask that he be permitted to carry Washburn through the blockade.

This delay angered Secretary Seward, who complained to his naval colleague in the cabinet. The latter, on April 26, 1866, ordered Godon to take Washburn to his post; but it was not until October 5 that Captain Pierce Crosby, commanding the *Shamokin,* received instructions to transport Washburn and his family to Asunción. A few days later Godon wrote a personal note to Crosby, indicating that he did not care whether the minister arrived or not. Nevertheless, Crosby was asked to pay every attention to the envoy. "Get me," Godon wrote, "a *dozen* of those *rings* made in Paraguay, marking *prices* on them—they are for others. Get me some of that Paraguaya *cordial* or *caña.*" So, on November 5, 1866, the *Shamokin* returned Washburn to his post, and, presumably, went back with rings and *caña* for Godon.

Washburn had no instructions to offer mediation in the war at the time he did so; but, on his own authority, he made an attempt to end the conflict in March, 1867. He conferred with López, then with Caxias, suggesting "reciprocal independence of the countries, including the retention of López himself as the head of the government of Paraguay." The Allies demanded that López resign as a *sine qua non* for peace. Washburn threw off common sense with a disdainful shrug when he wrote an indignant letter to Caxias. Why not ask Dom Pedro II to abdicate? Paraguay had been treated badly, the Allies had refused an honorable peace. By publishing this letter in *El Semanario,* the minister won temporary gratitude from López and permanent censure from the Allies, an attitude that served unjustly to damage his reputation for many years. López later charged that while in the Brazilian camp, Washburn had given advice on how to defeat the Paraguayans. This accusation seems less fantastic in view of Washburn's desire to tell Caxias everything he knew when he left Paraguay in 1868. Discretion was not one of his outstanding qualities.

One incident that helped to estrange López and Washburn was the case of Major James Manlove of Maryland, late a Confederate officer who had ridden with hero Nathan Bedford Forrest. This adventurer appeared in Buenos Aires, where the newspapers presented him as a sharpshooter specializing in Paraguayans. In August, 1866, Manlove arrived at Paraguayan headquarters, without benefit of passports of any kind, to offer López a plan that might help the landlocked republic, at least indirectly. Armed with letters of marque and reprisal, he proposed to assemble a fleet of privateersmen that would scour the seas for Argentine and Brazilian vessels. López, suspicious because Manlove had slipped through enemy lines so easily, laughed at the idea and sent its sponsor to Asunción, where he could be watched. Washburn, glowing with self-righteousness because he could forgive a former rebel, sought to help Manlove out of the trap he had entered so blithely. When his appeal to López met with a cold rebuff, the minister threw the protective mantle of the Stars and Stripes around this former follower of the Stars and Bars, but not even Old Glory could save the Confederate soldier from execution late in 1868.

When the Allied gunboats passed Humaitá in February, 1868, panic seized the capital. López ordered its evacuation, in spite of the fact that no preparations whatever had been made to receive the people who streamed out toward Luque, pushing their belongings in carts or carrying them on their heads and backs. Many people left their valuables in the American Legation. When Don José Berges, the minister of foreign affairs, relayed the evacuation order to Washburn, the American refused to leave. Other foreigners, among them the wives of many Englishmen employed by López, received asylum in the Legation until July 1. It was at this time that Manlove and Porter Cornelius Bliss became members of Washburn's staff. The two Allied gunboats bombarded Asunción harmlessly on February 24, then retired. Washburn stayed on, defying López to kick him out. Manlove violated the order to stay off the streets, fell into hands of the police, and passed from prison to prison before a firing squad ended his suffering in August. Washburn had tried repeatedly to help him.

The minister's most serious difficulty with López arose from having given asylum to the Portuguese acting consul, Senhor José María Leite-Pereira, whose exequatur was withdrawn in June, 1868. The consul had made the error of supplying Brazilian prisoners with money and food. Upon learning that he had taken refuge with Washburn, the Paraguayan foreign office demanded an explanation and was told that it was none of its business. A few days later, while the former foreign minister, José Berges, was in prison on a charge of treason, the government demanded a package of documents which Berges was suspected of having left with Washburn. Washburn replied that he had received none but official papers from Berges. Again the demand was repeated, together with a request that certain refugees suspected of conspiracy be expelled from the Legation. Not knowing how long Washburn would stay or how long López would respect legation immunity, the men decided to throw themselves on Paraguayan justice, confident that their innocence would be upheld. The Portuguese consul was among those who left the Legation on July 13.

Then came the great conspiracy fabrication: Washburn himself was the chief of a plot to assassinate the President. This entire conspiracy plot seems to have originated peculiarly. When the Brazilian ironclads had anchored off Asunción in February, 1868, government officials in the capital held a council to decide what to do. They knew that the one fort with its 150-pounder could offer token resistance and so ordered. When López heard about the meeting, his warped mind could place only one interpretation on the event—conspiracy! He summoned his brother-in-law, Saturnino Bedoya, put him to torture, and extracted the confession that a plot existed. Don Benigno López, the next witness, went through similar torture. Then the two were forced to name accomplices, who in turn named others, and in the end this round of extorted accusations centered on Washburn. Barrett, in his *Woman on Horseback*, would have us believe that Madame Lynch discovered plotting by the dictator's mother, brothers, and sisters. A novelist does have certain advantages. Juan Emiliano O'Leary, who wrote as though López himself were looking over his shoulder, flatly asserts that Washburn was "the soul of the movement."

These ridiculous conspiracy charges must have astounded Washburn, whose lack of discretion and diplomatic skill led him to blunder. Instead of ignoring the whole business, or merely calling it a stupid fabrication, he increased or created suspicion by replying to the monstrous lies in detail. Even the new minister of foreign affairs, Don Gumesindo Benítez, who drew up the original charge against Washburn, was later arrested and shot as a ringleader. Madame Lynch went to the Legation to urge Washburn to confess. The minister had, it is true, been very free in expressing his opinions about López and Paraguay in a way that made him a model of what a diplomat should never be; but to charge him with a plot to crown his career by eliminating López was utterly absurd. Even then he had written a large part of his *History of Paraguay*, using a long manuscript prepared by Bliss that carried the story to 1810. If spies of López, who certainly were in the Legation, had found that manuscript, it is doubtful whether Washburn ever would have bothered his brothers again.

People in the Legation were ostracized after the conspiracy concoction boiled so madly. Before a committee of the House of Representatives, Washburn testified: "There was a gloom that could be felt in the atmosphere. The Paraguayans whom I met in the street did not dare to look at me, and it was the same with some few Englishmen and others who were at work in the arsenal. ... All of us foresaw pretty well that Lopez was intending to kill us all if things continued so much longer." There was reason for this fear. Since June, López had been executing prisoners at an astonishing rate, according to General Resquín's diary. This document, captured by Brazilians after the battle of Lomas Valentinas, covers the period from May 31 to December 14, 1868, and is obviously incomplete. Resquín lists about four hundred Paraguayan criminal-traitors, deserters, and spies who were executed, died in prison, or died en route from one place of confinement to another. Three-fourths of the total were executed as criminal-traitors. Nor did foreigners escape similar treatment: thirty-three Brazilians, twenty-five Argentines, fifteen Italians, nine Spaniards, six Frenchmen, three Portuguese, two Germans, two Englishmen, and many more died or were executed. These incomplete figures are indicative of the López terror, rumors of which seeped into the beleaguered Legation surrounded by guards who were waiting for a chance to grab Masterman, Bliss, or other refugees. Every night, as soon as the windows and blinds were closed, Washburn "could hear the policemen whispering and their swords clanking beneath the window" of his bedroom. In this atmosphere of foreboding, Mrs. Washburn helped her husband move the pages of his precious manuscript from place to place until at last they rested under the cloth of a large table.

The Department of State was not unmindful of Washburn's predicament and its minister to Brazil, General James Watson Webb, was doing everything he could to rescue him. Rear Admiral C. H. Davis, Godon's successor, had sent the *Wasp* up the Paraguay, but the Brazilians refused to let it proceed beyond Curupaity, two hundred miles from Asunción. After General Webb threatened to break off relations with Brazil if there was any more interference, Admiral Davis ordered the *Wasp* to go through the blockade, and it did. Captain W. A. Kirkland, commanding the gunboat, sought out López and told him that Washburn was a friend of General Grant, and if anything happened to him, the United States would have the dictator's head. Besides, Kirkland said, six monitors were standing by, ready to knock Asunción around the López ears. López agreed to let Washburn go and issued passports for all of the legation except Masterman and Bliss. The *Wasp* anchored a few miles below Asunción on August 29, ready to receive Washburn and his party. The minister, reluctant to leave without the two men, conferred with them about the best course to pursue.

"Our united opinion," he testified, "was that if I could get away and give the alarm to our squadron as to their situation, it would be the best thing for me to do. They thought that probably before they would be killed, something would come to their relief. I started my family ahead of us so that they could not see anything of what might transpire. The French and Italian consuls went down to the steamer with us. We had got to the front door of my house, and just as we stepped off the corridor into the street, there were about 50 soldiers . . . who rushed in and caught Bliss and Masterman . . . and took them right off to prison." So Washburn got away. On the way downstream, he asked Captain Kirkland to let him go ashore at Humaitá to see Marshal Caxias, just to tell the Allied commander-in-chief all he knew about "Lopez's forces, their position and strength, and plan of operations." Kirkland quite properly refused to stop.

Porter Cornelius Bliss was something of a prodigy. This brilliant but erratic adventurer was the son of the Reverend Asher Bliss, a missionary among New York's Indians. Porter, born in 1839, entered Hamilton College in 1858 and Yale a year later. Although he did not finish his work at either institution, Hamilton awarded him an honorary Bachelor of Arts degree. Being short of funds, Bliss worked for various members of the Massachusetts Historical Society and earned flattering recommendations from Everett, Bancroft, Longfellow, and others by his unusual skill in historical research. With letters from eastern literati to show, he went to Washington to ask Lincoln for an appointment as Indian agent. But he met General Webb, forgot the Indians, and asked to be made secretary of the American Legation at Rio de Janeiro. Webb refused to ask for such an appointment but offered to take him along as tutor to his children and private secretary. Bliss accepted, left for England ahead of Webb, met the minister abroad, and proceeded with him to Brazil on the *Tyne*. The Appleton publishing house had made Bliss their agent to translate and introduce some of their books to South America. Washburn, also on the *Tyne*, formed an excellent opinion of Bliss and corresponded with him after they parted company at Rio. At the Brazilian capital Bliss moved in the best circles, and even Dom Pedro II "received him on different occasions, and exhibited great kindness toward him."

No one should blame Bliss if he preferred Pedro II's conversation to his duties as a tutor. Webb chided him for not devoting enough time to instilling in his children a high regard for truth, although the minister himself was hardly one to read moral lectures to a person of any age. This failing by no means meant that Bliss himself was a "natural liar," as some people charged. The minister had complete confidence in his secretary's sworn word, and admired him as a scholar who had an unusual ability to learn foreign languages. Bliss asked for his release, and in December, 1862, sailed with Webb on the U.S.S. *Jamestown* for Buenos Aires. He knew no Spanish; yet, within a month he was speaking the language "as well as most foreigners." Webb and Edward A. Hopkins persuaded the Argentine officials to put Bliss in charge of a party being sent to investigate Indian languages. Returning from a trip up the Bermejo for this purpose, he became editor of *The River Plate Magazine*. After a year in that work, he sailed for Paraguay on January 1, 1865, to get more information about Indians and other subjects before going back to the United States.

Asunción did not welcome foreigners in those days. Since Bliss on his way upriver passed Washburn, who was going out on leave, he had no friends in the Paraguayan capital. López set spies to watch this suspicious character, who frankly admitted his connection with Webb in Brazil and with the Argentine Government. In order to make a living and to quiet suspicion about him, Bliss proposed to López that he write a pamphlet on the boundary dispute with Brazil, a controversy in which his sympathies honestly lay with Paraguay. Upon completing this study, he undertook to write a history of Paraguay based on archival research. Since the nation's archives were not opened for his examination, Bliss interviewed many people who had known Francia and worked with secondary materials. This history reached the year 1810 in manuscript form. Naturally, López did not play a very prominent part in events of the colonial period, and Bliss had not mentioned the dictator. This oversight resulted in cancellation of the small salary he had been receiving. By this time Washburn had returned from his leave and needed a private secretary. He, too, was interested in Paraguayan history, especially when Bliss presented him with a long manuscript that made research seem unnecessary.

When the Allied gunboats approached Asunción, Washburn believed that troops would follow within a few days. Desiring to serve his friends, native and foreign, he provided the asylum already described and accepted the treasures of more than one hundred persons for safekeeping. These actions caused him to anticipate a heavier burden of correspondence, so he engaged Bliss as translator for the legation, a role that the amateur historian had been filling unofficially for some time. It was on this basis that Washburn had demanded a passport for him.

Masterman and Bliss may have paid heavily for having incurred a dictator's displeasure. Loaded with heavy irons riveted to their ankles, they were sent to headquarters at San Fernando and thrown into an open prison. There were at least sixty-five other victims—priests, Brazilian soldiers, native Paraguayans, and foreigners. Masterman saw that many "were in the last stage of misery, almost, some quite naked, covered with wounds." Bliss testified that they "received no food, except bits of entrails of animals thrown to them twice a day which they were obliged to cook for themselves." The infamous Father Fidel Maíz, himself once a prisoner, was chief inquisitor and devil's advocate. After extreme torture, Masterman and Bliss confessed to knowledge of the "conspiracy" which López used as an excuse to kill nearly everyone in Paraguay of any importance, however slight. Washburn had told his friends to say anything they liked against him if it would help them at all. No sane person would believe the torture-extracted confessions, anyway. According to their own stories, the two men resisted the *cepo uruguayana* for some time, then agreed that Washburn was indeed the center of a conspiracy against López. Bliss won time by agreeing to write a detailed biography of Washburn. This book, *The Secret History of the Mission of the North American Citizen Charles Amos Washburn*, was published by López. No intelligent person would accept it as being anything but a complete fabrication; for those who might be somewhat obtuse, Bliss not only misspelled Washburn's middle name but also threw in many stories and charges that obviously were fantastic. The result was a fascinating portrait that surely made its subject squirm more than once as he read the 323 pages. Immediately on reaching the United States in 1869, Bliss published complete retractions in the press, with explanations of how the fantasy came to be written. The book was completed on December 2, 1868. Two days later Bliss was out of irons, and soon United States naval officers rescued him along with Masterman.

So runs the tale as related to the House of Representatives committee. However, before throwing all caution aside in shedding tears for these interesting characters, note the sworn statement of one Thomas Q. Leckron, who talked with Bliss when he came aboard the *Wasp*: "I remarked . . . that after three months of torture and confinement which he had undergone it must indeed be a relief to find himself once more with those who had the power and the will to protect him. He then said that as far as torture was concerned he had never been subject to it, or even threatened with anything of the kind; that he had not been in irons; that he and Mr. Masterman had a hut as comfortable as any of those occupied by the Paraguayans; that they were given every day a sufficient allowance of beef and mandioca, as well as yerba; and that the only thing he complained of was that he could not go any distance from his quarters without being accompanied by a Paraguayan soldier."

Someone certainly was lying. Captain Ramsay reported that Dr. Frederick Skinner said Masterman and Bliss had not been tortured; Dr. Marius Duvall testified that they showed no signs of it. One thing is certain: Masterman, at least, was nearly scared to death. It is a shame to cast such doubt on stories so heart-rending; but even Washburn called Masterman "a notorious liar." And Bliss, whose memory was phenomenal, stated that Masterman's *Seven Eventful Years* was filled with inaccuracies. Dr. William Stewart, however, confirmed everything Bliss and Masterman said, and credited Washburn with having saved the lives of many foreigners. Perhaps we had better let the matter of veracity rest there.

Washburn had not forgotten these two controversial characters. After he reached Buenos Aires on September 20, he informed the British minister of their arrest, then proceeded to Rio de Janeiro. There he met General Martin T. McMahon, his successor, who was en route to Asunción with a naval escort. Rear Admiral C. H. Davis had the *Guerriere, Pawnee, Ouineberg, Kansas,* and *Wasp* in his squadron. He learned about the arrest of Masterman and Bliss on October 5, but it was not until December 3, 1868, that he reached Angostura, carrying McMahon, who first demanded, then merely requested, their release. The unfortunate men went aboard the *Wasp* on December 10 as prisoners, reached New York in February, 1869, and at once prepared a memorial to submit to Congress. Before leaving Paraguay, Bliss wrote to López asking what he should do with the thousands of dollars he had been charged with having received. Not to be outdone in this sort of grim humor, López told him to keep it and sent a few gold coins as a parting gift.

As a result of the Bliss-Masterman memorial, the House of Representatives resolved, on March 19, 1869, to investigate the acts of Washburn and the naval officers commanding the South Atlantic Squadron. Hearings begun in Washington on March 30, with Washburn as the first witness, and adjourned on April 27, were resumed by a subcommittee in New York on October 21, and ended in Washington in November. Upon presenting its report, the committee stated: "With reference to this testimony that much of it is of a conflicting character, and reveals a feeling of bitterness and animosity between different officers of the navy, and between the naval and diplomatic officers of the government . . . not creditable to the parties concerned, and subversive of that efficiency in the public service which the government has a right to expect from its officials."

The committee itself could not agree on what to recommend. A majority condemned Rear Admiral S. W. Godon for failing to help Washburn, resolved that the arrest and detention of Bliss and Masterman was "a gross insult to the honor and dignity of the United States," and read a lecture to naval officers for failing to co-operate with diplomatic officers. The minority report agreed that the arrest was an insult, that Washburn's acquiescence to that arrest compromised the flag "and could not be justified upon any consideration of personal safety," that Washburn should not have accepted a passport that did not permit his entire legation to withdraw, that Washburn had been imprudent in assuming a hostile attitude toward López "and in associating Bliss and Masterman with his legation, (one a British subject, suspected by Lopez of a conspiracy with his enemies and the enemies of his country—both adventurers and of doubtful reputation);" that Admirals Godon and Davis should not be censured.

No one except a "navy-first-and-forever" man can read the 314 pages of testimony and documents presented to the committee without concluding that many high American officers of the South Atlantic Squadron were insolent and overbearing, with hardly enough discretion to scrub a deck. For several months after General McMahon entered Paraguay, the Allies cut off all communication to or from him. At last, according to Dr. Marius Duvall, when Commander Francis M. Ramsay wanted to ask McMahon for permission to marry his sister, Admiral Davis let him go on a passenger vessel to Asunción. The Admiral's son went along. "Young Davis . . . when he came back spoke of having a splendid time, driving in a coach and four with Mrs. Lynch, and was particularly delighted with the little arrangements of Mrs. Lynch, when she had some of the prettiest girls in Paraguay to wait on the table, veiled very faintly indeed." Perhaps Ramsay and young Davis actually went to deliver dispatches.

General McMahon presented his credentials to López on December 12, 1868, after Bliss and Masterman had been surrendered. He did not agree fully with Washburn's course but determined to be on good terms with the dictator. After a few days at headquarters, the new minister went to Piribebuy where the Paraguayan Government was located. McMahon saw López four or five times and urged him to stop the war. In May, 1869, he received his recall but delayed leaving for a few weeks. His principal and almost sole service to the United States lay in securing freedom for the two notorious prisoners; but, if Washburn's charge is true, he rendered far more valuable services to López and Madame Lynch.

Perhaps General McMahon could tell how it was that Madame

Lynch managed to live in Europe after her expulsion from Paraguay. This peculiar diplomat, the rumored executor of the dictator's last testament, had a lot of baggage when he sailed from Asunción. "Among other things," Washburn asserts, "there were eleven tercios of the yerba maté, and also a great number of boxes and packages, besides the trunks supposed to contain his personal baggage which he had taken into Paraguay. On reaching the lines of the Brazilians, they provided him with the means of transporting these rewards of industry to Asunción, where he remained for several days; thence he took passage in a merchant steamer for Buenos Aires, where the greatest curiosity was felt to know what these boxes from the camp of López contained, and whether the yerba maté in the tercios was solid, or merely used as packing for ounces and the jewelry that had been stolen from the murdered victims of Lopez and Madam Lynch. He was, nevertheless, allowed to take everything away with him when he left the Plata for France." If this serious accusation were true, it would brand McMahon as the accomplice of Paraguay's two greatest scoundrels. He was, surely, completely unqualified for diplomatic service, a trait that he shared with Charles Ames Washburn.

# CHAPTER XVI

# A Half-Century Between Wars

PARAGUAY, ruined and dismembered, suffered fearfully to be rid of its criminal dictator. Territorial losses, a huge indemnity (which was never paid), and military occupation until 1876, were imposed upon the little republic by Brazil and Argentina. There had been hard times before, times when manufactured articles fell far short of actual need, when people went half-naked for want of textiles or wore leather garments, when clouds of locusts destroyed their crops. Those times were comparatively mild in their effects. There were few occasions when hunger stalked the land and actual famine had never swept the country. Things were different after the great war. Albert Amerlan, who visited Paraguay in those days of despair, found that "Poverty, want and corruption now reign. . . . Outcasts, tramps and adventurers corrupted with vices, the scum of humanity . . . removed here after the termination of the war, to appropriate to themselves the estates of the perished Guaranis and to console the hundreds of thousands of bereaved widows and maidens, over their losses." There was little sympathy in Brazil, where opponents of the monarchy did not let the people forget their losses in treasure and men, or in Argentina, where the conviction persisted that Paraguayans were all savages anyway. The former Allies looked upon each other with suspicion; and that distrust served to mitigate the effects of military occupation and kept Paraguay from disappearing altogether as an independent nation.

261

Paraguay was a pawn in the game of Brazil *vs.* Argentina in which each country feared that the other planned to absorb their former enemy. Military occupation, as Cárcano says in *Guerra del Paraguay*, was "a war between the Allies for liquidation of the contract." Brazil had the advantage since her troops held Asunción, her statesmen dictated to Paraguayan officials, and her officers fraternized with and even married native women hungry for men. Argentina's few troops held out disconsolately across the river at Villa Occidental, hoping for reinforcements that would extend their country's boundaries across the Chaco to Bahía Negra. The two great victors nibbled at Paraguayan territory but prevented each other from taking huge gulps, while Bolivia stood by nervously, hoping to make good her own nebulous claim to the Chaco. José María de Silva Paranhos, Viscount of Rio Branco, blandly fomented civil war in Entre Ríos and Uruguay, according to Argentine belief, to keep Argentina busy elsewhere.

For six years this cat-and-mouse game, a "cold" war, went on as negotiators and foreign ministers sought to end the occupation. A group of Paraguayan radicals tried to accomplish the same result in 1874. Jaime Sosa Escalada, Adolfo Alsina, and Nicasio Oroño communicated with Carlos Tejedor, Argentina's former foreign minister and then envoy to Paraguay. Their plot was simple: Jovellanos would resign the presidency, go to Buenos Aires with Francisco F. Fernández as secretary, sign a treaty of peace, then return with the document for approval by the Congress. But the Baron of Araguaya, Brazil's dictator in Paraguay, got wind of the plot and broke up the scheme. He had Juan Bautista Gill, a Brazilian puppet, lead a revolt against President Salvador Jovellanos, and sent Sosa to represent Paraguay in Brazil. Ignored at Dom Pedro's court, the brilliant and patriotic Sosa negotiated with Tejedor, who had been transferred to Rio de Janeiro, so successfully that the two men signed a treaty in May, 1875. The Conservative Brazilian cabinet, considering Sosa's act one of rebellion, sent a gunboat to Asunción to get President Gill's disavowal while Argentine newspapers hailed the Sosa-Tejedor treaty. President Gill obediently summoned Congress in June to reject the treaty and to declare Sosa a traitor to his country—Sosa, one of Paraguay's intensely loyal and patriotic men at a time when loyalty was almost impossible to find.

Argentina, balked by Brazilian control in Paraguay, transferred negotiations to other hands. Senator Dardo Rocha went to Villa Occidental to look over the Argentine occupation zone and on to Asunción, where he conferred with Gill and Facundo Machaín, minister of foreign affairs. Since neither would or could agree to the cession of Villa Occidental, he returned to Buenos Aires without accomplishing much. A change of ministries in Rio de Janeiro and Buenos Aires in 1875 promised an end to the diplomatic impasse. Brazil was tired of the expensive occupation, President Gill threw off his Brazilian shackles, and Argentina sent Manuel Derqui to represent her interest in Asunción. Derqui worked so smoothly that by the end of 1875, Machaín went to Buenos Aires to sign the definitive treaty. Brazil sent its minister to Uruguay to participate in the discussions which went along so satisfactorily that on February 3, 1876, the war of nerves came to an end. A few months later the last foreign troops left Paraguayan soil.

Political reconstruction began several months before López met his death at Cerro Corá. An ineffective provisional government, formed in August, 1869, under Allied supervision attempted to bring some sort of order into being. Cirilo Antonio Rivarola, Carlos Lóizaga, and José Díaz de Bedoya represented the people as a triumvirate. They summoned a constitutional convention to meet on August 15, 1870, and filled the interim with various decrees in an effort to recreate a government. They had to work under terrible handicaps. There were decrees to relieve hunger, to set up judicial and police officers, to open all ports to foreign trade, to remove restrictions on exploitation of natural resources, to found a ministry of agriculture, to establish a school system, to abolish slavery, and many more. Don Federico Guillermo Báez spoke hopefully to the convention when it assembled: a new era was dawning for a Paraguay freed from its tyrants, future development would be rapid, and expanding commerce would enable Paraguayans to take their proper place among civilized peoples. Working diligently under the guidance of José Segundo Decoud, the convention ended the triumvirate by electing Cirilo Antonio Rivarola as provisional president on September 1, 1870. He became president for four years on November 25, when the new constitution went into effect. Rivarola, son of an old opponent of the López family, had suffered imprisonment during the war and had fought heroically in the last battle. He made a poor president, had few social graces, smoked incessantly, and was indisposed to mental exertion. However, since Brazilians actually ruled the country, it did not matter what sort of president he was.

Paraguayans were politically immature in 1870, at least in the party system. Political parties never had advanced beyond the point of factionalism, had never existed as formal organizations, and had no traditional issues. Newspapers attempted to whip up enthusiasm for their publishers. *La Regeneración, La Voz del Pueblo,* and *La Opinión Pública* all endeavored to attract adherents. Juan José and José Segundo Decoud, brilliant descendants of a first family, were editors and politicians, as were Cándido Barreiro and Juan Silvano Godoy. Dr. Facundo Machaín, with support from young exiles who dribbled back to the country, formed the Great Club of the People; veterans rallied under Barreiro, head of the Club of the People. Radicals so plagued President Rivarola that, following Brazilian orders, he dissolved the Congress in October, 1871, and resigned when the new Congress assembled in December.

General Bernardino Caballero, greatest surviving hero of the war, founded the conservative Republican (or Colorado) Party about 1874 and controlled the government for thirty years. Caballero and General Patricio Escobar made and unmade presidents at will, with little interference from the Liberal party which Don Antonio Taboada organized in 1887 to give strength to demands for freedom of suffrage. A Liberal revolt from August to December, 1904, terminating in the Pilcomayo Agreement, turned the rascals out for about thirty years, but not without several bloody protests. "The revolution of August, 1904," says Juan José Soler, "was the first popular movement the Republic had known." Dr. Cecilio Báez and General Benigno Ferreira—a Liberal and a soldier in alliance—caused it; Manuel J. Duarte, Manuel Gondra, Elías Ayala, Eduardo Schaerer, Félix Paiva, and other Liberals carried it out; but Adolfo Soler was its soul. His son, Juan José, helped Antonio Taboada, Luís A. Riart, and others to found *El Liberal* as a vehicle to propagandize party principles. Liberals and Colorados sought unsuccessfully to regularize political affairs for the next eight years, while nine presidents came and went. Paraguay had twenty-nine presidents from 1870 to 1932, which means that on the average each served slightly more than one-half of his four-year term.

Paraguayan military power, destroyed by the war, remained insignificant until the conflict with Bolivia. Military training was haphazard, the army was held in low repute, and its ranks were filled with conscripts chosen arbitrarily by local authorities. The four-year "enlistment" was regarded as equivalent to a jail sentence. One battalion of infantry, two cavalry squadrons, two to four artillery batteries, and a company of machine gunners made up the army for about three decades. The government occasionally sent young men to Argentina and Chile for military instruction, under the theory that they would return to form officer cadres for old and new units.

After the revolution of 1904, the Liberals disbanded the army and started anew. They created a general staff and a military school, activated new units with modern equipment, and limited conscription to men of good character from eighteen to twenty years of age. Under the guidance of Argentine and Chilean instructors, the Liberal army made slight progress until 1908 when another revolution split it into factions. Major Albino Jara, leader of the rebels, became minister of war. He reorganized the army, divided the country into military zones, suppressed the general staff, closed the military school, and increased the number of men under arms. Compulsory military service began in September, 1909, to replace the conscript army. Two military tremors, one on January 17 and the other on February 11, shook the country slightly in 1911 without overthrowing the government. Anarchy prevailed in the army and continued until the army was again dissolved and reorganized in 1912 under Manuel Gondra, then minister of war. This reorganization marked the beginning of Paraguay's revitalized army, the creation of a force that was later trained by foreign missions and which gave such a good account of itself in the Chaco War.

Revolution itself is an old story in Paraguay. The custom goes back to that April day in 1544 when enraged royal officials hatched the plot that sent Álvar Núñez Cabeza de Vaca back to Spain in chains. People and livestock always bore the heaviest losses while real property usually escaped with little damage in the many military revolts (*cuartelazos*) against the existing regime in the six decades between real wars. These uprisings were not a passing phenomenon. They are a part of Paraguayan national life, an inalienable right of the people. Revolution in Paraguay, as in all of Latin America, is a social malaria, a fever that strikes almost without warning, subsides, then strikes again. Revolution is also a cure for governmental longevity and self-perpetuation, since it is an axiom in Latin American politics that the government does not lose an election. There has never been a civil war of long duration in Paraguay (that of 1947 lasted for five months), nor has there been one that substituted orderly progress in place of congenital chaos. There has never been a popular uprising against great landlords, or a war against clerical privilege, as in Mexico. Political and economic issues, until the last decade, have been submerged in personal issues. Even the Febrerista revolt against Higinio Morínigo in 1947, complicated as it may have been by Argentine interference, seems to have followed the pattern that became routine during those years when Paraguay was attempting to regain its balance after the War of the Triple Alliance.

Each revolution that occurred after 1870 had its fascinating stories, its heroism, terror, and sorrow. Alexander MacDonald, in *Picturesque Paraguay*, describes a *cuartelazo* of 1908 led by Major Jara, who represented a radical wing of the Liberal party. Long before dawn on July 2, Jara and a few companions captured the guard at the artillery barracks, mounted guns at street corners to command approaches to public buildings, posted an infantry regiment at key points, and waited for the shooting that would begin with daybreak. Police officers, when they discovered Jara's dispositions, displayed an understandable indignation, especially when the *Libertad* at anchor in the harbor bombarded their station. President Benigno Ferreira gathered about one hundred men to protect the palace, while the *comandante* at Villa Rica hastened to his aid with two hundred farmers who knew nothing about the revolt and cared less. Jara's men cut the railway and telegraph lines, started to storm various public places, and seduced a regiment that came from Concepción with the noble resolve to rescue their president. General Ferreira, himself the conqueror of the redoubtable Caballero, resigned after three days. This little fracas resulted in some four hundred casualties and was called "a political crime of fatal transcendency for the country."

A more violent revolt occurred in 1911, a troubled year even in Paraguay. President Manuel Gondra refused to keep Jara in his cabinet, so Jara compelled Gondra to resign on January 17, kept the job himself for a while, then gave it to Liberato Rojas in July. Followers of Gondra managed to overthrow Rojas. Rojistas accepted the challenge; and for two days street battles raged, in which four hundred were killed. Rojas returned to the capital and then attempted to drive the Gondristas out of Pilar, 250 miles from the capital. Three thousand men set out on this foray, seven hundred returned. General Gondra obtained more guns, including a naval piece mounted on a railway car. The attacking Rojistas seized a locomotive, packed it with high explosives, and sent it careening madly down the rails. A crew manning the naval gun fired desperately until a lucky shot struck the locomotive with rather startling consequences. The final scrap in this revolt apparently occurred in Paraguarí on May 11, 1912. Government troops defeated a small force of Gondristas outside of the town and then marched in confidently to celebrate their victory, mistakenly believing that they had defeated the main rebel force. They marched into an ambush. When Gondristas stopped shooting, "Piles of bodies choked the roads, doorways, and even window ledges. By sundown there was only one party

left in this decimated little South American state." The judgment
was too hopeful: there were still Radical Liberals, Democratic
Liberals, Common Liberals, and Moderate Liberals!

Hampered though Paraguay was by political chaos, economic
recovery could be observed in the founding of banks and large-
scale enterprises. The Banco Agrícola, opened in 1887, enlarged
its activities in 1894 through addition of the Council of Agriculture and Industries, and was active in promoting scientific exploitation of Paraguay's fertile land and in introducing new crops.
The Banco Francés del Río de la Plata in Buenos Aires assisted
the government in establishing the Banco de la República in
1908. Several private banks appeared, testifying to a faith in the
country's future. The Banco Mercantil del Paraguay, founded
with German capital in 1890, prospered sufficiently to establish
five branches by 1916. In that year, also, the Banco de España y
Paraguay opened its doors and soon had two branches. The
Banco de Londres y Río de la Plata introduced English capital
on a larger scale, and the Banco Germánico de América del Sud
set up a Paraguayan branch that soon gained an enviable reputation for sound practices and courteous treatment of its clients.
These institutions somehow managed to survive political uncer-
tainties, although their managers had many uneasy moments as
rebels scurried past shuttered doors.

Little effort was made for more than seventy years after the
War of the Triple Alliance to develop Paraguay's mineral resources. The country could have had heavy industries, but capital and enterprise were lacking. It was too busy to exploit an extremely fertile soil that produced fabulous yields of cotton, tobacco, corn, coffee, sugar cane, mandioca, rice, and citrus fruits, and
such forests products as yerba, rubber, quebracho, and lumber.
The government granted concessions to foreign capitalists to
exploit these natural resources. Packing plants, quebracho works,
and other enterprises appeared. Foreign capital completed the
railroad to Buenos Aires, provided funds to start the government
itself, inaugurated lines of river steamers, and invested in public
utilities. These developments were largely the work of individual
foreign immigrants, well-financed corporations, and agricultural

colonies. Investments were so well balanced among British, American, German, French, Italian, and Argentine companies that little antiforeign sentiment appeared among the people, who failed to realize how they were being exploited.

Paraguay offered undeniable advantages to the immigrant. His rights, in the most approved democratic manner, were protected by the constitution of 1870. Foreigners enjoyed all the civil rights granted to citizens, the inalienable protection of life, liberty, and property, the essential freedoms of religion, speech, press, and assembly. Only freedom from revolutionary disturbances was lacking. Favorable land laws encouraged both large and small scale colonization in the country's 150,000 square miles of territory. Heads of families need bring only $30 in gold. They would be housed temporarily by the government, their goods and implements would be landed free of charge and free of customs duties under a law of 1903. Moreover, the Paraguayan government would give free passage second class from Buenos Aires to Asunción. With about $340 in gold, it was estimated that an immigrant family of four could build a rancho, fence and clear about twelve acres, and live for eight months while waiting for a harvest. Immigration remained on a small scale in spite of propaganda and favorable laws. Although notable exceptions did occur, the most successful agricultural immigrants came in as members of colonies.

Population gains from immigration were slight. The total for the years 1905–25 reached only 13,258, and Germans, Spaniards, and Italians accounted for nearly 60 per cent of this figure. By 1928, according to Dr. Adolf N. Schuster's *Paraguay*, there were 8,000 Spaniards and nearly 20,000 Italians in the country. From Argentina came 1,659 settlers; from Brazil and Uruguay combined, only 323. Austria, Russia, Sweden and France were the only other countries to send more than 100 immigrants during the two decades. Considering only persons with occupations, farmers made up somewhat more than one-half of the total.

European immigrants, it is quite apparent, paid little attention to Paraguay from 1870 to 1929. The main stream flowed to the United States, smaller streams went to Argentina and to

Brazil, but only a trickle reached remote Paraguay despite the work of that country's champions. Among Englishmen who urged their compatriots to seek fortunes in the Guaraní paradise was Alexander K. MacDonald. After fourteen years in the country, he published his *Picturesque Paraguay* in 1911, in which he painted an attractive picture, especially of "A Village Belle," a lovely girl in long braids who holds a bouquet of flowers to set off long fringes of a black mantilla that drapes over her inviting shoulders. She would be worth emigrating for. This gorgeous beauty could hardly fit MacDonald's description: "Many of the daughters of Paraguay—out in the country—lead an ideal life, as far as health is concerned. She usually gets up at daylight in the morning and trips away to the nearest market, with a basket of fruit or vegetables upon her head, thinking nothing of carrying her burden several miles on the way to town. With shoulders squared and head erect, she inhales the fresh morning air with the delight of perfect life. Arrived in town, she does a pleasant gossip, disposes of her wares, buys a few pounds of meat and groceries—and flits away home with a good appetite for the homely meal which has been prepared by the old grandmother, who was left in charge of the house. Then she goes to the spring to wash her clothing, or, perhaps, to hoe the weeds in the family cultivation patch. A siesta in the middle of the day, and then the pounding of maize in a wooden mortar, for the evening repast. The use of the heavy wooden pestle strengthens the muscles of the arms and chest, and provides a splendid breathing exercise. Later on the cows are milked, supper partaken of by the simple folk, and away to bed—unless there is a dance at a neighbour's, when she tricks herself out in her finery . . . and no doubt enjoys her outing just as much in her own way as My Lady X—in pearls and diamonds—at a social entertainment in the West End. If the peasant girl's soul was looked after as well as her body, she might then have really a good time. Unfortunately, even in this matter Lady X is sometimes no more spiritual than our peasant girl in the backwoods." MacDonald did not mean to be funny; but if he had added that this little sprite, tripping off so gaily on her long hike, was barefooted, smelled of garlic, smoked a short black cigar, had hookworm, and actually worked like a horse, he would have been closer to the truth. At least, the bonny belle was a busy lass!

Immigration suffered somewhat from wild reports of unbearable heat, swarms of mosquitoes, man-eating jaguars, venomous spiders, deadly fevers, and terrible snakes. These exaggerations failed to discourage hardy enterprisers of several nationalities. A French botanist, Benjamin Balansa, began the petitgrain-oil industry in 1876, taking advantage of the great number of orange trees growing east of the river. A few years later another Frenchman, Domingo Barthe, began to exploit six hundred leagues of land bordering the Paraná River in the east. From yerba, bananas, timber, and other products he amassed such great wealth that his holdings soon extended into Brazil and Argentina. His commercial empire included ships, ports, sawmills, *estancias,* and haciendas. José Fassardi, Italian by descent, formed a partnership in 1897 to establish a steam sawmill. By 1914, José Fassardi y Cía. was recognized as one of the strongest firms in the country. Success stories like these could be multiplied many times. The failures will be omitted.

Corporations, dominated by few or many investors, engaged in so many activities that they assumed great importance in colonization, manufacturing and processing, and transportation. The Société Foncière du Paraguay owned the largest and best-organized *estancias* in eastern Paraguay. Occupying 234 square leagues near the Brazilian border a few kilometers east of the river, this French company revolutionized the cattle industry by crossing Argentine Hereford bulls with native cows. Their experiments in horse breeding also achieved great success. Across the river in the Chaco, William Cooper and Nephews, a British enterprise established in 1905, imitated La Foncière on eighty square leagues. Industrial Paraguaya, another British company, began operations in 1888. Primarily concerned with yerba production, this company alone was shipping about 5,000,000 kilograms of maté annually by 1910, drawing from 456 leagues of *yerbales.* Cattle, timber, and rubber were subsidiary enterprises carried on in another 684 leagues of forest and prairie. The Paraguay Land and Cattle Company held 1,687,500 hectares of land and ran 45,000 head of cattle; the New York and Paraguay Company exploited 375,000 hectares of Chaco land near Puerto Pinasco; the Gibson Paraguayan Estates Company held 150,000 hectares and ran 10,000 cattle. These are but examples of large-scale exploitation that contributed greatly to Paraguay's economic recovery. E. A. Hopkins had made his pioneer effort altogether too soon, and it is doubtful whether officials of the International Products Company, an American corporation, ever thought of him as they prospered where he had failed.

Paraguayan governments disposed of great tracts in the Chaco between 1880 and 1915. In those lush times, national patrimony disappeared in an orgy of speculation and sharp practices. Carlos Casado, Anglo-Paraguay, and "Tex" Rickard were among the men and companies who sought and received huge areas for practically nothing. As Hans Tolten remarked in *Enchanting Wilderness,* "Everything swam in gold. . . . Today they bought; tomorrow they sold. And the profits were squandered in dissipation. . . . To purchase at five gold *centavos* per acre was nothing extraordinary, and twenty *centavos* were only obtained after the tenth owner." Then there followed a scrip scheme, in which the same piece of land was sold to many buyers. This orgy ended with foreign financiers in control of far more land than was good for the country.

When Carlos Casado established Puerto Casado in 1886, he started the Chaco's most prosperous enterprise. Beginning with 3,000 square leagues, larger than Belgium and Luxemburg combined, the company disposed of parcels amounting to 1,200 square leagues to individual enterprisers and set up mills to process varied products of its princely domain. Puerto Casado was a town of 3,000 people by 1928, with electric lights, plumbing, schools, a hospital, a hotel, churches, and courts. A narrow gauge railway penetrated the interior for 150 kilometers, beyond which another 120 kilometers were under construction. More than 20,-000 head of cattle ran on the company's model *estancia;* from 7,000 to 15,000 tons of quebracho extract came annually from its tannin factory which employed 1,000 workers.

Foreign colonization, promoted for the most part by societies formed abroad, suffered somewhat from corporate competition. Nevertheless, each decade found more hopeful immigrants seeking wealth in Paraguay. In the half-century from 1870 to 1920, thirty-two colonies were begun, nine of them in 1918 alone. Some were primarily of one nationality; others were mixtures of foreign immigrants and Paraguayans; none was very large. San Bernardino, founded in 1881 by General Bernardino Caballero on the north shore of Lake Ipacaraí, counted Germans and Paraguayans among its moderately prosperous community in 1888. The Leipzig Company founded Nueva Germania about 210 kilometers northeast of Asunción in July, 1887, on a grant of 12 square leagues. Concentrating attention on plantations of oranges, bananas, coffee, cotton, yerba, and sugar cane, this colony had about 1,500 acres in cultivation by 1915. Germans obtained a grant of 295 square kilometers near Encarnación in 1898, and two years later settlers appeared to begin the Hohenau colony. The enterprise struggled along indifferently for a few years, then began to prosper on corn, yerba, wheat, grapes, mandioca, beans, and other crops. Hohenau, the village around which the colony centered, had about 1,000 inhabitants in 1915. Gaboto, begun in 1901 by Germans, Spaniards, Argentines, and Paraguayans between Asunción and the Tebicuary River, was larger than Hohenau in 1915 in spite of an unfavorable location.

Italian scholars turned more and more toward Paraguayan themes at the end of the nineteenth century. The prolific peninsula had been pouring prolific people into Argentina, Brazil, and the United States by the millions. Some of them found wealth in Paraguay operating banks, public utilities, and mercantile establishments. Celso Pusinieri e Hijos set up the first Paraguayan shoe factory; Dr. Stefano Paternó, prime mover in the Italo-American Colonization Society, founded two agricultural colonies. The first, Trinacria, was begun in 1898 with a grant of about 30,000 hectares, some sixty miles north of Asunción, which was excellent for cattle raising and general agriculture. By 1915, there were 145 homes in small clusters on this grant. Nueva Italia, begun in 1906 between Lambaré and Angostura south of Asunción, was one-half as large as Trinacria. Each colonist in Nueva Italia received, after three years' occupation, title to a 16-hectare lot upon which he had to plant 1,000 orange or other trees and 200 vines. After meeting these conditions, the colonist might buy another lot of the same size for $20 gold per hectare. A hundred families, cultivating 433 hectares, were prospering at Nueva Italia by 1915.

Nueva Australia, north of Villa Rica, had a slightly quixotic origin. William Lane, a Socialist free-lance journalist of Australia, looked upon Paraguay as a place where paradise might be regained after labor had made a stirring effort to win recognition of its rights in Australia by means of an unsuccessful general strike. Lane formed the Australian Co-operative Society, approached the Paraguayan government for a grant, and received 100 square leagues of excellent land. Lane's first batch of 250 immigrants arrived at Montevideo on the *Royal Tar* in 1893 and transferred to a river vessel for the trip to Asunción. These Socialists began to quarrel about how their Utopia should operate even before it was well started. Lane seceded from the group in disgust and founded Cosme in 1894, while Frederick Kidd directed the parent Nueva Australia along non-socialist lines. Both colonies prospered moderately.

Perhaps the most significant colonization scheme in the country's history is the Mennonite Chaco settlement west of Puerto Casado. General Samuel McRoberts, former president of New York's Chatham-Phoenix National Bank, bought 323,700 acres from Casado in 1921, then exchanged much of it for Mennonite wheat lands in Canada. Late in 1926, the paddle-wheel steamer *Apipé* carried the first contingent, 309 strong, to their promised land. By the end of April, 1927, some 2,000 of those religious exiles were settled in the Chaco at Colonia Menno. Seeking for 400 years to be let alone, followers of Menno Simons had moved often in search of a land where they might practice their religion undisturbed by war. They went to southern Russia in 1783, then to Canada and the United States, where industrious, sober people expected to live at peace. At last they found in Paraguay a government willing to grant them and their descendants perpetual military exemption. The charter, granted in July, 1921, guaranteed practical self-government, suspension of tariff duties on basic imports for ten years, freedom of taxation for a similar period, and complete freedom of immigration. Thanks to preliminary work by Fred Engen, the first arrivals avoided those hardships so often a part of new colonization efforts. At Puerto Casado a comfortable hotel, homes for transients, and other comforts provided quarters until dwellings could be built in the Chaco.

More and more Mennonites arrived from Russia, Poland, Germany, Manchuria, Canada, and the United States until there were 5,000 of them distributed in thirty-six villages in 1933. A number of cattle farms, stocked with high-grade animals, seemed to bear out the hope that this land was one where a man could murmur "with a sigh of relief: 'This is beautiful; this is wonderful.'" That was before the wells went dry and hordes of termites and locusts brought the plagues of Babylon. When the giant grasshoppers stripped crops to their stems, peanuts became a staple food; but there was little to the rumor, spread in 1933, that peanuts constituted the only food Mennonites had for long periods. Hardships certainly existed in the Chaco, and they were not eased by poor transportation that made it extremely difficult to move crops to market. Land acquired at three dollars an acre seemed expensive in the face of rising costs. The Chaco War threatened to engulf the Mennonite villages, causing the Paraguayan commander at one time to order their evacuation. Bolivians fell back before a determined attack, and the order was rescinded. The peaceful colonists were so grateful that they threw open their homes to entertain their saviors.

Not all of the Mennonites were willing to endure the Chaco trials. There were many desertions during the first year and later contingents had little of the forbearance shown by those from Canada. New colonists from Russia arrived in May, 1930, to form Colonia Fernheim on 60,000 acres. Some 800 of this group left in 1937 to found Colonia Friesland near Asunción east of the river, and a short time later more than 300 Hutterites bought 20,000 acres near Friesland. Colonia Fernheim in 1943 boasted a population of about 1,450.

Paraguay's public school system really dates from a decree issued by President Rivarola on March 7, 1870. Political chiefs (*jéfes políticos*) of each department and commandants of each villa were to establish one or more schools within their respective jurisdictions. All parents were required to send their children to these schools. Two years later, a Council of Public Instruction appeared to make recommendations for improvement, and a law authorized the president to engage foreign teachers. By that time the Colegio Nacional was functioning. After five years, in 1877, it was reorganized and continued as a secondary school. A normal school, connected with the Colegio, opened in 1874. Before the decade ended, there were eighty schools for boys and twenty for girls in rural areas. Still the educational system was in its formative period. Improvements continued intermittently. A School of Law, created in 1882, became the "illustrious mother" of the National University, which was provided for in a decree dated October 18, 1892. Fine lawyers, writers, and journalists, graduates of Paraguayan schools, appeared by 1900 to create a golden age of national literature—Manuel Domínguez, Cecilio Báez, Manuel Gondra, Fulgencio R. Moreno, Blas Garay, and many more. Contributions of these men in law, history, belles-lettres, geography, political science, and other fields justified the statement that, from 1870 to 1910, Paraguay made more intellectual progress than in the previous three centuries. Still there were no public libraries other than the struggling Biblioteca Pública, which had gained a museum in 1875.

The twentieth century opened with educational facilities woefully inadequate to meet the people's needs. The number of schools increased from 349 with 29,600 pupils in 1905, to 618 with 71,324 pupils in 1914. Quality of instruction left much to be desired, but the statistics indicate that some progress was being made. Education in public health, agriculture, mechanical arts, child care, and other broad fields lagged far behind the need.

The Rockefeller Foundation revealed an interest in the public health problem in the nineteen twenties, when it subsidized a *Campaña Sanitaria* (Health Campaign) which set up centers of instruction and clinics in various parts of the country. At the

The Presidential Palace in Asunción

A typical farm worker's home near Asunción

Photographs by Fenno Jacobs from Three Lions

Campaña's central office in Asunción, Rockefeller and native doctors labored with patience and skill to decrease the ravages of hookworm and other diseases that were sapping the nation's vitality. A brilliant young doctor, John Austin Kerr of Chicago, arrived early in 1928 to take over the work. His yellow Buick roadster with the right-hand drive became a familiar sight on Paraguay's few kilometers of improved roads and on the seemingly limitless stretches of wagon roads that connected the Campaña's field offices. Early in 1929, when President José P. Guggiari was more interested in building up armaments than in promoting health education, the Paraguayan government failed to provide its share of funds for the Campaña Sanitaria, and Dr. Kerr returned to Rio de Janeiro. There was altogether too much willingness in Paraguay to be helped and not enough desire by Paraguayans to help themselves. They had far more enthusiasm for swatting Bolivians in the Chaco than for warring against hookworms in their intestines.

Easily the best of all private schools in the country was the Colegio Internacional, supported by the United Christian Missionary Society. Clement Manly Morton was its director when the Colegio opened its doors in March, 1920. He started a building program, enlisted the support of government officials, and had enthusiastic backing from the small foreign colony. When Robert B. Lemmon succeeded Morton in 1926, the Colegio Internacional had become the finest primary and secondary school in the land. Slowly the curriculum expanded, enrollment increased, both Paraguayan and foreign teachers served on the faculty, and new buildings were added to meet the steadily increasing demands for admission. Other new schools in the twenties raised the cultural level considerably. The Medical School of the National University, dropped in 1908, was reorganized in 1928; a private agricultural college, which had an intermittent existence at Ipacaraí, was overshadowed by a government agricultural school in 1925, which was located in Asunción's beautiful Jardín Botánico. At the end of the decade, there were 45 private and 733 public elementary schools in the country with an enrollment of 104,089 pupils. Asunción and its suburbs, with a population of about 130,000, made a good showing with 10,894 pupils in intermediate and upper grades. The Colegio República de Argentina, which enrolled more than 1,000 pupils, was the largest elementary school.

Education, unfortunately, was not exempt from political considerations. Even in primary instruction, military chieftains interfered with texts for the purpose of eliminating the influence of regimes overthrown by the most recent *cuartelazo*. Juan José Soler, one of four teachers trained in Argentina on scholarships at the turn of the century, recalls how two readers he wrote for the first and third grades were discarded by a new government in 1908. Teachers did not despair when confronted by such officious interference from politicians who had no genuine interest in education but continued to work, through the Consejo Nacional de Educación, for educational advancement. Soler, Manuel Benítez, Manuel Gondra, and Eusebio Ayala were among educators who strove, in the first twenty years of the century, to provide for Paraguay that educational foundation upon which an adequately functioning democracy must rest.

Professors in the National University were too enthusiastic in urging impressionable young men to participate actively in politics. They needed little encouragement. Once begun, the habit became so deadly that even the university itself was divided by partisan groups, some of which were so strong that they could force professors either to resign or to collaborate in their program of social and political action. A number of students in 1927, observing university reforms in Argentina after 1918, demanded greater control, an end to faculty tyranny, a "university republic" with semiautonomous powers. A law of 1929 created, in response to this demand, an autonomous university. This autonomy meant student government, not the insipid, picayunish thing permitted by boards of timorous trustees in the United States, but a genuine self-control vested in the Consejo Superior with a minimum of legislative interference. Each college or faculty had its own directive council, composed of teachers and students; each college, the alumni, and the professors were represented on the Superior University Council.

278

Agriculture made great progress between the two great foreign wars but still had scarcely tapped available resources. Cotton, tobacco, rice, sweet potatoes, sugar cane, maize, peanuts, alfalfa, and a bewildering variety of fruits were produced on a fairly small scale for the most part. Mandioca led all crops in 1928 with nearly 600,000,000 kilos; sugar cane, maize, and sweet potatoes were the other leaders. Oranges, pineapples, and bananas were abundant. No one cared to count the orange trees, but a banana census revealed about 600,000 plants under cultivation in 1929.

Viticulture, which enjoyed a brief period of prosperity during colonial days, was revived by Carlos Voigt, an immigrant from southern Brazil in 1907, who began experiments with the vine to find a wine-producing grape that would flourish near Villa Rica. After two decades of effort, he produced 28,000 liters of wine from his own vineyards and those of neighbors who grew the grapes he had developed. Señor Voigt hoped that wine drinking might eventually displace the vice of *caña* drinking. As the Paraguayans would say, *Que esperanza!* Unfortunately, too, the fertile soil and a climate wonderful for certain crops also encouraged insect pests, like the ants *ysaú* and *akeké*, to multiply by the million.

Large-scale agriculture could flourish in spite of pests. The Paraguayan Sugar Company (Azucarera Paraguaya, S. A.) cultivated extensive fields along the Tebicuary near Villa Rica that produced more than 2,500 short tons of sugar in 1927. An affiliate of this company processed yerba, oil, soap, rice, and other products. In that year there were eight sugar mills in the country, compared with three in 1914, that had a combined production of 5,000 short tons. Cotton planting increased significantly under the guidance of the Banco Agrícola. This crop grows magnificently in several parts of the country, but its production had lagged far behind possibilities. The Banco Agrícola distributed several tons of seed with such good results that the yield had reached 17,500,000 pounds in 1934, and in 1935 about 100,000 acres devoted to the crop yielded an average of 625 pounds of raw cotton per acre.

Hogs were almost as important as Spaniards in the conquest

of America, although the more noble horse has received far greater plaudits. When Irala depopulated Buenos Aires in 1541, he left a boar and a sow to disport themselves on San Gabriel. Apparently, too, boars and sows accompanied the migrants to Asunción and proceeded at once to natural activity with such gusto that pork became a common food. Hog raising was not scientific. One may accept the statement that in 1928 there were more than 45,000 pigs in Paraguay and wonder why so few. A drive through the country would soon reveal the answer. Farmers made little effort to raise hogs or to control their breeding. On sunny, dusty roads a careless motorist might feel a sudden jolt as the car's wheels lurched over a bump in the deep ruts. The bump, more than likely, would be a pig without enough energy to curl his droopy tail, and every farmer knows that a happy pig likes to furl his caudal appendage. The pigs were almost entirely *criollos,* whose high arched backs, long legs, and bloated bellies gave little promise of succulent hams and savory bacon. Some 6,000 Yorkshires, 200 Berkshires, and a few Duroc-Jerseys formed the porcine aristocracy.

An agricultural census in 1928 revealed a considerable number of miscellaneous livestock. Irala's lieutenant, Nufrio Cháves, brought goats and sheep to Asunción from Peru in 1550. The goats, nearly all *criollo,* or native stock, numbered less than 14,-000 in 1928. Sheep did much better. The native breed numbered about 164,000, with a ratio of about one ram to seven ewes, which indicates an attempt at controlled breeding. More than 30,000 of the Romney-Marsh, Lincoln, and Rambouillet breeds were improving the general quality. Horses, mules, and asses were less numerous in 1928 than one might suppose. Still, with some 210,-000, there was about one animal to every five persons. Blooded stock made up a very small portion of the total.

Cattle raising, more typically a frontier occupation—and Paraguay retained many frontier characteristics four centuries after the initial conquest—offers a more imposing record. With about 15,000 cattle left in 1870, recovery was so rapid that the number grew to nearly 3,000,000 in 1926. Hereford, Polled Angus, Durham, and Zebú stock accounted for 10 per cent of the total. The rest were *criollos,* mixtures of everything that happened to be around at the opportune time. Paraguay was beginning to take advantage of its opportunity to become an important cattle producer. Its 220,000 square kilometers of good pasture lands could support much larger herds with no damage to the luxuriant grass. Carlos Casado, La Foncière, and International Products Company were but three large companies that exploited cattle. Many smaller outfits, such as the Estancia San Juan de Rigoberto Caballero, Estancia Fidela Rosas, Ganadera Mojoli, and Bottrell e Hijos made good profits in the business. The three principal meat processors were International Products, Liebig's Extract of Meat Co., Ltd., and Saladero de La Foncière. Liebig's produced 1,615,088 kilos of *harino de carne* and 592,390 kilos of extract, in addition to many other products, in 1927. International Products turned out 1,314,150 kilos of canned beef and La Foncière produced more than 1,200,000 kilos of dried beef (*tasajo*) in the same year.

Production of leather in great quantities was possible in Paraguay in the twenties, since the three necessary elements of hides, tannin extract, and skilled workers existed together; but concentration on shoe leather for export prevented the country from producing enough for its own needs. The tannin extract industry flourished in factories located in the Chaco near the Río Paraguay, where immense forests of *quebracho colorado* defied exhaustion. Puerto Casado, owned by Carlos Casado, Ltda., and Puerto Pinasco, built by the International Products Company, were small cities constructed to produce quebracho extract and meat products. From 1925 to 1927, quebracho-extract exports averaged 56,395,984 kilos annually, the bulk of which went to Argentina and the United States.

Another extractive industry of considerable importance developed in producing essence of petitgrain, taken from leaves of the bitter orange, to use in perfumes. In 1927 alone, the country exported 81,372 kilos of this oil. Lumbering, though still in its infancy, met the country's needs and provided large quantities for export. José Fassardi y Cía. alone had an investment of $1,-500,000 gold in its mills in the department of San Juan Nepomuceno. Most of Paraguay's fires of industry were fed by wood and charcoal.

The textile industry remained almost entirely in the handicraft stage. There were no modern mills until two were erected in the nineteen thirties, although wool and cotton production fully warranted their construction. Fine lace, the exquisite *ñandutí,* continued to come from homes, particularly in Itaguá, a town about thirty kilometers from Asunción.

Paraguay between wars experienced few of the difficulties that beset highly industrialized nations. Banking crises, labor troubles, unemployment, bread lines, and other refinements of balanced economies were noticeably absent. This lack of industrialization prevented the labor movement from attaining significance. The fourteen unions in existence in 1928 had no general federation, nor had they won very high wages for their members. Linotypists earned from 2,000 to 3,100 pesos a month equivalent to $45 to $75 in gold; carpenters and painters received $0.50 to $2.00 a day; shoemakers could make from $0.35 to $1.80 a day; river sailors were fortunate if they earned $20 a month, and a first-class cook could be had for $10 a month. These wages prevailed in Asunción; in smaller cities and villages they were considerably lower.

The country, with less than 1,000,000 people in 1928, could provide only a modest market for imports and a small volume of exports. It had, nevertheless, made tremendous strides toward recovery since the War of the Triple Alliance had turned the land into a vast cemetery. This recovery, as Dr. Pablo Max Ynsfrán states, "was a veritable miracle of vitality and energy." Foreign trade, aided though it was by outside capital and enterprise, amounted to about $26,000,000 in 1927. Imports, less in value than exports from extractive and agricultural enterprises, came principally from Argentina, the United States, England, and Germany, but more than forty countries in all were involved.

Transportation facilities remained inadequate between wars, although the republic was only a few years behind Argentina in opening its first section of railway. The present Ferrocarril Central del Paraguay reached Paraguarí, 45 miles from Asunción, in

1861 and rested there until work was resumed in 1885. The road finally reached the Paraná River at Itapuá where it connected with an Argentine railway running to Buenos Aires. Within Paraguay, this line accounted for 441 kilometers of a total of 723. The other 282 kilometers were narrow-gauge roads owned by private enterprise. River transportation was far more important than the rails. From Villa Hayes on the Chaco side, 20 kilometers north of Asunción, steamers called at twenty principal ports, the last call in the upper Río Paraguay being Bahía Negra, 860 kilometers upstream. Thirteen ports south of Asunción, from Lambaré to Itapirú, served the lower Paraguay for a distance of 330 kilometers. Encarnación on the Paraná was the dividing point for traffic on that river. Steamers went upstream, generally northeast, for 505 kilometers, to call at twenty-three ports, and west to the Paraguay for 350 kilometers, to make six ports. In all, then, the Paraguay and Paraná provided more than 2,000 kilometers of river transportation with sixty-two ports of call. The Compañía Argentina de Navegación (Nicolás Mihanovich), Ltda., was the most important line, with dozens of large and small steamers, launches, and motor boats, and cattle barges. Six comfortable steamers made the round trip between Asunción and Buenos Aires, a fascinating experience for any traveler. Another line, the Arce, Mosciaro y Cía., was much smaller. The Compañía Paraguaya de Navegación y Comercio Marcelino Camihort (S.A.) began operation in 1925 on the Paraguay with three steamers and three smaller vessels. The river system and its lines of steamers were all the more important since there were only a few kilometers of improved highway in the entire country. Indeed, the modern highway had to wait for 1939 before becoming more than a curiosity. Telegraph provided the only swift means for transmission of messages until Asunción installed a telephone system in 1928. There were about 3,000 kilometers of telegraph lines in 1926, with another 300 under construction.

Tourists, primarily from Uruguay and Argentina, seeking a touch of the exotic or fleeing from uncomfortable winter months on the Río de la Plata, visited Paraguay. They came in by rail, river steamer, and the airline from Buenos Aires, which was still in the experimental stage by 1928. Some made the excursion to the famous Falls of Iguassú before resuming their trip up the Paraguay past famed Humaitá and Lambaré to Asunción. Others, in smaller numbers, went on upstream to Concepción, an interesting small city founded in 1773 by Governor Agustín Fernando de Pinedo, from which they might make short trips into the mysterious Chaco to hunt, visit cattle ranches, or watch quebracho cutters at work. Those who knew little of Concepción were surprised at the activity in its port, the substantial and often beautiful homes, and the adequate supply of electricity generated by a plant constructed in 1918. Asunción, of course, was the center of attraction. A tourist could soon exhaust the city's points of interest, but not as quickly as a lady from Boston who was "doing" South America in three months and Paraguay in three days. In that short period there is hardly time to settle into the easy routine of relaxation at San Bernardino, the delightful resort on Lake Ipacaraí, or to enjoy excellent food at the hotels Paraguay and Oriental, not to mention a sampling of concoctions at the Bar Oriental, where one might hear gossip about what Bolivians were up to in the Chaco.

# CHAPTER XVII

# Whose Chaco?

THE CHACO WAR was a delayed reaction from the past, a carry-over from colonial boundary disputes that should have been settled by Bolivia and Paraguay soon after they won independence. It was an anachronism made possible by untidy diplomatic housekeeping and the interposition of two great conflicts, the War of the Triple Alliance and the War of the Pacific, in which Paraguay and Bolivia were victims of imperialistic powers whose insatiable appetite for territory made a mockery of that so dearly loved phrase, "transcendental confraternity."

For many years after the War of the Pacific (1879–83), Bolivians dreamed of recovering the ocean provinces lost to Chilean imperialism. Then came the Treaty of 1904, by which Bolivia came to realize an unpleasant fact: its lost territory would never be recovered. Bolivia's *integrismo territorial,* the spirit of revindication, died slowly. Throughout the long Tacna-Arica dispute between Chile and Peru, the hope flickered that somehow the Treaty of 1904 might be rectified. By 1928 that hope, too, had evaporated in the rare atmosphere of the altiplano, gone as a wisp of cloud disappears into the blackness of gathering night.

Beyond the mountains and the yungas lay the Chaco, a poor substitute for the Pacific littoral, but a region Bolivia might claim on the bases of maps, colonial jurisdictions, and explorations. This was the Chaco Boreal, the Chaco north of the Pilcomayo River, that spread its plains, forests, and marshes to the Río Paraguay, an outlet to the Atlantic by way of the Río de la Plata.

Scholars knew of the Chaco, but the people as a whole did not. Historians believed Bolivia's title to be indisputable, but a succession of petty dictators had failed to make good that claim. They had temporized, signed treaties and protocols with Paraguay that served only to postpone the inevitable conflict. Perhaps the scholars were wrong, or perhaps Paraguayans could find, by diligent search and careful selection of evidence, a title equally valid. Justo Rodas Eguino, in *La Guerra del Chaco,* complains that governmental myopia prevented a full realization of what the Bolivian East could mean for the future; but he fails to consider one pertinent fact: the Bolivian East was also the Paraguayan West. And Paraguay, too, had lost territory to aggressors after 1870 when the madness of 1864 died with Francisco Solano López. The Chaco Central, between the Bermejo and Pilcomayo rivers, went to imperialistic Argentina, which sought to square its boundaries, as Bartolomé Mitre admitted. Ownership of a large part of the Chaco Boreal, from the Pilcomayo to the Verde, was decided in favor of Paraguay by President Rutherford B. Hayes in 1878, but that arbitral award could not prejudice Bolivia's claims, if any, to the same region.

Paraguayans regarded the Chaco as their territory from time immemorial. Geographers and historians agree that from December 16, 1617, when Philip III divided Paraguay into two *gobernaciones,* the country has had to fight for its territory. It would be erroneous to accept charges, such as R. B. Cunninghame Graham has made, that Paraguayans before independence refused to resist aggression by Chaco Indians. Far from being apathetic, colonial governors vigorously if sporadically fought Guaycurús and other Chaco tribes. Some punitive expeditions also left garrisons in the Chaco; one of them, led by Lázaro Ortega Vallejos in 1662, left five *fortines* (fortified military posts) as a result of six months west of the Paraguay. Again, in 1675, Governor Rege Corvalán built a fort on the west bank opposite Asunción. These data, reviewed with others by Elías Ayala in *Paraguay y Bolivia en el Chaco Boreal,* could be supported by missionary work centered at Asunción. Guaycurús were poor prospects for Christianity; but the Mbayás, Abipones, Tobas, and others were more submissive. In 1787, Governor Pedro Melo founded the reduction of Melodía twenty miles north of Asunción on the west bank, site of the present Villa Hayes. Indian fighting in the Chaco was bad enough but a more dangerous enemy threatened Paraguay. Brazilians drove Jesuit missions out of Guayrá in 1629, from Itatín (northern Paraguay) in 1632, and forced the removal of Villa Rica and Ciudad Real to points west of the Paraná. By 1734, these Paraguayan areas were firmly in Brazilian hands. The Comunero confusion helped Brazil to secure its great theft. Agustín Fernando de Pinedo founded Villa Real de la Concepción in 1772 to contain this foreign threat on the north. In spite of these facts, Mariano Antonio Molas, a native of Asunción, wrote in 1840 that the Río Paraguay was the actual limit on the west.

Bolivia's claim to the Chaco rested primarily upon jurisdiction of the Audiencia of Charcas, a court district founded in 1559. There were various types of audiencias: viceregal, as in Mexico and Lima; pretorian (*pretoriales*), as in Buenos Aires and New Granada; dependent (*subalternas*), as in Quito and Charcas. Various decrees amplified or restricted the area served by the Audiencia of Charcas and its powers. In 1563, its eastern limits were La Plata (Chuquisaca), but later the Audiencia's judicial functions extended to Paraguay as well—judicial but not executive. It was as a judge-investigator that *oidor* Antequera had gone to Asunción to examine the rule of Governor Diego de los Reyes Balmaceda, and it was because Antequera had exceeded his judicial role by becoming governor that the Viceroy reprimanded the Audiencia, which replied that never had it assumed executive powers. The Bolivian René Moreno states that the Audiencia of Charcas was a court of appeal or supreme court of justice. Moreover, in April, 1783, Paraguay was placed under the Audiencia Pretorial de Buenos Aires and had nothing more to do with the Audiencia of Charcas.

Executive jurisdiction was poorly defined in Spain's colonies. Maps, drawn and redrawn, may be cited until one becomes hopelessly lost in a maze of irreconcilable lines. Dr. Cecilio Báez, educator, historian, and diplomat, published a map in his *Le Para-*

*guay* to show conclusively that in 1620 the Chaco was Paraguay's. Bolivian historians matched their opponents map for map in the cartographical contest without proving or disproving anything. The reason is clear. Except where the sea itself set the boundary, not one of Spain's former colonies began its independent career with clearly defined and clearly located boundaries. So the colonies adopted the principle of *uti possidetis:* what each had in 1810, that it should keep. A good principle, indeed, but for the fact that no one knew in 1810 exactly what anyone had. An impartial examination of maps and descriptions leads one to believe that Paraguay and Bolivia each had valid claims to the Chaco. These claims cancel one another, leaving as the best criterion the test of occupation. This statement will hardly satisfy Paraguayans; it could induce cerebral hemorrhages in Bolivia, a country desperate for an outlet to the sea.

Forget the maps and the old Audiencia of Charcas; forget explorers and missionaries; forget artificial lines on academic unreadable charts; and remember undeniable facts: Paraguay had settled, sparsely it is true, the fringe of Chaco bordering the river. Paraguay had exploited some of the hinterland, had granted concessions to foreigners for taking out and processing quebracho. Maybe all this was illegal. Bolivians thought so. But maybe it was done under color of a title just as good if not better than Bolivia's. Paraguayans thought so. Who was right? Unfortunately, this matter could not be decided by a court. Actually, neither country was right until the Chaco War decided the issue.

While Paraguayans were not unmindful of the Chaco, Bolivian leaders concentrated their attention on mining and on efforts to get a Pacific port. Bolivia, Rodas Eguino and other critics say, neglected the Chaco. This charge is by no means accurate. In 1879, a Bolivian diplomat persuaded a Paraguayan to sign a treaty renouncing title to part of the Chaco. And long before that time, Bolivians explored in the Chaco, set up missionary Indian reservations, and founded agricultural and military colonies that began to win the area, inch by inch, for civilization. It was inevitable that this civilizing work should eventually clash with similar Paraguayan efforts, especially since Bolivia's "inches" were measured in leagues. This movement into the Chaco apparently began in the north, in lands of Chiquitos Indians, about 1836, long before Bolivia had lost its Pacific provinces to Chile. Although not energetic in pushing their country's claims at all times, Bolivian politicians did not by any means neglect the Chaco. Their military colonies, like those of Paraguay, were called *fortines*. Primarily for protection against savages and cattle rustlers, they were not military fortifications in the true sense. Sometimes a trench surrounded the *fortín*, which was composed of a barrack for a company, huts for officers, a well, and a corral.

Some Bolivian writers, bitterly assailing their shortsighted or even blind *políticos*, complain of stupidity in high places. Rodas Eguino summarizes these charges neatly: Did it ever occur to Bolivian politicians, before the Chaco War, that Argentina would have a "transcendental, definitive" role in the conflict? Did they ever realize Argentina's role in the Plata area? Did the Bolivian foreign office ever study Argentina's influence in Paraguayan politics, economy, or destiny? Or did Bolivian diplomats ever plan a course of action toward Argentina? Never! Bolivia was isolated morally, spiritually, and commercially. There was no link with Argentina until the opening of a railway in 1925, and ties with other South American republics were so weak that Bolivia found herself friendless when the war began.

One need not wonder that Bolivian statesmen found it difficult to make a fundamental, *trascendental* adjustment in their thinking. Bolivia was Upper Peru in colonial times. Its orientation for nearly three centuries before the War of the Pacific had been toward the west, toward the Pacific, and habits of such long standing are not changed readily. Shut off from the Pacific, Bolivia was forced by Chilean conquest to seek new ties. Those ties could be only with countries of the Plata, and Argentina was the great power of that area. A newcomer to a Platine concert of powers, Bolivia inevitably must go through a period of painful readjustment, and the pain would be felt by others as well. True statesmanship would be required of Paraguay and Argentina if the new relationships were to be established without violent disturbances; but that statesmanship was lacking because public men in neither of those countries realized how important was Bolivia's forced reorientation. Indeed, few writers in recent years have shown any sign of appreciating the fact of this intensely significant reorientation in Bolivian interests and outlook. Paraguay, all but destroyed by the War of the Triple Alliance, could not be expected to develop thinkers who would observe the change. Argentina was too busy with its own marvelous economic development. Another half-century must pass before the light began to dawn, and another terrible war must be fought.

Why didn't Bolivia march an army into the disputed region in 1870, when Paraguay had no more military power than a dead *piranha*? There were three reasons: Bolivia, Argentina, and Brazil. Bolivia could not do it; Brazil and Argentina would not have permitted such a move in any case. Then came the War of the Pacific, and Bolivia's bellicose spirit all but disappeared, at least on the international level. Both countries recovered their ambition through the same years; both had foreign-trained armies at the same time; both dreamed of vast, undiscovered or nonexistent oil pools in the same place; both began to build outposts after 1907. The wonder is that war was so long in coming.

A recital in detail of the many fruitless efforts to settle the dispute would be boring and pointless. There were treaties: Aceval-Tamayo (1887), Decoud-Quijarro (1879), Benítez-Ichazo (1899), and the Soler-Pinilla protocol (1907). There was a conference in Buenos Aires in 1927 and 1928. There was a dreary exchange of notes. Lines were drawn on the maps, any one of which would have been far better than the war, which finally resulted in an agreement essentially like the boundaries drawn by negotiators on at least two occasions in the late nineteenth century. Why wasn't one of the treaties ratified by both parties? Bolivians believe that the only justification for Paraguayan political parties was the Chaco dispute. Settle that argument and Paraguay would lose the one issue, the one cohesive factor, that held the country together as a nation. After his term of office expired, José P. Guggiari declared that the Bolivian menace provided Paraguayan opposition parties with their principal issue. There is reason to credit Guggiari with having analyzed the situation correctly;

but Bolivians, too, could make a similar use of Paraguayan "aggression." There is nothing like a fire abroad to keep a dictator warm at home. Hernando Siles, president of Bolivia from 1926 to 1930, certainly conducted himself accordingly. Sampling the press of both countries supports the conclusion that parties made effective use of the Chaco conflict. Paraguayan newspapers, *La Patria, La Nación, La Tribuna,* and *El Diario,* kept up an agitation, extending over several years, supporting their country's claims, criticizing presidents for inaction, warning against Bolivian tricks, and urging military preparation. One particularly sarcastic writer for *El Orden,* who signed himself "O. I.," yelped and inveighed against Eligio Ayala—"Eligio the Short"—because that dapper statesman was too sensible to be jingoistic. Bolivian papers met this journalistic attack head on, quite in contrast to smooth words exchanged by diplomats.

Argentina's Radical president, Marcelo T. de Alvear, made an effort to settle the Chaco dispute by offering his country's mediation in 1924. As a result of this offer, the two countries signed a protocol on April 22, 1927, agreeing to a conference in Buenos Aires to decide on what was to be arbitrated. This conference met from September 29, 1927 to July 12, 1928, without reaching an agreement, partly because Bolivia insisted on arbitrating territory stubbornly claimed by Paraguay as beyond any question of ownership. Bolivia was agreeable to demilitarization; Paraguay insisted that she dismantle her *fortines.* Dr. Eusebio Ayala, the suave, cultured, cosmopolitan scholar, president-to-be José P. Guggiari, and Chaco expert Fulgencio R. Moreno represented Paraguay in these futile negotiations. They maintained that most of the region was not in dispute; that, since concessions to the Mennonites lay in territory undeniably Paraguayan, there was no threat to Bolivia in that enterprise. Bolivia could reply that its cession to the William H. Murray Company was also clearly within Bolivian territory. After reading scores of documents presented by each country in support of its claims, one inevitably reaches the conclusion that the Chaco dispute could not be settled by reference to history. There were four courses that could be followed by the disputants: direct agreement, arbitration, continued haggling, or war. They chose the last course. Incidents that started the war were not long in coming, and it was Paraguay, by its surprise attack on Fortín Vanguardia, that started the conflict. Even then Paraguayans insisted that Bolivians fired the first shots.

Since the Vanguardia incident precipitated the Chaco War, it is well to review contentions of both parties. Major Rafael Franco, later provisional president and still later a leader in a number of revolts, including the rebellion of 1947, commanded the troops at Bahía Negra, part of whom set out from Fortín Galpón at 9:00 P.M. on December 4, 1928. Bolivians reported that more than 400 Paraguayan cavalry and infantry demanded their surrender at Vanguardia early in the morning of December 5. A half-hour's fight followed in which 5 Bolivians were killed and 23 were captured. In the march back to Fortín Galpón, a Paraguayan corporal and a private shot two prisoners who were unable to go farther. Deny this incident as they might, Paraguayans—and Bolivians, too—were fully capable of such brutality. Bolivians charged that the attack on Vanguardia was part of a premeditated campaign. The military staff had set up headquarters at Concepción in November to be near Vanguardia. Bolivians retaliated quickly to avenge their loss. Before daybreak on December 14, a force of 150 attacked Fortín Mariscal López, routed its garrison of 35, captured a detachment moving in carts from Fortín Valois Rivarola to Fortín General Genes, and took Fortín Boquerón. A few more incidents of this kind would result in a spread of guerrilla fighting and eventually in a full-fledged war. Drops of blood again stained the soil of Paraguay, drops that soon became streams. Diplomatic relations were severed quickly. Dr. Bailón Mercado departed from Asunción on December 9, one day after Paraguay's chargé d'affaires was ordered out of La Paz.

At the very time when the first incident of the Chaco War occurred at Fortín Vanguardia, a Conference on Conciliation and Arbitration was meeting in Washington. Bolivia's envoy, Dr. Eduardo Diéz de Medina and Paraguay's chargé, Dr. Juan Vicente Ramírez, accepted the conference's offer of mediation.

Eusebio Ayala

Bolivia charged that Paraguay, violating the Buenos Aires agreement of July 12, 1928, attacked and razed Vanguardia on December 5; Paraguay denied the charge. A Commission of Inquiry was appointed to settle this peculiar argument. Pending a report from the nine-man commission, which included delegates from the belligerents, Mexico, Cuba, Colombia, Uruguay, Chile, and the United States, each country promised not to create any more incidents. Major General Frank R. McCoy presided over the commission, which began its labors in Washington on March 13, 1929. Rival delegations labored hard in presenting their cases to the commission. While this was going on, Paraguay sent a small party to ascertain the exact location of Vanguardia, and found a new post in the neighborhood. The party was fired on by Bolivians on May 4 and 5. Two horses became casualties. Concerning itself primarily with studying memorials and with efforts to repatriate nationals held by the disputants, the commission decided that reconciliation of divergent views was impossible and submitted a proposal for arbitration of the Chaco dispute. Each country reaffirmed its sincere devotion to arbitration, but neither would agree with the other on what to arbitrate.

It was inevitable, before and after the Vanguardia affair, that dozens of volumes should be written by scholars and pseudo-scholars to present their country's claims. Fulgencio R. Moreno's *El problema de las fronteras,* Manuel Domínguez' *El Chaco Boreal,* and Elías Ayala's *Paraguay y Bolivia en el Chaco Boreal* may be cited as among the best Paraguayan defenses. Rodas Eguino's *La guerra del Chaco* and Miguel Mercado Moreira's *El Chaco Boreal* and *El Chaco boliviano* rank high among Bolivian efforts. These and other writers, some of them excellent historians, mulled over the same ground, the same old documents, and came to conclusions in harmony with preconceived prejudices. One thing at least was accomplished: the histories of Bolivia and Paraguay were subjected to an intensive analysis, however confusing the results might be. Manuel Domínguez, for example, examined Bolivian arguments and decided that "Nothing but dust remains of the . . . Bolivian theses." Mercado Moreira put the dust together again.

Bolivians did not realize that Latin American sympathies would lie largely with Paraguay. Standard Oil had concessions in Bolivia, and so great was resentment against foreign exploitation that people in other countries easily believed the lie that Standard Oil was arming Bolivia, was encouraging the war to exploit the supposedly great petroleum deposits of the Chaco. The fact is that Bolivia's munitions came primarily from Vickers of London, although many Latin American republics had used United States loans to buy stocks of surplus armaments from countries involved in World War I. Paraguay's foreign office knew of the Vickers-Armstrong contract and loan; Dr. Gerónimo Zubizarreta, minister of foreign affairs in Asunción, presented details of how shipments, amateurishly camouflaged, proceeded from Buenos Aires overland or up the rivers. There was no need to drag Standard Oil into the picture. One should remember, too, that Bolivia expropriated Standard Oil properties in 1937, two years after the Chaco War ended. That would have been a fine reward for financing the war.

Among many charges against Standard Oil is one that would require considerable proof. Carlos Casado, runs the story, was a relative of President Justo of Argentina. Casado had the largest concession in the Chaco, hence was vitally interested in the war. Standard Oil was charged in August, 1935, with having piped 9,018,950 barrels of gasoline from Bolivian wells to the Argentine side of the Bermejo, whence it found its way into Paraguayan motors. Standard, the "black oil god," supplied Paraguay, while Bolivia had to buy from Peru, Argentina, and the United States. Royal Dutch Shell was thought to be financing Paraguay, encouraged by the Anglo-Argentine plutocracy. Another story is that Standard needed an outlet on the Paraguay for its wells in eastern Bolivia. Royal Dutch Shell tried to block this outlet. "That was the cause of the conflict that has bloodied the continent," Don Liborio Justo, son of the Argentine president, is reported to have said. On the other hand, the war is also charged to Anglo-Argentine companies that wanted possession of Standard's Bolivian wells. This explanation, Augusto Céspedes holds, is too simple. It overlooks Argentine backing of Paraguay, it denies "Argentine imperialism that has colonized, financed, and armed Paraguay and strangled Bolivia economically and diplomatically in order to take possession of the Chaco."

The whole question of oil in the Chaco has come up so often for discussion that it needs a little more attention. In the Chaco proper there might be oil, but geologists were and still are doubtful about it. The oil fields of Bolivia lay in the Andean foothills. Nine syndicates obtained concessions in a belt about 100 miles wide and 750 miles long. Standard Oil Company of New Jersey was the only one to take active steps to bring in a field. North of Villa Montes a few miles, in a concession of 860,000 acres, Standard began exploration in 1923, drilled several wells, and built two small refineries. When the Chaco War began, these wells were producing about 300 barrels daily, all of which went to Bolivia under terms of the concession. How could Bolivia get oil to market during peacetime? Argentina imposed a high tariff on shipments from Yacuiba, its railhead on the frontier south of Villa Montes, and refused to permit construction of a pipe line through Argentine territory to the Paraná. Why not a pipe line through the Chaco? Paraguay held the west bank of its river where such a line would end; Bolivia refused to negotiate for fear it would prejudice claims to the Chaco. In view of these factors, and of Standard's picayunish investment, charges that American oilmen were back of Bolivia are somewhat ludicrous.

Much larger and more populous than Paraguay, Bolivia could have maintained a comparatively large military establishment. To offset this potential advantage in men and material, Paraguayans took pride in their military psychosis, their legends of valor that grew rapidly after 1870. War with Bolivia was considered almost a certainty—even anticipated eagerly as a chance to prove that the French-indoctrinated and Argentine-trained Ibero-Guaraní was superior to the German-trained Ibero-Quechua and Ibero-Aymará. Paraguay's martial spirit was and is an undeniable fact: Paraguayans know that man for man they are in the top rank of the world's fighting men. True or not, the conviction exists.

Paraguayan writers overemphasize Bolivian military preparations, having been naturally deceived somewhat by visible signs of militarism and by knowledge of armament contracts with such concerns as Vickers-Armstrong. They are right in calling attention to those preparations; what they did not know, although their apparently but not actually inflated opinion of their own military prowess led them to the correct conclusion, was that Bolivia's army was inferior to Paraguay's potential. As Lieutenant General Angel Rodríguez, chief of the Operations Section of the Bolivian General Staff from 1931 to 1932, wrote in his *Autopsia de una guerra:* "The Bolivian Army has had a twenty-year propaganda, as a logical consequence of innumerable parades. The people believed in the organization of their military institution, it also knew that it boasted a good contingent of trained reservists; what no one knew was that he who had organized the Army had done so simply to show it in parades. The Army was a political instrument, it was never an instrument of war. The various Presidents of the Republic desired and considered it as such."

What would the great powers of South America do in case of a Paraguayan-Bolivian war? Chile had blindly and deliberately severed Bolivia's ties with the Pacific; but, to maintain a continental balance of power, she would have to lend at least moral support to Bolivia in order to counter Argentina's support of Paraguay. Brazil, a long-time rival of Argentina for influence in the Plata basin, might be expected to favor Bolivia. Indeed, citizens of the altiplano blindly longed for an alliance of some sort. They misinterpreted Brazil's position. That colossus intended to be friendly with everyone; its intervention in the Chaco War would be confined to mild diplomatic actions. Brazilians were devoting their energies primarily to internal problems, to filling out a vast, sparsely settled hinterland.

Argentina was definitely on an uncomfortable spot when the Chaco War began. Here were two important parts of the new Plata Basin Concert that Argentina was trying to form, each destined to be strongly dependent upon Buenos Aires, fighting over a large area. In 1928, the year of the Vanguardia incident, old Hipólito Irigoyen returned to power as the Radical president. Two years later, in September, 1930, the generals and Conservatives ended the Radical regime. General José Uriburu and his successor, General Agustín P. Justo, occupied the presidency until 1938, throughout the Chaco War. The revolution of 1930 initiated a period of militaristic nationalism led at first by Uriburu, Justo, and Carlos Saavedra Lamas. A skillful diplomat, Saavedra Lamas resented the efforts of American neutrals and the League of Nations to mediate the dispute. Failure to do so left Argentina with enhanced prestige. When the war began (June, 1932) Saavedra Lamas obtained the unanimous adherence of the American republics to the declaration of August 3, 1932: no territorial conquest by force of arms would be recognized. Even if Bolivia should defeat Paraguay, no American republic would recognize the fruits of victory. This declaration was directed against Bolivia, the belligerent favored to win. But Paraguayans surprised the self-styled experts, defeated Bolivia, and occupied territory indisputably Bolivian. The declaration of August 3, 1932, served to protect Bolivia in the truce signed on June 12, 1935, and the additional act of January 21, 1936. Saavedra Lamas got credit for ending the war, to him went the Nobel Peace Prize. The field of candidates was slim indeed.

Argentine sympathy definitely lay with Paraguay. The Argentine press, as Rodas Eguino says, was far from neutral and tried to show that the "Chaco War was explained only by the ambition and plan of conquest with which Bolivia, a great country, a military power supposedly of the first order, trained in the principles of military discipline and, in addition, with a German general at the head of its troops, launched a surprise attack against a small country like Paraguay, poor, without a peso, without arms, without credit, a confirmed pacifist people, surprised overnight by the Bolivian invasion, an instrument of foreign capitalism, particularly of the Standard Oil Company." The great newspapers, *La Presna* and *La Nación*, leaned more toward Paraguay in the conflict, but their editors made sincere efforts to be impartial. That was a difficult task for men of a class that stood to lose heavily if Bolivia won the Chaco.

# CHAPTER XVIII

# The Chaco War

THE last two years of José Patricio Guggiari's administration were extremely difficult. He had taken office in August, 1928, after Eligio Ayala had given the country its first four years of internal peace since 1899. Like Herbert Hoover, he began in a period of prosperity that had run its course and fell headlong into a world depression that certainly was not of his making. Guggiari continued and ended the constitutional period that began in 1870; he made no effort to suppress political opposition, strove to unite the Liberal party, and saw most of his work destroyed by the Chaco War.

While hotheads were clamoring for war, Guggiari earnestly worked for peace. The Vanguardia incident in December, 1928, had inflamed public passion to a dangerous degree and fixed too much attention on the Chaco at a time when public revenues were too low to provide adequate schools, public health services, and internal improvements. The country had begun to remodel the Asunción port in 1927, a work completed four years later with considerable difficulty. Plans for highways, bridges, schools, and hospitals went back into their pigeonholes as war with Bolivia appeared increasingly unavoidable. Moreover, since many of the countries in South America experienced revolts in 1930, Guggiari would have to be unusually astute or lucky if he were to end his term peacefully. Even the garrison at Campo Grande on the outskirts of Asunción was so restless with "revolutionitis" that anarchy threatened in March, 1931. José Félix Estigarribia, deputy commander of the armed forces, ordered the disaffected regiments to the Chaco and went to Puerto Casado himself in April "to continue his country's history."

Shortly after Estigarribia reached Puerto Casado, the Bolivians advanced a patrol to occupy Fortín Masamaklay (Agua Rica), which lay close to Paraguay's southwestern Chaco base of Fortín Nanawa (Ayala). This encroachment was another of those incidents that inflamed the public. It gave enemies of "the regime"—the Liberal–wealthy–foreign-interests group—a chance to demand action. Guggiari wanted to arm the country gradually, following a plan laid down by Eligio Ayala, and the General Staff was willing to shrug off the Masamaklay affair after a reconnaissance in force failed to recapture the post. Increasing belligerency on both sides in the Chaco was so obvious by August, 1931, that the powers involved in conciliation in 1929 suggested a nonaggression pact. Clashes, a small-scale war at various points, occurred in September. Negotiators redoubled their efforts; so did the militarists. While talking went on in neutral capitals, troops moved into the Chaco. A mob of excited superpatriots rioted in Asunción on October 23, 1931, to express discontent with Guggiari's pacifism. Only loyalty in the armed forces, revitalized after the revolution of 1922–23, prevented a serious revolt, which, Justo Pastor Benítez believed, would have meant loss of the Chaco to Bolivia.

There seemed to be good reason for this opinion. By April, 1932, according to press dispatches, Bolivia had 7,000 or more troops near or in its *fortines,* was mobilizing for war, and was feverishly adding to its armament. Confident of quick victory, politicians of the Andean country refused all concessions offered to avoid the conflict. President Daniel Salamanca and his military advisers thought they could sweep through the Chaco with 4,000 men, which explains, General Rodríguez wrote, why Bolivia began the war with three regiments of infantry, one of cavalry, and one artillery battery. These units, sadly undermanned, mustered less than 2,000 men instead of the 7,000 reported by the newspapers. Bolivia's General Staff begged for matériel, prepared plans that President Salamanca disregarded, tried to mobilize resources for "Salamanca's war," and watched helplessly while ultimate defeat was in the making.

Bolivians on duty in the Chaco in 1931 knew full well that a war was under way. Conscripts fought with ax and machete to cut *picadas* (trails) through brush and forest that would link their *fortines* in the heart of the Chaco. This chain of posts might control Paraguayan infiltration. President Salamanca saw clearly the strategic value of such trails to contain Paraguay's future invasion; but, Augusto Céspedes complained, not even that illustrious citizen suspected "that behind the implied objectives of that advance, there hides a powerful capitalistic oligarchy that is preparing, from desks and offices in Buenos Aires, to pull out chestnuts with the hands of half-naked Paraguayan soldiers and, in time, to use the very roads built by Bolivian soldiers to reach the monopolized oil in the mountain folds of Bolivia."

The Ingaví and Florida regiments, later destroyed in combat, worked in small detachments to build these roads. Among their officers, whose deeds became legendary, were heroes Major Francisco Manchego and Germán Busch. November rains flooded the *picadas,* oxcarts mired in clinging mud. "Water dripped from the gray sky, flooding the inextinguishable forest in cloud. Marshes spread like blotches of oil and united to form an immense lake 20 centimeters deep over the plain, above which grass and trees leaned earthward, bent by weight of the water." November's rains were but showers compared with December's floods. Six months later the earth, robbed of its water by hungry rays of an insatiable sun, lay baked and cracked. Clouds of dust mingled with swarms of blue-green flies, while the heat closed over men and beasts "like a cloak of hot rubber."

Summer in the Chaco was a long nightmare of waiting for rain to bring temporary relief, of sinking deep holes in search of water, of watching buzzard shadows. "Someone should open a window somewhere to let in the air. The sky is an enormous stone under which the sun is imprisoned," wrote one who survived. On one occasion in 1933, a Bolivian detachment spent seven months in digging a well. Thirty, forty, fifty meters and more they went down without finding water. Rumors of this well reached the *patapilas,* as Bolivians called their enemies, who attacked in an effort to capture such a valuable prize. The excavators defended their hole as fiercely as they would have protected a gushing fountain. Eight of them and five of the enemy found a common grave in the deep, dry hole.

Mass meetings in La Paz, mass meetings in Asunción . . . presidents on their balconies . . . national honor . . . deceitful enemies . . . our fatherland in danger . . . bells to ring, bells to toll . . . cymbals to crash and bugles to blare. War! Throw the flowers on Andean streets, on wooden blocks and cobblestones leading to the Río Paraguay. War! Take the Aymará and Quechuá from their high plateaus, send them down into the Green Hell. Take the Guaraní from his patch of mandioca, let him hear the *urutaú* mourning, forever mourning in his dim retreat. War in the Chaco, in that hell of green and gray, of mud and swamps and dust. And after the thousands of conscripts have spilled out their blood, let their masters gather around and draw lines on maps, on maps that will never show where brown men died for nothing.

Paraguay was fortunate when Dr. Eusebio Ayala succeeded Guggiari on August 15, 1932, to continue the Liberal party's work. No newcomer to the position, the fifty-eight-year-old executive had served as provisional president from 1921 to 1923. A lawyer, journalist, educator, and banker, he had achieved distinction in every endeavor toward which he had directed his magnificent abilities. At the age of thirty-five, he was chosen president of the National Chamber of Deputies, later served in the Senate, was minister to the United States, ambassador to Peru, and won the presidency in a quarrelsome election on May 8, 1932. No man in Paraguayan political life was better qualified for high office than this brilliant, honest, cultured son of Barrero Grande. He was to be heckled and goaded by fiery nationalists because of moderation in handling the Chaco dispute, he was to be pilloried by the mob for hesitating to declare war, and he was to be overthrown by the Febreristas because he dared to sign a truce with Bolivia in 1935. When he died an exile in Buenos Aires on June 4, 1942, Paraguay and South America lost one of their truly great men.

José Félix Estigarribia, joint architect with Eusebio Ayala of Paraguay's eventual victory, was born at Caraguatay on February 21, 1888, to a Basque family of colonial antecedents. Perching firmly on high branches of the family tree could be found such names as Dr. Juan Vicente Estigarribia, friend of Francia, and Colonel José Antonio de la Cruz Estigarribia, who had surrendered his army at Uruguayana during the War of the Triple Alliance. Don Mateo, father of the Chaco hero, was a farmer and silversmith, a mestizo with considerable Guaraní blood. Doña Casilda Insaurralde, the mother, could also boast of prominent ancestry. Caraguatay, eighty kilometers east and slightly north of Asunción and near Ayala's birthplace of Barrero Grande, is noted for its beautiful women and strong men, who are largely white. It is a prosperous community that somehow escaped the worst effects of the great war, nestling among low hills where the rich red soil yields abundant crops of tobacco and cotton to supplement a thriving cattle industry. Here young José Félix spent his youth "as one of the country boys close to nature," and grew up to be a handsome man whose regular features, chestnut eyes, sensitive lips, and wavy black hair gave him the appearance of a cinema star. One of his good friends has asserted that Estigarribia smoked only one or two cigarettes a day and never drank maté.

Estigarribia enrolled in the Agricultural School of Santísima Trinidad, directed by Dr. Moisés S. Bertoni, in 1903. Completing his studies there, he went on to attend the Colegio Nacional in Asunción. The revolution of July 2, 1908, found the young man in rebel ranks, and two years later he entered the army. One revolt later, in August, 1911, he went to Chile for further military training. After two years abroad, Estigarribia returned to Paraguay and became a first lieutenant in 1914. Customary assignments kept him occupied. He remained steadfastly loyal to the government during the turmoil of 1921–22, a fact that Provisional President Ayala would not forget, and directed the Escuela Militar through 1923. As a reward for faithful service, Captain Estigarribia received a trip to France for further military study in 1924, and studied under Marshal Foch. While in France he became convinced that the Paraguayan Army had two historic functions: to save the Chaco and to reconstruct the country. As its leading officer, he carried out the first mission and was well along in the second when death ended his career in 1940. Returning to Asunción in 1927, he became chief of the General Staff a year later, and inspector general of the army in 1931.

These were the two men, Ayala and Estigarribia, upon whom Paraguay was to depend most in the war years. The country, "born under the sign of Mars," rallied behind them to defend the Chaco. People and government gave proof of their vigor in the crisis, and even those discontented elements who had no love for Ayala refrained from attempting a revolt that would have delivered the Chaco to Bolivia. Only a united country could win this second war in less than seventy years.

Military and civilian leaders alike failed to foresee the type of war that impended. They expected a series of clashes between small detachments of riflemen or cavalry, in which heavy artillery and automatic weapons would have little use. Motorized equipment was at first thought unnecessary and not feasible since the Chaco had no road system. Instead, the war was to be modern, with heavy equipment, trucks, artillery, machine guns, and even airplanes playing a prominent role. Neither Bolivia nor Paraguay believed it would be possible for each to maintain 50,000 men in combat and another 50,000 in supply and other auxiliary services; nor did either combatant appreciate the extent to which the other could arm. The Liberal government, Policarpo Artaza assures us in *Ayala, Estigarribia y el Partido Liberal,* bought munitions on seven occasions from 1906 to 1932, in Germany, England, Chile, Spain, Belgium, and Switzerland. These purchases included 46,100 rifles and carbines, 268 heavy and 572 light machine guns, 36 mortars, 32 military aircraft, 3,000 trucks, vast quantities of cartridges and shells, clothing, medical supplies, and other equipment. One suspects that when the full story is told, Argentina and perhaps Brazil will not be missing from the list of countries that aided Paraguay directly or indirectly.

Ayala, when he took office, inherited a conflict slowly growing in scope. One might select any of several dates for the war's beginning, from December 5, 1928, to September 9, 1932, depending on whether a pro-Bolivian or a pro-Paraguayan date is desired. Preferring the latter, we shall accept June 15, 1932, for the transition from a war of incidents and clashes to a war of campaigns. On that date Bolivia's Major Oscar Moscoco led 300 men in a successful attack against Fortín Pitiantuta which lay some one hundred miles north of the Mennonite colonies. By the end of July, the legendary Captain Victor Ustares Arce had paced Bolivians in the capture of several posts in the central Chaco, where most of the war would be fought and where the *fortines* were most thickly clustered. On the next day, August 1, the Congress at Asunción told President Guggiari to proceed with mobilization, and in less than two months Estigarribia had 15,000 conscripts in his First Corps. Again the neutral powers begged the belligerents to sign a truce. A two-day lull occurred in the fighting on August 10 and 11. Paraguayans insisted that Bolivia return Boquerón and other recently captured posts; Bolivians refused. That ended the lull. On August 12, Paraguayans recaptured Pitiantuta; three days later, Eusebio Ayala became president of Paraguay. Again the neutrals began to hope. Why not set up a neutral zone in the Chaco and agree to a truce of one, two, or three months? Neither country would agree to the other's terms and each continued its efforts to put on a full-scale war. Estigarribia, now a lieutenant colonel, already was planning a counterattack against Boquerón, and Plácido Jara, the heroic Gaucho of the Chaco, was leading his hard-riding Guerrilleros de la Muerte on demoralizing raids into Bolivian positions.

Justo Pastor Benítez, in *Estigarribia el soldado del Chaco*, tells an interesting story of how his hero treated superiors. On July 30, 1932, an officer from the General Staff flew to the First Corps command post 145 kilometers west of Puerto Casado to deliver secret instructions. Colonel Estigarribia read the order carefully, then said that no rear-guard action, such as that contemplated, should be considered. Instead, he wanted to strike at once to prevent full mobilization of Bolivia's Fourth Division. "Tell the High Command to send me two more divisions and artillery!" he ordered. And he wrote to the Commander-in-Chief that it was necessary to send all possible aid within twenty days if the country were to be saved. The Chief of Staff himself reached Puerto Casado a few days later and had a telephone call sent through to Estigarribia. The Colonel listened briefly, then said: "Tell him to go back to the capital to hurry mobilization and to send me a map of the Chaco. I haven't anything to say to him; I am very busy."

His plans disagreed with those that called for defense along the river, a policy that he felt would have abandoned the entire Chaco to Bolivia. Estigarribia wanted to advance, to strike the enemy along the entire front; but all he had late in 1931, when he urged such action, was a force of 500 men scattered in small groups over a large expanse of territory. A year later, with a small army at his command, he favored the same strategy. He counseled audacity while the General Staff wanted to fight a defensive war; he wished to defend by attacking before the enemy columns could unite anywhere in vital territory and reduce Paraguay to a "paralytic coastal [river] defense"; he believed victory possible in spite of limited resources, and he knew the Chaco well. President Ayala had complete confidence in this daring soldier, defended him from his enemies and granted him freedom from political influence. When Estigarribia wanted to recover Boquerón, the President told him to go ahead.

Bolivians planned to follow their easy capture of Boquerón on July 31 with an attack on Isla Poi, Estigarribia's headquarters, on September 11. Estigarribia learned of this plan and beat the enemy to the offensive by attacking from Isla Poi on September 9 with about 8,000 men of the First Army Corps. The Bolivians believed that Boquerón was invested by 11,000 to 14,000 men; nevertheless, they sent small detachments from Fortín Arce, thirty miles to the southwest, in vain efforts to relieve the garrison. After twenty days of fighting, Estigarribia's soldiers marched in triumphantly and claimed to have taken 1,000 prisoners, although the garrison probably was less than 600 at the start. The defenders, of the Fourth Bolivian Division, had been defeated by hunger and thirst. Bolivians then concentrated their forces at Arce, their Chaco headquarters. This post fell on October 23 and yielded many prisoners. Just how many men Bolivia had at Arce is hard to say. General Rodríguez can account for only 1,200 divided among fourteen posts. This Bolivian officer also condemned the Boquerón siege as a Paraguayan tactical error. Estigarribia should have immobilized Boquerón with a small force while sweeping over Arce, Muñoz, and Platanillos; but the error is excusable since Paraguayans believed they were fighting a very strong enemy, a belief engendered by propaganda. West of Boquerón the Paraguayan drive continued for fifty miles, but the southern offensive, aimed at Fortín Muñoz, bogged down in November before reaching Saavedra. President Ayala flew to the front, promoted his commander to colonel, and said, "You are worthy of commanding Paraguayan soldiers."

General Hans Kundt, who had trained the Bolivian Army under President Hernando Siles, was on his way to take over Bolivia's military effort. He left New York on November 17, 1932, for La Paz, which he reached on December 6, and then went on to set up headquarters at Muñoz. The German's arrival revitalized Bolivian efforts on the Saavedra or southern front. Bolivians surged back, recaptured several posts in the north, and threatened Paraguay's Nanawa base in the south. Their road building, heavy artillery, and air power helped to stop the Paraguayan offensive on December 10, with heavy casualties on the Alihuata trail. By that time casualties on both sides were about 30,000 for the war period. All the horrors of war were unleashed at Kilometer Seven, a small clearing on the road from Saavedra to Alihuata. Bolivian trenches and machine-gun nests faced similar Paraguayan installations. Long-range mortars of Belgian make dropped shrapnel on the Paraguayans, while heavy artillery answered. At least 20,000 men were engaged in this one battle.

Two Bolivian divisions had been badly cut up in this fighting. The men wandered in the brush in small groups, seeking their way back to their own lines. One band of possibly 100 men, with not even a compass among them, sought to break through an almost complete envelopment. A guide led them through fairly open woods into heavy brush where matted bushes ten feet high forced them to cut a path with machetes. Two days of this sort of work brought them close to Paraguayan patrols. The guide changed his direction, only to meet other patrols of *pilas*. The men lost their sense of time, threw away empty canteens and useless knapsacks, cursed Hans Kundt for a blundering Boche, and died one by one. Caked with sweat and dust, lips cracked and drawn in a lunatic leer, backs and arms scratched deeply, the survivors pushed on. Seven of them reached Saavedra.

Bolivian strategy, if President Salamanca's scatterbrained schemes may be called such, required an effort to recover Boquerón, so forces were brought down from the north by a circuitous route to join others in attack against Corrales and Toledo, sixty-five miles west of their objective. Although exhausted by their forced march, the troops went forward "under a burning sun that scorched their brains, coagulating the blood in the arteries of many soldiers who died in the brush like scorpions surrounded by live coals. . . " This assault, begun on December 31, 1932, would enable the Bolivians to threaten Isla Poi and to flank Boquerón if it succeeded. Colonel Félix Cabrera, one of the principal founders of *fortines* when Paraguay began in 1924 to occupy the central Chaco, held Corrales with 300 men. At dusk on January 1, 1933, Cabrera ordered his men to fall back on Toledo, twenty-five miles to the north, to aid in its defense.

Paraguayans had no intention of giving up Toledo, a miserable collection of huts protected by trenches, automatic weapons, and howitzers which slaughtered Bolivians creeping through the brush or crawling like snakes along the ground. Whole companies were decimated in the attack, ammunition was exhausted, and water failed. Bolivian artillery tried to open a way for infantry to advance; but those deadly Paraguayan machine guns refused to be silenced. Bolivian infantry broke at one point, were halted only by their commanding colonel, then broke again. On the night of January 2, 1933, the Bolivians fell back to Corrales. On the following day, the sky was filled by "the mourning constellations of buzzards." Céspedes, in his *Sangre de mestizos,* gives a graphic account of this battle of Toledo.

Bolivia in the meantime had been so successful in the north that Paraguay rushed reinforcements from the south to protect Bahía Negra and the railway to Concepción. Jubilant as 1933 opened, Bolivians expected the war to end quickly. Now that the Paraguayan positions in the southern sector had been weakened, General Hans Kundt ordered a new offensive against Nanawa. Heavy rains brought a lull in the fighting until January 8, when an outpost of Nanawa fell; but subsequent assaults failed, as did attacks on Boquerón and Arce in the center. Rain again halted operations on January 28.

Fortín Nanawa was a crude post characteristic of Chaco fortifications, surrounded by clumps of bushes and islets of trees in a vast sea of scrub. Bolivians laid siege to the post after they failed to take it by storm, and constructed a twenty-kilometer semicircle of trenches that approached within one hundred meters of the *fortín* at one point. Paraguayans had built a strong machine-gun post, called "Fortified Island," in a small grove in front of the main position and about eighty meters from a Bolivian-held strong point protected by quebracho logs. These two positions suffered reciprocal fire for several months without serious damage to either.

Fighting around Nanawa was so severe that journalists began to call that *fortín* the Verdun of South America. There, and in other sectors, the war had settled down to a series of futile but costly attacks and counterattacks. Nanawa was able to hold out against the Bolivians and Muñoz against the Paraguayans partly because they were the only heavily fortified and carefully prepared positions in the Chaco. Nanawa remained defiant during the Bolivian offensive of March, 1933, which captured Alihuata, Saavedra, and bloody Kilometer Seven. Rains again held up the "final" assault on Nanawa while Paraguayan morale sank deeper into the Chaco morass.

All of this fighting occurred before war was declared. In March, the Paraguayan Congress authorized President Ayala to issue a declaration of war; on May 10, 1933, he did so. Paraguay had ratified the Kellogg Pact; Bolivia had not. Hence, there was no violation of that white hope of eternal peace. With war formally under way, Argentina, Uruguay, Chile, Peru, and Brazil hastened to reassure one another by declaring their neutrality while leaving their ports open for the most part to both belligerents.

Fort Esteros on the bank of the Pilcomayo River in Gran Chaco, won from Bolivia early in 1934

Bolivian mortar battery in the advance lines near Nanawa, Gran Chaco

Photographs from Wide World Photos, Inc.

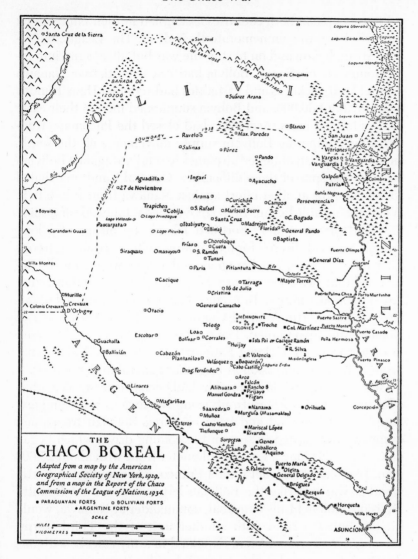

THE
# CHACO BOREAL

*Adapted from a map by the American
Geographical Society of New York, 1929,
and from a map in the Report of the Chaco
Commission of the League of Nations, 1934.*

● PARAGUAYAN FORTS □ BOLIVIAN FORTS
● ARGENTINE FORTS

SCALE

MILES
KILOMETRES

Pious people in both countries assembled in their churches on June 15, 1933, to commemorate their dead. The League of Nations struggled on and on to stop the war but always ran into insurmountable obstinacy. Bolivia had lost its initiative; Nanawa still held out; sickness and casualties had reduced Hans Kundt's force to about 30,000, and Bolivia summoned men in their early thirties to bear arms. Argentina had closed the Pilcomayo frontier, thus hampering Bolivian supply movements on the south, and Paraguay had obtained airplanes to retaliate against Bolivian bombing. In spite of these difficulties, General Kundt marshaled 25,000 men for another effort against Nanawa from July 6 to 9. When the assault began, Bolivian engineers touched off a mine they had placed under "Fortified Island" by means of a long tunnel. A rain of dirt fell for ten minutes on the advancing troops after the explosion; but Paraguayan defenses were so well constructed that two enemy tanks, heavy artillery, and infantry fire failed to break through. In August, General Kundt shifted his attack against Fortín Manuel Gondra, about ten miles north of Nanawa, and again failed. The reason was primarily to be found in clever work by Colonel Estigarribia, whose skillful defense brought him a commission as brigadier general in September.

General Estigarribia for months had been preparing a counteroffensive on the southern front, using Nanawa as his main base. Supplies from abroad and from captured Bolivian troops and dumps were hoarded to sustain the coming drive, which began on October 23 along a seventy-kilometer front with about 25,000 men. Lieutenant Colonel Rafael Franco, commanding at Fortín Gondra, was to strike the Bolivian left with the First Infantry Division; Colonel Luis Irrazábal, commander at Nanawa, would hit the Bolivian right with another unit of the Third Corps; *Comandante* Torreani Viera remained in army reserve with one division. Covered by dense underbrush, Paraguayan troops hacked passages through the brush and came out behind several Bolivian positions. By December 12, 1933, Alihuata, Masamaklay, and Saavedra were all in Paraguayan hands, as were 8,000 Bolivian prisoners, many of them clad in United States uniforms, and a considerable quantity of equipment and munitions. Those uniforms caused all too many people to jump at a stupid conclusion: the United States must be providing for the Bolivians. They forgot that after World War I surplus supplies were sold by nations and individual merchants to any country that would take them. One may as well conclude that Great Britain was backing Bolivia simply because Vickers-Armstrong of London sold large quantities of munitions to that country.

That was all for General Hans Kundt, who had "directed the war with a stupidity worthy of a William II." A Bolivian, General Enrique Peñaranda, took over the command when disaster threatened. Two divisions had been cut to pieces, leaving only one to protect Fortín Muñoz. Fortunately, a truce on December 19, arranged by the League's Chaco Commission while the Pan American Conference was meeting at Montevideo, saved Peñaranda for the time being. When hostilities were resumed on January 8, 1934, Estigarribia began to drive toward Fortín Ballivián, far up the Pilcomayo River, toward which the Bolivians withdrew as rapidly as possible. At Ballivián, 130 miles southeast of Villa Montes, Peñaranda made a magnificent stand. The heaviest fighting of the war, worse than at Nanawa, occurred there from March to July. Persistent Paraguayan assaults broke time and again against stubborn Bolivian defense. While the battle of Ballivián was going on, other Paraguayan forces swept westward on the northern end of their fluid line, and by the end of September had nearly cut off Villa Montes, Bolivia's general headquarters on the Pilcomayo, and threatened to invade the oil lands that lay well beyond the disputed territory. Paraguay had captured 20,000 square miles since June 15, 1932, at a cost of about three Bolivians and two Paraguayans dead per square mile.

There were some signs in July and August, 1934, that the Paraguayan tide might be forced to recede rapidly. At the southern end of the line, the Third Corps was held up before Ballivián; the Second Corps was falling back from Carandayty under a persistent Bolivian attack; and the First Corps was in retreat at the north end without having reached Parapití. At this time Estigarribia had about 21,000 men to oppose an estimated 50,000 of the enemy (probably much too high), and to man a front of well over two hundred miles. He regrouped the First and Second Corps north and south of Picuiba, after Bolivia's Colonel David Toro had failed to trap the Second Corps, and then resumed the attack. The First Corps struck first on the north and, in a battle from November 9 to 16, succeeded in capturing 7,000 prisoners at El Carmen. Ballivián fell on November 17 and President Salamanca resigned eleven days later.

By mid-December the Paraguayans were again within reach of the Parapití River and the oil fields. Bolivia now ordered a general mobilization, calling young boys and old men to the ranks. President José Luis Tejada Sorzano hoped to build up an army of 100,000 men to continue the futile struggle, and Bolivian writers fondly believe that their forces were on the verge of turning the tide, that the Paraguayans had run out their string of victories.

Certainly it was time that Paraguay be stopped. Since the Pilcomayo River runs diagonally, the fall of Ballivián shortened the front considerably and enabled Estigarribia to concentrate more and more men against Villa Montes and the oil region. Further advances carried his troops to the Parapití River on January 16, 1935, and enabled them to cut the road from Villa Montes north to Boyuibe. The League of Nations threatened to lift the arms embargo, supposedly in effect against both belligerents, and Paraguay announced its resignation from that ineffective world organization on February 23; Chile and Argentina, favoring Bolivia and Paraguay respectively, began to glare balefully at each other. Even Agustín Edwards, the great Chilean historian and diplomat, declared that Argentina had been prolonging the war.

While South American neutrals became more and more restless, Bolivians in February held on to Villa Montes and began to drive the Paraguayans back from the Parapití River. Extended lines, transport difficulties, and an aroused Bolivia had halted Estigarribia's great advance. General Angel Rodríguez modestly proclaimed himself as the savior of Villa Montes. The hard fighting was over, and on June 12, 1935, a truce was signed which went into effect two days later.

Why had previous efforts to stop the war failed so miserably? The answer is that political recalcitrance in Asunción and La Paz was responsible. Some cynical observers insist that Argentina did not want the war ended until Paraguay had won the Chaco; others point out that the United States made abortive every effort by the League of Nations. Certainly, the United States preferred to see the Pan American system rather than the League in control, but that is a far cry from actively opposing a settlement regardless of who were the mediators. The League's Chaco Commission had succeeded in getting an armistice from December 19, 1933 to January 8, 1934; but the League could supply little except talk and tremendous sincerity, and neither was effective. When Paraguay withdrew from the League, Argentina, Chile, Uruguay, Brazil, and the United States were assembling the Mediation Commission that brought the truce of June. The Bolivian Rodas Eguino quotes an unnamed neutral military observer as stating "that it is absolutely necessary to reach an agreement, above all to cease hostilities, in order to avoid not only a Paraguayan disaster but also the destruction of Paraguay's internal political force." That statement could bring little applause in Asunción, where newspapers gave hardly a hint of impending disaster. It is true that Bolivia's high command fully expected to win a glorious victory; but a three-year performance gave little reason to expect Paraguay's veteran divisions to disintegrate in response to a foreign observer's opinion.

Bolivia's minister of foreign relations, Dr. Tomás Manuel Elío, thought in May that the truce was to be arranged in Rio de Janeiro. Getulio Vargas would have enjoyed the role of supervising dove, but Argentina's Carlos Saavedra Lamas, who had sponsored an antiwar pact to compete with the Kellogg Pact, had been smoothing his own feathers for the part. Chile's foreign minister suggested Buenos Aires as the natural site for the mediation conference; Argentina's minister to the United States urged Cordell Hull to discourage Brazil's ambition. These various measures, according to Rodas Eguino, succeeded. Not to Rio de Janeiro but to Buenos Aires went Dr. Elío, former President Dr. Bautista Saavedra, and the learned Dr. Carlos Calvo, together with the usual experts. Elío, as an opposition deputy in 1933, had charged Argentina with being unfriendly to Bolivia and had consistently favored the League as the proper conciliatory agency.

The truce ended hostilities and provided that each army was to withdraw to lines to be fixed by a neutral military commission. A peace conference was to settle all disputes by direct negotiations; if these negotiations failed, arbitration would decide the issues. Paraguay, therefore, was left in possession of its conquests for the time being, and no one supposed that she would fail to take the opportunity to consolidate and strengthen those positions. The Argentine General Rodolfo Martínez Pita headed the Neutral Military Commission which discharged its delicate task with skill and extreme patience. Its principal work was to arrange for repatriation of prisoners and to persuade the armies to withdraw from their advanced positions. The commission's fairness is shown by charges from each side that it favored the other. Bolivians were particularly incensed because Paraguayans retained control over the road from Villa Montes to Boyuibe.

The situation was touchy in the Chaco for many months while neutrals labored with official delegates of the belligerents on a peace treaty. Bolivia and Paraguay finally agreed to renew diplomatic relations on August 25, 1936, and Dr. Elío bestowed Bolivia's Grand Cross of the Condor of the Andes on Saavedra Lamas. More negotiating finally resulted in the treaty of July 21, 1938. The boundary was to be arbitrated within fixed limits which would leave Paraguay with most of its conquests. Presidents, ministers, and delegates of the neutrals and belligerents were present at the signing. It was a happy hour, when one might hope that "blood so heroically shed . . . will not have been shed in vain." Dr. Roberto M. Ortíz, president of Argentina, said: "America and the whole world know that both the Bolivian and Paraguayan combatants fought with epic heroism, but without hatred or desire for vengeance." Heroism, yes; but no one ever fought any war without hatred. Let the good words fall over unburied corpses in the Chaco—they could do no good now, nor could they bring back the thousands of men who had died in one of the most senseless wars in history.

# CHAPTER XIX

# The New Paraguay

THE DECADE following the Chaco War was one of political anarchy that resulted from social unrest. Although long in power, the Liberal party had failed to provide answers to pressing questions being asked with ever increasing emphasis. The Liberals had brought a form of political democracy; but they were an oligarchy, not a popular party, and suffered from factional strife. Ordinary Paraguayans had little influence in the government and could see no chance to get action on the reforms they demanded. That the reforms were needed no sensible person would deny. Too much land was held by too few; standards of living were terribly low; public welfare services were woefully inadequate; working conditions, especially in the *yerbales*, were atrocious; the educational system probably was the poorest in South America; and perhaps the country suffered from the "heavy weight of powerful economic interests" that were taking away far more than they contributed. There were other complaints, but these will serve to indicate, by antitheses, what the common man wanted.

Who had the answers to Paraguay's problems? Would the "foreign interests" permit any drastic politico-economic changes? Could a restless people be kept quiet long enough for any program to function? Rafael Franco tried on the presidential sash in February, 1936, only to have it torn from his military shoulders in August, 1937. Then the Liberals returned to power, with Dr. Félix Paiva applying balm to old wounds. The Liberals made

Estigarribia president two years later; but this soldier proclaimed a new kind of state in an effort to reconcile new demands with old forms, then died in an airplane crash before he had time to implement his ambitious program of national rejuvenation. That brought Higinio Morínigo to power, the third Chaco hero in four years to be the chief executive, and perhaps the most astute politician ever to crush a Paraguayan *cuartelazo*.

That Paraguay would escape influences at work in the world and in Latin America was too much to expect. During the nineteen thirties, her neighbors were in turmoil, either hesitating between political extremes or definitely embracing them. Argentina had a revolution that eliminated Hipólito Irigoyen and installed General Agustín P. Justo, who held on until 1938, then gave way to Dr. Roberto M. Ortíz, a genuine democrat whose ill health was an Argentine disaster. When Dr. Ramón S. Castillo took over as acting president in 1940, Argentina's swing toward some form of native-foreign totalitarianism was more pronounced. This swing was too clear to be ignored when, on June 4, 1943, General Arturo Rawson led a revolt that was to culminate in a "new" state under guidance of the virile Colonel Juan Domingo Perón, a caudillo in modern dress. Brazil, too, had its troubles, with Getulio Vargas endeavoring to breathe life into a sculptured corporate state. Politics were even more topsy-turvy in Bolivia, where Italian and German totalitarianism found many admirers. And one should not forget that the New Deal, with its governmental controls and public-works programs, seemed to many Latin Americans to fit into a general plan of state socialism or something similar to it. Young Paraguayans, with a corps of Chaco veterans easily mobilized, thought about these things. If they were good for Argentina, Brazil, and the United States, why not for Paraguay?

Closely connected with political ideologies was the new economic nationalism apparent in many countries. This movement took various forms: increased emphasis on immigration, industrialization, expropriation of foreign properties, large-scale enterprises financed by a central government, agricultural expansion, and several auxiliary developments such as social welfare programs and adult education. Economic nationalism is a plant whose roots are sunk deeply in Latin American history, but one whose trunk had been stunted by long exposure to an unfavorable climate. Invigorated by the great depression, it grew rapidly in many countries. In Paraguay, the Franco, Estigarribia, and Morínigo administrations tried with indifferent success to nurse it along under the aegis of a super-nationalistic state. That state, the politicians and political philosophers proclaimed, was the "New Paraguay."

Dr. Juan Stefanich, perhaps more than any other contemporary Paraguayan, has attempted to explain the philosophical basis of what he calls *"El Paraguay nuevo."* His own training and career, notable for teaching, writing, and statesmanship, have qualified him eminently for a role as philosopher of the revolution begun by Franco and his Febreristas in 1936. If anyone could explain the Febrerista concept of democracy, Stefanich did so in *El mundo nuevo* and *El Paraguay nuevo*. These two books, published in 1941 and 1943 respectively, are the apology and the explanation of the Febrerista movement.

Stefanich has a philosophy of society, derived from various sources, which he thinks applicable to Paraguay's needs. He is a peculiar combination of incurable idealist and stern realist, with the idealist in the fore. "We have faith," he wrote, "in the power of thought and in the creative virtue of ideas, we believe in the generous conjectures of the spirit and in the optimistic conceptions of life, in individual effort and in collective action, and we accord high place to the will that does not surrender, to the hope that does not decline, and to the ideal that lights the paths of human existence with lovable images." He envisioned a new world of justice that might come from turmoil, tragedy, death, and sorrow, and he called for a new democracy that would preserve past victories while going beyond the theorists of 1789, a democracy that would be in harmony with the "world rhythm."

All of this was in September, 1940. Stefanich was looking back as well as ahead. Two months later, he recalled that on February 17, 1936, "a new era in the national life began." Paraguay had again answered the call of destiny to make its contribution to that new and better world in which peace would prevail. "The dawn beats of a great movement of political, social and historic renovation opened new horizons to the country." One suspects that Stefanich was thinking about a new democracy in which nineteenth-century liberalism and personal liberties were to be subordinated to national interests, as interpreted for the moment by a ruling clique, in order that nothing might hinder achievement of social objectives. That could be totalitarianism. Or was it just authoritarianism?

This new ideology did not spring upon Paraguayan thinkers without preparation. Some events grow in importance with the passing years, although at the time of their occurrence they may have appeared of significance only to a limited number of participants. Paraguay was on the eve of celebrating its centennial in the midst of troubled times that prevented realization of ideals and fulfillment of glowing promises. All this disturbed five youthful thinkers, to whom May 14, 1911, was a date of great importance in spite of contemporary dictatorship. The young men signed a pact dedicating themselves to public service. The five of 1911 became twelve in 1912, a liberal group determined to publish an independent paper dedicated to national rejuvenation. The twelve of 1912 became one hundred in 1925, determined on a program of "moral, political and social redemption." They began *La Nación* to propagandize their ideas. The one hundred of 1925 became one thousand in 1928, with adherents from the intelligentsia. There appeared the Liga Nacional Independiente, not a political party but an association to prepare for the future, "to give Democracy a new orientation and a new perception." The hour had come in 1931, Stefanich believed, for Paraguay to consummate its great democratic transformation, without sacrifice of public liberties. The country must be united, fratricidal strife must cease, foreign enemies must be repulsed, foreign totalitarian ideologies must be combatted. Stefanich, Adriano Irala, and other members of the Liga Nacional inspired a "student" demonstration on October 23, 1931, which miscarried and resulted in several deaths. Stefanich then attempted without success to form a "national front" of opposition journalists, student leaders, and workers. Then came the Chaco War that killed Adriano Irala and so many more, but the "New Democrats" did not forget.

The Chaco War did great things for the people; it "was the great laboratory of the Revolution. It put in motion all the powers of the country, polarized collective energies, organized material resources and called forth the deepest moral and spiritual reserves of the nation, displaced masses of people from all interior regions, infused in them a strong feeling of their solidarity and their strength and gave them ... confidence in their own strength and the civic courage to face the future." Political partisanship, says Stefanich, disappeared on the battlefields, where it all seemed so stupid and where the New Paraguay matured. Before the strength of ideas ripened in bloody conflict, the old regime "fell like a rotten fruit" in the revolution of February, 1936. Even though the new men, followers of Rafael Franco, had no platform and no program, they were energetic and realistic. In less than two years the Febreristas re-established order in economic and administrative matters, or so it is asserted. But had they? Was Paraguay ready for the New Era?

There was an ideological ferment in the New Paraguay. Fascism, communism, nazism, and the old partisanship struggled to control the current. Vagueness and resounding phrases were not enough; the Febreristas had neglected to adopt a definite program in advance to implement their philosophy; there was no unity on just what should be done, but Franco proclaimed that the New Paraguay would be a natural democracy for the benefit of the people, a "representative and functional" democracy, established by a new constitution. The Unión Nacional Revolucionaria emerged formally on November 15, 1936, and adopted a platform which the powerful National Veterans Association (*Asociación Nacional de Ex Combatientes*) endorsed. Now the work of the old Liga Nacional Independiente was complete, and the group extinguished itself.

Why the emphasis on *new* democracy? Dr. Stefanich examined the old bases and found something lacking. Man is free, man is social. What more? Man is *solidario*, inextricably united with his fellows. This condition of *solidaridad*, of solidarity or community of interests, "is the new principle and the new regulatory truth of the political and social order. It is the vertebral column of the new democracy." Perhaps if one accepts this definition, one is a Febrerista; but there is far more to Stefanich's thought that warrants a serious study by political philosophers. In brief, and perhaps by doing an injustice to an excellent thinker, one may say that *Democracia solidarista* seeks to extract all that is good from individualistic democracy, fascism, nazism, and communism and to weld them together to form a political philosophy valid for American realities and capable of answering needs created by complex modern societies. Perhaps that is why so many Febrerista actions appeared to be totalitarian.

Paraguay's losses in the Chaco War deepened economic depression and increased discontent in the country. Army leaders, adherents of the "new democracy," opposed Eusebio Ayala's handling of negotiations with Bolivia and his confirmed democratic bias that was anachronistic according to Febrerista concepts. Ayala as a Liberal was also friendly with agents of foreign companies, a characteristic of most Liberal leaders who were quite happy to have Paraguay continue as a political and economic colony of Argentina. Colonel Rafael Franco, hero of the Chaco War, supported by 300 army officers and 40,000 veterans, capitalized on discontent to overthrow Ayala on February 17, 1936. Only eleven days before, Ayala had exiled Franco, saying that he was a Communist! The Febreristas won their revolt without Franco, but he returned and assumed power with little trouble. Although this revolt was widely considered as the army's repudiation of the Chaco truce negotiated by Ayala, Franco assured the delegates, before he left Buenos Aires on February 19, that his regime would respect agreements that had been made.

Franco had the support of discontented pressure groups who hailed his efforts to create a new state along totalitarian lines. University students, Chaco veterans, labor leaders, and a large part of the armed forces saw in him the strong man who would end Liberal "betrayal" of the fatherland. Just what Franco would do was rather doubtful. He talked about a corporate state, suspended political liberties, called up new classes for the army, frowned on foreign capital, and ordered his National Labor Department to take care of labor troubles. Apparently the Unión Nacional Revolucionaria was going places fast with its "new democracy" that looked much like a poor imitation of big-time fascism. There was something ominous about Franco's efforts to make a national hero of Francisco Solano López, the one strong man who might be used as a symbol of a militarized Paraguay. He completed the Pantheon begun by López and had the tyrant's bones placed in the central hall.

Franco made the balcony popular again. Standing on a projection of the Government House on February 24, 1936, he proclaimed a new era, a restoration of glory known under the dictators, Paraguay's return to its destiny. He made his intentions clearer on March 10 with a decree that set up either a totalitarian or an authoritarian state. The "liberating revolution" and the state were one in the New Paraguay, all political activities outside the Party were forbidden for one year, all industrial disputes were to be settled by the minister of the interior. Newspapers had been seized on February 18 to establish censorship, and this gag on freedom of the press was made even tighter by forbidding anyone to discuss the totalitarian decree in print. At last it seemed that the Chaco Veterans Association and the National Federation of Students might have their way in driving foreign capital out of the country. Franco's aims, however, failed to meet with full approval by all the veterans. Friends of General Estigarribia, in exile and at home, plotted to rebel in May, but Franco moved fast enough to save his job for the time being. A new batch of Liberals, prospective leaders of a revolt, headed for Buenos Aires at official request; Eusebio Ayala and General Estigarribia soon joined them, being released from custody for the purpose.

Febreristas recognized the need for better relations with Paraguay's neighbors and were determined to support a continental policy. Dr. Stefanich, minister of foreign affairs, attended the Buenos Aires Chaco Conference and the Inter-American Conference on the Maintenance of Peace in December, 1936. He sought better commercial relations with Argentina and signed a convention on December 31 that provided for an Argentine-Paraguayan commission to study mutual problems and to recommend ways to improve commercial intercourse. Political changes in the two countries nullified the work. Stefanich went to Montevideo in January, 1937, to sign a similar accord, and Dr. Isidro Ramírez, Paraguayan minister at Rio de Janeiro, signed a third with Brazil in April. These three basic agreements augured well for the future of commercial and political relations which Febreristas hoped would restore Paraguayan economy and promote intra-continental commerce.

Discontent with the Chaco truce had been the means of starting the short-lived New Era; discontent with peace negotiations killed it. The war ended with Paraguayan forces in control of the road from Villa Montes to Boyuibe. On January 9, 1937, Franco agreed to withdraw his troops from this road in accordance with suggestions of the Neutral Military Commission. Unfortunately, he had encouraged the belief that a smashing military victory had been prevented by Ayala's signing of the truce. The same theme caused rebellions in Bolivia and had been played upon so much in both countries that neither dared to sign a definitive peace. Franco ordered the army to withdraw from the road in June, 1937, and Dr. Stefanich delivered a three-hour speech in a theater at Asunción in a vain effort to explain why the withdrawal was necessary and why it did not violate Franco's promises.

The order caused Franco's downfall. Chaco commanders refused to obey their president, and on August 13, 1937, Lieutenant Colonel Ramón Paredes executed a *cuartelazo* that forced Franco's cabinet to resign. This coup, which left Franco in office for two more days, was carried out to "reimpose the ideals of February, 1936," and clearly revealed that a group of officers controlled the country's immediate future. Who controlled the officers? Perhaps the Liberals, who in turn were controlled by sinister foreign influences. Dr. Stefanich called the revolt a great national disgrace and its government the acme of stupidity. The rebels certainly were not Febreristas, however they might attempt to win support by prating about the ideals of February.

Dr. Félix Paiva, dean of the National University's Law School, replaced Franco on August 15. Paiva was a handy man to have available. His first experience as acting president came in 1920 when, as vice-president, he had held the reins briefly after Eduardo Schaerer's followers had rebelled against President Manuel Gondra.

Why had Franco failed? Foreign observers attributed his fall to lack of popular support. His promises of land, of better social conditions, were not carried out because he dared not confiscate foreign holdings, principally Argentine, to distribute among the landless. He had signed a law in May, 1936, authorizing the government to expropriate 5,000,000 acres not under cultivation, to pay for it with bonds, and to sell it in plots of 25 to 250 acres to farmers. The *Bulletin* of the Pan American Union reported that land for 15,000 families had been taken over by August, and that 10,000 families had been settled on 207,048 acres at the end of the year. Surely this was a splendid beginning, but national socialism had little chance in a country dominated by foreign capital in league with a small upper class whose economic interests demanded the *status quo*. A would-be dictator acceptable to the good people and to the foreign interests could hold on for years; without such support, there could be no successful dictatorship of any stamp, whether one called it *Democracia solidarista* or anything else.

Paiva's provisional regime did not satisfy the Chaco War veterans, university students, and factions in the armed forces. They charged that Franco's overthrow was a Liberal party maneuver to return to power, and it was well known that Liberal leaders were closely identified with foreign interests. Franco had been unable to bring state socialism to Paraguay; now his supporters were determined to keep the Liberals from perpetuating their old control. For this reason, apparently, a counterrevolt took place on September 7, 1937, under the leadership of Lieutenant Colonel Julio Jara and Colonel Federico Weddell Smith. They demanded Paiva's resignation and Franco's return. After fighting sporadically in Asunción during the night, Paiva's supporters threw out the rebels; Colonel Franco climbed from his plane in

Asunción and then climbed back again. His Febrerista followers did not stop plotting. Anarchy must cease but not until Febreristas were in control. Less than two months later, on November 2, a state of siege was enforced in Asunción to meet a *cuartelazo* that occurred far upstream at Concepción. One regiment also revolted in the capital, but the Chaco Division remained loyal, and the uprising fizzled to a sputtering end.

General Estigarribia seemed to be far removed from Paraguayan political troubles as he enjoyed the hospitality of Buenos Aires, Rio de Janeiro, São Paulo, and Montevideo. He lived in the Uruguayan capital from April, 1937 to February, 1938, teaching in the Escuela Superior de Guerra. In August, 1937, military leaders of the anti-Franco forces sent him a telegram inviting his return from exile. The famous soldier docked at Asunción on February 9, 1938, to find a grand welcome organized by Archbishop Juan Sinforiano Bogarín. Veterans, students, cadets, and plain people were in a gathering of 50,000 enthusiastic Paraguayans who came to pay homage to the architect of so many victories against Bolivia.

President Paiva offered the hero his country's diplomatic post in Washington, which Estigarribia accepted. Dr. Pablo Max Ynsfrán, a brilliant Liberal statesman and linguist, went with him. He interrupted this mission to sign the treaty of peace with Bolivia at Buenos Aires on July 21, 1938, then returned to complete negotiations for a loan from the United States to build the Asunción-Caaguazú highway and for other purposes.

Félix Paiva's administration was noted for two important achievements: a lull in the period of anarchy and peace with Bolivia. Estigarribia, at the request of Dr. Cecilio Báez, became chief of the Paraguayan delegation. He knew the advantages of a definite settlement with Bolivia and did not hesitate to sign a treaty when opposition was certain to appear in Asunción. This decision saved the treaty from going the way of all previous efforts. A plebiscite ratified the document by a vote of 135,385 to 13,204.

While Estigarribia was in Washington, he became the Liberal party's candidate for the presidency, with Dr. Luis A. Riart as

Signing the "Treaty of Peace and Friendship" to end the Chaco dispute between Bolivia and Paraguay is Dr. Cecilio Báez, Paraguayan minister of foreign affairs. On his left is General José Félix Estigarribia of Paraguay

his running mate. He was a popular, unopposed nominee. When he returned to Asunción on an Argentine warship for the inauguration, the entire capital seemed to be waiting to welcome him. His inauguration on August 15, 1939, promised a more liberal regime that would try to take over certain Febrerista ideals.

This second new era within four years scarcely survived inaugural festivities. Discordant elements were too numerous to be welded together easily into a co-operative, peaceful society. The Colorados, on a political strike since 1931, refused to participate in a government whose cabinet and congress were solidly Liberal. A student strike, a vicious opposition press, and many Febrerista plots disturbed the country. Franco's talk about a new Paraguay had awakened or had taken advantage of latent hopes for a better life among thousands long submerged and oppressed by colonial exploitation. A new phase in the country's history had begun in the nineteen thirties and probably would have made itself apparent before the Febreristas erupted in 1936 had it not been for the Chaco War. Estigarribia felt that he would have to lead, to guide this surging spirit in order to avoid anarchy, even though it meant some form of state socialism, a desertion from the Liberals to the Febreristas.

On February 18, 1940—the month had become propitious for new departures—President Estigarribia issued a proclamation. He had endeavored to restore the Political Charter of 1870, the press had enjoyed unlimited freedom, opposition parties had been encouraged, and the government had promoted a public-works program "of fundamental importance to the national economy in a scope never before attempted in the country." Now, after six months of futile effort to establish the constitutional ideal, the nation teetered on the verge of social anarchy. "Hatred divides Paraguayans. Respect for the Magna Carta, law, and authority has been lost." Stern measures were necessary to prevent endangering the country's future. "The individualistic democracy of 1870 has fulfilled its mission." Now social and economic democracy must be attained. Political rivalries must end, a national convention would be summoned to draw up another constitution "that responds to the [people's] needs and to their democratic ideal." Therefore, the President proclaimed, "In view of the collective resignation of Congress [February 17], basing my attitude on the services I have rendered to the country with devout conviction, inspired in my conscience as a loyal soldier and citizen, and seeking the help of Almighty God in my acts, I assume from today the total responsibility of political power for the time necessary to assure the Paraguayan nation order and stable peace and to insure its greatness and prosperity."

The President's words were intended to be noble and sincere, devoid of the deceit commonly found in such pronouncements. There was to be no proscription of prominent men, no interference with the courts and the university. Political contention was to cease, but the cabinet would represent a wide spread of opinion. "The movement of February 18," Justo Pastor Benítez wrote, "was not a step backward toward regimes of force, but a parenthesis, a maneuver to halt anarchy, a revision of juridical statutes that merited not only the support of the army but also of the most representative men of the country." Estigarribia believed his mission to be one of starting the country along new paths toward prosperity. He wanted to be president of all the people, not the mouthpiece of a favored minority.

As temporary dictator, Estigarribia acted vigorously. While a new constitution was in the making, he reopened the university, put the Banco de la República on its feet, promoted public works, strengthened the Office of Lands and Colonies, funded the floating debt, and revised municipal administration. These measures won support among all classes, particularly the workers, and they were very similar to Franco's policies. An agrarian law, effective March 1, provided that land be expropriated to give every Paraguayan family a bit of earth. The 178,000 acres of abandoned land taken over in the department of Encarnación by the Office of Lands and Colonies were to be given to 1,800 families. Estigarribia also echoed Franco when he issued a decree-law in June, 1940, to stifle the press. Absolute freedom of the press, the decree stated, is an attribute of juvenile minds.

One who is not too critical may readily accept the praise of Benítez, a co-worker in the regime: "Estigarribia was the most

American Paraguayan who ever lived." He was American, not in the sense of being like statesmen of the great northern republic but in his detached patriotism, his unselfish devotion to Paraguay, his loyalty and honesty. He knew that "There is always a dynamite bomb under the presidential chair," but the knowledge served as a challenge to regularize political affairs, even at the expense of liberty. He had great plans for Paraguay, plans that might have been carried out had he ruled for more than a few months. The country needed fuel other than wood, customs agreements, lower transportation costs, a modern highway system, a better monetary standard, a merchant marine, a railway to Brazil, a pipe line across the Chaco to Bolivia's oil fields. Estigarribia planned these things; Higinio Morínigo was to accomplish most of them.

Estigarribia's government was a dictatorship with its orientation toward totalitarian methods. So much emphasis has been placed on Morínigo's "reign of terror" that there is an inclination to forget its origin under Estigarribia, who protected Axis groups. The experience of a student, Calixto Bogado, may be taken as typical. He was arrested on July 18, 1940, by secret police, and beaten and tortured for three days by Adriano Quevedo. Then, with eight workers, he was sent to Peña Hermosa, where hundreds of others soon enjoyed the benefits of Estigarribia's glorious regime. Freed in January, 1941, Bogado was too ill to resume his anti-Fascist work. Periodically thereafter the secret police molested him and eventually sent him into exile.

Estigarribia used the press, mass meetings, the radio, and other means of publicity to indoctrinate the people with his brand of diluted *Democracia solidarista.* Typical of this propaganda are the short articles and speeches by José Antonio Pérez Echeguren, published as *Relieve y categoria de la revolución paraguaya,* which identify Estigarribia with the Febreristas. Civil turmoil must end to permit progress; political forms must be changed to meet new conditions; democracy of the nineteenth century, with its emphasis on individualism, must give way to a new democracy in which the state intervenes to solve political, social, and economic problems. A genuine revolution had taken place in Paraguay; the country had been born again, to a new destiny in which individuals must subordinate their selfish interests to national welfare, with Estigarribia leading the way into a grand future with culture, bread, liberty, and justice for all. All this was to be done not through a totalitarian state but through a strong national state. The revolution was not a mere episode but a major phase that began on February 18 and could not end until Paraguay had been completely remodeled. The constitutional framework would be provided. This propaganda was definitely official and anticipated the prologue, published over Estigarribia's name, that was bound with copies of the constitution of 1940.

The frame of government provided by the constitution of 1870 was too slow in solving problems and in meeting critical situations. "The present reform," Estigarribia announced, "refers more to organization than to content; we shall continue to be a representative democratic republic in conformity with our tradition." Not a totalitarian state but a perfecting of the democratic regime, was the objective of the new basic law. "Paraguay needs a constitution more genuinely its own, without diminution of the cardinal principles of the American democracy consigned in the Constitution of Philadelphia and in the Argentine Constitution of 1853, and adopted by our country in the Constitution of 1870, because of a great disaster. . . . The new Charter bestows on the Administrative Power a greater breadth of functions in homage to the general good and not to benefit persons, parties, or any social class. It seeks an Executive Power strong but not despotic; to greater responsibility must belong more ample possibilities to meet it." The modern state must not be a mere policeman, but a means of regulating and defending society. Economic interests, class conflicts, and diverse ideologies require a strong, efficient, and respected executive. The executive power in the present epoch must assume responsibility; there is not always time to deliberate "when problems knock at the gates of the government demanding solutions." Congress, therefore, must be a legislative collaborator instead of a recalcitrant, slow, political forum. The judiciary will continue its historic role and needs the least modification; commercial and civil codes need attention; courts must be a neutral zone in which individual rights are protected. The old congress was unrealistic: the senate was merely another chamber of deputies, reduced in number, not a body representative of states as in a federal republic. To have a check on the chamber, the Council of State is created as an intermediary between the legislative and executive division. Under the old system there were too many elections, too much incitement to anarchy, that gave rise "to a class of professional politicians who definitely are not the statesmen a country needs." The new document provides for general elections every five years, and thus discourages *caudillismo*. It protects the traditional liberties of man but does not place them above society; it does not suppress them as in an absolute state but improves them by protecting them from anarchy. Private initiative must be controlled in a country like Paraguay. "A new direction must be given to political organization. It is necessary to replace the classic theory of absolute equilibrium of powers with the more modern one of specialization of functions, without prejudice to the checks and balances so dear to the constitutionalists of the past century."

Paraguay's new constitution resulted from hard work by Estigarribia and a commission of jurists headed by Dr. Cecilio Báez. There was an attempt to include only broad powers in the document, properly leaving to laws the role of putting flesh on the basic skeleton. Military and naval leaders, the council of ministers, and noted public figures approved the instrument before it was published on July 10, 1940. A plebiscite on August 4 found more than 160,000 voters in favor of the charter, which was formally promulgated in a ceremony eleven days later. This overwhelming approval was a vote for Estigarribia more than an endorsement of the document itself.

The constitution of 1940 made drastic changes in Paraguay's fundamental law. Congress was to be unicameral, with one representative to each 25,000 citizens, and it was to meet annually. The Council of State was to be made up of executive ministers, the rector of the university, the archbishop of Paraguay, a representative of business, two representatives from agricultural industries, one representative from processing industries, the president of the Banco de la República, and two officers from the armed forces (who must be retired from active duty). It was, in effect, an official "brain trust" with advisory functions. Economic activities, from enterpriser to laborer, would be strictly controlled. There was to be no more class war, no more monopoly, no more manipulation of prices, and all citizens were expected to earn their living through useful work. There were freedoms: "to choose a profession; to work and to engage in every legitimate trade and industry, except for limitations that, for social and economic reasons of national interest, [may be] imposed by law; to publish their ideas in the press without prior censorship, provided that they deal with matters of general interest; to dispose of their property; to associate for legitimate purposes; to practice any religion freely; to learn and to teach." Suffrage was universal and obligatory for citizens eighteen years of age and over.

In Paraguay as in many other countries, unfortunately, people have learned how to make constitutions while lacking the determination to live by them. Just how this document would have functioned under Estigarribia is a matter of conjecture. Fate gave it no chance.

Escape from the worries of public affairs was possible on week ends, when Estigarribia and his wife, Doña Julia Miranda Cueto, flew to San Bernardino to rest at Lake Ipacaraí. On Saturday, September 7, 1940, the first family of Paraguay prepared for the customary trip, a flight of fifteen minutes. The morning was cloudy and hazy when the President and Doña Julia appeared at the airport and found that their plane, en route from Puerto Pinasco, was late. Thereupon Estigarribia ordered his pilot, Major Carmelo Peralta, to take off in an old survivor of the Chaco War. A few miles out of Asunción the plane crashed. By executive decree the Chaco hero became Marshal Estigarribia, the new highway to Villa Rica received his name, and Doña Julia was laid to rest beside him in the Panteón Nacional.

# CHAPTER XX

# *Morínigo*

AMONG the *conquistadores* who sailed with Mendoza was one listed as "myn de moringo"—Martín de Morínigo. This obscure figure, whose role in the conquest most certainly was by no means outstanding, was the first of that name to live in Paraguay. Perhaps he was the remote ancestor of Higinio Morínigo, a faithful and safe army officer upon whom fell Estigarribia's mantle.

Liberals in the government probably felt that they could control the man whom Estigarribia had made his minister of war and navy on May 2, 1940. This position placed him in control of the support necessary for a chief executive and probably caused his appointment as provisional president for two months. Morínigo had to feel his way carefully. Army leaders were not satisfied with Liberal policies. There were some who thought that Estigarribia had not gone far enough toward a totalitarian state, and others who thought he had ignored their sacred interests. Febreristas, in and out of the army, were waiting for a chance to reimpose themselves upon the country, convinced that they and they alone were worthy of being trusted with their country's future. Among these and other factions Morínigo had to tread warily if he hoped to remain in power.

Trouble developed in the cabinet almost at once. The four Liberal ministers resigned on September 30, and military men, with Colonel Ramón Paredes playing a prominent role, replaced them. Another cabinet shake-up brought another army group to the front on November 25, when Paredes went out. Five days later Morínigo assumed full powers of government "to orientate once for all the Paraguayan revolution." This sounded like Febrerista talk; surely Liberals did not hear Estigarribia's shade speaking with his successor's voice, and they objected to being orientated. On the charge that Liberals were plotting to overthrow the government, Morínigo rounded up most of the prominent ones on December 25, threw 180 into jail, and sent others to the Peña Hermosa military prison.

For a while in 1941 it was doubtful whether the president could squelch *cuartelazos* as fast as they appeared. Two examples must suffice to illustrate the plotting that went on constantly within the country and abroad. An attempted Febrerista *coup d'état* failed on April 18, and Morínigo requested the Uruguayan government to place the exiled Franco under home arrest. The entire cabinet resigned, and ten army and navy officers, suspected of disloyalty, lost their commissions. In the second *cuartelazo*, the garrison at Pilar attempted a revolt that was crushed easily on July 4. This uprising apparently resulted from Morínigo's action in sending three former rebel leaders to prison for a cooling-off period. The dictator on July 26 issued a decree that detailed a long list of punishments to be meted out to future rebels: death for attempting to kill the president, twenty-five to thirty years' imprisonment for attempting to overthrow the government, five to ten years for conspiracy, two to four years for sending unfavorable information abroad, and so on.

There had been a general exodus of Liberal leaders soon after Morínigo took office. Following the mass imprisonment, the President suppressed the Liberal party in May, 1942, and its greatest leader, Eusebio Ayala, died in exile in Buenos Aires on June 4. Supported by his "boy heroes," the dictator had a precarious but heavy hold on the country. He felt so secure that on September 29, 1942, he announced that his military friends insisted on his staying in office until 1948. From Montevideo, where Colonel Rafael Franco was said to be running a soap factory while longing to blow bubbles through a *bombilla* in Asunción, came word that the Febrerista leader wanted to vote in the peculiar

Higinio Morínigo

one-candidate election that continued on week ends from January 16 to February 14, 1943. Franco started back to vote. At Buenos Aires the Argentine Government restrained him at Morínigo's request. Still, while there was Franco, there was always hope for a revolt, despite Morínigo's inauguration on August 15, 1943, for a five-year term. Odds were heavy against his completing the period.

No country, apparently, could have been more remote from World War II than Paraguay. Without ocean shipping and lacking essential war materials, the republic's interest in the conflict was almost wholly political or ideological. A major war, at last, was to be economically profitable for Paraguay, not because the country was important in itself but because it happened to be in Latin America. Lend-Lease goods and American money; increased markets for its canned beef, hides, cotton, and quebracho; higher prices and higher wages; public-works programs paid for largely by Brazilian and American loans; and numerous foreign commissions, all brought a spirit of prosperity that could not fail to aid Estigarribia and Morínigo politically.

The war found Paraguay with at least the rudiments of a price-control system that dated back to April, 1936. All necessities of life could be controlled under the sweeping decree issued by President Franco. Practically nothing was done with this power until World War II began, then ceilings were clamped on foods, textiles, clothing, and other items. A new law in November, 1939, changed the situation little, except to broaden the law's scope. These powers, wielded by the Ministry of Agriculture, Commerce, and Industry, were used lightly until 1941. Rationing, allocation, and export controls were even more important than price fixing. Agricultural minimum prices were set in July and August, and minimum prices were later extended to other products; maximum prices for many goods were set in January at approximate market levels, and were advanced from time to time to permit a reasonable profit. Outside of Asunción, price-fixing had little success because there was practically no popular support for it. There was such a demand for meat exports that, after January, 1942, growers had to sell 60 per cent of their animals

333

for domestic use. Cost of living increased sharply in spite of controls. A steady rise in prices from 1939 to 1941 was followed by steep increases that caused some commodities to double and triple their prewar prices by 1944. The many Americans who went to Paraguay in various capacities spent freely and bid up rents until ordinary houses brought $100 a month in Asunción. Cost of living went up 300 per cent for the city dwellers with money and 50 per cent for the poor people.

Morínigo displayed considerable skill in dealing with foreign countries, in playing upon their mutual jealousies and ambitions. Brazil wished to increase its influence in the country to break the Argentine stranglehold, and the United States sought to wean Morínigo away from Axis affiliations. The dictator stood to gain much and to lose little. United States money in 1939 had paved the road from Asunción to Villa Rica; another credit, this time for $4,000,000, in 1942 completed the highway to Encarnación and left some money for various other projects. From Brazil came a credit of $5,000,000 for a six-year public-works program. Fortunately, there was no dollar debt, other than Export-Import Bank credits, profits were coming in from increased traffic on the Paraguay Central Railway, and the first six months of 1942 accumulated a favorable trade balance of about $1,000,000.

Achievements in 1942 were but an indication of what was to come in 1943. Somehow Morínigo had to appease Argentina and at the same time apply pressure where it would hurt. Argentine finance dominated the country through such firms as Casado, Bunge-Born, Mihanovich, Domingo Barthe, and the Francisco Mendes-Banco de Buenos Aires group. Of some $60,000,000 in foreign investments, Argentina controlled fully 75 per cent. Brazil's principal interest was the huge Companhia Matte Larangeira which had large holdings in northern Paraguay. The President went to Brazil in January to talk things over with Getulio Vargas. He returned with a free port zone at Santos, a promise for an extension of the São Paulo railroad to Concepción, and projects for a new trade and navigation treaty that was signed later in the year. Then he traveled to the United States, defying his enemies to start a rebellion during his absence. The official record of this visit remains secret, but it is known that a reciprocal trade agreement was discussed and Lend-Lease equipment began to move to Asunción in such quantities that by July 1, 1945, its worth amounted to $1,387,000.

Among the more entertaining features of Morínigo's visit to the United States was his reception by Fordham University, which could have been prompted by the Department of State. The Reverend Robert I. Gannon, president of the university, conferred an honorary LL.D. on Morínigo and said: "As a university, Fordham has been gratified to see in this new energetic executive the exceptional type of soldier who has won glory on the field of battle, but who values learning and who considers the fostering of true education to be the principal concern of government; a man of valiant judgment who can appreciate the dreadful abuses of the absolute state as exemplified in Nazi Germany [Was this satire?], and at the same time emphasizes the necessity for a mental outlook based on the stern ideal of duty and responsibility." Then at St. Patrick's Cathedral, Bishop John F. O'Hara praised the spirit of Morínigo's rule as being fundamentally that of the Jesuit missions. No comment is needed, but it might be suggested that the Bishop would profit from a more careful reading of Paraguayan history.

Financial changes and agreements with Bolivia further improved Paraguay's international position. An expert from the Federal Reserve System studied the country's finances while the government was endeavoring to discard the depreciated paper peso. On November 7, 1943, the *guaraní* became Paraguay's monetary unit at an initial exchange value of 3.07 to one United States dollar and one *guaraní* to 100 of the old paper pesos. A year later, in response to recommendations of the Federal Reserve expert, the Banco de la República was streamlined and renamed the Banco del Paraguay.

These financial changes were still brewing when Morínigo visited President Enrique Peñaranda at La Paz in July, 1943, to pave the way for a better relationship with the former enemy. Four months later the two presidents, their chiefs of staff, and foreign ministers erected a cross to the Chaco War dead, then adjourned to Villa Montes, where they signed commercial agreements. Especially significant was the provision for a pipe line to carry Bolivia's landlocked oil to the Paraguay River.

Foreign loans and increased revenues should have put Paraguay in a favorable financial position, but the treasury was in constant difficulties. The budget was too large for the poverty-stricken country, and it increased steadily—from about $5,000,-000 in 1943 to $10,000,000 in 1945. Dr. Juan Plate, minister of finance, objected to the army's share of the 1945 budget, which was 37 per cent of the 28,274,000 *guaranís*, not counting heavy extraordinary expenses. The chief of staff, Colonel Bernardo Aranda, did not like to be told that out of a primary school population of 163,000, about 74,000 could find no educational facilities; that one-half of the children dropped out at the end of their first year; that five-sixths got no farther than the second year. Aranda was not worried about illiteracy. "Look at the international situation!" he cried, and Plate became an ex-minister. The Frente de Guerra, a group of politically powerful officers, did not care what happened to the country so long as its leaders could remain in power.

Aside from Lend-Lease aid to bolster Morínigo's hold on the country, the United States made its greatest contribution in public health. The Inter-American Public Health Service opened its Asunción office on July 1, 1944, under the direction of Dr. Richard J. Plunkett. Working with an initial gift of $1,000,000, the service constructed hospitals, set up laboratories, provided filtration plants for drinking water, laid water mains, organized public health centers, and initiated a program of public health education. In spite of these contributions, Paraguayan intellectuals were skeptical about the United States, whose ambassador was more interested in social work than in defending political liberties. After all, the situation was somewhat touchy. Fascist organizations were prominent, Morínigo and his gang wanted to stay in Argentina's good graces, and no matter who headed Paraguay's government he was almost certain to be a dictator. Perhaps the best policy was to buy good will, a precarious and ephemeral business at best.

Not even this apparent and crude appeasement can explain the amazing case of Pablo Stagni, chief of Paraguay's air force and an avowed Axis sympathizer. American officials knew that Stagni had on occasions dealt with Yankee experts in a most unfriendly manner. J. Edgar Hoover did not like the man's record, G-2 knew about him, and so did the Department of State. Still, according to the *Inter-American,* Colonel John Considine of the United States Army mission in Asunción, recommended that Stagni be invited to tour United States airplane factories in the fall of 1944. The War Department seems to have been willing, but Cordell Hull's underlings objected, just the reverse of what one might expect. Nevertheless, Stagni made the trip early in the spring of 1945. Again the State Department officials said "no"—that is, all but the naïve Avra Warren. So Stagni saw the Canal Zone defenses and the airplane factories, and J. Edgar Hoover disclaimed all responsibility for what might happen. When asked why Stagni had been allowed to make the junket, War Department spokesmen (conveniently anonymous behind their silver and brass), reportedly shrugged off the inquiry with the remark: "It's quite a story." It must have been, but all the facts may never see the light so far as this or the next generation is concerned.

Morínigo's affiliation with the United Nations was sheer hypocrisy since Paraguay, to her eternal shame, was a stronghold of Axis sympathizers and agents. On December 10, 1941, the dictator announced his solidarity with the United States; on January 25, 1942, he "severed" diplomatic relations with the Axis; on February 8, 1945, he declared war on the Axis; on February 14, 1945, his ambassador to the United States signed the Declaration of the United Nations; in March, 1945, his delegates signed the Act of Chapultepec, which included nice words about International Protection of the Essential Rights of Man; and in June, 1945, his delegates signed the United Nations Charter. It was not necessary to ask Morínigo if he would sign anything recommended by the United States—he seemed to keep ready one of those pens that can write under any circumstances.

Paraguay's support of hemisphere solidarity could be explained in part by foreign control over quebracho, from which the country derived considerable income. The American International Products Company and the British Forestal Land, Timber and Railways, Ltd., had a cartel that monopolized production and distribution of Argentine and Paraguayan quebracho. Morínigo, by playing along, received Lend-Lease army equipment that enabled him to smash strikes and revolts. It made him strong enough to dissolve trade unions, to keep a thousand potential leaders in concentration camps; but no amount of Lend-Lease could keep Morínigo from falling in line with Argentina's colonels.

Higinio Morínigo certainly had peculiar ideas about democracy. If one could believe his radio address of December 23, 1940, another new era was opening for Paraguay, in which there would be no place for selfish interests, intrigue, deception, demagoguery, and traditional Paraguayan politics. He hoped to create a real democracy: "The fundamental political dogma of the Paraguayan Revolution is the predominance of the national interest over the selfish, grasping interests of individuals." His program for the nation during the expected three years of his tenure was broad, laudable, and missed little in showing what the country needed in economic and social improvement. This Three-Year Plan would be wonderful if it worked; but there was no place in it for traditional democracy.

A few revolts later, Morínigo spoke sweet words to the United States Congress on the occasion of his visit in June, 1943. "New theories in the field of law inspired the reform of 1939," he said, "which sought to harmonize the Constitution with modern trends and assure greater general welfare. The problem was not to abandon the road followed theretofore and to travel by a different one, but to straighten the route and to expedite our progress in a desirable way, avoiding both obstacles and illusions and advancing in accordance with modern ideologies and in line with the procedure that other American countries had established." As an apology for dictatorship, Morínigo's explanation was extremely weak. He was much more explicit a month later in remarks published by a Peruvian paper: "An exclusively electoral democracy for a people not yet educated to vote conscientiously and freely is a farce. It does not assure government for the people but only for dictators and demagogues. . . . We reject liberalism, a product of the nineteenth century, because it does not admit of the positive intervention of the state in satisfying human needs. . . . We propose interventionist methods, above all in the field of economics and especially in the relations between capital and labor in order to rectify social injustices. The inertia of the liberal state must give way to the dynamism of the state as protector and leader." These statements show clearly how far the Morínigo government had progressed toward totalitarianism; or, perhaps, it had accepted the principal tenets of Stefanich's *democracia solidarista.*

The bare record of documents signed looks good for hemisphere solidarity; but how did Morínigo really feel about it all? Wesley Frost, first American ambassador to Paraguay, discovered that the dictator was not willing to implement his oral protestations with physical manifestations. Morínigo, like Perón, provided refuge for Axis spies, he protected their espionage ring, he followed their advice, he refused to expel known spies, he encouraged German colonies to fall in line with Axis propaganda, he suppressed pro-Allied demonstrations, and he fomented anti-Semitism.

The Nazi web in Paraguay was notorious and important, although its ramifications in other Latin American countries received more attention. The Deutsche Winterhilfe collected considerable sums from Germans, immigrants or their descendants, and delivered the money to Karl Thomas, a clever fellow who went to Asunción in the nineteen twenties and made the Banco Germánico a favorite among foreigners. Karl seemed to be a nice chap when the writer met him in 1928. He was not a Nazi then, of course. What happened to Karl Thomas probably was typical of what happened to hundreds of Germans in Paraguay: Go along with Hitler, or else.

Many other Nazi organizations had Paraguayan branches. The Opferring carried on Nazi political activities under the guidance of Dr. O. Huber; the Sociedad Alemania de Gimnasia y Deportes was the Hitler Youth organization, with more than five hundred members; the Colegio Alemán (*Deutsche Schule*) was a center of Nazi propaganda; the Frente Nacional Socialista del Trabajo was a Nazi labor union of German workers; the Asociación Femenina Nacional-Socialista, with more than five hundred members, was a counterpart of the N. S. Frauenschaft; the Coro Masculino Alemán (German Male Chorus) was another propaganda agency; the Unión Germánica del Paraguay (*Deutsche Volkbund*) distributed propaganda; the Club de Amigos de Alemania counted among its members the chief of the secret police, Marcos Fuster; and there were Spanish Falange and Italian groups to round out the list. At Luque, Villa Rica, and other cities, Nazi activities were carried on openly. German colonies on the southeastern frontier served as links with Nazi groups in Argentina. Eugene Frank, German consul at Encarnación, directed a system of propaganda distribution centers, aided by the *Gauleiter* of Encarnación, Wilhelm Gunther. Radio-transmission stations operated at many points. Before taking over Argentina in June, 1943, pro-Nazi militarists said with reason: "We already have Paraguay."

Government attitudes toward labor organizations may be examined as a further means of testing Morínigo's adherence to democratic principles. Labor unions in Paraguay had entered a new period of development in the nineteen thirties, a period of rapid growth and radical tendencies that caused their leaders to be called Communists. The Workers' Council (*Consejo Obrero*) became affiliated with Lombardo Toledano's Confederation of Latin American Laborers (CTAL) and had sent a delegate to the Cali, Colombia, meeting in 1944. This Second General Congress favored destruction of Latin American dictatorships, a stand that would hardly win favor with Morínigo whose record was definitely antilabor. The general strike in January, 1941, was a labor declaration of war against the regime and resulted in more than two hundred arrests. Outbreaks occurred again in August and December, followed in each case by more arrests. An attempt to establish complete government control (Morínigo called it *"fiscalización"*) in November, 1943, brought on the general strike in the following February. Morínigo then appointed Lieutenant

Colonel Basiliano Caballero Irala to head the Departamento Nacional de Trabajo. This enlightened officer attempted to swim with the labor current and proposed a democratic labor law that earned for him the privilege of exile in Montevideo. New outbreaks of violence on February 15 and 16 and May 1 to 3, 1945, testified to labor's strength in the face of oppression and imprisonment of leaders in concentration camps.

The labor program was not particularly radical in most of its aspects. Workers demanded freedom of organization, the right to strike, social reforms, restoration of democratic government, and support of the United Nations. Working conditions certainly needed improvement, judging by what went on at one of the largest foreign enterprises. About one thousand of the International Products Company's workers belonged to a union. Most of these men were receiving 1.60 *guaranís* per day in 1945, less than 55 cents; the union wanted an increase to 2.50 *guaranís*. At Puerto Pinasco, where workers generally lived in one-room houses, purchases at the company stores kept them perpetually in debt. Conditions in the other quebracho works were similar and help to explain why the general strike of February, 1945, gained such strong support in the foreign enterprises.

Freedom of the press may not be an infallible gauge of the democratic current, but it has never been tolerated by dictators. Estigarribia in June, 1940, had set up a limited censorship under which the Ministry of Government and Labor might dictate how certain matters should be treated, compel the press to print its propaganda free of charge, and take over any papers it desired. Morínigo was the minister who signed that decree, later modified by the constitution of 1940. As president, he established full censorship through a series of laws dating from October 22, 1941, and amplified by frequent regulations issued by the Departamento Nacional de Propaganda (Denapro), which was organized under a decree of December 11, 1944. An underground press, of course, appeared at once to fight the Nationalist Revolutionary Movement. Denapro's vigilance extended to all phases of publishing, radio, entertainment, sport, tourism, and social organizations. No public officials could release information without

Denapro's approval; all presses and printed matter had to be licensed; all organizations had to register and report regularly on their activities. No one could broadcast without Denapro's consent, all radio programs and commercials were censored, and all musical broadcasts must be at least one-third native music. Cinemas could show only approved films; even dance halls and playgrounds had to be licensed.

Captain Manuel W. Cháves, director of Denapro, told Carlos Borche that he had no intention of restricting thought as expressed by newspaper editorials. Those editors who wrote lovingly about the temperature, the rise and fall of the river, and the locust plagues were being guilty of pure deviltry. Why couldn't they write criticisms of things they were told to criticize? The Captain thought it all very sad. More sad, and with reason, was Dr. Policarpo Artaza, owner of the influential Liberal organ *El País*. Morínigo, not satisfied with his official *El Paraguayo*, seized *El País*. The formerly pro-Democratic paper became pro-Nazi, and the German minister visited its editorial offices frequently. Foreign correspondents found little encouragement to exercise their talents. Carlos Borche's fact-finding trip was a great concession that may have led Diarios Asociados of Brazil to send a correspondent, Edmar Morel, to Paraguay in February, 1946. This ungrateful reporter published violent attacks against Morínigo when he returned to Brazil. Then Senhor Pedro Motta Lima, editor of the Communist *Tribuna Popular* of Rio de Janeiro, tried his hand at reporting on Paraguay. *El Paraguayo* published a warm editorial welcome when Motta Lima arrived in Asunción in March, but police quickly hustled him off to the Argentine border. Morínigo did not like foreign newsmen.

Carlos Borche made his trip to Paraguay under rather unusual conditions. It was inspired on July 3, 1945, when the reporter for *El País* sat at his desk in Montevideo, probably wondering where his next story would come from. He raised his head to see before him a group of Paraguayan political exiles, among them a student refugee named Badri Yampey. This unfortunate youth told a story that made headlines. He had been arrested in February and was sent with thirty-two other students and workers to a Chaco concentration camp, where he suffered two months of rigorous treatment by the camp's commander, Lieutenant Colonel José Segunda Dacosta. On a diet of corn and *galletas* (small, hard biscuits), with little water, no medical care, and forced labor, Yampey still found enough strength to escape to Asunción where he took refuge in the Uruguayan Legation.

Morínigo's minister to Uruguay, Dr. Juan Natalico González, read this account on July 4 with considerable indignation. Perhaps he found time to obtain instructions from his superiors; at least, on the same day he wrote a letter to the editors of Montevideo's *El País* in which he denied the existence of such camps in Paraguay and invited the paper to send a reporter on a fact-finding trip under a guarantee of complete freedom of movement. Carlos Borche accepted the challenge, specifying the types of persons he wanted to interview. A score of Argentina's secret police were on the *Bruselas*, an advance guard preparing for Edelmiro Farrell's visit to Asunción, when Borche and a photographer left on July 28, hardly believing that Morínigo really meant it. How could a dictator be so bold, or so stupid? He would not be again, not after Borche published his *Campos de concentración en América*.

Agents of the Departamento de Propaganda met Borche at Asunción, probably to keep members of the opposition from getting in touch with him too soon, and perhaps just to be polite. Within an hour after the reporter was settled in his hotel, the clandestine democratic movement had established contact with him. A student, Ricardo Franco, called to see Borche and was arrested by Morínigo's secret police (*pyragües*) when he left. Undismayed by Franco's fate, a delegation of women whose relatives were prisoners in the Chaco called to show hundreds of letters received from their men. On the following day, August 3, Borche called on Morínigo after obeying a guard's command to take off his hat, button his coat, and throw away his cigarette. The pompous ruler received him cordially and answered questions politely. Would elections be permitted for a congress? Maybe. When? Probably in 1948. Would the Constitution be restored? Perhaps, with modifications. What parties would be permitted to participate in an election? The Colorados or some newly organized groups; but not the treacherous Liberals. The dictator took advantage of the interview to say a few things in self-defense: "My government believes that harmony should be sought between capital and labor. But there are many agitators among the workers and also among the students. All of them are detained and are confined in their home towns. You will see them yourself. They are all right. Pretty little towns, surrounded by vegetation. As to those in the Chaco, according to General Andino, many of those who are held there have definitely resolved to settle in that place to work honestly. It is said that I am a dictator. That is not true. You see how the common people come to see me. It is only that I need no political parties to act as intermediaries. I work directly with the people. Many come from far away and even with complaints against the authorities. I attend to everyone. I never need special guards. I go along and show myself as I am."

The Uruguayan reporter enjoyed freedom of movement, but he was not permitted to be lonely. *Pyragües* were everywhere—in cafes, taxicabs, streetcars, on the streets, and even in hotel corridors. In spite of such shadowing, Borche talked to many workers and students, obtained lists of prisoners and names and locations of concentration camps. He flew to the Chaco on August 5 in a plane manned by two Americans and two Paraguayans. The first stop was at old Fortín Camacho, now modernized as Fortín Mariscal Estigarribia, from which Colonel Augusto Guggiari commanded the Chaco Military Zone. The colonel assured Borche that he had only sixty-odd prisoners, which hardly agreed with the list supplied by the Asunción Labor Council. When pressed on the point, he admitted that others were at Ingavi, Irendagüe, and Puesto Muñeca. Borche rode with Guggiari in his jeep to Puesto Muñeca, several miles to the east along the road leading to Puerto Casado. There the journalist held a roll call while Colonel Guggiari stood by. There were 103 names on Borche's list, most of them workers or students. Some had been distributed among eleven other camps, some had fled, some had died, and a few had been set free. Why were they held?

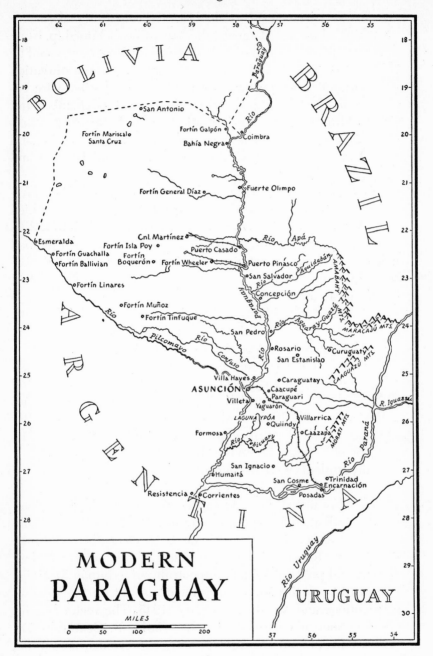

MODERN
PARAGUAY

MILES

0    50    100    200

Because they were anti-Nazi, had favored constitutional government, or had protested against the Argentine dictatorship. None
had been given formal trials, none knew how long they would be
held and all were forced to work without wages on a starvation
diet without receiving issues of clothing. No barbed-wire en-
closures marked the camp, nor was there a torture chamber; but
Puesto Muñeca was a concentration camp, better than others
in the Chaco, all of which were under the command of General
José Andino, a soldier with a reputation for moderation and
democratic tendencies.

Most notorious of all Paraguay's prisons was Isla de Peña Hermosa near the confluence of the Apá and Paraguay rivers, which
became a military prison in 1933. This rock, according to Indian
legend, appeared overnight after the girl Camelote had jumped
to her death in the river to escape being ravished. Many intellec-
tuals, political leaders, and former government officials had
known incarceration there.

At Villa Rica, Borche talked freely with opposition elements.
No labor unions, no political parties existed there or anywhere
else in Paraguay. The Asociación Aliada Americana and three
educational centers were the only survivors of democratic expression. On August 12, 1945, the day of Borche's visit, several
students had been arrested. Pro-Axis sympathizers were not
bothered in Villa Rica, as shown by a celebration at the Bar
Austria, attended by Inspector of Schools José P. Montiel, on the
occasion of Franklin D. Roosevelt's death.

Many students were in concentration camps because they led
the movement for democracy and later the underground activity
against Morínigo. Late in October, 1944, high-school and university students held separate congresses that condemned military intervention in the government. In December, Dr. Juan
Boggino, rector of the university, most of his faculty, student
groups, and political leaders respectfully urged upon Morínigo
a return to constitutional government and set off the wave of
persecutions and arrests in January, 1945. The rector lost his
position; such noted scholars as Dr. Carlos R. Centurión, Dr.
Carlos Carrera, and Dr. Agustín Morales were discharged and

exiled. Dr. Antonio Taboada, a law professor and president of the Supreme Court, cravenly delivered an *"Acuerdo Extraordinario"* on January 12 to condemn the petition. Juan Domingo Perón had shown his Paraguayan friend how to deal with professors and students. Nevertheless, the University Student Federation called a strike in protest against Farrell's visit in August. Morínigo's *pyragües* surrounded the institution and sent Domingo Bañuelos, president of the federation, to a concentration camp.

And what of the political leaders? Dr. Federico Cháves, chief of the Colorado party, asserted categorically his party's opposition to Morínigo, and affirmed that since the party's beginning it had steadfastly opposed the Liberals. Since the constitution of 1940 was undemocratic, a reversion to regimes of force, a new constitutional convention must be called. Leaders of the Liberal party were all in exile: Dr. José Patricio Guggiari, Dr. Vicente Rivarola, Dr. Gerónimo Riart, and many more who called Morínigo's regime one of violence and terror that denied fundamental rights of citizens. The nation, these exiles declared, was bankrupt: "Managed economy has punished the producer and impoverished the people." To restore democracy, the party proposed an immediate call for a constitutional convention, the union of all democratic forces, proportional representation, the restoration of public liberties, and the liberation of all political prisoners.

Colonel Rafael Franco, leader of the Febreristas, was in exile in Montevideo. He believed that a powerful desire existed for a return to constitutional methods, although it was this same Franco who had initiated the period that made Morínigo possible. He insisted that Lieutenant Colonel Victoriano Benítez Vera, chief of the Frente de Guerra, controlled Paraguay. Franco denied having dissolved the old parties during his brief tenure of office; the Unión Nacional Revolucionaria was formed to contend with them at the polls. He favored throwing out the pseudodictatorial constitution of 1940, calling a constitutional convention, and re-establishing democratic institutions. Perhaps someday a genius may be able to tell us just what a Paraguayan politician means by "democracy."

Paraguay's Communist party, small but active, infiltrated into labor unions and was a disruptive factor in them. The party stood for "democracy," demanded a general amnesty, called for a constitutional convention, approved the United States' opposition to Argentina after the San Francisco meeting, and hailed Nelson Rockefeller's resignation as an end to the policy of appeasing reactionary Latin American dictators.

What would these parties do if Morínigo did call a convention? Probably they would co-operate in forming a new fundamental law, then proceed to fight one another bitterly as in the past. Whoever controlled the most guns would govern the country, and there is little in Paraguayan history that leads one to believe that genuine freedom would result. Oppression, exile, violence, and petty revolts would be the norm. So long as Communists found for their propaganda mills inexhaustible grist among exploited people, they could win support for their own totalitarian doctrines. Perhaps Utopia might someday come to Paraguay, but the Communists would not bring it.

Democratic, Liberal, and Communist Paraguayans were not alone in causing trouble for General Morínigo. A trio of native Fascists, leaders of the Frente de Guerra, felt that the President should follow the line they laid down. Colonel Victoriano Benítez Vera, chief of staff in 1946, found support from his cronies, Colonels Bernardo Aranda and Pablo Stagni. These three men seem to have dictated to Morínigo for about five years. They opposed the *Tiempistas,* a group that favored a "Catholic social-service state" and took their name from the paper *El Tiempo* founded in 1939. Dr. Luis Argaña, minister of foreign affairs in the 1943 cabinet, was a leading *Tiempista* and anti-Nazi. The Frente forced his resignation in March, 1944. Morínigo waited patiently for a chance to throw off the fetters forged by the Paraguayan colonels.

Inaugurations of Latin American presidents are always occasions for the gathering of the continental elite. Juan Domingo Perón was to be installed as Argentina's president on June 4, 1946, and someone must represent Paraguay. Acting under a happy inspiration, Morínigo sent Benítez Vera to Buenos Aires, seized control of the Campo Grande garrison while he was away, and sent word to Stagni and Aranda that he wanted to see them. The two colonels, knowing what to expect, sought refuge beyond their friend's reach. Morínigo then shook up his cabinet and waited for the next move in the game of belling the cat. He had seen some two dozen revolutionary attempts to overthrow him, and more might well be in the making. Events in Bolivia soon caused the dictator to pass his hand lovingly over his neck, just to be sure there were no rope marks.

Occasionally an oppressed people, maddened by repeated attacks on their liberties, will turn savagely upon their tormentors when the breaking point has been reached. Bolivians passed that point in July, 1946, a month that brought ignominious death to many murderers and left the seminude remains of President Colonel Gualberto Villarroel hanging from a lamp post in La Paz. Morínigo took heed a day before Villarroel's last public appearance, although events in Bolivia may not have been a deciding factor in his sudden love for democracy. On July 20, he gave political parties the right to criticize the regime; on July 22, he named a new cabinet in which Colorados and Febreristas might be represented; on August 1, the Communist proscription ended and hundreds of political refugees began to return. Among the latter was Colonel Rafael Franco, back from making soap in Montevideo. Perhaps Morínigo was trying to get all the mice nibbling on the same piece of cheese before he pounced; perhaps he really meant his promise to turn the government over to officers chosen freely in an honest election. No one knew, but everyone who had any kept his shoes on, ready to run if it became necessary.

Morínigo, displaying amazing skill as a political strategist, organized his cabinet on July 26 by persuading Colorados and Febreristas to take posts in a coalition government under the promise that elections would be held within a few months. This move probably saved him from a fate somewhat similar to Villarroel's in Bolivia. Three cabinet posts went to each of the parties, while the ministry of the interior, most important of all, fell to General Juan Rovira. Truly, the old dictatorship appeared to have ended; Morínigo said he was ready to get out, he wanted the army to stop playing politics, and he hoped that the Liberals would stop playing with the army.

What would Franco do when he returned from exile? The question was answered, it seemed, on August 4. Morínigo executed a piece of showmanship rare in any Latin American country: he sent an aide to greet the exile and stayed at home. With a crowd of 20,000 supporters on hand at the docks, Franco could have said: "To the Palace! Down with Morínigo!" But he didn't. The famous Febrerista spoke briefly and soothingly to the crowd and then went home. Maybe Franco was tired; maybe Paraguay was growing up politically; but more than likely the Febreristas wanted to see what the next few months would bring.

They were uneasy months, a time in which cynical observers predicted that a revolt would break out momentarily. Their prophetic warnings apparently were vindicated on the night of December 12, 1946, when "anarchist elements" failed in an attempt to seize the prison, police headquarters, and the military school. This effort to be rid of Morínigo came at a time when the Colorado-Febrerista coalition broke up. Military leaders seem to have wanted the cabinet to hold on until elections could be called, but the cabinet resigned on January 11, leaving Morínigo no choice but to form a military government. He declared a state of siege on January 13, and kept an eye on young officers of Febrerista leanings. Something certainly was brewing, but few people seemed to know what it was. Nine members of the Liberal party were arrested on January 23, charged with plotting a revolution, and were released a short time later.

The big show of 1947, long planned by Febreristas, began at Concepción on Friday, March 7, when the First Infantry Division raised the standard of rebellion. At the same time a weak effort to seize Asunción failed. Morínigo did not underestimate the danger while the rebels appealed for support of other military units. Loyal planes bombed wildly near rebel headquarters where Major Cesar Aguirre soon had more than 1,500 supporters whom he used in attacks to gain control over territory north of Concepción. What was Aguirre fighting for? New elections and a new constitution, he said. Who was back of this latest *cuartelazo* that threatened to become a long and costly civil war? Even its military leadership was uncertain. Colonel Alfredo Galeano, former commander of the First Cavalry Division, had been sent as a prisoner to Peña Hermosa in September, 1946. When rebels captured the island, he was released and took command of the revolutionary forces. Opponents of Morínigo rallied to Galeano's support, and when the fugitive Communist leader, Obdulio Berthe, appeared at Concepción, there was added proof that Communists and Febreristas were co-operating. Liberals, too, took part in the committee formed to direct the revolution. Galeano lasted until March 24, when Colonel Fabian Zaldívar Villagra became commander-in-chief. Colonel Rafael Franco, no matter how much he remained in the background, was the real leader of the revolution and was the man who would be president if it succeeded.

Military events during the revolt of 1947 offer the general pattern of confusion typical of civil wars. Rebels won control over most of Paraguay north of Concepción before Colonel Federico Weddell Smith, a Chaco War hero, could stop them and prepared for an all-out attempt against Asunción. Colonel Alfredo Ramos led this southward thrust. Out of the welter of claims and counterclaims, one fact emerged clearly: the rebels failed to capture the capital. Several small detachments manning river posts south of Asunción pronounced for the rebels in April, but they succeeded only in causing fear that supplies might be cut off. Part of the navy rebelled and attacked Asunción unsuccessfully on April 27, a bold stroke that apparently caused Colonel Smith to give up his command in favor of an Argentine refuge. He left too soon. After a series of minor victories in June, loyal troops captured Concepción on July 31 and expected to end the war quickly.

Morínigo was jubilant. Bells rang and whistles tooted in Asunción for this hollow conquest, hollow because the rebels cared nothing for Concepción after it had served as a base of operations. A token resistance by a holding force had kept Morínigo's First Army Corps at bay while the main rebel army, protected by two gunboats, headed downstream for Asunción. Foreign diplomats hurried out of the capital to escape the siege and Morínigo desperately assembled a Second Army Corps to fight an estimated 10,000 rebels. This siege did not last long. On August 20, rebels were in full flight, their leaders hurrying to be the first to take refuge in neighboring countries. Franco himself returned to exile on August 19.

Foreign efforts to mediate in the civil war all failed because Morínigo refused to believe that the rebels could win. Brazilian and Uruguayan efforts, most notable of these attempts, met courteous but firm rejections. In Brazil, there was some feeling that Argentina's Perón was helping Morínigo, and General J. A. Flores da Cunha charged Perón with plans to attack Brazil if necessary to form his so-called Iberian bloc, and that Brazil's mediation attempts, headed by Ambassador Francisco Negrão de Lema, failed because of Perón's aid to Morínigo. Perón's government, of course, denied plans for an Iberian bloc or designs against Brazil. Early in August, when matters seemed critical for Morínigo, the Inter-American Defense Conference at Rio de Janeiro urged Paraguay to accept mediation, and the United States instructed its chargé, Edward Trueblood—one of the few diplomats who did not run in panic when rebels approached the capital—to offer his good offices.

Political conditions after the revolution were somewhat confused, but by November it was clear that Morínigo had adopted the Colorado party and that either he or Juan Natalicio González would be the Colorado candidate in elections promised for February 15, 1948. Federico Cháves, Bernardo Campos, and other prominent Colorados were skeptical of Morínigo's conversion, especially since it was accompanied by a neat political coup that wrested control from the acknowledged directors. When 296,000 registered voters went to the polls on the appointed day, they found only one name on the ballot—Juan Natalicio González. Then why vote? Suffrage is compulsory in Paraguay, and the voter proves participation by showing his registration certificate stamped at the time of voting. This certificate must be presented whenever a Paraguayan male of voting age desires to obtain any document issued by the government—no stamp, no document. Therefore, the regime could claim, Paraguayans overwhelmingly endorsed Morínigo by electing his candidate for a five-year term starting on August 15, 1948.

Higinio Morínigo could review his eight stormy years in office with considerable satisfaction. He had been stern without being unusually bloody, he had defeated every attempt to overthrow him, and, thanks to foreign loans and gifts, the country had made considerable economic and social progress. Politically, Paraguayans had advanced little, if any, toward enlightened self-government. No man since Carlos Antonio López had been as successful in dealing with foreign governments. Morínigo had fallen in line with Argentina's colonels far enough to appear as one of them; at the same time he convinced United States officials of his good intentions sufficiently to receive sizable crumbs from the Lend-Lease cake. His flirtations with Brazil looked toward eventual freedom, in part, from Argentine domination of Paraguay's foreign commerce, and his arrangements with Bolivia might eventually result in acquiring petroleum products in satisfactory quantities. In these matters he had labored for the welfare of his country, not for personal glory. Perhaps Paraguay paid heavily in the loss of individual liberties; the loss was not as great as it would have been under a continuation of Febrerista supremacy. No one can say how good or how bad Morínigo was until we have the tests of time and the contrasts of things to come.

So far as man is concerned, there is no end to history. Thus, no matter how neatly one may summarize what has happened, the summary concludes nothing and offers little basis for anticipating future events. Fortunately, the historian need not be a prophet, nor a maker of programs, nor a self-appointed Messiah who points to four centuries of history and shakes an admonishing pen at heirs of the past. Paraguay has known glory and despair but never disgrace. There is an inherent vitality in her people that has led the country slowly forward, that has overcome tremendous handicaps and healed terrible wounds. So long as that vitality endures, Paraguayans can hope that their land may yet become the paradise of Guaraní legend.

# Governors, Dictators, and
# Presidents of Paraguay, 1536-1948

| | |
|---|---|
| 1536 | Pedro de Mendoza |
| 1538 | Domingo Martínez de Irala |
| 1541 | Álvar Núñez Cabeza de Vaca |
| 1544 | Domingo Martínez de Irala |
| 1548 | Diego de Abreu |
| 1549 | Domingo Martínez de Irala |
| 1557 | Gonzalo de Mendoza |
| 1558 | Francisco Ortiz de Vergara |
| 1574 | Juan Ortiz de Zárate |
| 1581 | Juan de Torres |
| 1586 | Alonso de Vera y Aragón |
| 1592 | Fernando de Zárate |
| 1597 | Juan Ramírez de Velasco |
| 1598 | Hernando Arias de Saavedra |
| 1599 | Diego Rodríguez Valdez |
| 1602 | García Mendoza |
| 1605 | Hernando Arias de Saavedra |
| 1606 | Francisco Alfaro |
| 1611 | Diego Martínez Negrón |
| 1619 | Manuel de Frías |
| 1629 | Pedro de Lugo y Negrón |
| 1634 | Luis de Céspedes Jeray |
| 1636 | Martín de Ledesma Valderrama |

1641  Gregorio de Hinestrosa
1647  Diego Escobar Osorio
1649  Bernardino de Cárdenas
1649  Sebastián de León y Zárate
1650  Andrés de León Garabito
1653  Cristóbal de Garay y Saavedra
1656  Juan Blásquez de Valverde
1659  Alonso Sarmiento y Figueroa
1663  Juan Diez de Andino
1671  Francisco Rege Corvalán
1673  Diego Ibañez de Irala
1681  Juan Diez de Andino
1684  Antonio de Vera Múgica
1685  Francisco Monforte
1692  Sebastián Félix de Mendiola
1696  Juan Rodríguez Cota
1702  Antonio Escobar Gutiérrez
1705  Sebastián Félix de Mendiola
1706  Baltazar García Ros
1707  Manuel de Robles
1713  Gregorio Bazán de Pedraza
1717  Diego de los Reyes Balmaceda
1722  José de Antequera y Castro
1725  Bruno Mauricio de Závala
1725  Martín de Barúa
1731  Ignacio Soroeta
1733  Manuel Agustín de Calderón
1735  Bruno Mauricio de Závala
1736  Martín Echáuri
1740  Rafael de la Moneda
1747  Marcos José Larrazábal
1749  Jaime Sanjust
1761  José Martínez Fontes
1765  Fulgencio Yegros
1766  Carlos Morphi
1772  Agustín Fernando de Pinedo
1778  Pedro Melo de Portugal

1781   Joaquín Alós y Bru
1796   Lázaro de Ribera y Espinosa
1806   Bernardo de Velazco y Huidobro
1807   Manuel Gutiérrez
1809   Eustaquio Giannini
1809   Bernardo de Velazco y Huidobro
1811   *May 15.* Triumvirate: Bernardo de Velazco, José Gaspar Rodríguez de Francia, Juan Baleriano Zeballos
1811   *June 19.* Junta: Fulgencio Yegros, José Gaspar Rodríguez de Francia, Pedro Juan Caballero, Francisco Javier Bogarín, Fernando de la Mora
1813   *October 15.* Consulate: José Gaspar Rodríguez de Francia, Fulgencio Yegros
1814   *October 30.* Dictator for three years: José Gaspar Rodríguez de Francia
1816   *June 6.* Dictator for life: José Gaspar Rodríguez de Francia
1840   *September 20.* Junta: varying membership
1841   *March 12.* Consulate: Carlos Antonio López, Manuel Roque Alonso
1844   *March 12.* Carlos Antonio López
1862   *September 10.* Francisco Solano López
1869   *August.* Triumvirate: Cirilo Antonio Rivarola, Carlos Loizaga, José Díaz de Bedoya
1870   *September 1.* Cirilo Antonio Rivarola
1871   *December 18.* Salvador Jovellanos
1874   *November 25.* Juan Bautista Gill
1877   *April 12.* Higinio Uriarte
1878   *November 25.* Cándido Barreiro
1880   *September 4.* Bernardino Caballero
1886   *November 25.* Patricio Escobar
1890   *November 25.* Juan Gualberto González
1894   *June 9.* Marcos Morínigo
1894   *November 25.* Juan Bautista Eguzquiza
1898   *November 25.* Emilio Aceval
1902   *January 9.* Hector Carballo
1902   *November 25.* Juan A. Escurra

1904    *December 19.* Juan Bautista Gaona
1905    *December 9.* Cecilio Báez
1906    *November 25.* Benigno Ferreira
1908    *July 2.* Emiliano González Navero
1910    *November 25.* Manuel Gondra
1911    *January 17.* Albino Jara
1911    *July 5.* Liberato Rojas
1912    *March 1.* Pedro Peña
1912    *March 15.* Emiliano González Navero
1912    *August 15.* Eduardo Schaerer
1916    *August 15.* Manuel Franco
1919    *June 9.* José Montero
1920    *August 15.* Manuel Gondra
1921    *November 7.* Eusebio Ayala
1923    *April 11.* Eligio Ayala
1924    *March 17.* Luis A. Riart
1925    *August 15.* Eligio Ayala
1928    *August 15.* José Patricio Guggiari
1932    *August 15.* Eusebio Ayala
1936    *February 17.* Rafael Franco
1937    *August 15.* Félix Paiva
1939    *August 15.* José Félix Estigarribia
1940    *September 7.* Higinio Morínigo
1948    *June 3.* Juan Manuel Frutos
1948    *August 15.* Juan Natalicio González

# Bibliographical Essay

An annotated bibliography of works relating to Paraguay would require a volume of considerable proportions. In view of the abundance of periodical literature, biographies, formal histories, published documents, and monographs, it is remarkable that there is no satisfactory bibliography of that sort. Although the present volume might be described as a labor of love for a country too little known in the United States, not even that affection has reached the stage of blind infatuation necessary for the compilation of a much-needed complete bibliography of Paraguayan history. I have, therefore, restricted this note to include only the majority of books upon which the narrative rests. Periodical literature, to which I am greatly indebted, has been omitted because only a sampling could have been given without making the bibliography unduly long.

Among the more important general histories, one may consult three studies by the prolific and brilliant Cecilio Báez: *Historia diplomática del Paraguay* (2 vols., Asunción, 1931–32), *Le Paraguay, son évolution historique et sa situation actuelle* (Paris, 1927), and *Resumen de la historia del Paraguay desde la época de la conquista hasta el año 1880, seguido de la historia particular de la instrucción pública desde el gobierno de Domingo Martínez de Irala hasta nuestros días* (Asunción, 1910). While not a history, Guillermo Tell Bertoni's *Geografía económica nacional del Paraguay* (Asunción, 1940), offers a penetrating analysis of economic geography. C. W. Thurlow Craig wrote two interesting travel accounts, *Land of the Far Distance* (New York, 1934) and *Paraguayan Interlude* (New York, 1935). José Segundo Decoud's *History of Paraguay* (Washington, 1902), has performed yeoman service. Readers with a knowledge of French should consult Alfred

Demersay, *Histoire physique, économique et politique du Paraguay et des établissements des Jesuites* (2 vols., Paris, 1860–65). João Pedro Gay provides a critical Brazilian view in *Historia da republica jesuitica do Paraguay desde o descubrimento do Rio do Prata até nossos dias, anno 1861* (Rio de Janeiro, 1863), which may be somewhat balanced by reading Juan Andres Gelly's essay, *El Paraguay, lo que fué, lo que es, y lo que será* (Paris, 1926), a volume published first in Portuguese in 1848 and in Spanish a year later. Two volumes by W. H. Koebel, *In Jesuit Land* (London, 1906) and *Paraguay* (London, 1916), are competent but thin. Charles Ames Washburn's apology, *The History of Paraguay, with Notes of Personal Observations and Reminiscences of Diplomacy under Difficulties* (2 vols., Boston, 1871), may be read with profit and must be read with caution. Much reliable data on governors and presidents is found in Antonio Zinny, *Historia de los gobernantes del Paraguay, 1535–1887* (Buenos Aires, 1887).

Descriptions of Paraguay occur in the above titles and in standard geographies. Among the latter are Fred A. Carlson, *Geography of Latin America* (1st ed., New York, 1936); Preston E. James, *Latin America* (New York, 1942); and R. H. Whitbeck, *Economic Geography of South America* (1st ed., New York, 1926). Pedro Lozano's *Descripción corográfico* (Córdoba, 1733), is an early work. C. B. Mansfield published *Paraguay, Brazil and the Plate* (Cambridge, 1856) for the edification of English readers. Many of the titles mentioned below include accounts of the Indians. An excellent summary is in volumes I and III of Julian H. Steward (ed.), *Handbook of South American Indians* (Smithsonian Institution, Bureau of Ethnology *Bulletin 143*, 4 vols., Washington, 1946–48). In describing the Indians of Paraguay, I have generally followed accounts contemporary with the colonial period, which undoubtedly would be the cause of anthropological apoplexy in a scientist. A Paraguayan interpretation highly favorable to the Guaraní Indians is in Moisés Santiago Bertoni, *Civilización guaraní . . .* (Puerto Bertoni, 1922). Eloy Fariña Núñez, *Conceptos estéticos; mitos guaraníes* (Buenos Aires, 1926), and Ernesto Morales, *Leyendas guaraníes* (Buenos Aires, 1929), have accounts of Guaraní legends.

Paraguay's long colonial period has not suffered from lack of attention, although there is ample room for scholarly monographs. Félix de Azara produced several volumes, among which the *Descripción e historia del Paraguay y del Río de la Plata* (Madrid, 1847; 2 vols., Asunción, 1896) is indispensable. Considerable fiction crept into Martín del Barco Centenera's *Argentina y conquista del Río de la Plata* (Lisboa, 1602; Buenos Aires, 1912). For discovery and missionary work, there is the delightful if somewhat prejudiced Pierre François Xavier de Charlevoix, *The History of Paraguay* . . . (Tr. from the French, 2 vols., Dublin, 1769). Luis L. Domínguez edited *The Conquest of the River Plate, 1535–1555* (Hakluyt Society Publications, 1st Series, No. 81, London, 1891), and Manuel Domínguez, in *El alma de la raza* (Asunción, 1918) has several studies on the colonial period. Dean Gregorio Funes, *Ensayo de la historia civil del Paraguay, Tucumán y Buenos Aires* (3 vols., Buenos Aires, 1816; 2d ed., 2 vols. in 1, Buenos Aires, 1853), properly relates Paraguay's colonial history to the larger picture. Juan Natalicio González, before he started dodging revolutions, wrote the excellent *Proceso y formación de la cultura paraguaya* (Asunción–Buenos Aires, 1938 [1940]) and *Vida, pasión y muerte de Güyrá Verá* (Buenos Aires, 1939). Among the few accounts in English is R. B. Cunninghame Graham's *The Conquest of the River Plate* (London, 1924).

Students of the colonial period must also refer to José Guevara, *Historia de la conquista del Paraguay, Río de la Plata y Tucumán* (Buenos Aires, 1882). Historical novelists should consider Irala as a subject and begin their reading with Ricardo de Lafuente Machaín, *El gobernador Domingo Martínez de Irala* (Buenos Aires, 1939). In a class with Guevara but better are Pedro Lozano's *Historia de la conquista del Paraguay, Río de la Plata y Tucumán* (5 vols., Buenos Aires, 1873–75), and *Historia de las revoluciones de la provincia del Paraguay* (2 vols., Buenos Aires, 1905). Mariano Antonio Molas whiled away time in prison by writing *Descripción histórica de la antigua provincia del Paraguay* . . . , which was later edited by Justiniano Carranza (Asunción, 1880). Fulgencio R. Moreno's *La ciudad de la Asunción* (Buenos Aires, 1926) is far broader than the title indicates. Domingo Muriel's monograph *Historia del Paraguay, desde 1747 hasta 1767* (Tr. by Pablo Hernández, Madrid, 1918) is valuable for the period covered.

Many writers have devoted their efforts to defending or attacking the Jesuit missions. All colonial histories mentioned above and many more deal with the problem in some detail. One may select the following titles as representative of this field, whose possibilities have not been exhausted. Pablo Hernández is bitter toward enemies of the Jesuits in *El extrañamiento de los Jesuítas del Río de la Plata y de las misiones del Paraguay por decreto de Carlos III* (Madrid, 1908) and defends the Jesuits in *Misiones del Paraguay; organización social de las doctrinas guaraníes de la Compañía de Jesús* (Barcelona, 1913). José Sánchez Labrador lived among the Mbayá, a branch of the Guaycurú linguistic family, from 1760 to 1767 and has left a splendid account in *El Paraguay Católico* (3 vols., Buenos Aires, 1910–17). A sad tale is told by V. Martin de Moussy, *Memoire historique sur le decadence et la ruine des missions des Jesuites dans le bassin de la Plata . . .* (Paris, 1864). The best Jesuit view is given by Lodovico Antonio Muratori in *Il cristianesimo felice nelle missioni de' padri della Compagnia di Gesu nel Paraguai* (2 vols. in 1, Venice, 1743–49). To this title some prefer Nicolás del Techo, *Historia de la provincia del Paraguay y de la Compañía de Jesús* (Tr. from the Latin by Manuel Serrano y Sáenz, Madrid, 1897). B. Capdevielle's *Misiones Jesuíticas en el Paraguay* (Asunción, 1923), Blas Garay's *El comunismo de las misiones* (Asunción, 1921), and R. B. Cunninghame Graham's *Vanished Arcadia* (London, 1901), should also be mentioned.

Paraguay's movement for independence is inseparable from the career of José Gaspar Rodríguez de Francia, a founding father to whom the efforts of many writers have been devoted. A basic study is that by Cecilio Báez, *Ensayo sobre el Doctor Francia y la dictadura en Sud-América* (Asunción, 1910). Lewis W. Bealer has a good brief survey, based upon reputable sources, in A. C. Wilgus (ed.), *South American Dictators . . .* (Washington, 1937). Justo Pastor Benítez, a productive scholar and statesman, wrote sympathetically yet critically in *La vida solitaria del Dr. José Gaspar de Francia* (Buenos Aires, 1937). Guillermo Cabanellas has a very readable biography, *El dictador del Paraguay, Dr. Francia* (Buenos Aires, 1946). Julio César Chaves performed a brilliant piece of research and writing in producing his definitive *El supremo dictador, biografía de José Gaspar de Francia* (Buenos Aires, 1942). José Segundo Decoud pays homage to leaders of the independence movement in *Recuerdos históricos. Homenaje á los próceres de la independencia paraguaya* (Asunción, 1894), and Alfred Demersay provides a critique in *Le docteur Francia, dictateur du Paraguay: sa vie et son gouvernement* (Paris, 1856). Blas Garay's *La revolución de la independencia del Paraguay* (Madrid, 1897), provides a fair perspective, as does Fulgencio R. Moreno's, *Estudio sobre la independencia del Paraguay* (Asunción, 1911).

There are a few enlightening references in Woodbine Parish, *Buenos Ayres and the Provinces of the Rio de la Plata* (London, 1834). After Johann Rudolph Rengger and Marcelline Longchamps were allowed to leave Paraguay, they published their *Essai historique sur la révolution du Paraguay* (Paris, 1827), and Rengger, with due credit to his former companion, published an English version as *The Reign of Doctor Joseph Gaspard Roderick de Francia, in Paraguay; . . .* (London, 1827). The brothers J. P. and W. P. Robertson wrote entertaining *Letters on Paraguay: Comprising An Account of A Four Years' Residence in that Republic, under the Government of the Dictator Francia* (2 vols., London, 1838) and followed it with *Francia's Reign of Terror, Being a Sequel to Letters on Paraguay* (2 vols., Philadelphia, 1839). H. Sánchez Quell has written a good study of the *Política internacional del Paraguay (La junta de 1811, Francia y los López)* (2d ed., Buenos Aires, 1945), and there is an excellent essay and collection of documents in Benjamín Vargas Peña (ed.), *Paraguay-Argentina, correspondencia diplomática 1810–1840* (Buenos Aires, 1945). An excellent historical novel is Edward Lucas White's *El Supremo, A Romance of the Great Dictator of Paraguay* (New York, 1916). Enrique Wisner de Morgenstern wrote a biography in the eighteen sixties which appeared as *El dictador del Paraguay, Doctor José Gaspar Rodríguez de Francia* (Concordia, Argentina, 1923).

People like the López' call forth the highest praise and the most bitter denunciation. A few of their biographers tried to be fair. Cecilio Báez used his blackest ink effectively in *El Mariscal Francisco Solano López* (Asunción, 1926). William E. Barrett was perhaps too sympathetic in *Woman on Horseback, the Biography of Francisco López and Eliza Lynch* (New York, 1938). Héctor Pedro Blomberg offered a different view of Eliza in *La Dama del Paraguay* (Buenos Aires, 1942). R. B. Cunninghame Graham's *Portrait of a Dictator, Francisco Solano López (Paraguay, 1865–1870)* (London, 1933), also considers the War of the Triple Alliance. George Frederick Masterman was still angry when he wrote *Seven Eventful Years in Paraguay; A Narrative of Personal Experience Amongst the Paraguayans* (London, 1870). Juan Emiliano O'Leary pulled out all stops in his eulogy *El Mariscal Solano López* (2d ed., Madrid, 1925). Thomas Jefferson Page described his relations with the elder López in *La Plata, the Argentine Confederation, and Paraguay; being a Narrative of the Exploration of the Tributaries of the River La Plata and Adjacent Countries during the Years 1853, '54, '55, and '56, under the Orders of the United States Government* (New York, 1859). Carlos Pereyra must have hoped for a Paraguayan decoration for his *Francisco Solano López y la guerra del Paraguay* (Madrid, 1919). Adverse Argentine views are expressed by Arturo Rebaudi in *El lopizmo* (Buenos Aires, 1924) and *Un tírano de Sudamérica, Francisco Solano López* (Buenos Aires, 1925). Héctor Varela wrote an early biography anonymously in *Elisa Lynch* (Buenos Aires, 1870).

We can do no more than sample other literature relating to the War of the Triple Alliance. The great Argentine Juan Bautista Alberdi favored Paraguay in his *El imperio del Brasil ante la democracia de América* (Paris, 1869), and *Las dos guerras del Plata y su filiación* (Paris, 1867). Gregorio Benítes published *Anales diplomático y militar de la guerra del Paraguay* (2 vols., Asunción, 1906) and *Guerra del Paraguay; las primeras batallas contra la Triple Alianza* (Asunción, 1919). Pelham Horton Box gave us the definitive study of causes in *The Origins of the Paraguayan War* (2 vols., Urbana, 1927). Richard F. Burton was something of a war correspondent in *Letters from the Battle-fields of Paraguay* (London, 1870). Some Brazilian background is in Pedro Calmon, *O rei filosofo: vida de Dom Pedro II* (2d ed., São Paulo, 1939). Argentine views are presented in Ramón J. Cárcano, *Guerra del Paraguay, acción y reacción de la Triple Alianza* (2 vols., Buenos Aires, 1941), and *Guerra del Paraguay, orígenes y causas* (Buenos Aires, 1939). J. A. Cova added little with his sketchy *Solano López y la epopeya del Paraguay* (Buenos Aires, 1948). José Ignacio Garmendia, Argentine glorifier of war, studied one campaign in *Campaña de Humaytá* (Buenos Aires, 1901). Brazilian views are given competently by a participant in E. C. Jourdan's *Guerra do Paraguay* (Rio de Janeiro, 1871), and *Historia das campanhas do Uruguay, Matto Grosso e Paraguay* (3 vols., Rio de Janeiro, 1893-94). Juan Emiliano O'Leary wrote *Nuestra epopeya (Guerra del Paraguay, 1864-1870)* (Asunción, 1919), and Benjamin Poncel's *Le Paraguay moderne* (Marseilles, 1867) provides a contemporary view. One should note four studies by Arturo Rebaudi: *La declaración de guerra de la República del Paraguay a la República Argentina* (Buenos Aires, 1924), *Guerra del Paraguay; la conspiración* (Buenos Aires, 1917), *Guerra del Paraguay, vencer o morir* (Buenos Aires, 1920), and *Lomas Valentinas* (Buenos Aires, 1925). George Thompson was reliable in *The War in Paraguay, with a Historical Sketch of the Country and its People and Notes upon the Military Engineering of the War* (London, 1869).

Many Paraguayans are still convinced that Charles Ames Washburn plotted to overthrow López, but no one has come close to proving it. The best sources on Washburn's activities are his unpublished dispatches in the National Archives, Washington, D. C. Writers on López find it necessary to include the United States minister in their biographies, usually to discredit him. Results of the Congressional investigation were published in *Paraguayan Investigation* (*H. R.*, 41 Cong., 2 sess., Report No. 65, Vol. II; Washington, 1870), and Washburn offered his own defense in *The History of Paraguay, with Notes of Personal Observations and Reminiscences of Diplomacy under Difficulties* (2 vols., Boston, 1871).

Materials are scanty for the interesting half-century of reconstruction between wars, but the gaps are being filled slowly. Albert Amerlan wrote *Nights on the Río Paraguay; Scenes of War and Character Scetches* [*sic*] (Tr. from the German by Henry F. Suksdorf, Buenos Aires, 1902). Cecilio Báez and José Rodríguez Alcalá collaborated on *El Paraguay moderno . . .* (Asunción, 1915). Cultural development is traced by Justo Pastor Benítez in *El solar Guaraní (Panorama de la cultura paraguaya en el siglo XX)* (Buenos Aires, 1947), which should be read with Carlos R. Centurión's *Historia de las letras paraguayas* (Buenos Aires, 1947). There are interesting details of revolutions in C. W. Domville-Fife, *Modern South America* (Philadelphia, 1931). Arthur Elwood Elliott prepared a survey of *Paraguay, its Cultural Heritage, Social Conditions and Educational Problems* (New York, 1931). Indispensable is Juan Natalicio González and Pablo M. Ynsfrán, *El Paraguay contemporáneo* (Asunción, 1929). Sportsmen will enjoy John Waller Hills and Ianthe Dunbar, *The Golden River; Sport and Travel in Paraguay* (London, 1922). A few immigrants might have been attracted by Alexander K. Macdonald's *Picturesque Paraguay . . .* (London, 1911), and surely by H. Mangels' *Paraguay; wirtschaftliche, naturgeschichtliche und klimatologische abhandlungen* (Munich-Freising, 1919). W. L. Schurz has a compact and valuable *Paraguay: A Commercial and Industrial Handbook* (Washington, 1920). By far the best survey for immigrants and merchants was Adolf N. Schuster's *Paraguay; land, volk, geschichte, wirtschaftsleben und kolonisation* (Stuttgart, 1929). An earlier study is E. de Bourgade la Dardye, *Paraguay: the Land and the People, Natural Wealth and Commercial Capabilities* (London, 1892). Otto Bürger's *Paraguay, der "garten Südamerikas"; ein wegweiser fur handel, industrie und eniwanderung* (Leipzig, 1927) supplements Schuster.

The Chaco boundary dispute called forth a number of studies. Among those presenting the Bolivian side, one may cite José Aguirre Achá, *The Arbitration Zone in the Bolivian-Paraguayan Dispute through the Diplomatic Negotiation* (La Paz and New York, 1929), and the same author's *El desacuerdo y el conflicto entre Bolivia y el Paraguay* (La Paz, 1929); *Bolivie-Paraguay, le conflit de délimitation de frontières, ses origenes et son état actuel* (Paris, 1929); *Documentos relativos a la agresión del Paraguay contra el fortín boliviano Vanguardia* (La Paz, 1929); Telmo Ichazo, *Cuestión de límites, exposición de 1894* (La Paz, 1894); two volumes by Miguel Mercado Moreira, *El Chaco boliviano (Antaciones al alegato paraguayo)* (Cochabamba, 1928), and *El Chaco Boreal (Litigio boliviano-paraguayo)* (La Paz, 1929); and Ricardo Mujía, *Bolivia-Paraguay; anotaciones a la "réplica" del Señor Fulgencio R. Moreno* (La Paz, 1916). These studies present the Bolivian case adequately.

On the Paraguayan side, many historians, diplomats, and journalists entered the argument to defend their country's claims. The following titles are representative of their efforts: Benjamín Aceval, *Chaco paraguayo* (Asunción, 1896); Alejandro Audibert, *Los límites de la antigua provincia del Paraguay* (Buenos Aires, 1892); the same author's *Cuestión de límites entre el Paraguay y Bolivia* (Asunción, 1901); Elías Ayala, *Paraguay y Bolivia en el Chaco Boreal* (Asunción, 1929); two studies by Cecilio Báez, *The Paraguayan Chaco* (New York, 1904), and *Paraguay-Bolivia: su cuestión de límites* (Asunción, 1917); Marcelo de la Place Chauvac, *Gran Chaco—Chaco Austral, Chaco Central, Chaco Boreal* (Asunción, 1916); Manuel Domínguez, *El Chaco Boreal fué, es y será del Paraguay* (Asunción, 1927), and his *El Chaco Boreal. Informe del Doctor Manuel Domínguez, miembro de la Comisión Asesora de Límites que arruina las tesis bolivianas y expone los títulos del Paraguay sobre dicha zona* (Asunción, 1925); Rogelio Ibarra, *Paraguay-Bolivia: cuestión de límites* (Asunción, 1924); *Libro blanco. Documentos relativos a las conferencias de Buenos Aires sobre la cuestión de límites paraguayo-boliviana y algunos antecedentes* (Asunción, 1929); two works by Fulgencio R. Moreno, *Diplomacía paraguaya-boliviana. Antecedentes de los tratados de límites y causas de su fracaso* (Asunción, 1904), and *El problema de las fronteras* (Buenos Aires, 1927); *Paraguay-Bolivia; cuestión de límites* (Asunción, 1917); Raul del Pozo Cano's two studies, *Paraguay-Bolivia; nuevos documentos que prueban la jurisdicción del Paraguay en el Chaco* (Asunción, 1927), and *Paraguay-Bolivia: el Chaco paraguayo y el Vaticano* (Asunción, 1927); and Francisco Rolón, *El Paraguay y Bolivia: cuestión de límites* (Asunción, 1903).

After wandering through these books, the student will find welcome relief in Hans Tolten, *Enchanting Wilderness, Adventures in Darkest South America* (Tr. from the German by Ferdi Loesch, London, 1936). Arguments of both countries may be found in such reports as *Commission of Inquiry and Conciliation, Bolivia and Paraguay, Report of the Chairman* (Publications of the Department of State, Latin American Series, No. 1; Washington, 1929); *Documentation Concerning the Dispute between Bolivia and Paraguay* (League of Nations, Geneva, 1928) and the *Supplement* (Geneva, 1929); *The International Conference of American States on Conciliation and Arbitration, Washington, December 10, 1928–January 5, 1929* (Washington, 1929); and *Proceedings of the Commission of Inquiry and Conciliation Bolivia and Paraguay, March 13, 1929–September 13, 1929* (Washington, 1929).

A really good history of the Chaco War remains to be written. Justo Pastor Benítez eulogizes *Estigarribia, el soldado del Chaco* (Buenos Aires, 1943). Augusto Céspedes gives us an impressionistic story in *Sangre de mestizos, relatos de la guerra del Chaco* (Santiago de Chile, 1936). Philip de Ronde attempted to arouse sympathy with his *Paraguay, a Gallant Little Nation; the Story of Paraguay's War with Bolivia* (New York, 1935), which was hardly worth the effort. Perhaps the best account is Manuel María Oliver's *La guerra en el Chaco Boreal, como se defiende el Paraguay* (Buenos Aires, 1935), although it leaves ample room for improvement. Justo Rodas Eguino provides a criticism of Bolivian diplomacy in *La guerra del Chaco; interpretación de política internacional americana* (Buenos Aires, 1938). Angel Rodríguez presents the views of a disgruntled Bolivian general in *Autopsia de una guerra (campaña del Chaco)* (Santiago de Chile, 1940).

Interpretations of the New Paraguay are mostly journalistic, but a good beginning has been made. Policarpo Artaza defends *Ayala, Estigarribia y el partido liberal* (2d ed., Buenos Aires, 1946) against the Febreristas. Carlos Borche presents a damaging indictment of Morínigo in *Campos de concentración en América (Misión en Paraguay)* (Montevideo, 1945). For the reconstructed state under Estigarribia, one may read with profit the *Constitución de la República del Paraguay* (Asunción, 1940). Some light is shed on economic problems by Seymour E. Harris (ed.), *Economic Problems of Latin America* (New York, 1944). Simple editorial lessons are found in José Antonio Pérez Echeguren's *Relieve y categoria de la revolución paraguaya* (Asunción, 1940). Immigration is discussed by Walter Quiring in two books, *Deutsche erschliesen den Chaco* (Karlsruhe, 1936), and *Russlanddeutsche suchen eine Heimat* (Karlsruhe, 1938). Juan José Soler indulges in memoirs in *Hacia la unión nacional, 40 años de vida pública* (Buenos Aires, 1943). Juan Stefanich explains the philosophical bases of Febrerismo in *El mundo nuevo: una nueva teoría de la democracia* (Buenos Aires, 1941), and *El Paraguay nuevo, por la democracia y la libertad hacia un nuevo ideario americano* (Buenos Aires, 1943). There is also valuable information in Arthur P. Whitaker (ed.), *Inter American Affairs* (5 vols., New York, 1942–46), which covers the years 1941–45.

# Index

74; sends aid to Doña Mencia
Calderón, 75; sends expedition to
Guayrá, 76; becomes governor of
Río de la Plata, 77; death of and
evaluation of his work, 79; will of,
79–80; children of, 80
Irala, Ginebra Martínez de: 80, 133
Irala, Isabel de: 80, 133
Irala, Juan de: 133
Irala, María de: 80
Irala, Martín Pérez de, father of
Domingo Martínez de Irala: 68
Irala, Martín Pérez de, son of Domingo
Martínez de Irala: 80
Irala, Pedro de: 68
Irala, Ursula de: 80, 133
Irendague: 344
Irigoyen, Hipólito: 296, 316
Irrazábal, Luis: 310
Isarakí, myth: 19–20
Isla Poi, Fortín: 305, 307
Itaguá: 282
Italo-American Colonization Society:
273
Italy: 6, 49, 51, 269
Itapirú: 194, 195, 228, 230
Itapuá: 147, 172, 227, 228, 283
Itatín Indians: 21; attack Inca empire,
23; attacked by Mbayás, 31; Jesuit
missionaries withdrawn from, 108,
287
I-Yara, myth: 12
*Izapí*, tree and myth: 17

*Jamestown*: 255
Jara, Albino: 265, 266–67
Jara, Julio: 323
Jara, Plácido: 304
Jardín Botánico, Asunción: 12, 34, 277
Jeffers, William N.: 194
*Jejui*: 226
Jejui River: 131
Jérez de la Frontera, Andalucía: 51
Jesuit Colegio, Asunción: 83, 103, 105,
108, 120, 139, 164
Jesuits: 5, 14, 28; Tape missions of, 23;
among Guaycurús, 31, 57; invited to
Paraguay, 82; in Brazil, 82; in the
Chaco, 83; arrive at Asunción, 83;
recalled from Paraguay and return
of, 84; colonial opposition to, 84,
101, 110, 111, 121, 128, 129; at
Bahia, Brazil, 87; withdraw from

Guayrá, 89; establish missions in
Uruguay-Paraná area, 89–90;
mission duties, 92–93; accomplishments, 96; responsibility for War of
the Seven Reductions, 98; expelled
from Spanish dominions, 98–99, 122,
182; supported by Governor
Hinestrosa, 102; opposed by Bishop
Cárdenas, 104–105; and "gold
mines of Paraguay," 106–107;
missionaries withdrawn from Itatines,
108; charged with seducing Governor Victoria, 111; expelled from
Colegio in Asunción, 113, 120; expulsion recommended by Asunción
cabildo, 115; driven from Asunción,
116; opposition of Governor Burúa,
117; Francia's opinion of, 154–55;
*see also* missions; Society of Jesus
Jesús-María, mission: 87–88
João, Portuguese regent: 146
John VI, king of Portugal (1816–26):
*see* João
Johnson, Cave: 195, 196
Johnson, María Irene, quoted: 197
José Fassardi y Cía.: 281–82
*Juniata*: 248
Junta of Asunción: formation, 146–47;
calls general congress, 147; recon-
stituted, 148; swears loyalty to
Ferdinand VII, 148; signs treaty
with Buenos Aires, 149
Junta of Buenos Aires: sends agents to
Asunción, 145; seeks to coerce
Paraguay, 145–46; sends agents to
Paraguay, 149
Justiniano, Bartolomé: 77
Justo, Agustín P.: 294, 297, 316
Justo, Liborio: 294

*Kansas*: 258
Kellogg Pact: 308, 313
Kerr, John Austin: 277
Kidd, Frederick: 274
Kilometer Seven, struggle for in Chaco
War: 306, 308
"King Joseph of Paraguay": 117; *see
also* Antequera y Castro, José de
Kirk, Robert C.: 210
Kirkland, W. A.: 253, 254
Kundt, Hans: 306, 307, 308, 310, 311

*La Decidée*: 204–205

254, 256, 257, 258; quoted, 163, 182, 199–200, 206, 226, 241
Maté: *see* yerba maté
Matto Grosso province, Brazil: 187, 188, 218, 224; invasion of, 219–20
Mayas: 30, 100
Mayra, Galiano de: 126
Mbaeveraguasú: 21–22
Mbayá Indians: 31, 59, 70, 122, 286
Medicine men: 25
Medina, Juan: 125
Melo, Pedro: 287
Melodía reduction: 287
Méndez Caldeira, Manuel: 174
Mendoza, Andrés Hurtado de: 32
Mendoza, Diego de: 40; killed by Querandís, 41
Mendoza, Francisco de: 66; commands at Asunción, 71; overthrown by Abreu, 73
Mendoza, Gonzalo de: 60, 133; sent to search for Ayolas, 45; aids in founding Asunción, 45; in charge of Asunción, 48, 58; commands rearguard of Chaco expedition, 62; forages for supplies, 63, 65; succeeds Irala as commander of expedition to Peru, 73
Mendoza, Hernando de: 133
Mendoza, Pedro de: 68, 69, 72, 125, 126, 127, 130, 135; leads expedition to Río de la Plata, 40 ff.; orders execution of Osorio, 41; sends Ayolas to explore rivers, 44; departure from Buenos Aires, 45; death of, 45, 51; promises reinforcements for Buenos Aires, 46
Mendoza, Chief Pedro de: 80, 133
Mennonite colonies: 31, 274–75, 291, 304
Mercado, Bailón: 292
Mercado Moreira, Miguel: 293
Mestizos: 49, 133, 134; morals of, 137
Mexico: 100, 122, 127, 141, 266, 293
Mexico, Audiencia of: 287
Meza, Pedro Ignacio: 189, 225–26
Miguel, Indian guide: 521
Mihanovich, firm of: 334
Militia, Guaraní: in missions, 95; aid against Colonia do Sacramento, 97–98; aid against Guaycurús, 102; summoned by Governor Hinestrosa, 105, 107; escorts Governor Osorio to

Asunción, 108; aid to León y Zárate, 108; protect Asunción, 109; defeated by Comuneros, 116; aid to Governor Závala, 117; support Governor Ruiloba, 120; aid against Chaco Indians, 122
Mineral resources: 127, 268
*Mineros,* yerba workers: 129
Miranda, Lucía: 39, 40
Miranda Cueto, Julia: 330
Misiones province, Argentina: 13; migration of Itatines to, 31; mission ruins in, 84–85; Paraguay surrenders claims to, 186
Missions, Jesuit: 85 ff., 335; begun in Guayrá, 85–86; as barrier to Brazil, 86, 89; attacked by mamelucos, 86 ff.; population of, in Guayrá, 87, 89; withdrawn from Guayrá, 89; established in Uruguay-Paraná area, 90; population of, 90, 92, 99, 100, 122; form of, 92; agricultural production in, 92; handicrafts, 92; religious instruction, 93; education, 93; morals, 93–94; festivals, 94–95; government, 95; militia, 95; influence on Paraguay, 95–96, 100; among Chiquito Indians, 98; wealth, 99; decline, 99–100; visited by Governor Reyes, 112; threatened by Antequera, 115; placed under control of Buenos Aires, 117; Indians ordered from, 182
*Mita:* 135
Mitre, Bartolomé: 210, 238, 286; praises Francisco Solano López as mediator, 209; rejects offer of mediation, 211; seeks understanding with Brazil, 211; agrees to Brazilian intervention in Uruguay, 212; neutrality policy, 215–16; enters Triple Alliance, 222; relations with Urquiza, 223; as allied commander, 222, 223–24; invades Paraguay, 228, 230; attacks Curuzú, 235; confers with López, 235; orders assault on Curupaity, 235
Melo, Pedro de, at mission San Antonio: 87
Molas, Mariano Antonio: 148, 287
Molines, Felipe de: 125
Mompóz y Zayas, Fernando: arrives in

UNIVERSITY OF OKLAHOMA PRESS

NORMAN